Thinking with a Pencil

About the Author

As the illustrations in *Thinking with a Pencil* indicate, Henning Nelms has enjoyed an unusually wide range of education and experience. He won his letter in college and holds degrees from three universities. He has worked as a sailor, bookkeeper, editor, and managing director of an advertising firm. He has been a practicing lawyer, a college professor, and an active director in two real estate companies. His travels have covered twenty-one countries. He spent ten years in the theater as producer, director, designer, technician, and actor. He has produced and written two radio programs. Drawings by him have appeared in national magazines and on the jackets of books issued by major publishers. His published works have been translated into Arabic, French, Portuguese, Spanish, and Swedish. They include two novels and the standard handbooks *Lighting the Amateur Stage, A Primer of Stagecraft, Play Production, Magic and Showmanship,* and *Scenery for the Stage.* Their combined sales have long since passed the quarter-million mark. His plays include the burlesque melodrama, *Only an Orphan Girl,* which has been a perennial favorite with amateurs wherever English is spoken. Recently, he has divided his time between preparing a handbook on technical writing and providing the scripts for a series of audio/visual programs, many of which have had international distribution.

Thinking with a Pencil

by Henning Nelms

With 692 Illustrations of Easy
Ways to Make and Use Drawings
in Your Work and in Your Hobbies

Ten Speed Press

1☺

TEN SPEED PRESS
P O Box 7123
Berkeley, California 94707

Library of Congress Catalog Number: 81-84867
ISBN: 0-89815-052-3

Cover Design by Brenton Beck

To
Lloyd George Venard
a small payment on a great debt

Foreword

This book is intended for two groups: (1) those who wish to use drawing as a tool for thought and communication but lack knowledge of how to make drawings and (2) those who are accustomed to draw but want to enlarge their graphic vocabularies and extend the range of fields in which they can apply the abilities that they already possess.

The book has been planned for self-instruction. This treatment meets the needs of the person who works alone. It is equally valuable when the book is used as a supplementary text for courses—such as those in the biological and medical sciences, drama, and home economics—where drawing is either required or is obviously important, but where there is little or no time for instruction in the methods of making drawings. *Thinking with a Pencil* is also recommended as a main text in freehand technical sketching.

Students of Economics and Business Administration, and those studying sciences which use many charts, diagrams, and graphs, will find the elements of those subjects amply covered in Chapters 3, 10, and 11. The material in these chapters is adequate for a short course in abstract graphics.

Thinking with a Pencil begins with types of drawing which require no skill whatever, but which can be of practical everyday use to the artist, the draftsman, and the person who "can't draw a straight line." Each principle is introduced in its simplest, most basic form. Each chapter explains new uses for material already learned and thus serves as an effortless review. Experienced artists and draftsmen will find that the fundamentals of drawing take on fresh interest when they are employed in unfamiliar ways; the book makes its chief claim to the attention of experts by pointing out new applications for standard techniques. For example, more than a hundred illustrations are devoted to showing how the methods of the technical draftsman can simplify problems involved in drawing people, animals, clothing, and landscape. Nevertheless, new techniques are not lacking; *Thinking with a Pencil* provides a comprehensive treatment of the principles underlying charts, diagrams, and graphs, the use of tracing as a tool for creating original drawings, and the ways in which three-dimensional objects can be represented without the use of perspective. The book also contains an approach to figure drawing which greatly simplifies this field for the beginner, and which culminates in a method that I believe will prove of value to beginner and expert alike. The new material and its applications are ample to satisfy the requirements of a two-semester course in technical sketching.

Learning to draw is much easier when you take only one step at a time. You need not master each chapter before going on. However, do not leave a chapter until you have found new applications for the principal types of drawing described and have made at least a few sketches for practical use in your own work or hobbies. If you try to progress too rapidly, you will miss much and learn little. You will also find that the material in the later chapters seems "technical" and difficult, whereas it will all be easy when you make each step provide a firm foundation for the next. Such a slow-but-steady procedure will not prove wearisome if you really think with a pencil and put drawing to actual use in your work and in your hobbies. *Every* chapter in this book illustrates methods of drawing which can be applied by *everyone* in some way that is either practical or amusing.

When the book is used as a supplementary text, little or no class time needs to be spent on teaching drawing. However, the assignments should not only cover the basic field but should also provide graded exercises in drawing. This means that assignments must be planned with the problems of drawing in mind. A course in Elementary Biology, for example, might begin with a survey of the text [Fig. 110]. Charts modeled after Figs. 113 and 114 might come next. These could be followed by simple diagrams like Figs. 72–75, 126, and 136. Students should then master the techniques of tracing, transferring, redrawing, using contours, and accenting [Figs. 42 and 184–189]. Labeling these tracings furnishes separate, and valuable, assignments [Figs. 137–140 and 200]. Creative tracing can be taught by assigning exploded views [Fig. 137] or a series showing how a paramecium divides. Any of these tracings may be enlarged to provide exercises in measurement and proportion [Fig. 271]. Laboratory assignments should begin by tracing the subject from the text. It may then be traced from life [Fig. 190] and, finally, constructed freehand [Fig. 34]. These assignments take the student through Chapter 9. Any student who completes them will find them both more interesting and more instructive than conventional assignments.

Instructors in such fields as French and Accounting will not be able to make so many drawing assignments as those in, say, Anatomy or Home Economics. But with a little ingenuity, they can find a fair number. Even a few will add interest to the course, and every drawing a student makes leaves a far deeper impression on his mind than a written paper or a series of numerical computations.

Most of the illustrations are devoted to ways of using drawing rather than to ways of making them. In order to emphasize the fact that drawing has practical applications in *every* field, I have chosen examples from the widest possible range of topics. My own knowledge is much less extensive. Hence, I gathered much of my data from books. As I may have chosen poor sources or misinterpreted good ones, my illustrations cannot be regarded as authoritative in their respective fields. This does not affect their value as examples of drawing. However, you cannot afford to think of them as lessons in, say, Conchology or Cybernetics unless you check with someone who knows far more about the field represented than I do. If you catch an error, you will earn my gratitude by setting me right.

My thanks are due to John W. Barnes, my publisher, for his vision and support during the eleven years that the book has been in preparation. Dr. Gladys Walterhouse not only contributed invaluable editorial assistance but served as a guinea pig in experiments designed to make sure that the methods in the book can be used effectively by a person with no previous experience in drawing. Louise B. Hinds, of Barnes & Noble, Lawrence Cohen, and the staff of General Offset Company, Inc. have earned my praise and gratitude for seeing the book through the press and for their patience with my efforts to convert pencil drawings into that very different commodity "art work suitable for reproduction." Joseph Carlance has done far more to make the photographic illustrations adequate than a casual glance can reveal. John Carlance drew Figs. 187 and 584 and aided me with technical advice in preparing my own drawings for reproduction. My invaluable secretary, Mary Ellen Moran, has contributed so much to my work that no expression of appreciation is adequate.

A glance through the illustrations makes it obvious that one person could never have gathered information in such a wide variety of fields without unstinting aid from many people. My principal debts in this connection are to the staff of the Public Library of the District of Columbia and to that of the Cherrydale Branch of the Arlington County, Va. Library. Capt. John Barleon,

Jr. (Ret.) not only contributed much himself but dragooned his many friends, in and out of the Navy, into supplying information tnat I could never have obtained by my own efforts. M. Louise Curley worked out the data for Fig. 430 and the explanation of why continuous and integral data produce different curves on a graph. Clifford Hinds, Jr., was kind enough to prepare the architectural renderings in Fig. 174 from my rough sketches. H. T. E. Hertzberg provided many of the measurements from which I compiled the table in Fig. 623. However, he is not responsible for the final figures, which are also influenced by other sources. Rudy Oetting of Keuffel & Esser Co. graciously permitted me to use the drawings of scale rules in Figs. 272–274. Fig. 125 is the outcome of a suggestion from William P. Halstead. The improved Venn chart in Fig. 133 was originated by Edmund C. Berkeley. I am also indebted to Mr. Berkeley for catching and correcting a number of errors in earlier printings of this book.

Many others have aided me with advice, encouragement, and information. I would like to mention all of them and describe the contribution of each in detail. But if I did so, this foreword would be longer than the book itself. I have space to list only the names of those whose assistance meant most to me: Douglas P. Adams, James M. Alexander, Stanley Andrews, Richard R. Armacost, Capt. Louis L. Bangs (USN), Clarence E. Bennett, Calvin C. Bishop, Dr. Arthur H. Bryan, Elizabeth L. Burckmyer, Samuel M. Burt, Dr. Fitch Cheney, Cooper-Trent, S. L. Coover, E. R. Cornish, Dr. Lester D. Crow, Anna Espenschade, James E. Foy, Paul R. Frey, Werner P. Friederich, Catherine Glidden, Frederick Goff, Eric V. Greenfield, Theodore Guerchon, Dr. John Z. Hearon, Dr. Myron S. Heidingsfield, Robert Hornung, Sampson W. Horton, Frank W. Hubbard, Dr. Edward E. Hunt, Jr., Dr. Willard J. Jacobson, Dr. Clifford L. James, M. Kendig, Walther Kirchner, Dr. Scott L. Kittsley, Herbert C. Kluge, Malcolm S. Knowles, John Learmont, Alfred McClung Lee, Dr. Robert D. Leiter, Dr. John R. Lewis, Dr. Harry M. Love, Eleanor Luette, Dr. Josiah Macy, Dr. Donald Maley, Charles Martin, Ernest E. McMahon, Cmdr. Leo Meacher (USN), Joseph T. Merden, Dr. Hugh M. Miller, Alvin C. Moran, Dr. Edith E. Mortensen, Dr. George Fox Mott, Dr. Dorothy Mulgrave, Dr. Elwood Murray, Dr. Kaj L. Nielsen, Edward M. North, Cletus O. Oakley, Earl R. Pinkston, Dr. Marion Richter, Herbert C. Rosenthal, Harold R. Rowe, Capt. J. S. Schmidt (USN), Willis Shook, Steve M. Slaby, John J. Smiles, Harvey K. Smith, Nicholas Soutter, Murray R. Spiegel, Dr. Bernhard J. Stern, Mrs. Shirley Duncan Stout, J. Taylor, Walter A. Taylor, Merritt M. Thompson, Buckner B. Trawick,

Dr. Beno Vajda, Dr. Coolie Verner, Charles Warner, Stephan Warshal, Gilbert G. Weaver, and Rex E. Wright.

I cannot close this foreword without expressing my indebtedness to Louise B. Hinds and Grace R. Cosgrove for their work on my previous book *Play Production*. When that was published, I was not aware of how much I owed them. This is my first opportunity to acknowledge the obligation.

HENNING NELMS

Table of Contents

DRAWING NEED NOT BE PRETTY TO BE USEFUL

None of these sketches required either skill or artistic ability. Nevertheless, each of them played an important part in one of the world's major discoveries, designs, or inventions.

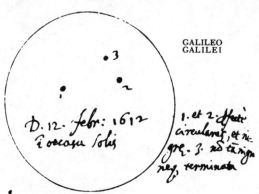

GALILEO GALILEI

1.
SKETCH OF SUNSPOTS
One of a series that inaugurated scientific astronomy.

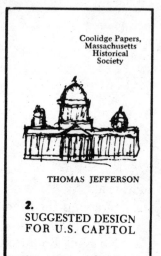

Coolidge Papers, Massachusetts Historical Society

THOMAS JEFFERSON

2.
SUGGESTED DESIGN FOR U.S. CAPITOL

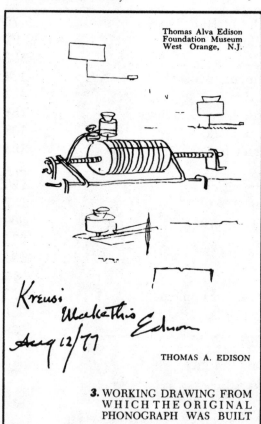

Thomas Alva Edison Foundation Museum West Orange, N.J.

THOMAS A. EDISON

3. WORKING DRAWING FROM WHICH THE ORIGINAL PHONOGRAPH WAS BUILT

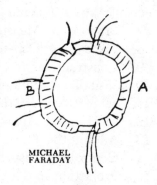

MICHAEL FARADAY

4.
LABORATORY NOTE ON BASIC EXPERIMENT IN ELECTRICAL INDUCTION
Most practical applications of electricity use this principle.

Sketches are reproduced at their original size, except that those made by Edison have been reduced one-third.

1

DRAWING FOR
PRACTICAL USE

Do the heads
you draw now
look like this?

HAIR

EQUAL

EQUAL

TOP OF
SKULL

If you learn that
the eye is midway
between the top of
the skull and the
chin, you can draw
a head like this.

6.

Gray line is the
same as Fig. 5.

5.

IF you have enough skill with a pencil to write your own name, you can make drawings like those in the frontispiece. They may be crude, and they certainly do not pretend to be artistic. Nevertheless, their value is proved by the fact that each of them served its purpose in a work of major importance. Practical drawings are mental tools. Once you have learned to make them, you will find that they are as useful in solving problems as saws and hammers are useful in carpentry.

UNDERSTANDING DRAWING

When you want to make more elaborate drawings, knowledge can usually provide an adequate substitute for skill. I have no natural talent for drawing, but all my life I have been placed in situations where I required pictures or diagrams and could not persuade anyone else to make them. This forced me to search for methods of producing drawings without skill. The present book is evidence that I found a great many.

Although there are substitutes for skill, *there is no substitute for understanding*. A collection of methods is of little value unless you have a firm grasp of the principles on which they are based and are able to recognize opportunities for putting them to actual use.

Need for Data. If you have found drawing difficult, you probably attributed this to a lack of skill. Actually, part of the trouble was almost certainly due to something quite different—lack of knowledge about the thing you were trying to draw. The heads

1

in Figs. 5 and 6 give some idea of how serious a handicap this can be and show how much even a little knowledge may help.

If there is any question in your mind about whether you can learn to draw, try sketching a head right now. Make it face left; for some reason, that is easier. Place the eye half way between the top of the skull and the chin. See how much more effective this is than the heads you have drawn in the past. Then find a drawing of a profile head and copy that. The copy will be better than your first sketch. This is not because your skill has miraculously increased, but simply because you have more data to go on.

No one can draw any object unless he either has it before him as a model or is sufficiently familiar with it to create it from imagination or re-create it from memory. Leonardo da Vinci was an infinitely better draftsman than Galileo, but he could not have made Galileo's sketch in Fig. 1 because he never saw a sunspot.

If you are not accustomed to drawing, your memory for graphic facts is probably unreliable. Do not trust it. Work from a model, from a snapshot, or from *copy* (which is the term applied by commercial artists to pictures clipped from magazines and newspapers). Diagrams and graphs can be based on verbal descriptions, mathematical formulas, or statistics.

Unfortunately, there is no one term that covers all forms of graphic data. Some of them, like "model" and "copy," have other meanings, and these may cause confusion. For this reason, we shall use the word *source* to include everything that supplies us with the information we require.

As you gain experience, you will find that many of the facts

READING DRAWINGS

You may need to know certain facts before you can interpret a drawing. If you have not studied geology, you cannot expect to learn much about offset strata from this diagram.

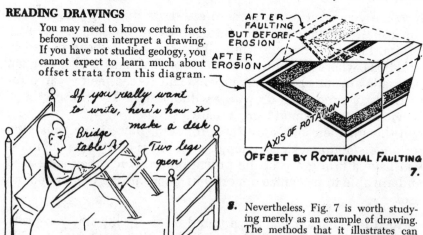

OFFSET BY ROTATIONAL FAULTING

7.

8. Nevertheless, Fig. 7 is worth studying merely as an example of drawing. The methods that it illustrates can be used to draw many things which have no connection with geology—such as the bed and table in this suggestion, sketched for a sick friend.

Fig. 8]   Drawing for Practical Use   **3**

you need can come out of your own head. But *they must be in your head before they can come out of it*. If you know the facts about geological strata, you can visualize some of them in a diagram like Fig. 7. If you have memorized many details about Renaissance architecture, you can combine them in a new way —as Jefferson did when he designed the Capitol [Fig. 2]. Nevertheless, if you lack even one basic fact, you can no more make the drawing than you can give an accurate verbal description of something about which you are ignorant.

Reading Drawings. Those who are accustomed to work with drawings speak of *reading* them, and they use the term in much the same way that other people do when they speak of reading a printed text. A drawing is said to "read well" when its meaning is clear. Thus, a fashion sketch reads well when it tells the dressmaker everything, except the measurements, that she needs to know in order to make the garment.

Reading a drawing is easier than making one. You can read drawings that you cannot make, but you cannot make a drawing unless you could read it if it were made by someone else. For this reason, *learning to make drawings begins by learning to read them*.

Every illustration in this book is an exercise in reading. Study each one to make sure that you understand it thoroughly. This is usually easy; a drawing like the bed in Fig. 8 can be read at a glance. But others, like the geological diagram in Fig. 7, may puzzle you at first. These are the ones from which you can learn most about drawing. Do not skip an illustration because you are not interested in the subject matter or because you never expect to make that particular type of drawing. Experience in reading unfamiliar varieties of drawing will not only increase your ability to draw but will enlarge your graphic vocabulary. This will help you to find applications for drawing in fields which you had previously overlooked.

Visualization. The first step in reading a drawing is to visualize the objects represented. Galileo's sketch in the frontispiece is a circle, but the caption tells us that it represents the sun. We must therefore see it as a sphere.

Fig. 7 is more complex. The near object is a rectangular block. The shading shows three oblique layers of different thicknesses. The dotted lines represent a similar block that has been rotated slightly about the axis on the right-hand face. If your visual imagination is weak, you may see these blocks merely as an arrange-

ment of lines on flat paper—but you must visualize them as blocks
before you can read the drawing.

Whenever you have trouble in seeing drawings as solid objects,
compare them with drawings that you can visualize easily. Thus,
the bed in Fig. 8 is obviously solid. If you get this firmly in mind
and then look at Fig. 7, the blocks there will probably also seem
solid.

You do *not* need to understand the meaning of a drawing
before you can visualize it. If you see Fig. 7 as two blocks with
oblique layers, you have visualized it even though you know
nothing of geology and have no idea of what the term "fault"
means.

Conventions. All drawings involve conventions. You must become familiar with these before you can read the drawings. In
some fields, such as electrical engineering, the conventions are
elaborate and must be memorized—just as you need to memorize
technical terms in order to read a book on the subject.

Fortunately, most drawings depend on a few simple conventions, and you are already accustomed to reading these. Thus,
solid objects are normally depicted from a viewpoint high enough
to show the top surface. You are so used to this that you visualize
the bed in Fig. 8 as though you were looking down on it, even
when the illustration is actually above your line of sight. Again,
you are accustomed to the idea that *solid* (continuous) lines
represent real objects, and that dotted lines (which are normally
composed of dashes) represent lines that are imaginary or have
specialized meanings.

The more you learn about such conventions, the easier it will
be for you to read drawings made by other people—and to make
drawings of your own that other people can read.

Functions of Drawing. Nearly everyone with whom I talked
while I was preparing this book spoke of drawing as a tool for
communication and seemed unaware that it has other functions.
Although drawing is certainly an effective and sometimes indispensable toool for expressing ideas, this is not its only use or
even its most valuable one.

My own experience has convinced me that practical drawing
is primarily a *thinking* tool. It can be used for taking notes, for
learning, for planning, and for computation. Perhaps no one of
these functions by itself is as important as communication. But
when we consider them all, there is little doubt that the ability
to think with a pencil is even more valuable than the ability to

Fig. 9] **Drawing for Practical Use** **5**

talk with one. Certainly this is true in my case. Ninety percent of my drawings are made entirely for my own use, and no one else ever sees them.

Many drawings fill several functions. Galileo's sketch [Fig. 1] is part of a series made originally as notes. These sketches then became learning tools in his investigation of sunspots. Later, he no doubt used them to communicate his theories to his friends.

Edison's drawings for the phonograph must have been made to guide his own planning [Fig. 3]. Only after he was satisfied with his plan did he decide to use this sheet of sketches as a means of communication.

None of the drawings in the frontispiece was intended for computation, but many graphs are made for this purpose. Working drawings often serve as devices for calculating lengths and angles without resorting to arithmetic. In fact, the process is so natural and easy that we may fail to recognize it as a form of computation.

Limitations of Drawing. Although drawing is an immensely valuable tool for thought, it is by no means a universal one. The fact that two-thirds of the space in this book is taken up by the text and captions demonstrates that, even in the field of communication, most drawings need to be supplemented by words. Again, although drawing is an extremely handy method of making certain computations, this does not alter the basic truth that the great majority of computations can be carried out much more easily and accurately by mathematics.

Perhaps the chief virtue of drawing is that it is most useful in the very places where language and mathematics fall short.

There is virtually no danger of becoming so fascinated by drawing that you will attempt to use it where language would be a better tool. No doubt, such a mistake could be made, but I cannot even imagine an example.

Unfortunately, situations do arise in which you may try to make computations and solve problems by drawing when mathematics would be the wiser choice. In most such cases, the selection of an approach depends on so many factors that no general principles can be laid down. However, for ordinary purposes, the following rules will usually suffice: When the problem offers an obvious attack by drawing, this approach is likely to be both quicker and easier than one based on mathematics. But when generality or accuracy is important, either approach the problem by mathematics or at least check your result by making numerical calculations.

Types of Drawing. We frequently speak of charts, diagrams, maps, pictures, and so on as though they were separate types of drawing. But these types overlap in complex ways, and the distinctions between them are vague. Maps, for example, combine features of both diagrams and pictorial drawings—and they can be drawn by the methods used to make graphs. This is fortunate; it means that everything we learn about one type of drawing can be applied to many other types as well.

9. TWO KNOWN POINTS FIX THE POSITION OF A STRAIGHT LINE Children connect points like these in numerical sequence to draw pictures. Scientists and businessmen follow the same procedure when they make graphs. Surveyors also join points in this way in order to draw maps.

Elements of Drawing. Instead of classifying drawings by types, it is normally more helpful to think in terms of their elements. *Every drawing is composed of points, lines, and the relations between them.* If we have two points, we can connect them with a straight line [Fig. 9]. When we know that two lines cross at a point, we can locate the point by drawing the lines [Points A and B, Fig. 10]. In most cases, we use these principles alternately. We draw points to fix lines and then use the lines to fix more points; these in turn fix more lines until our drawing is complete.

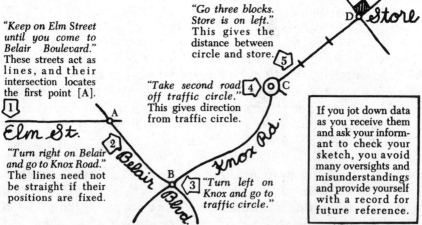

"Keep on Elm Street until you come to Belair Boulevard." These streets act as lines, and their intersection locates the first point [A].

"Go three blocks. Store is on left." This gives the distance between circle and store.

"Take second road off traffic circle." This gives direction from traffic circle.

"Turn right on Belair and go to Knox Road." The lines need not be straight if their positions are fixed.

"Turn left on Knox and go to traffic circle."

If you jot down data as you receive them and ask your informant to check your sketch, you avoid many oversights and misunderstandings and provide yourself with a record for future reference.

10. TWO KNOWN LINES FIX A POINT   A point can also be fixed by its distance and direction from a given point.

Fig. 10]   Drawing for Practical Use   7

Fig. 10 also illustrates how a point [D] can be located by establishing its distance and direction from some other point [C] that has already been fixed. This is normal procedure in freehand work.

If we can fix enough points, we can draw lines to mark the boundaries of such geometrical shapes as squares and triangles, and such irregular shapes as those in Fig. 9. Thus, drawing resolves itself into a matter of fixing the right points and drawing the right lines between them.

HOW TO MAKE DRAWING EASIER

The difficulty of making any particular drawing depends on the accuracy with which the points and lines must be fixed and on how hard this accuracy is to achieve.

How to Make Drawing Easier—
A. Decreasing the Need for Accuracy

Anything that lowers the need for accuracy decreases the need for skill. *If the standard of accuracy can be set low enough, anyone can draw anything for which he has the necessary data.*

Choosing Standards of Accuracy. We seek accuracy for two reasons: clarity and appearance. When you make a sketch—either to guide your own thinking or to explain a point in conversation —appearance is not important, and clarity can usually be secured by a very low standard of accuracy. The drawings in the frontispiece were easy, because the standards chosen were low.

Try to establish a slightly higher standard than your purpose seems to require. This helps to avoid forming a habit of careless drawing. It also provides a margin for error in case you have underestimated the need for accuracy or let yourself fall below the standard you have set.

Unnecessary accuracy is a waste of effort; unnecessary carelessness can defeat the purpose of a drawing. I have drawn many notes which were perfectly clear to me at the time, but which conveyed no meaning at all when I tried to consult them several months later. Jefferson's sketch of the Capitol [Fig. 2] leaves many points vague that could have been made clear by even a slight increase in the accuracy of his drawing.

Broadly speaking, we can divide drawings into three classes according to their standards of accuracy:

Roughs. These are offhand sketches made for immediate use [Fig. 11]. Appearance is not important, and explanations are either unnecessary or can easily be supplied. *Roughs* are invaluable tools for communication both in teaching and in conversation. They also help you to clarify your own ideas (learning) and to make plans.

Drawn on chalkboard

11.

ROUGH MAP TO SHOW THE ROUTE OF XENOPHON IN *THE ANABASIS* This cannot be understood without a verbal explanation or some familiarity with the subject matter represented.

SEMIFINISHED DRAWINGS. Notes and working drawings must explain themselves, but they need not attract the eye except by their neatness and clarity. Fig. 12 is a representative example.

There is no sharp break between roughs and *semifinished drawings*. Galileo's sketch in Fig. 1 looks crude, but it is really "semifinished" because neither improving the accuracy nor adding notes would make it clearer. The other sketches in the frontispiece are borderline cases. They undoubtedly served their respective purposes, and both Edison's and Faraday's drawings were clear to the people who actually used them. However, a typical semifinished drawing would be clear to anyone who was familiar with the field illustrated.

12.
SEMIFINISHED MAP MADE WHILE STUDYING *THE ACTS OF THE APOSTLES* AND SHOWING THE MISSIONARY JOURNEYS OF ST. PAUL Route maps are useful in many fields. Thus, a student of Greek might make his reading more vivid and interesting by tracing a map and marking each stage of the route taken by Xenophon and the Ten Thousand as it appeared in his text.

Fig. 13]   **Drawing for Practical Use**   **9**

FINISHED DRAWINGS. A drawing made for display or publication must catch and please the eye before it can instruct. This requires a fair degree of technical finish [Fig. 13]. Such *finished drawings* are no clearer than semifinished drawings—they are merely more attractive.

Drawings made for computation normally require the greatest attainable accuracy. However, as these are almost always mechanical, it is more convenient to treat them as a special variety of working drawings than to regard them as a separate class.

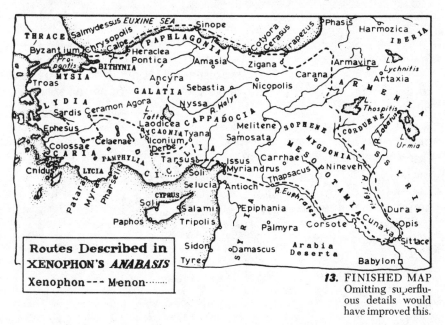

Routes Described in
XENOPHON'S *ANABASIS*

Xenophon --- Menon ·······

13. FINISHED MAP
Omitting superfluous details would
have improved this.

Eliminating Complications. Every complication adds to the need for accuracy and hence to the difficulty of drawing. The map in Fig. 11 serves its purpose, but if we tried to add the details shown in Fig. 13, they might not fit. Inaccuracies which were harmless in Fig. 11 would then become serious faults.

Omitting the useless is as important as including the essential. Aristotle stated a fundamental truth when he said that *everything which does not add will detract.* Fig. 12 supplies all the information we need to follow St. Paul's route—and nothing more. Fig. 13 includes a great deal of information which serves no purpose but which clutters the map and makes the important points hard to find. It also suffers from a common fault by omitting several places mentioned in the *Anabasis.* A map made to accompany a particular text should label every point mentioned in the text and nothing else—except that one or two well-known places may be added to help the reader fit the map into his general knowledge of geography.

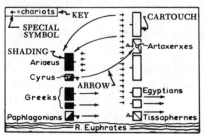

14. LABELS AND SYMBOLS
Plan of battle of Cunaxa
described in *The Anabasis*

Labels and Symbols. When we can treat an item as a unit, we are concerned only with its identity and do not need to draw a picture. In fact, labels and symbols enable us to draw things that cannot be pictured at all. In the battle plan [Fig. 14], groups of soldiers are represented by generalized symbols known as *cartouches*. As a cartouch can represent anything from an oyster to an abstract idea, we shall find many applications for them in later chapters.

Some of the elements in the battle plan are labeled. In other cases, symbols eliminate the need for labels. Thus, troops of cavalry are indicated by little pennons and diagonal lines, and the army of Cyrus is distinguished from that of Artaxerxes by shading. The arrows representing movement are also symbols, and ones for which we shall have much use.

Most of the symbols in Fig. 14 are standard. The rest are either labeled or explained in a *key*.

Left-Handedness. This is not a handicap in drawing. In fact, it appears to be an asset. The percentage of successful artists who are left-handed is surprisingly large.

15.
EFFECT OF
LINE ANGLE

Lines from "southwest" to "southeast" or from "northeast" to "northwest" are much easier to draw than those in any other direction. When a line gives trouble, bring it to this angle by turning your paper.

LINE BEING DRAWN

LINES ALREADY DRAWN

There are not many differences between left- and right-handed drawing. But if you are left-handed, you should reverse any instructions in this book which speak of "left" and "right" and make corresponding changes in interpreting the illustrations. Thus, left-handed readers will find it easier to draw lines that run from "southeast" to "northwest" [Fig. 15].

Fig. 18]   Drawing for Practical Use   11

TRICKS OF THE TRADE
If you think you can't draw
a straight line, try one of
the easy methods shown here.

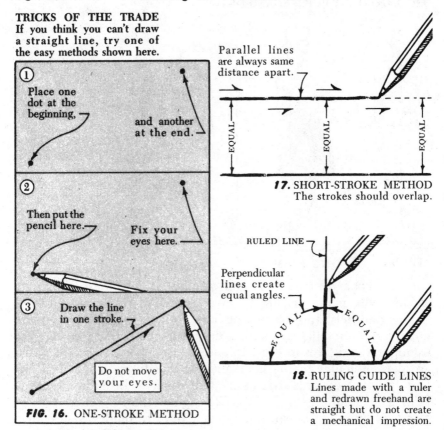

① Place one
dot at the
beginning, ⌐
and another
at the end. ⌐

② Then put the
pencil here. ⌐
Fix your
eyes here. ⌐

③ Draw the line
in one stroke. ⌐

Do not move
your eyes.

FIG. 16. ONE-STROKE METHOD

Parallel lines
are always same
distance apart. ⌐

EQUAL   EQUAL   EQUAL

17. SHORT-STROKE METHOD
The strokes should overlap.

RULED LINE ⌐

Perpendicular
lines create
equal angles. ⌐

EQUAL   EQUAL

18. RULING GUIDE LINES
Lines made with a ruler
and redrawn freehand are
straight but do not create
a mechanical impression.

How to Make Drawing Easier—B. Making Accuracy Easier

After we have reduced our need for accuracy to an adequate minimum, the next objective is to achieve that minimum with the fewest demands on our skill and the least expenditure of effort. Much of this book deals with methods of making accuracy easier. Those in Figs. 15–18 are especially useful to the beginner. Others are explained in every chapter.

Parallels and Perpendiculars. Readers familiar with either geometry or mechanical drawing may feel that parallels and perpendiculars are too elementary to be worth mentioning—and that illustrations like those in Figs. 17 and 18 overemphasize the obvious. However, when we undertake the study of practical drawing in general, it pays to rethink even the most commonplace ideas. Otherwise, we are apt to overlook important ways in which they can be applied.

Thus, an architect, who automatically thinks in terms of parallels and perpendiculars when planning a house, may neglect them

WHY PARALLELS AND PERPENDICULARS
ARE IMPORTANT IN FREEHAND DRAWING

High hip is under the low shoulder

When a figure runs, line of balance slants.

LINE OF BALANCE

19.
ERECT FIGURE

20.
WEIGHT ON ONE FOOT

21.
RUNNING FIGURE

22.
TOPPLING FIGURE

entirely when he tries to sketch a man or a woman. This may explain why many architects have trouble with figure drawing.

The parallels and perpendiculars used for this purpose are imaginary, but that does not diminish their importance. For example, the figures in Figs. 19 and 20 must balance on lines that are perpendicular to the floor and parallel to each other. If the *line of balance* slants, the figure will seem to be either running [Fig. 21] or falling over [Fig. 22]. Again, the soldier in Fig. 19 stands at attention because imaginary lines through his shoulders and hips are perpendicular to his line of balance. The correspond-

DRAWING CIRCLES
WITH A COMPASS

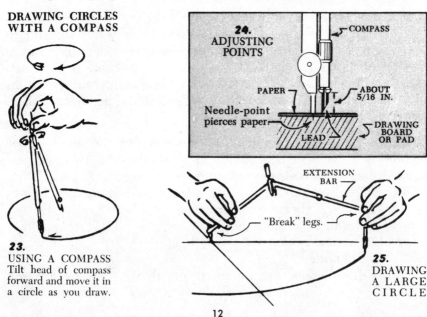

24.
ADJUSTING POINTS

COMPASS

PAPER

ABOUT 5/16 IN.

Needle-point pierces paper.

LEAD

DRAWING BOARD OR PAD

EXTENSION BAR

"Break" legs.

23.
USING A COMPASS
Tilt head of compass forward and move it in a circle as you draw.

25.
DRAWING A LARGE CIRCLE

Fig. 27]   **Drawing for Practical Use**   **13**

ing lines in the girl are *oblique* [Fig. 20]. That makes her weight seem to rest on one foot. Even in this case, you must be able to imagine perpendiculars and parallels; otherwise you cannot tell whether your oblique lines are really slanting, let alone judge how much they should slant.

Similar considerations apply to the rudiments in any specialized field. If you have had even a little experience in some particular type of drawing, at least a few of my remarks on that type may seem so elementary that they are almost an insult to your intelligence. When a principle appears overobvious, stop and ask

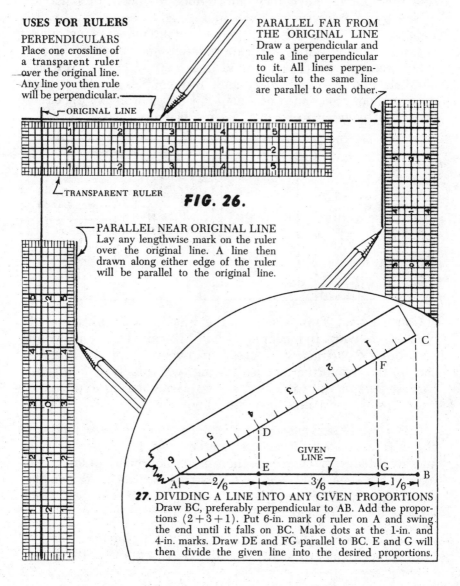

USES FOR RULERS

PERPENDICULARS
Place one crossline of a transparent ruler over the original line. Any line you then rule will be perpendicular.

—ORIGINAL LINE

—TRANSPARENT RULER

FIG. 26.

PARALLEL FAR FROM THE ORIGINAL LINE
Draw a perpendicular and rule a line perpendicular to it. All lines perpendicular to the same line are parallel to each other.

PARALLEL NEAR ORIGINAL LINE
Lay any lengthwise mark on the ruler over the original line. A line then drawn along either edge of the ruler will be parallel to the original line.

GIVEN LINE

A ⊢—2/6—⊣ ⊢——3/6——⊣⊢1/6⊢ B

27. DIVIDING A LINE INTO ANY GIVEN PROPORTIONS
Draw BC, preferably perpendicular to AB. Add the proportions (2 + 3 + 1). Put 6-in. mark of ruler on A and swing the end until it falls on BC. Make dots at the 1-in. and 4-in. marks. Draw DE and FG parallel to BC. E and G will then divide the given line into the desired proportions.

yourself how you would apply it in an unfamiliar field. If you know all about drawing graphs, how would you use the principle in Fig. 9 when drawing a map—or an elephant? You have not really mastered a principle of drawing until you can apply it to many different types of subjects.

Mechanical Aids. Art teachers in grade schools often condemn the use of compasses [Figs. 23–25] and rulers [Figs. 26 and 27]. Perhaps this is one reason why so few of us learn to draw. From a practical standpoint, compass and ruler are valuable tools. They save time, increase accuracy, and reduce the need for skill.

The transparent ruler shown in Fig. 26 is especially helpful. It is the handiest tool I have found for offhand drawing, and it enables anyone to draw accurate parallels and perpendiculars.

Squared paper acts as a kind of built-in ruler [Fig. 28]. It fixes parallels and perpendiculars and also enables us to estimate measurements. Sketching on squared paper is probably the easiest way for a beginner to develop a sense of proportion.

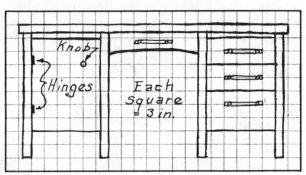

28.◊
SQUARED PAPER AS
A MECHANICAL AID
It provides a quick and
easy way to plan home-
workshop projects—like
this desk. It is much
easier to correct errors
with an eraser than to
use a saw or a hammer.

Construction. This is one of the fundamental procedures of practical drawing. In fact, it may almost be called *the* fundamental procedure. *Construction* is based on two principles: (1) If we can fix the proportions of a drawing, we usually find that the hardest part of the work is done. (2) Drawing an approximate line helps us to visualize the correct line.

FIXED VS. FREE LINES. If we cannot draw straight lines and circles freehand with sufficient accuracy, we can always fall back on straightedge or compass. There is an enormous practical difference between *fixed lines* like these, which *can* be drawn mechanically, and the *free lines* of a tree or a pin-up girl, which *must* be drawn freehand.

CONSTRUCTIONS FOR FIXED-LINE DRAWINGS. Anyone who can draw a rectangle, a triangle, and a circle can draw all the shapes

Fig. 31]   Drawing for Practical Use   15

CONSTRUCTION FOR FIXED-LINE DRAWING

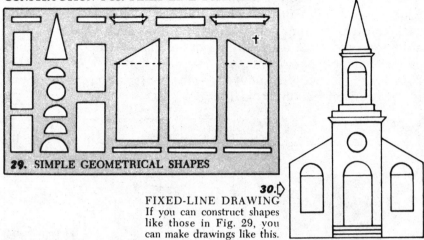

29. SIMPLE GEOMETRICAL SHAPES

30.
FIXED-LINE DRAWING
If you can construct shapes like those in Fig. 29, you can make drawings like this.

in Fig. 29. Anyone who can draw these shapes can put them together and "build" the church in Fig. 30. No single line presents any difficulty, and the construction is made by adding one line to another until we get through. When we think of it in this way, drawing a church requires no more ability than drawing a rectangle. Walking a mile employs the same process as walking across the road—it just takes more steps.

If you have skill, it may be convenient to fix some points by eye and to draw lines freehand. But all you really need is a knowledge of the facts about the object and familiarity with the methods of construction.

CONSTRUCTIONS FOR FREE-LINE DRAWINGS. When we complete the geometrical construction of a church, or any other fixed-line subject, we automatically complete the drawing. But for free-line subjects, such as the elephant [Fig. 31] and the moth [Fig. 34], the geometrical construction is only the first step. Such constructions act as scaffoldings. They fix the proportions of the drawings and the positions of the parts. The accuracy problem is reduced to a minimum. We can no longer make serious mistakes.

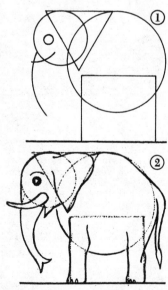

FIG. 31.
HOW CONSTRUCTION WORKS
Once a framework of geometrical shapes has been constructed, a child can complete the drawing —if he has a source to follow.

Although drawing a geometrical construction is a mechanical matter which demands no skill whatever, the ability to design such constructions must be learned because each object requires a different construction. Learning to design constructions is much easier than it looks. Moreover, you will find that every bit of knowledge you acquire about fixed-line construction prepares you for the study of free-line construction.

CONSTRUCTION PROCEDURE FOR FREE-LINE DRAWING

32. SOURCE — TIGER MOTH

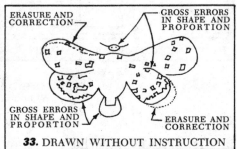

ERASURE AND CORRECTION · GROSS ERRORS IN SHAPE AND PROPORTION

GROSS ERRORS IN SHAPE AND PROPORTION · ERASURE AND CORRECTION

33. DRAWN WITHOUT INSTRUCTION

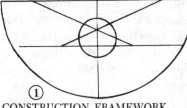

① CONSTRUCTION FRAMEWORK

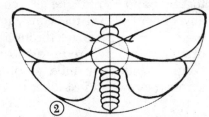

② **FAINT-LINE CONSTRUCTION**
After the framework is drawn, it acts as a guide and the contours can be sketched without trouble.

③ **CORRECTION AND DETAILS**
Correct errors in construction. Adding details may reveal minor mistakes. Erase this stage until it is barely visible. It then serves as the construction over which the final drawing is made.

④ COMPLETED DRAWING

FIG. 34.

FAINT-LINE CONSTRUCTIONS. Construction enables us to make drawings one step at a time. To take full advantage of this principle, the geometrical construction for a free-line drawing should be followed by a *faint-line construction* [moth, Step 2, Fig. 34] in which the lines of the object are sketched lightly freehand. After comparing this construction with the source and making whatever corrections seem desirable [Step 3], the final drawing is easy [Step 4].

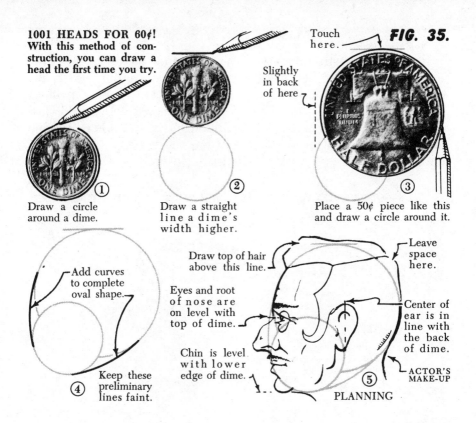

1001 HEADS FOR 60¢! With this method of construction, you can draw a head the first time you try.

Touch here.

Slightly in back of here

FIG. 35.

① Draw a circle around a dime.

② Draw a straight line a dime's width higher.

③ Place a 50¢ piece like this and draw a circle around it.

④ Add curves to complete oval shape. Keep these preliminary lines faint.

Draw top of hair above this line.

Eyes and root of nose are on level with top of dime.

Chin is level with lower edge of dime.

Leave space here.

Center of ear is in line with the back of dime.

ACTOR'S MAKE-UP

⑤ PLANNING

This step-by-step procedure is not just a crutch for the beginner; it is the quickest way to draw with a reasonable degree of accuracy. Cartoon animators work in this fashion, using red pencil for the stages of construction and black for the final drawing.

SIXTY CENTS A HEAD. Not all constructions are so specialized as those for the elephant and the tiger moth. Fig. 35 shows a construction on which you can draw any profile head. Sketching heads in this way is real fun. It can also teach you a great deal about drawing. Try to vary the features. Start with men; women's hair may cause trouble.

Heads provide far more than a combination pastime and drawing lesson. Figs. 35–39 illustrate how heads can serve all five functions of practical drawing. See how many different applications you can find in fields that interest you.

While studying Figs. 36–39, note the various ways in which faint and dotted lines can be used to subordinate certain features of a drawing or diagram. Fig. 36 stresses the drawing by showing the construction in gray. Fig. 37 achieves a similar, but not identical, effect by the use of dotted lines. A third technique is to use a color for the construction and make the drawing in black.

Both the construction and the drawing were given equal emphasis in Fig. 38 because I wanted to illustrate how neatly the construction fits a skull. Fig. 39 shows the construction in black and the drawing in gray. This stresses the construction and calls attention to the fact that the two-circle trick is useful even though the circles are far from perfect and the subject has unusual proportions which do not fit the framework closely.

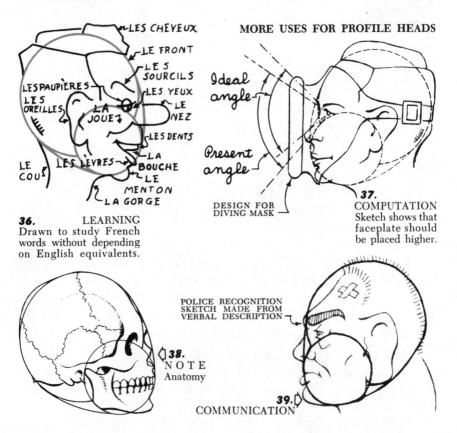

MORE USES FOR PROFILE HEADS

36.   **LEARNING**
Drawn to study French words without depending on English equivalents.

37.
COMPUTATION
Sketch shows that faceplate should be placed higher.

DESIGN FOR DIVING MASK

38.
NOTE
Anatomy

POLICE RECOGNITION SKETCH MADE FROM VERBAL DESCRIPTION

39.
COMMUNICATION

TRACING AS CONSTRUCTION. If you have ever tried to trace a picture freehand, you have probably been disappointed by the result and concluded that effective tracing requires almost as much skill as freehand drawing. Actually, it requires more. Few people can copy a picture exactly by direct tracing.

The reason for this is that the lines of the source vary in width. If you attempt to trace the whole line, you are likely to get the ragged effect in Fig. 41. If you draw uniform lines [Step 1, Fig. 42], they will not produce a true copy. Also, your line may fall anywhere within the broad part of the line in the source.

Fig. 45]   Drawing for Practical Use   19

However, tracing permits us to take a short cut by making a faint-line construction [Step 1, Fig. 42] without starting with a geometrical construction. After this faint-line construction has been traced, it is lifted from the source and laid on a sheet of white paper. The sketch is then redrawn freehand, using heavy lines and following the source as a model [Step 2].

This procedure of tracing a faint-line construction and then redrawing freehand with heavy lines is the secret of successful tracing. Even when you are trying to copy your source exactly,

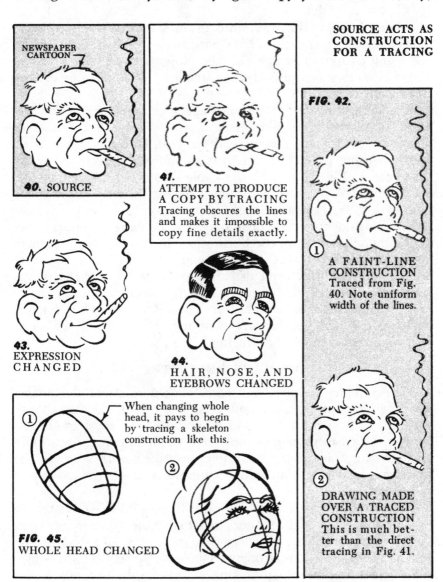

SOURCE ACTS AS CONSTRUCTION FOR A TRACING

NEWSPAPER CARTOON

40. SOURCE

41. ATTEMPT TO PRODUCE A COPY BY TRACING Tracing obscures the lines and makes it impossible to copy fine details exactly.

43. EXPRESSION CHANGED

44. HAIR, NOSE, AND EYEBROWS CHANGED

FIG. 42.

① A FAINT-LINE CONSTRUCTION Traced from Fig. 40. Note uniform width of the lines.

When changing whole head, it pays to begin by tracing a skeleton construction like this.

①

②

FIG. 45. WHOLE HEAD CHANGED

② DRAWING MADE OVER A TRACED CONSTRUCTION This is much better than the direct tracing in Fig. 41.

redrawing can do as much for a tracing as baking does for a cake (compare Fig. 41 with Step 2, Fig. 42). Tracing is by no means limited to copying. It can be as creative as you like. Figs. 43–45 show how new, and even completely original, heads can be drawn over traced constructions. This method enables us to draw any head from any angle for which we can find a source.

The same technique was used to produce the simplified map in Fig. 12, which was traced from the complex shore line of the map in Fig. 13. You will find it an excellent procedure for getting rid of unwanted details.

When tracing in this way, think of the source as though it were a geometrical construction like that for the moth in Step 1, Fig. 34. Use it as a guide which fixes the proportions of your drawing, but which does not restrict your freedom to simplify or change any element you wish.

It is both ethically wrong and legally dangerous to copy pictures from books or periodicals if you display the results or employ them for any commercial purpose. However, there is no harm in using published drawings as sources for original work. The head in Fig. 43 was clearly copied from Fig. 40, but no one could object if you turn a cartoon like Fig. 40 into a sketch like Fig. 44 or the girl's head in Fig. 45.

Some idea of the value of tracing may be gained from the fact that although nearly all the illustrations in this book are original, every one of them (except a few rough sketches) was traced at some point in its history. This is partly due to the fact that I was preparing illustrations for reproduction, which is a much more elaborate matter than ordinary drawing. But even when I make semifinished sketches for my own use, at least half of them involve a certain amount of tracing.

DRAWING UNLIMITED

The examples in this book were chosen to cover the widest possible range of types and subjects. The fact that I was able to make them does not show unusual versatility on my part. If you master the basic principles and methods of drawing, and apply them to everything that comes along *regardless of type or subject,* you can draw anything which interests you—if you have the necessary facts.

You would not learn one kind of arithmetic to make change in dollars and cents and another kind to handle measurements in feet, inches, and fractions. There is no more reason to study drawing in watertight compartments labeled "mechanical drawing," "charts and graphs," "map-making," "costume design," and so on.

Fig. 46]   Drawing for Practical Use   21

Some subjects may seem harder to draw than others. However, the difference is in the subject itself rather than in the drawing. Human figures, for example, require a fairly high standard of accuracy. Furthermore, the facts about the figure are subtle. They are not easy to master, even when you sketch from life. If you knew as much about the structure of the human figure as you do about the shape of an egg, you could draw one as easily as the other—*with the same degree of accuracy.*

You can convince yourself of this by noticing that familiar subjects seem easier than unfamiliar ones. As your skill does not vary with the subject, the difference must lie in your knowledge of the facts. Again, it is much easier to copy a drawing freehand than to sketch from life. The reason for this is that the artist who made the drawing has already gathered the pertinent facts and revealed them in his picture. When you copy it, you take your facts from him instead of having to dig them out for yourself. This makes your drawing seem easier—although the real difference is that the facts are more accessible.

If you want to produce expert drawings in a professional field, you must concentrate on the applications of drawing that it requires. This may involve taking a specialized course. Nevertheless, the important things to learn in such a course are *not* specialized methods of drawing—they are the facts about the subject matter, the conventions used in that type of drawing, and the most efficient ways of *applying* the general methods of drawing to problems that arise in the field covered by the course.

When you are not specializing, put drawing to work in every way you can. This will make it more useful. As you will do more drawing, you will get more practice. You will understand drawing better because you will employ each principle and method in many different ways and can therefore see it from every aspect.

Mastering Principles. Half the difficulty of learning anything comes in grasping the principles upon which it is based. Knowing a specialized trick—like the coin construction for heads—will not get you very far. But when you master a principle, you take a stride in seven-league boots. I have attempted to explain the principles of practical drawing in this book. However, you will not really master them until you can apply them to your own problems.

Suppose you want to draw two heads for a poster. The heads should be about 8 in. high. Coin heads are barely 1½ in. high, and you cannot find suitable heads to trace. What can you do?

The only reason for using coins is to draw circles of the right proportions. The smaller (dime) circle is half the height of the head. Therefore, for an 8 in. head, the smaller circle should have a 2 in. radius. If you can find the right radius for the larger circles, you can draw the circles with a compass and apply the principle of the coin method to your 8 in. heads. Finding the radius is a problem in proportion, and Fig. 27 shows how to solve such problems. Once you recognize these facts, large heads are as easy to draw as small ones [Figs. 46 and 47].

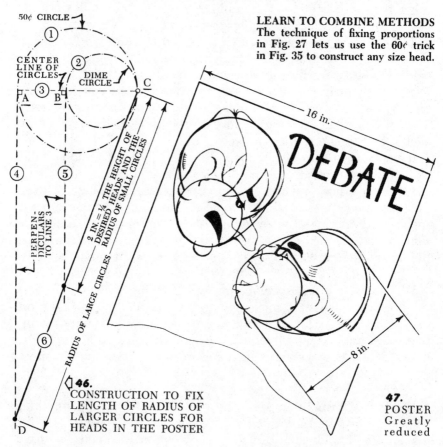

LEARN TO COMBINE METHODS
The technique of fixing proportions in Fig. 27 lets us use the 60¢ trick in Fig. 35 to construct any size head.

46. CONSTRUCTION TO FIX LENGTH OF RADIUS OF LARGER CIRCLES FOR HEADS IN THE POSTER

47. POSTER Greatly reduced

But why limit the coin method to profile heads? Fig. 48 demonstrates that it works equally well for three-quarter heads and even for cartoon bodies.

By changing the positions of the circles, you can draw a Neanderthal man or a baby [Figs. 49 and 50]. Note how these circles reveal the structure of the heads and help us to compare one with the other. Varying both the positions and proportions of the circles provides constructions for heads as different as those

Fig. 53] Drawing for Practical Use **23**

of an embryo [Fig. 51] and a unicorn [Fig. 52]. If you use a quarter instead of the 50¢ piece, you can make constructions for front views of adult human heads [Fig. 53]. By substituting ellipses for circles, you can construct the body of any animal, real or fabulous [Fig. 52].

Variations like these are not so easy as profile heads. They may be beyond your reach until you have had more experience.

EXPLORING MODIFICATIONS OF THE COIN-CONSTRUCTION METHOD

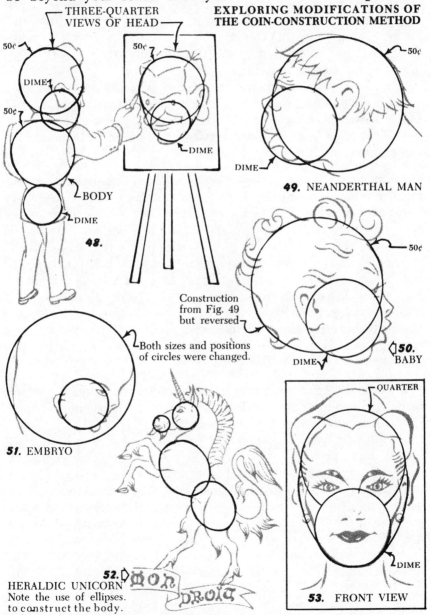

THREE-QUARTER VIEWS OF HEAD

50¢
DIME
50¢
BODY
DIME
48.

50¢
DIME
DIME

50¢
DIME
49. NEANDERTHAL MAN

Construction from Fig. 49 but reversed — Both sizes and positions of circles were changed.

50¢
DIME
50. BABY

51. EMBRYO

52. HERALDIC UNICORN
Note the use of ellipses to construct the body.

QUARTER
DIME
53. FRONT VIEW

Nevertheless, they are worth noticing; they bring out the difference between the 60¢ *trick*, which is good only for profile heads, and the two-circle (or ellipse) *principle*, which enables us to construct any head or body in any position.

How to Practice without Practicing. We cannot learn to draw without practice, but practice is dull and no one enjoys it. If you study some individual type of drawing, you must begin with formal exercises which have no value except as practice material. In general drawing, however, you can start by making charts, diagrams, and tracings that you can actually use. You will then get your practice by drawing these.

Another painless method of practicing is to doodle with a purpose. You can doodle coin heads well enough now to get a lot of fun out of it. As you learn new methods, invent doodling "exercises" for yourself. Do not repeat the same doodle endlessly; draw something different each time.

Learning to Draw by Drawing. This book has been arranged to introduce each principle in its simplest form. The material in one chapter prepares you for the next and acts as a review of the principles previously explained. If you take each step as it comes and take only one step at a time, no step will be difficult in itself. You can learn to draw by drawing; formal practice will not be needed except in a few special cases where experience has shown that it is worth the effort.

Nevertheless, you cannot have it both ways. You cannot skip the material on charts and diagrams, skim lightly over that on tracing, and then expect to master construction with ease and draw figures without formal practice.

Technical Terms. Although there are many ways in which drawing becomes easier to learn when we do not confine it to a single kind of subject matter, there is one aspect that becomes more difficult. We do so much of our thinking in words that we have trouble understanding anything which cannot be explained in simple, appropriate terms. The terms used in any one field of drawing are adequate for that field. But if we consider drawing as a whole, we find that some basic ideas are described by a variety of terms and that some terms have many different meanings.

When we do have a single term with a clear meaning, it has often been taken from mathematics—where the simplest ideas are apt to be weighted down by the longest names. Thus, *orthographic projection* sounds like something that only a Giant Brain could handle. Actually, it is a technical term for the most elementary type of picture. Galileo's sunspot sketch is an orthographic projection. He could almost have made the drawing while he was pronouncing its name.

Sometimes we shall meet important ideas for which there are no accepted terms at all. Thus, although we have words for model, copy, data, description, and so on, I had to go outside the usual vocabularies of drawing to find the general term "source."

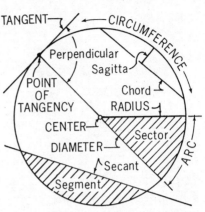

I have tried to minimize the problem of nomenclature by using the simplest, most descriptive terms I could find and by using only one term for each concept. This may confuse you if I happen to employ an unfamiliar term for some idea that you

54. TECHNICAL NAMES FOR PARTS ASSOCIATED WITH A CIRCLE
Memorize the ones in capitals. We shall need them in later chapters.

already understand. But if I attempted to list every synonym for every term, I would confuse every reader. Whenever a point seems obscure, I suggest considering the possibility that the difficulty is in the words rather than in the ideas.

2

GETTING STARTED

55. WRONG

56. CORRECT

ALTHOUGH the essential pre-
liminaries of drawing are
few and simple, beginners show
great ingenuity in getting them
wrong. If you have tried to draw
and failed, your failure was at least partly due to starting off on
the wrong foot.

WORKING CONDITIONS

Experts sometimes turn out good drawings when working
under difficulties. The rest of us cannot afford to burden ourselves with unnecessary handicaps.

Working Surface. When you draw on a level surface, such as
the top of a table, the movements of your hand are hard to
control. Also, you must compensate for the fact that you see your
work in perspective. You can avoid both difficulties by using an
auxiliary table top [Fig. 56]. A large *drawing board* is ideal, but
a bread board or a sheet of plywood will do nicely. It should be
at least ½ in. thick to resist bending and at least 16 in. by 21 in.
in size. Prop the rear of the board up on a small box or a block
of wood. The board in Fig. 56 is tilted enough to let you work in
comfort. A steeper angle would not interfere with your drawing,
but a pencil or ruler placed on the board would slide down it.
Make sure that your table or desk is solid. Trying to draw on
rickety furniture is as frustrating as trying to write in a cross-
town bus.

Light. The light should come over your left shoulder so that it
will neither shine in your eyes nor cast the shadow of your hand
on your work. Most lamps need to be adjusted before they are

26

suitable for drawing. The one in Fig. 55 will be adequate if it is placed on a small table behind your left elbow with the shade tilted to throw the light over your shoulder. Use at least a 100-watt bulb with this type of lamp as you will need a strong light —especially for tracing.

Fig. 56 shows a standing lamp equipped with a swivel socket and a 75-watt *reflector-flood* or *projector-flood* bulb. These are silvered on the inside and are much more efficient than household bulbs.

EQUIPMENT AND MATERIALS

The choice of materials and equipment varies with the kind of drawing. Also, technical specifications are of little interest except when a purchase is contemplated. I have therefore grouped all such data in the Equipment and Materials Supplement [pp. 322–329]. Every item mentioned in this book, no matter how casually, is described there. In cases where the text refers to only one piece of equipment or type of material, the Supplement often lists three or four and compares their respective merits. *Always refer to the Supplement before making a purchase.* The present section is confined to a description of papers, pencils, and a few items directly associated with their use.

Paper. Most pencil drawing calls for a paper that is opaque, strong enough to resist buckling and tearing, and hard enough to keep pencil strokes from leaving grooves. The surface should have sufficient *tooth* to *take* pencil marks, though it must not be so rough that a line drawn on it is ragged. Erasure should be easy and should neither leave a smudge nor damage the surface for future drawing.

The fear of making mistakes is a serious handicap to the beginner. Even when his fear is entirely subconscious, it causes strain which reduces his ability to draw. Expensive paper aggravates this fear. It seems a pity to spoil the beautiful white surface with a poor drawing. For this reason, it is well to make your first sketches on the cheapest paper you can find that meets the specifications I have listed. Good quality 32-pound *newsprint* is ideal. Do not buy the rough-surfaced trash sometimes sold as "sketch pads." The smooth-finished, 16-pound *sulfite paper* commonly used for scratch pads is also good. Many 3 x 5 index cards take pencil nicely. Use them to practice "60" heads. Practice on postal cards. When you add a short note, you save writing a letter. Experiment with every cheap paper you can find and then adopt the ones that suit your needs.

TRACING PAPER. This should have all the qualities specified above, except that it must be transparent instead of opaque. Test the transparency by placing a sheet of the paper over the reverse of a dollar bill. Examine the scroll in the eagle's beak under a strong light. If you cannot read the word "UNUM," the paper is too opaque.

SQUARED PAPER. The type illustrated in Fig. 28, which has eight squares to the inch, is the only one that you need consider at present. Many other varieties are available, and we shall find use for them later.

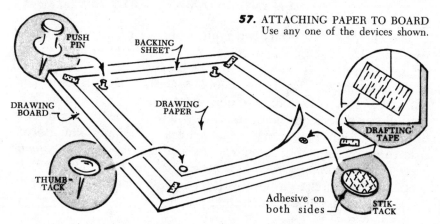

57. ATTACHING PAPER TO BOARD
Use any one of the devices shown.

ATTACHING PAPER TO BOARD. Pads are convenient for freehand work. They hold the paper flat, provide a smooth drawing surface, and permit turning the paper to bring each line into the easiest position.

When you use a single sheet of paper instead of a pad, you will need a *backing sheet* [Fig. 57]. This is a piece of smooth, white paper placed under the drawing to keep it from being affected by irregularities in the surface of the supporting board.

Both the backing sheet and the drawing or tracing paper can be fastened to the board with *thumb tacks* or *push pins*. Another common method is to use small strips of *drafting tape*, which is similar to cellophane tape but is opaque. A fourth method is to place one of the little wax disks, called *Stik-tacks*, under each corner of the sheet. These methods are largely interchangeable, but push pins are unsatisfactory for the lower corners as they interfere with the movements of your hands.

Paper fastened directly to the auxiliary table top cannot be turned to bring a line into the easiest position for drawing. For that reason, you may want to buy a separate drawing board and affix your paper to it. When tracing free-line subjects, you can attach a sheet of tracing paper to your source with Stik-tacks. The two sheets then stay together without being fastened to a board and can be turned to any position you choose.

Pencils. Many kinds of pencils are made, but only a few are important for practical drawing.

Leads. The graphite *leads* in ordinary pencils may be of good quality, but they are usually limited to three degrees of hardness. Even these are not standardized. The leads made for drawing pencils come in seventeen different degrees, marked as follows:

HARDEST   SOFTEST

9H, 8H, 7H, 6H, 5H, 4H, 3H, 2H, H, F, HB, B, 2B, 3B, 4B, 5B, 6B

The choice of a lead depends on the paper. The lead should be soft enough to leave a clear mark without undue pressure but hard enough not to wear rapidly or to smudge when rubbed lightly with the fingers.

Newsprint calls for a B or 2B pencil, and sulfite demands an F or HB lead. Tracing paper usually has more tooth; try a 5H or 4H lead for construction tracing and a 3H or 2H for the final drawing. These, however, are mere suggestions. Papers of the same general type vary greatly, and something depends on your personal *touch*. If you are choosey, a change in the weather may make a difference of one degree because it affects the tooth of the paper.

Colored leads are useful to color drawings made in lead pencil or ink. They can also distinguish lines that have different meanings. The leads are of two types: waterproof and water-soluble. Both types come in a wide range of colors. Unless you need the waterproof feature, choose the water-soluble type. The colors are brighter, and the leads are less fragile. Furthermore, after shading the area, you can smooth the color with a damp brush. This is easier than using regular water color.

Holders. Leads are too fragile to be used without some form of support. The wood in an ordinary pencil forms a built-in support. Wooden pencils come with all grades of lead and are preferred by some artists and draftsmen for that reason. Both the wood and the lead must be sharpened [Figs. 58 and 59]. However, mechanical and electrical sharpeners are available.

Mechanical holders made especially for draftsmen also take all grades of lead. You will need a different holder for each grade as the diameter varies with the grade. These holders have screw clutches to permit adjusting the length of the lead for sharpening. The holders do not carry erasers.

For general drawing, I find mechanical pencils with screw feed ideal. They have sturdy, usable erasers and pocket clips that also serve to keep them from rolling off your drawing board. Each pencil of this type takes only one diameter of lead. Although several grades of lead are made for each diameter, the choice of a diameter is important.

Only three of the available diameters deserve serious consideration for practical drawing, "Standard" lead measures 0.046 in. This is too blunt for many uses, but it can be sharpened to the needle points required for accented lines like those in the push pins of Fig. 57 and the hands in Fig. 58. Extend the lead, sharpen it, and then retract it. Sharpening can be done with a *sandpaper block, magneto file* [Fig. 58], or even a sheet of fine *sandpaper* held on the edge of your desk. Sharpening may seem like a nuisance at first, but experience makes it quick and easy. "Thin" leads are 0.036 in.; *Autopoint* makes pencil that take 0.5 mm. leads. Both types draw lines thin enough for roughs and most diagrams. Adjust the lead so that the tip barely shows, or it will break. Neither type can be sharpened.

Colored leads made for mechanical holders break easily and cannot be sharpened.

Erasers. The erasers sold for Scripto-type pencils, those made in pencil form, and the block eraser known as Pink Pearl are all good and have much the same characteristics. Magic-Rub is softer and produces exceptionally clean erasures.

Art Gum is useful for erasing large areas but will not remove strongly marked lines. A device known as an ABC Dry-Clean Pad, which consists of a stockinet bag filled with crumbs of Art Gum, can be employed to clean pencil drawings.

A draftsman's *erasing shield* is often helpful. This is like the shields used by typists but has many more holes.

PROCEDURE

Artists have developed techniques that use pencils for both lines and shading. For practical purposes, however, you can work almost entirely in line. Use uniform lines for roughs, offhand sketches, and technical drawings. Finished free-line drawings call for accented lines.

Technical drawings often need to distinguish between lines that differ in importance or that have different meanings. The easiest way to distinguish this is to use lead pencil for the principal lines and draw the others with colored pencils. When

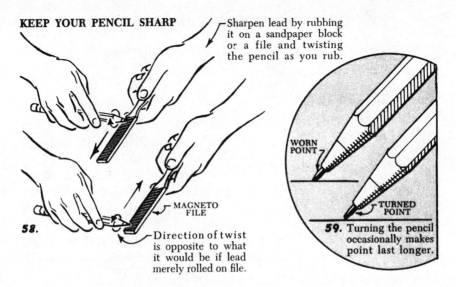

KEEP YOUR PENCIL SHARP

Sharpen lead by rubbing it on a sandpaper block or a file and twisting the pencil as you rub.

MAGNETO FILE

58.

Direction of twist is opposite to what it would be if lead merely rolled on file.

WORN POINT

TURNED POINT

59. Turning the pencil occasionally makes point last longer.

you make drawings for reproduction, either as blueprints or white prints or on an office duplicator, you cannot use color. Either rule lines with pens of different widths or draw with leads of contrasting grades, such as 2H and 3B. Ordinary mechanical

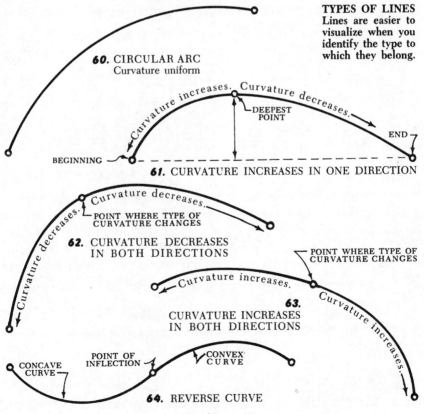

TYPES OF LINES
Lines are easier to visualize when you identify the type to which they belong.

60. CIRCULAR ARC
Curvature uniform

Curvature increases. Curvature decreases.

DEEPEST POINT

BEGINNING

END

61. CURVATURE INCREASES IN ONE DIRECTION

Curvature decreases.

POINT WHERE TYPE OF CURVATURE CHANGES

Curvature decreases.

62. CURVATURE DECREASES IN BOTH DIRECTIONS

POINT WHERE TYPE OF CURVATURE CHANGES

Curvature increases.

63.
CURVATURE INCREASES IN BOTH DIRECTIONS

Curvature increases.

CONCAVE CURVE

POINT OF INFLECTION

CONVEX CURVE

64. REVERSE CURVE

31

pencils are not suited to this work. You need either the wooden pencils made for draftsmen or the type with screw clutches that take leads of different diameters.

65. PRACTICE STROKE
Keep the pencil point
a little above paper.

Types of Curves. Although every curve seems to be in a class by itself, curves actually form only five distinct types. The first is the circular arc [Fig. 60]. This has a uniform curvature throughout and can be drawn with a compass. The other four types are free lines [Figs. 61–64]. The speed and regularity with which the curvature changes will vary widely from one curve to the next. However, if you can identify the general class to which a curve belongs, you will find it easier to visualize the curve.

You cannot draw a line properly until you know where to put it. Visualizing the line becomes easier if you place a dot at both ends of the curve [Fig. 61]. It also helps to put another dot at the deepest point of the curve [Fig. 61] or at a *point of inflection* where the type or the direction of the curvature changes [Figs. 62–64].

Practice Strokes. When you have placed the dots for a line, turn your paper to bring it into the easiest position for drawing and try a practice stroke [Fig. 65]. Move the pencil as you

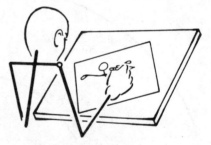

66. SWING FROM SHOULDER

would in actual drawing, but do not let the point touch the paper.

The movement should start from the shoulder, and the fingers should play no part in it [Fig. 66]. This is difficult at first. Once mastered, however, it enables you to draw with greater freedom and improves the appearance of your work. When your practice stroke is satisfactory, you can proceed to draw the actual line.

If you still have trouble after three or four practice strokes, you are probably attempting too long a line. Put a dot at the midpoint of the line you originally planned. Then try a new practice stroke extending only to this point.

Speed. Although I hope that even your earliest drawings will be made for practical use, remember that they must also give you

Fig. 67]   Getting Started   33

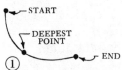

START

DEEPEST
POINT

END

① VISUALIZING A LINE
Imagine where the line
should go and then mark
main points with dots.

DRAWING PROCEDURE

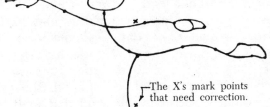

The X's mark points
that need correction.

② FAINT-LINE
CONSTRUCTION

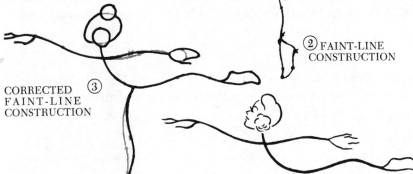

CORRECTED ③
FAINT-LINE
CONSTRUCTION

FIG. 67.

④ COMPLETED
DRAWING

practice in drawing. Learn all you can
from every one. Take your time and
think out each line. Be sure you understand its function and exactly where
you want it to go.

After the dots have been placed, however, the line should be
drawn in one swift stroke. A line that is drawn slowly is apt to
waver, but a swift line must follow a smooth curve—just as a
thrown ball cannot move in zigzags.

Stages of Drawing. Free-line drawings should normally be
made in four stages: (1) fixed-line construction, (2) faint-line
construction [dancer in Step 2, Fig. 67], (3) correction of faint-
line construction [Step 3], (4) final drawing [Step 4]. The fixed-
line stage is usually omitted in figure sketches, and it serves no
purpose when a faint-line construction is traced. In roughs, where
speed is more important than accuracy or appearance, all construction stages may be skipped and the final drawing made at
once. Nevertheless, you will often find that it pays to begin even
a rough with either a simple fixed-line construction or a crude
preliminary sketch which serves as a construction.

Line Quality. Concentrate on getting your lines in the right places without worrying much about technique. However, as it is easy to fall into bad habits and hard to correct them, the quality of your lines deserves some consideration.

Scratching in the lines with short, feeble strokes like those in Fig. 68 is definitely bad. Artists often *swing in* a number of construction strokes and then darken the best one [Fig. 69]. This method is adequate when all that matters is the general effect, but it encourages fuzzy thinking. That is a fatal habit for anyone who draws for practical use.

The ideal method is to complete each line in a single stroke. Unfortunately, this requires real skill when the lines are long and the standard of accuracy is at all high. Should lack of skill compel you to use short strokes, keep them in line and make them overlap at the ends [Fig. 70].

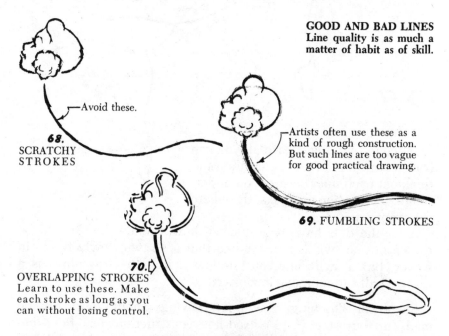

GOOD AND BAD LINES
Line quality is as much a matter of habit as of skill.

—Avoid these.

68. SCRATCHY STROKES

—Artists often use these as a kind of rough construction. But such lines are too vague for good practical drawing.

69. FUMBLING STROKES

70. OVERLAPPING STROKES
Learn to use these. Make each stroke as long as you can without losing control.

VISUALIZING IDEAS

Nothing will do more to clarify your ideas than visualizing them through drawings. You do not need either skill or practice for this because most ideas can be visualized with sketches that are as easy as doodles. Here are a few suggestions to get you started. You will find more in every chapter.

Testing Your Understanding. We often assume that we understand a passage in some book when we have either formed a false

Fig. 70]　　　　　　Getting Started　　　　　　35

idea of it or have missed the point entirely. We can test our understanding by trying to visualize the ideas of the text, and the easiest way to do this is to make one or more rough sketches. Those in Figs. 72 and 73 were drawn to test my grasp of a paragraph that I found in a syllabus dealing with experimental psychology [Fig. 71].

When I read the paragraph, I thought I understood it, but my first drawing [Step 1, Fig. 72] undeceived me. Nevertheless, it compensated for this by showing me where the trouble lay.

Although my second sketch [Step 2] carried me farther, it revealed that the paragraph does not explain the mechanism at Point B. In order to complete my drawing, as I did in Step 3, I had to look up alternation mazes in another textbook.

Even without that information, I was able to test my grasp of the psychological principles explained in the paragraph by making diagrams [Fig. 73] showing the possible paths of the rat.

This may seem like too much trouble merely to check a single paragraph. But reading without understanding is worthless and often misleading. Also, the trouble was not caused by the drawing but by my failure to understand what I read. If I had been correct in my belief that I knew the facts, I could have completed the drawing in less than a minute. Finally, making the drawing left a much more vivid impression on my memory than reading could possibly have done.

Most, though by no means all, drawings tend to correct mistakes in this way. The tendency is due to two things: (1) Drawings make ideas clear. Poets, perjurors, and politicians do not always regard clarity as an asset, but it is the chief requirement in useful thinking. As Sir Francis Bacon sagely remarked, "Truth is more apt to emerge from error than from confusion." Thus, my first sketches of the rat maze presented my ideas clearly. They also made it obvious that my ideas were wrong. (2) When our ideas contradict each other, the discrepancy usually shows up in a sketch because it is difficult to draw inconsistent lines. Unfortunately, this does not help when the mistake is not an inconsistency. A ballerina may criticize the position of my *stick-figure* danseuse in Fig. 67; if the position is wrong, there is no way to tell whether the illustration is a bad drawing of a good dancer or a good drawing of a bad dancer.

Collecting Information. Simple drawings are equally useful in classifying and recording any information we obtain. When someone gives you route directions, sketch a crude map like Fig. 10 and ask him to check it. He may catch errors, or the map may remind him of points which he overlooked in his verbal directions. Another advantage is that you have the map for reference and do not need to rely on your memory of his words.

The same method may be put to good use in gathering geographical data for historical research. If you study the southern campaigns of the American Revolution, for example, you will read about many places like Cowpens and Hobkirk's Hill which

---

DO YOU UNDERSTAND WHAT YOU READ?
A quick sketch will serve as a check. If you are confused or mistaken, your drawing will indicate the points that require further thought. See text.

"The alternation maze consists of pathways arranged like two squares adjacent to each other and with a side in common. The animal (rat) can start at one end of the pathway corresponding to the common side, and at its end can turn either left or right in order to return to the starting point. With this arrangement, the animal could theoretically run continuously around a given square or could alternate between the two squares. A 'choice point' is designated as the far end of the common side. In alternation problems, the animal must learn to turn right at this choice point, then turn left at the choice point, in order to receive a food reward upon reaching the starting point."

71. SOURCE PARAGRAPH
Taken from a syllabus on experimental psychology.

①

"Two squares . . . with a side in common.' But where is the path?"

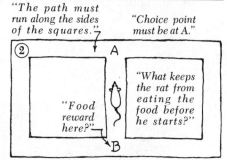

"The path must run along the sides of the squares."

"Choice point must be at A."

"Food reward here?"

"What keeps the rat from eating the food before he starts?"

"B must be the starting point. But why isn't it also a choice point when the rat reaches it after completing one circuit?"

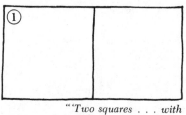

③

Gates to be controlled by experimenter

Experimenter places food here when rat succeeds

To complete this sketch, I had to collect data from outside sources.

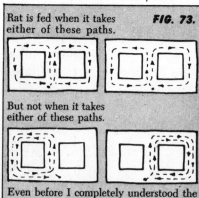

Rat is fed when it takes either of these paths.   **FIG. 73.**

But not when it takes either of these paths.

Even before I completely understood the maze, I could make these sketches to study the problem that it offers the rat.

FIG. 72. SKETCHES MADE TO TEST MY UNDERSTANDING OF THE PARAGRAPH IN FIG. 71

Fig. 74]   Getting Started   37

ordinary maps omit. Even maps in histories of the period do not contain them all. By drawing a rough map of your own and mark-

ing each site as you locate it, you can provide yourself with an invaluable aid to understanding what happened.

Abstract Ideas. Concrete objects, such as rat mazes, are easy to visualize because we can imagine them as they would appear. But how can we visualize abstract ideas that no one can see?

EXAMPLES. One solution is to portray some application of the idea. Thus, Fig. 74 represents $(a+b)^2$ as an area.

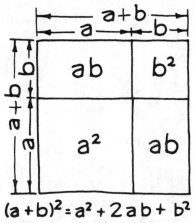

$$(a+b)^2 = a^2 + 2ab + b^2$$

74. ABSTRACT IDEA VISUALIZED BY SKETCHING A POSSIBLE APPLICATION

When you use an example to illustrate an abstract idea, remember that it is only one of many possible examples and not the idea itself. Thus, $(a+b)^2$ has an infinite number of other applications, most of which have nothing to do with area. For instance, with the ten digits of the decimal system, we can write a hundred two-digit numbers (including 00). If we added two more digits to make a duodecimal system, we could find the new total of two-digit numbers by letting a equal 10 and b equal 2. Then: $(a+b)^2 = (10+2)^2 = 12^2 = 144$, or $a^2 + 2ab + b^2 = 10^2 + (2 \times 10 \times 2) + 2^2 = 100 + 40 + 4 = 144$.

Students of advanced mathematics often find it difficult to free themselves from conceptions which they took from the drawings they made in elementary geometry. Avoid this by using example-drawing merely as an aid to understanding, and resist any temptation to assume that the drawing adds new facts to your data.

GRAPHIC METAPHORS. The number of purely abstract words is so limited that abstract verbal thinking is done largely in metaphors. Thus, we say that a set of account books "balances" when the sum of the debits is numerically equal to the sum of the credits. No one imagines that the ledger has been placed in one pan of a scale (or "balance") and found to balance the journal placed in the other pan. When the verbal metaphor represents a physical object, we can visualize the abstract idea by drawing the object [Fig. 75].

SYMBOLS VS. FACTS. Some abstract diagrams are so vivid that we come to regard them as pictures of actual objects. School children may believe that Ohio is blue "because it is blue on the map." Professors of Physics talk about "lines of magnetic force," and their students are led to think that magnetism actually "flows" along definite lines. This unfortunate misconception may well be due to the widespread custom of representing magnetism by lines in diagrams like Fig. 76.

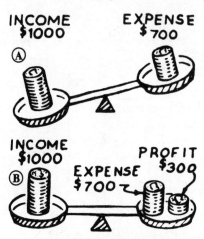

You are unlikely to be misled by one or two sketches. Many people must have made drawings like Fig. 77 without coming to believe in "lines of gravitational force." Nevertheless, whenever you have occasion to draw a number of abstract diagrams in the same field, remind yourself

75. GRAPHIC METAPHOR USED TO VISUALIZE AN ABSTRACT IDEA
Metaphores are as helpful in drawing as they are in writing. Here, a pair of scales is used to show why accountants must put "Profit" with "Expense" rather than with "Income" in order to balance their books.

every so often that a pencil is only a tool for thought and not a magic wand that can transform a symbol into a fact.

SYMBOLS VS. FACTS

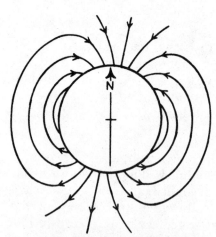

76. "LINES" OF MAGNETIC FORCE
These are purely symbolic. They show the direction of the force from point to point, but they have no counterpart in nature.

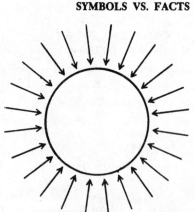

77. "LINES" OF GRAVITY
If we drew many diagrams like this, we might imagine that gravity acts in lines and that the spaces between them are free from gravity.

Fig. 81]   Getting Started   39

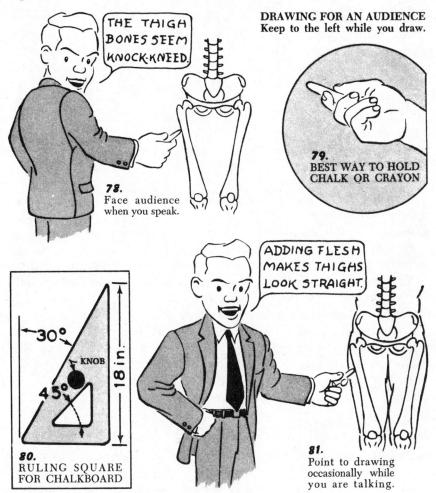

78. Face audience when you speak.

THE THIGH BONES SEEM KNOCK-KNEED.

DRAWING FOR AN AUDIENCE
Keep to the left while you draw.

79. BEST WAY TO HOLD CHALK OR CRAYON

80. RULING SQUARE FOR CHALKBOARD

30° KNOB 45° 18 in.

ADDING FLESH MAKES THIGHS LOOK STRAIGHT.

81. Point to drawing occasionally while you are talking.

DRAWING AND TALKING

If you spend much time explaining things to other people, you will find that the ability to draw as you talk is a major asset. Not only can drawings make your ideas clear, vivid, and convincing, but they help you to take and hold attention. I know one teacher who sketches two crude heads on the chalkboard and then uses these as characters in an anecdote that illustrates some point he wants to make. The heads have no real sigificance, but they supply an excuse for movement. When attention lags, he can always recapture it by pointing to one of the heads.

Drawing as you talk involves a number of special methods. These give no trouble when you know the tricks, but they may be difficult if you try to make up your procedure as you go along.

Offhand Drawing. This is easy because the sketches are always rough. Also, you can—and should—explain each line as you draw it, so that your audience cannot fail to understand. A second advantage is that a free-arm swing comes more naturally when you draw in a standing position. Hold the chalk as shown in Fig. 79. This may seem awkward at first. But when you become accustomed to it, you will find that it gives more freedom than the grip used in writing.

If accuracy is important, you can equip yourself with a compass made to hold chalk or crayon. You can also make a *ruling square* like that in Fig. 80.

Stand well to one side as you sketch [Fig. 78], so that the spectators can see what you are drawing. When you face the chalkboard, the audience may have trouble in understanding your words. This means that you should not talk while you are actually drawing. But if you are silent for any length of time (thirty seconds is about the maximum), your audience will become bored. The proper procedure is to stop after every three or four lines and explain them over your shoulder.

Should the sketch or diagram be at all elaborate, break off after drawing (and explaining) a dozen or so lines. Face the audience and talk for a minute or two. When you mention some part of the sketch, point to it with your left hand [Fig. 81]. Then go back and add another set of lines.

Rehearsed Drawing. If you are self-conscious about sketching in public, work out your drawings in advance and rehearse them with your talk. Do not memorize anything. That is apt to make you seem stilted. Simply speak and draw as you would before an audience. Repeat your talk until you can give it without a hitch. Lack of adequate preparation is the chief cause of stage fright.

Prepared Drawings. When your talk, or any part of it, calls for something more than a quick sketch, you can prepare drawings in advance and use them in many ways. These drawings need not be entirely homemade. Fig. 82 shows how a few "home-drawn" lines give meaning to pictures clipped from magazines and assembled in a *paste-up*. The "art work" in this example was prepared so that it could be displayed on television or photographed for use on 35 mm. slides, on 16 mm. film, or for display on television. Even when your immediate purpose is confined to slides, you will be wise to follow the limitations shown in Fig. 82. Then, if you or some colleague has a chance to use it on television, it will not need to be remade.

Elaborate chalkboard drawings can be produced by making a sketch on wrapping paper or heavy tracing paper. Prick holes along the lines one inch or less apart. Attach the sketch to the chalkboard with drafting tape and run a dusty eraser over it. When the sketch is removed, there will be a gray dot on the board corresponding to each hole. The dots serve as a construction over which the drawing can be completed freehand.

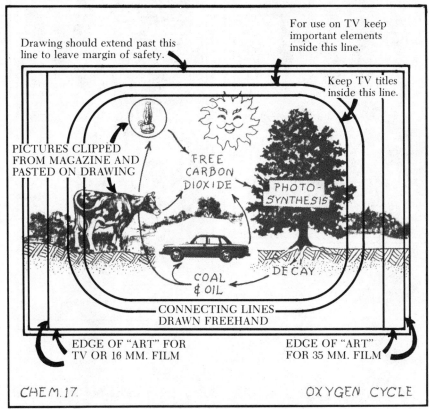

82. PASTE-UP DIAGRAM FOR SLIDES

Another plan is to make placards and either hang them on the wall or display them at appropriate points in your talk. If a map or diagram is to be used in a number of talks, you can draw it on a white window shade. Use india ink, and color the drawing with drugstore dyes. A shade mounted at the top of a chalkboard can be pulled down or rolled up at your convenience.

Most prepared drawings are static. If you prefer diagrams that can be built up and rearranged as you talk, a *flannelboard* will meet your needs. This is merely a piece of wallboard faced with cotton flannel [Figs. 83 and 84]. Small strips of sandpaper are glued to the back of each drawing and block of lettering [Fig.

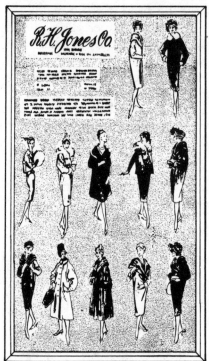

83. *"Placing similar items in rows is dull and wastes valuable space."*

STRIPS OF
SANDPAPER

85.
REAR VIEW OF
PAPER FIGURE

FLANNELBOARD "DRAWING"
This allows you to rearrange your material during your talk. The example illustrates one point in a lecture on layout for advertising.

84. *"Overlapping figures placed on diagonals are more interesting."*

85]. When the sandpaper is pressed lightly against the flannel, it adheres as though magnetized.

Slide- and *opaque-projectors* must be operated from the rear of a darkened room. Under these conditions, it is hard to hold the attention of your audience and impossible to be sure you are holding it. Also, the dark keeps listeners from taking notes. *Overhead projectors* [Fig. 86] eliminate these difficulties. Furthermore, you can switch from prepared slides to original drawings and back again, or you can draw over a prepared slide as you talk. That enables you to bring out important points or to turn a drawing into a diagram. The drawing can be done on an overlay of *clear acetate,* which is similar to cellophane. As this leaves the prepared slide untouched, it can be used for future

Fig. 86]   Getting Started   43

talks. Ordinary pencils will not mark acetate, and those made for
the purpose are not really adequate. A better device is the *felt-
tipped pen*. This has the added merit of using transparent inks
which are projected in colors, whereas pencil marks always show
as black.

86. OVERHEAD PROJECTOR IN OPERATION
This device works in daylight and can be used
for either prepared slides or freehand sketches.

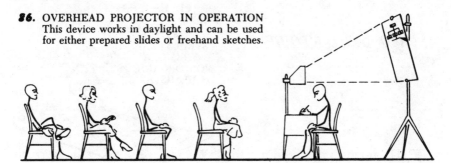

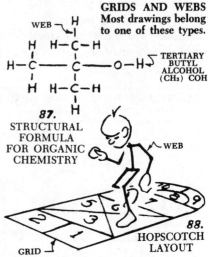

GRIDS AND WEBS
Most drawings belong to one of these types.

3

No Skill Required

87.
STRUCTURAL FORMULA FOR ORGANIC CHEMISTRY

88.
HOPSCOTCH LAYOUT

THE forms described in this chapter are so far from being pictures that you may find it hard to think of them as drawings. Nevertheless, they are true drawings because their meaning depends on the arrangement of points, lines, and shapes.

They are the most widely useful type of drawing as well as the easiest. Charts and diagrams help you to classify and organize your ideas. They are the basis of all graphs and many maps. They introduce at least half the methods and principles needed for any sort of practical drawing, and they present these in their simplest forms. Even the most untalented beginner can make useful charts and diagrams without the preliminary practice that other types of drawing require. Indeed, experience with charts and diagrams provides this practice and prepares the learner for the next step in his study of practical drawing. These features make them an ideal starting point for anyone who wants to master practical drawing with a minimum of effort, and who hopes to get the most out of it after he has mastered it.

When you draw a chart or diagram to guide your own thinking, *the mental process involved is more important than the drawing itself*. Work on a chart or diagram often makes your ideas so clear that you have no further use for the drawing; most of the examples which I drew to organize the material for this book were thrown away as soon as they were made.

These drawings need not be complete to be useful. You can stop at any point and still have a clearer idea of the subject than you had when you began. Even listing items that might fit into a chart will teach you something.

Although charts are easy to draw, we cannot get the full benefit from them without a thorough understanding of the prin-

Fig. 91]   No Skill Required   45

ciples upon which they are based. These principles are not easy to grasp. In fact, they require more real thought than anything else we shall encounter until we come to graphs in Chapter 10.

There is a way to dodge the necessity of mastering these principles. Look through the illustrations in this chapter until you find an example which meets your needs. Then use that as a model for a chart or diagram of your own.

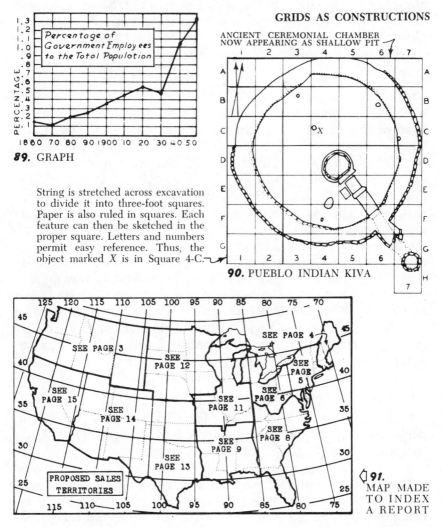

89. GRAPH

Percentage of Government Employees to the Total Population

GRIDS AS CONSTRUCTIONS

ANCIENT CEREMONIAL CHAMBER
NOW APPEARING AS SHALLOW PIT

String is stretched across excavation to divide it into three-foot squares. Paper is also ruled in squares. Each feature can then be sketched in the proper square. Letters and numbers permit easy reference. Thus, the object marked X is in Square 4-C.

90. PUEBLO INDIAN KIVA

PROPOSED SALES TERRITORIES

91. MAP MADE TO INDEX A REPORT

I mention this expedient because you might otherwise become discouraged by some of the sections in this chapter and give up before reaching the easier material that follows. Nevertheless, it is only an expedient. I hope you will not adopt it. If you really master the principles of charting now, you will equip yourself with a set of problem-solving tools which will be of the utmost usefulness as long as you live.

All charts—and in fact nearly all drawings—can be classified as *webs, grids,* or a combination of both. In drawing webs, we first set out points and then connect these with lines. Thus, in the chemical formula [Fig. 87], the "points" are labeled with symbols representing elements, and the lines show how these elements are related. The points of the stick figure in Fig. 88 are mere dots on the paper; the lines seem to constitute the entire drawing. Grids reverse this whole process; we fix the relations by drawing the grid and then fit *data items* into the spaces.

GRIDS

Grids take many forms, including the hopscotch-layout at the head of the chapter and the constructions in Figs. 31, 34, and 35. The examples in Figs. 89–91 demonstrate that simple grids provide all-purpose constructions on which we can base any free-line drawing. The map in Fig. 91 is especially interesting. The grid is made to follow the conventional lines of latitude and longitude. This enables us to fix points, such as cities, on the grid by taking the data from any other map—even one where the lines of latitude and longitude are drawn on a different principle. Note also that the sales territories have no names. The only way to index items of this sort is by making a drawing.

For the present, we shall confine ourselves to the grids known as *tabular charts* or simply as *tables.* The rectangular table in Fig. 92 is typical. Round and triangular tabular charts also occur [Fig. 94 and Fig. 96]. A few take other forms, though these are so rare that they can almost be regarded as freaks.

Grids—A. Elements

A table consists of a set of interlacing lines, usually parallel and perpendicular. These lines divide it into vertical *columns* and horizontal *rows* [Fig. 92].

Labels. Each row and each column requires a label called a *tab.* Note that the row tabs form a vertical column, and that the column tabs form a horizontal row. Each set of tabs should be labeled with a *tab designation,* and the whole table should be given a *title.*

When a title or a tab designation is obvious and too long to be stated briefly, it may be omitted. However, the only way to be sure that it really is obvious is to word it in your own mind.

Fig. 92]   No Skill Required   47

Finding suitable titles and tab designations is part of the mental process of making tables. If you slight it, you may work for some time on a table, only to discover that you have been charting the wrong thing.

For example, books on the piano or organ normally tabulate the major chords by notes, as I have done in Fig. 97. This is the right plan for the student of harmony but a poor one for the person who wants to learn which keys to strike. For that purpose, the chart in Fig. 98 is far more helpful. This chart provides a visual representation of the keys to be struck. It reduces the twelve chords to six finger positions. Furthermore, only two positions are needed for the six most common chords. Such simplification is a valuable memory aid, even though a chord is not always struck with the same fingers. By charting finger positions instead of notes, we also bring out several points of theoretic interest. Observe the symmetry in some places and the curious departures from symmetry in others.

Data. When a table is first laid out, the spaces in the body of the grid are blank. Filling a space with its corresponding data item shows that one step of the project has been completed.

The spaces which remain blank at any particular time serve an important purpose. They furnish a list of the points that still need attention. Thus, the gaps in the golf-match chart [Fig. 96] are reminders that Tim still has to play matches against Dot, May, and Sam.

The periodic table of elements, used in chemistry and physics, illustrates the value of such an automatic check list. Until this table was devised, no one could even guess how many elements exist or how they are related. The gaps in the original table not only pointed to unknown elements but enabled scientists to predict their properties.

GRIDS—B. ORDER

The order in which items are arranged is a matter of basic importance. The choice of an order depends upon both the nature of the items and the purpose of the chart. Thus, Fig. 93 shows pigments and colors placed as they appear in the spectrum. Although a physicist might consider this order inevitable, the circular arrangement in Fig. 94 has decided advantages for the artist and the interior decorator. A paint manufacturer may list his pigments alphabetically in his catalog. But when he takes an inventory, he may find it more convenient to classify them by their chemical compositions. Again, the alphabetic arrangement

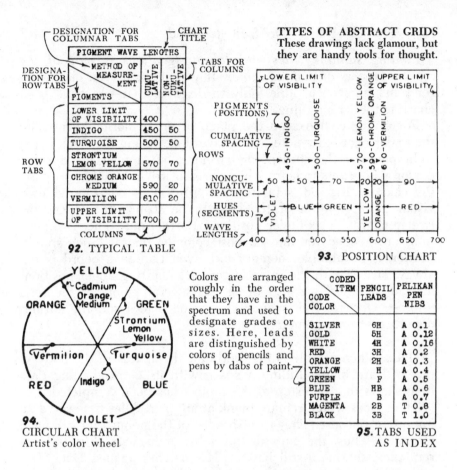

TYPES OF ABSTRACT GRIDS
These drawings lack glamour, but
they are handy tools for thought.

92. TYPICAL TABLE

93. POSITION CHART

Colors are arranged roughly in the order that they have in the spectrum and used to designate grades or sizes. Here, leads are distinguished by colors of pencils and pens by dabs of paint.

94. CIRCULAR CHART
Artist's color wheel

CODED ITEM CODE COLOR	PENCIL LEADS	PELIKAN PEN NIBS
SILVER	6H	A 0.1
GOLD	5H	A 0.12
WHITE	4H	A 0.16
RED	3H	A 0.2
ORANGE	2H	A 0.3
YELLOW	H	A 0.4
GREEN	F	A 0.5
BLUE	HB	A 0.6
PURPLE	B	A 0.7
MAGENTA	2B	T 0.8
BLACK	3B	T 1.0

95. TABS USED AS INDEX

of the chords in Fig. 97 is "natural" from one standpoint, but the arrangement by chord-progression (F – C – G – D – and so on) in the row tabs of Fig. 98 is equally "natural" from another standpoint.

Sets. A *set* is a collection of items which are related in some way (or at least have some common quality), but which are distinct from each other and do not blend or overlap. Thus, the pigments in Fig. 92 form a set, but the various degrees of sweetness in candy do not—there is no fixed point where "slightly sweet" stops and "medium sweet" begins.

Lists. Where the items in a set have no natural order, or at least none that suits the purpose of the chart we have in mind, they comprise a *list*. The golfers in Fig. 96 make up a list. Each one is a separate individual, and the order in which they are named is arbitrary.

Sequences and Series. When a set does have a natural order, it can be classified as one of two types. If we have *all* the items

48

Fig. 98]   No Skill Required   49

of a set, we can arrange them in *sequence*, and be sure that there are no gaps. But if the set *may* not be complete, we must allow for the possibility that gaps exist. In that case, the order will be a *series* and not a sequence. Thus, I can arrange the cards of a deck in sequence by deciding on some conventional order for the suits. If I shuffle the deck and take half of it, the best I can do is to arrange the cards in series.

The distinction between a sequence and a series is seldom important. Nevertheless, we should always consider it. When it does need to be made, it is apt to be vital. For example, the kings of France are all known. They therefore constitute a sequence, and a historian can plan his work around them. Early Egyptologists tried to do the same thing with catalogs of pharaohs. Unfortunately, the catalogs were incomplete. This meant that a gap of unknown length might exist between one name and the next. Attempts to treat the series of pharaohs as a sequence led to some highly erroneous ideas about Egyptian history.

MORE TYPES OF ABSTRACT GRIDS

Each member is to play against each of the others. Scores show total number of strokes for 18-hole match.

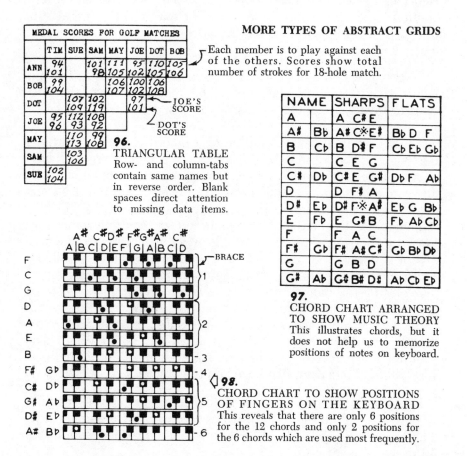

MEDAL SCORES FOR GOLF MATCHES

	TIM	SUE	SAM	MAY	JOE	DOT	BOB
ANN	94 101		101 98	111 105	95 102	110 105	105 106
BOB	99 104			106 107	100 102	106 108	
DOT		107 109	102 119		97 101		
JOE	95 96	112 93	108 92				
MAY		110 113	99 108				
SAM		103 106					
SUE	102 104						

— JOE'S SCORE

— DOT'S SCORE

96.
TRIANGULAR TABLE
Row- and column-tabs contain same names but in reverse order. Blank spaces direct attention to missing data items.

NAME	SHARPS		FLATS	
A		A C♯ E		
A♯	B♭	A♯ C✳ E♯	B♭ D F	
B	C♭	B D♯ F	C♭ E♭ G♭	
C		C E G		
C♯	D♭	C♯ E G♯	D♭ F A♭	
D		D F♯ A		
D♯	E♭	D♯ F✳ A♯	E♭ G B♭	
E	F♭	E G♯ B	F♭ A♭ C♭	
F		F A C		
F♯	G♭	F♯ A♯ C♯	G♭ B♭ D♭	
G		G B D		
G♯	A♭	G♯ B♯ D♯	A♭ C♭ E♭	

97.
CHORD CHART ARRANGED TO SHOW MUSIC THEORY
This illustrates chords, but it does not help us to memorize positions of notes on keyboard.

A♯ C♯ D♯ F♯ G♯ A♯ C♯
A B C D E F G A B C D

F
C
G
D
A
E
B
F♯ G♭
C♯ D♭
G♯ A♭
D♯ E♭
A♯ B♭

BRACE
1
2
3
4
5
6

◁ **98.**
CHORD CHART TO SHOW POSITIONS OF FINGERS ON THE KEYBOARD
This reveals that there are only 6 positions for the 12 chords and only 2 positions for the 6 chords which are used most frequently.

The difference between a series and a sequence often depends on the point of view. A traveler must regard the trains in a time-table as a sequence. To the train dispatcher, they form a series; he runs freight trains whenever he sees a chance and adds extra passenger sections if the traffic demands it.

Continuities. The tabs and data items of a chart are always separate units. This causes no difficulty when we want to chart a set, but a problem arises when we try to chart a *continuity*—such as sweetness, time, or the spectrum—which has no divisions between any one part and those on either side of it.

Cases like these are handled by making arbitrary divisions. Thus, the spectrum in Fig. 93 is divided by the pigments. Some divisions of this type have become so conventional that we tend to think of them as inevitable, but this is never the case. Even time is not naturally divided into days; a calendar day is an artificial period (see the article "Time Measurement" in the *Encyclopaedia Britannica*). When you chart material based on a continuity, it is essential to choose a system of division that suits the purpose for which the chart is made.

POSITIONS AND SEGMENTS. Fixing points on a continuity gives us two sets. The points themselves form a set of *positions;* the pigments in Fig. 93 are an example. The spaces between the positions are called *segments;* the hues in Fig. 93 make up a set of segments.

The sets formed from a continuity are not themselves continuities, and can be treated like any other set. For instance, I have a box of colored pencils which comprises the whole line sold under one brand name and is therefore complete. Each lead corresponds to a position in the spectrum, and I arrange them in sequence on this basis. The manufacturer could also arrange them by the spectrum. However, he would then regard them as a series, because he can add or discontinue colors at will. He could also ignore the spectrum and arrange the pencils alphabetically by the names of the colors. Actually, he arranges them at random. In either of the last two cases, they constitute a list.

A series or sequence need not be restricted to a particular continuity. I could have arranged my colored pencils on a light-dark continuity. The result would still have been a sequence but a very different one from that based on the spectrum.

MEASURING POSITIONS. Positions on a continuity can be specified in two ways. Both of these are illustrated in the pigment wave-length charts [Figs. 92 and 93]. One method, called *cumulative*

Fig. 99]   No Skill Required   51

spacing, measures all distances from some fixed zero point. The other method merely gives the distances between each pair of positions; such distances are said to be *noncumulative.* Similar methods of spacing could be applied to positions on a continuity of time, temperature, or weight.

Uniform spacing is normally desirable, but exceptions are far from rare. Thus, the pigments in Figs. 92 and 93 were chosen because they seem equally far apart to the eye, although this makes the distances between them highly irregular when they are located by their wave lengths.

NONNUMERICAL SCALES. It is not always necessary or even possible to specify positions numerically. The wave lengths in Figs. 92 and 93 were determined by experts in a laboratory. If I wanted to locate a pigment with an unknown wave length, I would have no number to fix its position. If I wished to chart types of candy by sweetness or odors by their strengths, I would not have even a numerical framework in which to place them.

Although a numerical framework is highly desirable, it is far from essential. Even without knowing the wave lengths of the pigments, I could have arranged them in order. My eye tells me that vermilion is farther from indigo than it is from turquoise. Hence, turquoise must come between the other two colors. I can add as many pigments as I like in this way. Red lead fits between chrome orange and vermilion but is nearer the orange. Ultramarine is about half way between indigo and turquoise.

Basis of Arrangement. The flexibility of the charting process is increased by the fact that we can use order in several different ways when we design a chart.

INDEXING ARRANGEMENTS. A large chart must be self-indexing if we are to find wanted items with reasonable ease. This is less important in small charts. But whenever there are more than half a dozen items, some sort of order is highly desirable.

The row tabs in the golf-match chart [Fig. 96] are arranged alphabetically and therefore index the data. The pigment charts in Figs. 92 and 93 are also indexed by their tabs, which are arranged as the hues appear in the spectrum. Both pigment charts follow the same order except that Fig. 93 is turned around so that its columns correspond to the rows of Fig. 92.

The row tabs in the color code [Fig. 95] were chosen solely because of their value as an index. No "natural" relation connects the columns in this chart. Their arrangement is based on three different continuities—the spectrum (eked out with silver, gold, white, and black), hardness, and line width (each nib makes a line of different width). There is no reason, except convenience, for applying the same code to both leads and nibs.

The relation between colors and leads is arbitrary. I could have reversed the order of one column, making silver correspond to 3B and black to 6H. If I used my pencils only for mechanical drawing, I would not have needed the B leads. I would therefore have started by making silver represent 9H and gone up the scale until black represented HB. Or I might have coded a full range of leads but left out certain grades—say 8H, 6H, 4H, 2H, F, and B. Similar things could have been done with the pen nibs.

As the pigment chart in Fig. 92 and the chord chart in Fig. 97 have only two columns apiece, there was no point in trying to find an indexing order for their column-tabs. In the golf-match chart [Fig. 96], the column-tabs are listed in reverse alphabetic order; a direct alphabetic arrangement would have placed large gaps between one set of tabs and the corresponding data items. Note also that Ann's name does not head a column and that Tim's name does not head a row.

FINAL GOLF SCORES BY RANK		
	TOTAL STROKES	AVER-AGES
JOE	669	95.6
TIM	683	97.6
ANN	717	102.4
SAM	726	103.7
BOB	736	105.1
SUE	747	106.8
MAY	756	108
DOT	790	112.9

◁ **99.**
FINAL SCORES
OF GOLFERS
IN FIG. 96

ARRANGEMENT BY RANK

100.▷
COMPARATIVE RANKING CHART
Both lists are arranged by rank. Differences of opinion are indicated by connecting each pair of old masters with a solid line and each pair of modern painters with a dotted line.

In the finger-position chart [Fig. 98], the row tabs follow the order of chord progressions to bring similar finger positions together. The columnar tabs, on the other hand, are arranged alphabetically—following the positions of keys in the keyboard. If the same plan had been employed in both cases, the chart would have been much harder to read.

Fig. 100]　　　　　No Skill Required　　　　　53

RANK. Anyone charting the heights of mountains or the melting points of metals may be more interested in their relative *ranks* than in finding the names of a particular mountain or metal. Fig. 99 shows a golf chart arranged by rank. The golfing scores were first listed in numerical order, and the arrangement of the names was then made to correspond.

The *ranking chart* in Fig. 100 illustrates a further development of this idea. Each column is essentially a set of tabs listed by an observer in the order of his personal preference. The columns are placed side by side, and the corresponding items are connected by lines. If the observers agree perfectly, all the connecting lines will be horizontal. Slanting lines show differences of opinion; the more a line slants, the greater the difference is. Where the true ranks of the items are known, a ranking chart can be used to test an observer's judgment. Thus, a person might be asked to arrange a set of advertisements in the order that he estimates will represent their pulling power. By comparing his list with one based on actual sales records, we can form an intelligent opinion of his ability to select profitable advertising.

GROUPING. The tabs in a set often fall into definite groups. The nature of these groups usually reveals important information, and the value of the chart will be enhanced if we indicate the grouping. Thus, similar finger positions are shown by the *braces* and numbers on the right of the finger-position chart [Fig. 98]. A more common method is illustrated in Fig. 102, where each set of related columnar tabs is grouped under a main tab. A chart with grouped tabs is said to be *compound*.

When the grouping is completely regular, as it is in the *schedule* [Fig. 103], the arangement can be reversed. Thus, the days of the week could have been used as main tabs with the semesters grouped under them. This plan might be better for someone who was considering a part-time job that would keep him busy three days a week, and who wished to avoid conflict between his work and his studies.

Grouping enables us to combine different types of data in the same table. Fig. 102, for example, tells us the subject of each course, its catalog number, the hours and the semester in which it is taught, the number of credit hours, whether the course is major, minor, or elective, and whether it is completed, required, or desired.

Ingenuity in grouping makes it possible to compress an enormous amount of information into a small area. But remember that the more complex a chart becomes the harder it is to read.

GROUPING TABS

DAYS / HOURS	MON WED FRI	TUE THU SAT
8:00 to 8:55	A	B
9:00 to 9:55	C	D
10:00 to 10:55	E	F
11:00 to 11:55	G	H
1:30 to 2:25	I	J
2:30 to 3:25	K	L
3:30 to 4:25	M	N

101.
KEY TO LABEL
CLASS PERIODS

	1	2 COURSES COMPLETED				3 COURSES REQUIRED				4 COURSES DESIRED				5	6	7	8
TYPE OF COURSE (FIELD)		Fall	Spring	Key	Hours	Fall	Spring	Key	Hours	Fall	Spring	Key	Hours	MAJOR	MINOR	REQUIRED*	ELECTIVE
CHEM.										1	2	G (J.L)	10				10
ENGLISH		1		C	3	2 / 13 14		C / F	3 / 6	21 22 / 37 38 / 41 42		D / F / A	6 / 6 / 6	12 12 6			
FRENCH		1		F	3	2 / 25 26		F / F	3 / 6					6 6			
HISTORY						3 4		G	6	45 / 34		I / C	3 / 3		9 9		
MATH.		15		G	3	16		G	3							6	
Totals		14				31				79	30	24	27				43

*Does not include courses required for major or minors.

102. PRELIMINARY CHART

PLANNING A SCHEDULE

Use this method to devise any sort of program from a sales campaign to a circus. This example shows how a freshman can select the rest of his college course at the end of his first semester. College requirements vary so widely that charts must be adapted to suit the regulations of any particular institution.

List the types of material (fields of study) in Col. 1, Fig. 102.

Place items over which you have no control (courses completed or required) in the next columns (2 and 3).

Put desired items in Col. 4. Add footnotes if there are any restrictions, such as prerequisite courses.

Select a major and two minors. Choose courses for these and list corresponding credit hours in Cols. 5 and 6.

Mark credits for any other required courses in Col. 7 and for electives in Col. 8.

SEMESTERS		8:00–8:55	9:00–9:55	10:00–10:55	11:00–11:55	1:30–2:25	2:30–3:25	3:30–4:25	HRS.
1		Completed							14
2	MWF		Eng.2		Math16	Munc2			17
2	TTS			Fr.2		Rel.2	Phys.Ed.2		
3	MWF			Drama1	Hist.3				20
3	TTS	Eng.21	Eng.13 (Fr.35)		Pol.Sc.5		Drama1 (lab)		
4	MWF			Phil.12	Biol.10	Hist.4			23
4	TTS	Eng.22	Eng.14 (Fr.26)		Pol.Sc.6		Biol.10 (lab)		
5	MWF			Soc.11		Psy.13	Econ.1		14
5	TTS	CONFLICT			Eng.37		Psy.13 (lab)		
6	MWF			Logic15		Psy.14	Econ.2		14
6	TTS				Eng.38		Psy.14 (lab)		
7	MWF	Eng41 Hist.45			Chem1				11
7	TTS					Chem1 (lab)			
8	MWF	Eng.42			Chem.2		Hist.34		11
8	TTS					Chem.2 (lab)			

(Vertical note rows 3–5: OVERCROWDED; rows 7–8: TOO LIGHT)

ELEMENTARY COURSE PUT OFF UNTIL SENIOR YEAR

103. FIRST DRAFT OF SCHEDULE

This sorts the data in Fig. 102. Each course is assigned to a specific semester, but that is the only matter left to choice. The example reveals many flaws. Some of these can be corrected by rearranging the schedule, but others will require changes in the list of courses elected (Col. 8, Fig. 102).

My original illustration for Fig. 102 was a masterpiece of compression; it contained examples of every question that can arise in selecting a college course. Nevertheless, I had to abandon it; the chart was so involved that no one else could make heads or tails of it.

GRIDS—C. USES

Tabular charts crowd a maximum of information into a minimum of space. Their value for this purpose is universally

Fig. 103]   No Skill Required   55

recognized; most published tables are little more than compact collections of data. You can prepare similar data charts for your own needs, but the real virtues of tabular charts will not appear until you employ them as tools for thought.

Planning. Many kinds of planning involve schedules [Fig. 103]. These are best presented in the form of tables. Furthermore, the easiest way to plan a schedule is to work out a preliminary table like that in Fig. 102. Space-consuming data (in this case, class hours and the days of the week) can be included by supplying a key [Fig. 101]. Railway timetables make extensive use of this device.

If you schedule a manufacturing process, a scene shift for the stage, or a military operation involving an entire army, you will have to deal with different items in each case—but the basic procedure is the same as that used to schedule a college course.

Classifying Material. When you want to clarify your ideas on any subject, nothing is so helpful as dividing the material into classes. Even breaking a subject into only two classes may mean a great step forward. My own ideas about drawing became much clearer when I found that all drawings could be classified into fixed-line and free-line types, and again when I learned to think in terms of grids and webs.

Classification is essentially a cut-and-try process. The charting method illustrated in Fig. 104 may appear tedious, but it is quick and easy compared to any procedure that will achieve equally good results either mentally or in writing.

We begin by making two lists of items and use these as tabs in a chart [Step 1]. We then try to fit actual examples into the data spaces. Ideally, each example should fit one data space. Something is wrong with the lists if: (1) an example will not fit at all, (2) an example fits two or more spaces that are not adjacent to each other, (3) there is any doubt as to the space into which an example should fit, (4) two examples overlap. In these cases, we must rearrange the tabs, find new ones, or both.

Examples that fit prove nothing; a fit may occur by accident. Try to find examples which will not fit as these prove that the classification is wrong in some way. This may seem like looking for trouble, but it is better to find trouble than to have it find you. For instance, I attempted to write the section on order in this chapter before I made the charts. My ideas on the subject were so vague that I turned out no less than seven drafts without getting anywhere. Then I began charting (which I should have had sense enough to do in the first place). It was not until I hit on

ORDER OF TABS \ FORM OF CHART	RECT-ANGULAR	TRI-ANGULAR	COM-POUND
RANDOM	COLLEGE COURSES		COLLEGE COURSES
INDEX		BOWLING SCORES	
RANK	CORRECT		
GROUPED	COLLEGE COURSES		COLLEGE COURSES
SERIES			

COLOR WHEEL?

FIG. 104.

TABULAR CHARTS USED AS TOOLS FOR CLASSIFYING AND CLARIFYING IDEAS These are some of the charts I made while trying to understand the principles of order.

UNCERTAIN — SEEMS TO FIT FOUR SPACES EQUALLY WELL

① FIRST ATTEMPT

RANDOM / ORDER OF TABS \ FORM OF CHART	RECTANGULAR	TRIANGULAR	CIRCULAR
GROUPED	COLLEGE COURSES CHORD CHART	CORRECT	
UNGROUPED			
INDEX	COLOR CODE CHORD CHART	BOWLING SCORES	
RANK		EXAMPLES OVERLAP	
SERIES	COLOR CODE CHORD CHART		COLOR WHEEL

②

CHART REARRANGED AND A FEW TABS CHANGED
1. Some altogether different approach is obviously required.

BASIS OF ARRANGEMENT \ ORDER	RANDOM	SYSTEMATIC		SERIES	SEQUENCES		
		INDEX	RANK		UNITS	CONTINUITIES	CLASSES
NOT GROUPED	ANY ITEMS CAN BE ARRANGED AT RANDOM	RIVERS, ALPHABETIC	RIVERS BY LENGTH	PHARAOHS, CHRONOLOGICAL	FRENCH KINGS CHRONOLOGICAL	SEGMENTS ?	POSITIONS ?
GROUPED / IRREGULAR		RIVERS BY CONTINENTS		PHARAOHS BY DYNASTIES	FRENCH KINGS BY DYNASTIES		
GROUPED / REGULAR / LARGER		MEN & WIVES BY SEXES			DECK OF CARDS BY SUITS		HUES, BY WARM COOL
GROUPED / REGULAR / SMALLER		MEN & WIVES BY COUPLES			DECK OF CARDS BY VALUES		HUES, BY COMPLEMENTS

③ A NEW ATTACK ON THE PROBLEM

I dropped the idea of form. Some examples still overlap, but I seem to be on the right track.

TYPES OF ORDER IN WHICH SETS MAY BE GROUPED							
TYPES OF SETS \ BASIS OF ARRANGEMENT	INDEPENDENT UNITS			DERIVED FROM CONTINUITIES (1)			
				POSITIONS		SEGMENTS	
	SEQUENCE	SERIES	LIST	SEQUENCE	SERIES	SEQUENCE	SERIES
UNGROUPED / RANDOM	ANY LIST CAN BE ARRANGED AT RANDOM BUT A SEQUENCE OR SERIES CANNOT.						
UNGROUPED / INDEX	FRENCH (2) KINGS, CARON	PHARAOHS CHRONO-LOGICAL	RIVERS, ALPHABETIC	(3) BY WAVE LENGTH	(4) BY WAVE LENGTH	HUES BY SPECTRUM	EGYPTIAN REIGNS. CHRON. (2)
UNGROUPED / RANK	TRAINS LEAVING STATION	(5)	RIVERS BY LENGTH	A SET BASED ON A CONTINUITY CAN BE ARRANGED BY RANK ONLY WHEN THE CONTINUITY IS IGNORED. (5)			
GROUPED / IRREGULAR	FRENCH KINGS BY DYNASTIES	PHARAOHS BY DYNASTIES	RIVERS BY CONTINENTS	(3) BY HUES	(4) BY HUES	FRENCH REIGNS BY DYNASTIES	EGYPTIAN REIGNS BY DYNASTIES
GROUPED / REGULAR / BY LARGER GROUPS	FULL DECK CARDS BY SUITS	HALF DECK CARDS BY SUITS	MEN AND WIVES BY SEXES	(3) BY WARM-COOL	(4) BY WARM-COOL	HUES BY WARM-COOL	(5)
GROUPED / REGULAR / BY SMALLER GROUPS	FULL DECK CARDS BY VALUES	HALF DECK CARDS BY VALUES	MEN & WIVES BY COUPLES	(3) BY COMPLE-MENTS	(4) BY COMPLE-MENTS	HUES BY COMPLE-MENTS	(5)

(1) WHEN A SET IS TREATED AS A LIST, THE CONTINUITY IS NO LONGER IMPORTANT.
(2) KINGS ARE INDEPENDENT UNITS, BUT REIGNS ARE SEGMENTS OF A CONTINUITY OF TIME.
(3) PAINTS FROM STANDPOINT OF CUSTOMER, WHO MUST TREAT LINE AS COMPLETE.
(4) PAINTS FROM STANDPOINT OF MANUFACTURER, WHO MAY INTRODUCE CHANGES.
(5) BLANK SPACES DO NOT NECESSARILY INDICATE MISTAKES IN CLASSIFICATION. THERE MAY BE LOGICALLY SOUND CLASSES FOR WHICH NO EXAMPLES EXIST.

④ MY LATEST CHART ON *ORDER*

This may not be ideal, but I have not been able to improve it so far.

the classification in Step 4, Fig. 104, that I managed to produce a satisfactory version of the section.

Classification charts are made solely for the purpose of selecting the best tabs and arranging them in the most logical way.

Fig. 104]　　　　　No Skill Required　　　　　57

The examples placed in the data spaces merely test the tabs and have no value in their own right.

A completed classification chart is almost never used *as a chart;* it may have served its function by clarifying our ideas, or we may turn the tabs into an outline for something that we want to write. Thus, the tabs in Step 4, Fig. 104, became the headings for the section on order in this chapter. I used some of the examples in the chart as examples in my text, but that was a by-product; I originally thought of these examples only to test the validity of the tabs.

Unlike scheduling, classification does not proceed on any set plan. Each case must be worked out on its own merits. Furthermore, no two people think along the same lines when charting the same material. This makes it impossible to give a clear-cut example. You may not be able to follow the details of my thinking as I made the charts in Fig. 104 because much of it went on in my head and does not appear in the charts. However, if you will experiment with this method by using it to classify some of your own ideas, I believe you will find that it almost explains itself as you go along.

I started with little more than a vague feeling that order and chart form are related. Some idea of my mental confusion at this stage is shown by the fact that I placed "Grouped Charts" in one set of tabs and "Compound Charts" in the other. As compound charts are really grouped charts, this means that I made the mistake of including the same basic idea in both sets of tabs. Such foggy thinking is common in the early stages of classification —which is one reason why it pays to make charts.

When I found that the color wheel would not fit into any space and that the college-course chart fitted into four different spaces, I tried to correct matters by rearranging the tabs and changing a few of them [Step 2]. This often works well, and in this case it eliminated some of the difficulties in Step 1. However, as soon as I tried to fit in other examples, I saw that my new chart was as bad as my old one. A more drastic revision was obviously needed.

Although my tentative charts did not work, I had (in Paul de Kruif's phrase) "failed forward." My ideas on order had been brought into focus, I had eliminated a number of mistaken beliefs, and I had recognized the need to distinguish between series and sequences.

I experimented with several other schemes before I hit on the idea of charting "Order" against "Basis of Arrangement" [Step 3]. Although my new chart still showed serious faults, I had learned enough to feel that I was working along the right line.

Unfortunately, there is no way to be sure that a classification is complete. One of the charts that I made following the one shown in Step 3 satisfied me so well that I used its tabs as an outline for a draft of my section on order. When this draft showed serious flaws, I went back to charting and produced Step 4.

DIAGRAMS VS. WORDS
Verbal statements often tend to obscure the relationships between ideas because the words must follow one another and also because artificial rules of grammar must be observed. In a diagram, however, ideas are arranged to stress the connection between them.

We can diagram an idea like this:

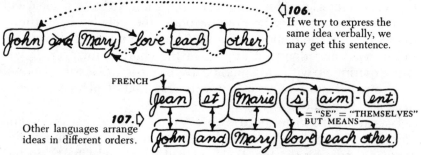

106.
If we try to express the same idea verbally, we may get this sentence.

FRENCH

107.
Other languages arrange ideas in different orders.

= "SE" = "THEMSELVES" BUT MEANS

When we diagram the *grammatical* relations in Fig. 106, we get this:

108.
Which gives a false picture of the *idea*-relationships involved.

REED-KELLOGG DIAGRAMS
Drawn to bring out grammatical relations, which may have little connection with the idea that the words express. These diagrams are highly specialized.

109.
If we express the same thought in other words, we have a different grammatical diagram:

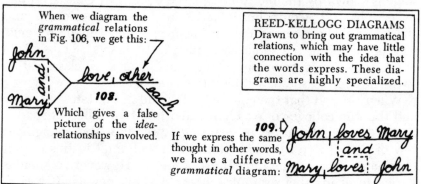

WEBS

Abstract webs are far more flexible than grids. They have a much wider range of usefulness, and they can probably serve you in more different situations than all other types of drawing combined. Such webs require no advance planning. We can set down anywhere from two to thirty items and then work out their relationships by connecting them with lines. Another advantage of webs over grids is that we can add a new classification, or change a relationship, without needing to remake the old chart.

Fig. 109]   No Skill Required   59

A table shows the relation of each data item to two tabs. But when different data items are connected to their tabs in different ways, tables provide no convenient method for indicating this. Webs permit us to distinguish types of relationships and also to represent several different relations at the same time. Thus, Figs. 105 and 106 use solid lines for John's attitude toward Mary and dotted ones for Mary's attitude toward John.

Organization Charts. Most people seem to think of organization charts merely as devices for showing the structure of business, political, or military organizations. Actually, organization charts are far more than that. They are tools for organizing ideas—any ideas. Even electrical wiring diagrams are essentially organization charts.

SURVEYS. The charts in Fig. 110 show how you can use organization charts to survey a subject *before* you begin any formal study of it. The easiest way to start is to find a textbook on the subject. The example is based on the book that you hold in your hand.

Write the name of the subject at the top of the chart. List the chapter titles below. Abbreviate long titles [A, Step 1]. If a title is not clear, read the first paragraph of the chapter and glance at the headings and illustrations. This will usually indicate the nature of the material. You can then substitute a more descriptive title in your chart [B]. If two chapters deal with the same topic, use only one title [C]. When a chapter obviously covers two or more topics, list these separately [D]. Enclose each title in a cartouch.

Draw lines to mark the relationships between the items. These lines will probably reveal a different pattern from the one given by the author of the book. As a book must follow a single sequence, the writer may be forced to separate material that logically belongs together; the chart-maker can show as many relationships as he likes.

Some of your lines will cross without connecting [E, Step 1, Fig. 110]; others will connect [F]. Fig. 111 shows the best method of distinguishing these when you draw for your own use or for anyone familiar with the symbols. However, when drawing for laymen, the fact that some lines do not connect should be stressed by adding little humps [Fig. 112].

In your first draft, you may not be able to find connections for a few of the items—such as "Rudiments" and "Short Cuts." This calls attention to the fact that these items deserve further study.

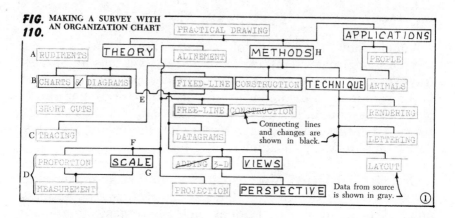

FIG. 110. MAKING A SURVEY WITH AN ORGANIZATION CHART

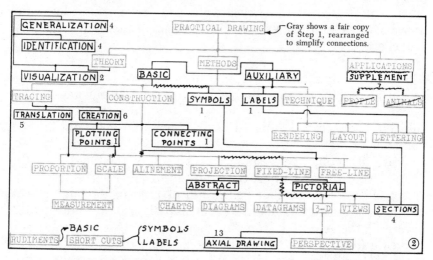

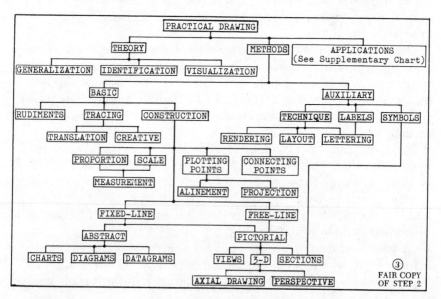

Fig. 112]   No Skill Required   61

If you already have some knowledge of the field, you will probably add items of your own [G, Step 1, Fig. 110]. You may also want to include *grouping items* like "Methods" [H].

Even while the chart is in this rough state, your work on it will have given you a much clearer grasp of the subject than you had when you started. You will have acquired a bird's-eye view of the whole field, and this is perhaps the most valuable asset that a beginner can possess. You also have a mental filing system in which to arrange new facts as you learn them. For example, to anyone who studies Chapter 1 without first charting this book, "Connecting Points" may come as an isolated bit of information —worth learning perhaps, but not associated in any special way with drawing as a whole. However, if he had charted the book before beginning to read it, he would have seen at once that "Connecting Points" is a method of construction. He would then be prepared to use it as such [Step 2, Fig. 110].

SYMBOLS TO DISTINGUISH BETWEEN LINES WHICH DO AND DO NOT CONNECT

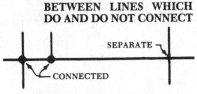

111. FIRST METHOD

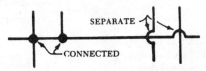

112. SECOND METHOD

The relationships shown in Step 1 are those that you might work out by glancing through the book without reading it. Prepare a *fair copy* of this without erasures or corrections and with the items arranged to make the connecting lines as simple as possible. The gray version in Step 2, Fig. 110, shows the result. This completes your preliminary survey. If a book is not too thick nor the subject too abstruse, you can do the job in an hour.

Anyone who makes such a *survey chart* begins his study with a clearer view of the subject than many people have when they finish. He knows the principal topics and sees how they fit together. He is prepared to learn details efficiently. As each one appears in his work, he has a mental pigeonhole in which to put it. It is no longer an orphan fact; it is related to all the other facts. This makes it more interesting, more useful, easier to learn, and harder to forget.

As you study the subject further, you will undoubtedly want to make changes in your chart. The black markings in Step 2, Fig. 110, show changes that you might make while studying the chapters indicated by the numerals. Thus, you would probably add "Translation" and "Creation" after reading Chapters 5 and 6. Step 3, Fig. 110, shows a fair copy of the revised chart.

Although organization charts are useful for reference, their chief value lies in the mental process involved in making them. If you study a textbook which already contains a chart, do not be content with this; make your own and keep it abreast of your advancing knowledge. Your chart will differ from the author's because your viewpoint is different. Also, if you want to study a subject from several viewpoints, make a separate chart for each viewpoint.

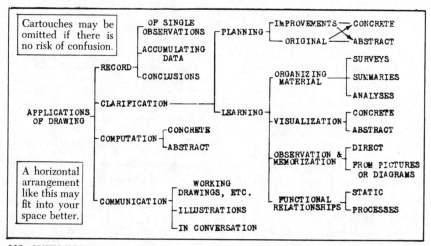

113. SUPPLEMENTARY CHART

This one expands the item *APPLICATIONS* shown in the chart at Step 3, Fig. 110.

No chart is final. You may study a subject for a lifetime without learning all there is to know about it. Any important new knowledge calls for modifications of your chart. Regardless of how thoroughly you believe you have mastered a subject, I doubt if you can spend twenty minutes in charting it without discovering something that you did not know before.

When dealing with a field for which no textbook is available, you will not have a ready-made list of titles. But if you know enough about the subject to consider charting it, you must be able to think of four or five headings. These will give you a start, and your study of the relations between the items will automatically suggest more.

If, on the other hand, you already know a good deal about the subject, you can save trouble by tentatively grouping related topics as you set them down instead of merely listing them in columns.

Fig. 114]   No Skill Required   **63**

OUTLINES. You cannot prepare an outline for a speech, or for any form of writing, until you decide on the basic organization of the material. If you try to find the proper arrangement by making a rough outline, you may work for an hour or more only to discover that you have been using the wrong plan and must start again from scratch. If your ideas are extremely vague, you may want to make classification charts, but an organization chart is easier and will usually serve your purpose. You will still need an outline to bring the items into a single sequence. However, once you know how your headings are related, writing the outline becomes a straightforward matter.

SUPPLEMENTARY CHARTS. Whenever a subject requires more than twenty or thirty headings, organize the main topics on a key chart and work out further subdivisions of these topics on *supplementary charts*. Fig. 113 shows how the heading "Applications" in Step 3, Fig. 110 may be analyzed in such a supplementary chart.

The use of supplementary charts can be carried as far as the material requires. In fact, the science of biological classification consists essentially in making an enormous series of organization charts to cover the thousands of plant and animal species studied by botanists and zoologists.

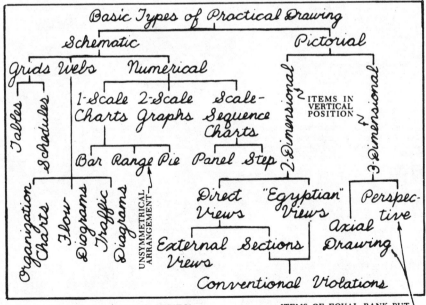

114. A CHART DRAWN TO STUDY ONE ASPECT OF A SUBJECT
Note devices used to crowd the material into a restricted space.

ITEMS OF EQUAL RANK PUT AT DIFFERENT LEVELS SO THAT THEY CAN OVERLAP

CHARTS FOR SPECIAL TOPICS. Organization charts are not limited to cases where you must deal with whole subjects. They are equally applicable to a single chapter or even a single paragraph. Furthermore, you can use them to analyze special aspects of the subject which may not be covered by the chapter- or section-headings of any book. Fig. 114 shows how I would chart the main types of Practical Drawing. This classification covers the same ground as Fig. 110, but it is based on types of drawing instead of on methods of drawing. Hence, the two charts bear little resemblance to each other.

When you study a subject intensively, it usually pays to chart it from several different viewpoints. You can learn much from the "Types" chart that is not brought out by the "Methods" chart and vice versa.

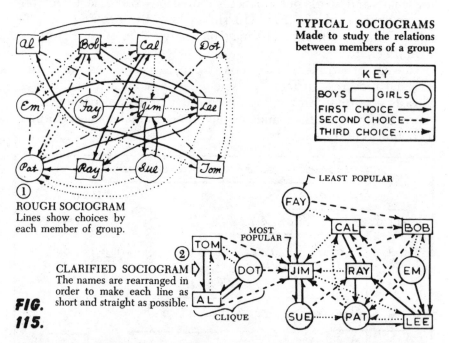

TYPICAL SOCIOGRAMS
Made to study the relations between members of a group

KEY		
BOYS ☐	GIRLS ○	
FIRST CHOICE	——→	
SECOND CHOICE	– – ➤	
THIRD CHOICE	·····➤	

① ROUGH SOCIOGRAM
Lines show choices by each member of group.

② CLARIFIED SOCIOGRAM
The names are rearranged in order to make each line as short and straight as possible.

FIG. 115.

LEAST POPULAR

MOST POPULAR

CLIQUE

Direction. Organization charts convey no sense of direction. If Fig. 113 were reversed, right to left, it might look odd but the meaning would still be clear. Instead of saying, "Clarification is divided into Planning and Learning," we would say, "Planning and Learning involve Clarification." However, in the John-loves-Mary diagrams [Figs. 105 and 106], the direction of the lines is of basic importance and must be shown by arrows.

SOCIOGRAMS. A more elaborate example of direction is provided by the *sociograms* in Fig. 115. These are ranking devices used to

Fig. 120]   No Skill Required   65

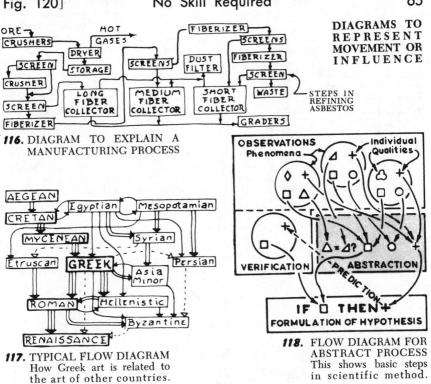

116. DIAGRAM TO EXPLAIN A
MANUFACTURING PROCESS

DIAGRAMS TO
REPRESENT
MOVEMENT OR
INFLUENCE

STEPS IN
REFINING
ASBESTOS

117. TYPICAL FLOW DIAGRAM
How Greek art is related to
the art of other countries.

118. FLOW DIAGRAM FOR
ABSTRACT PROCESS
This shows basic steps
in scientific method.

study the relations between the people in a group. Each person
is asked to give his first, second, and third choice among the
other members of the group. The names are written down and
enclosed in cartouches. The choices are then marked by lines
with arrows.

A rough chart like Step 1 is not very revealing. However, when
the names are rearranged to make the lines as short and straight
as possible, the structure of the group becomes clear [Step 2].

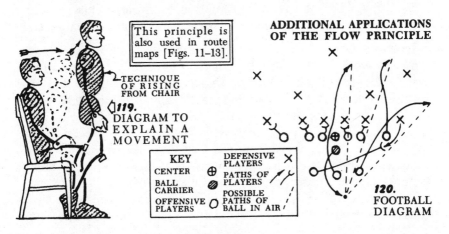

This principle is
also used in route
maps [Figs. 11–13].

TECHNIQUE
OF RISING
FROM CHAIR

119.
DIAGRAM TO
EXPLAIN A
MOVEMENT

ADDITIONAL APPLICATIONS
OF THE FLOW PRINCIPLE

KEY	DEFENSIVE PLAYERS ✕
CENTER ⊕	PATHS OF PLAYERS
BALL CARRIER	POSSIBLE PATHS OF
OFFENSIVE PLAYERS ○	BALL IN AIR

120.
FOOTBALL
DIAGRAM

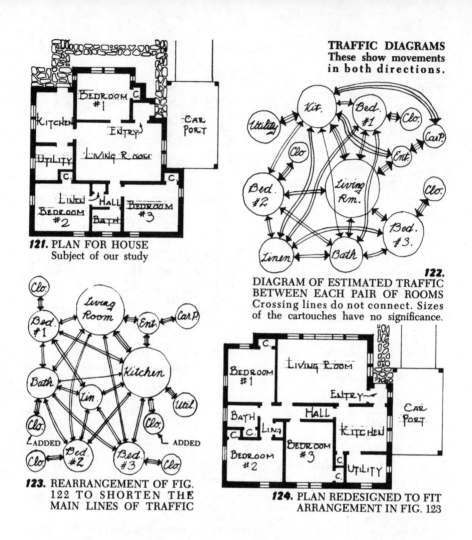

TRAFFIC DIAGRAMS
These show movements
in both directions.

121. PLAN FOR HOUSE
Subject of our study

122.
DIAGRAM OF ESTIMATED TRAFFIC
BETWEEN EACH PAIR OF ROOMS
Crossing lines do not connect. Sizes
of the cartouches have no significance.

123. REARRANGEMENT OF FIG.
122 TO SHORTEN THE
MAIN LINES OF TRAFFIC

124. PLAN REDESIGNED TO FIT
ARRANGEMENT IN FIG. 123

FLOW DIAGRAMS. When directional arrows show either physical movement or a sequence of events, the result is a *flow diagram*. Figs. 116–118 are representative examples. This principle has a wide range of applications, as Figs. 119 and 120 suggest.

TRAFFIC DIAGRAMS. When double-headed arrows represent actual movement in both directions, we have a *traffic diagram* [Figs. 122 and 123]. Webs of this type enable us to find the arrangement that gives the heaviest traffic the shortest paths. You can appreciate the value of this if you attended one of those high schools where you had to walk half a mile between classes because the rooms were not laid out with the traffic in mind. Mistakes in planning a factory to suit the traffic requirements of its operation may cost thousands of dollars a year.

The use of traffic diagrams is not confined to large-scale situations. They can improve the efficiency of any routine operation,

Fig. 124] No Skill Required 67

including the family dishwashing and the technique of a single worker on an assembly line.

CHOICE AND DESIGN OF TYPES

The main types of charts and diagrams are illustrated in this chapter. One or another of these types will fit most situations, although you may have to adapt it to meet special requirements.

Definitions. The terms "chart" and "diagram" are often used interchangeably. This is unnecessarily confusing. I hope that the following comments will help to clarify the situation.

Charts tend to be nonrealistic; diagrams tend to be pictorial. A chart may be dressed up with pictures to catch the eye, but this is mere decoration; the pictorial elements can always be replaced by labeled cartouches without loss of meaning. If the picture is essential, the drawing is not a chart but a diagram.

Charts are static; diagrams tend to be dynamic. A drawing that contains arrows which indicate change is a diagram. However, when the arrows merely show relations, the drawing should be classified as a chart. On this basis, Figs. 116–120 are diagrams. Most of them represent physical movement, and all of them indicate change. The arrows in Fig. 125, however, symbolize fixed relationships. This classifies it as a chart. The Reed-Kellogg diagrams in Figs. 108 and 109 are a border-line case. Although I would classify them as charts, they are always called "diagrams" and they certainly convey a sense of movement as one word follows another. Fine distinctions are of little value. Nevertheless, the practice of using the terms "chart" and "diagram" without discrimination will undoubtedly tend to confuse your thinking in a field where clear thought is essential.

We need a general term to cover all forms of practical drawing that are not primarily pictorial. This would include charts, diagrams, maps, graphs, and many types of working drawings. The best term for this purpose seems to be *schematic drawings,* or *schematics* for short.

Symbols. Only five different types of symbols are available for charting. Each type can be varied to some extent. But even by ringing all possible changes, we cannot provide enough different symbols to give each one a standard meaning which will apply to every schematic we may wish to make.

This means that the same idea may be expressed by different symbols in different drawings. As part of my purpose is to enlarge your graphic vocabulary by showing a wide range of symbols and by letting you compare various methods of symbolizing

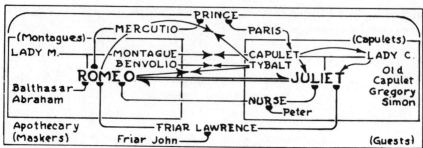

125. CHART TO INTERPRET THE RELATIONSHIPS
BETWEEN THE CHARACTERS IN A DRAMA

ideas, I have deliberately avoided any attempt to standardize one set of symbols for this book. In a few cases, two or more drawings in the same plate use different symbols to express similar ideas or use the same symbols in different ways (see Figs. 36–39). However, this is an exceptional situation. Unless you are preparing a book on practical drawing, you should adopt a fixed set of symbols for each drawing, or set of drawings, and employ them consistently throughout.

CONNECTING LINES. These may be varied to show emphasis, rank, or different types of relationship. Almost every drawing on pp. 58–68 offers examples. The dots, humps, and breaks used to indicate whether lines join or pass each other deserve careful study [Figs. 111, 112, and 118].

ARROWS. Adding arrows to connecting lines greatly enlarges their range of meanings. Fig. 125, for example, uses several types of symbolic arrows in the same chart. Single arrows show "influence" (Capulet influences Juliet). Arrows that meet indicate "conflict." Half-arrows with double lines represent "love." By substituting black half-circles for arrowheads, I have been able to show that some characters support others (the Nurse supports both Romeo and Juliet). The football diagram in Fig. 120 contains another type of "arrowhead" with a specialized meaning.

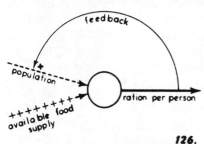

126.
DIAGRAM TO ILLUSTRATE
PRINCIPLE OF FEEDBACK
Any increase in the ration will
increase the population which,
in turn, decreases the ration.

The shaft of the food-supply arrow in Fig. 126 is made up of plus signs to show that any increase in the supply increases the ration per person. The "population" arrow has a shaft composed

Fig. 127]　　　　　No Skill Required　　　　　69

of minus signs to remind us that any increase in the population decreases the ration per person. The "feedback" arrow means that any increase in the ration increases the population which, in turn, decreases the ration. This is an exceptionally flexible diagram. No less than eighty-five versions of it are used by Pierre de Latil in his book *Thinking by Machine* to explain points ranging from the psychology of love to the functions performed by the tail vanes of a windmill.

CARTOUCHES. Fig. 127 emphasizes "PRACTICAL DRAWING" by weighting the outline of the cartouch. The sociograms in Fig. 115 distinguish the sexes by using cartouches of different shapes. These cases, however, are exceptions. Most cartouches have uniform outlines, and neither their shapes nor their sizes are significant.

The cartouches in Fig. 125 group items and separate the Montagues on one hand and the Capulets on the other from the rest of the characters in the play.

In Fig. 127, the cartouches overlap to show that the items blend into one another. Do not confuse this with the symbolism in Fig. 130, where the overlapping cartouches divide the chart into completely separate compartments (in logic, there is no middle ground between an item which is "Both A and B" and one which is "A but not B"). These *Venn charts*—named for their inventor, John Venn—label their cartouches by breaking the outline and placing the letter or name in the break. Any other arrangement may lead to confusion.

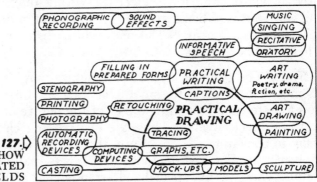

127.
CHART TO STUDY HOW
A FIELD IS RELATED
TO SIMILAR FIELDS

SHADING. This is used for emphasis in the movement diagram [Fig. 119], and it sets off one area from the rest in the scientific-method diagram [Fig. 118]. The Venn chart in Fig. 130 employs shading to show that the classes corresponding to the shaded compartments are empty. However, the southwest-

VENN CHARTS
These are used
to illustrate the
rules of logic.

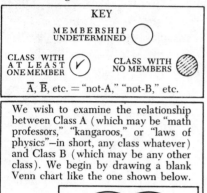

KEY

MEMBERSHIP
UNDETERMINED ◯

CLASS WITH
AT LEAST ⓥ
ONE MEMBER

CLASS WITH
NO MEMBERS ▨

$\overline{A}$, $\overline{B}$, etc. = "not-A," "not-B," etc.

We wish to examine the relationship between Class A (which may be "math professors," "kangaroos," or "laws of physics"—in short, any class whatever) and Class B (which may be any other class). We begin by drawing a blank Venn chart like the one shown below.

A — B

A BUT | BOTH A | B BUT
NOT B | AND B | NOT A

NEITHER A NOR B

129.◊
BLANK
CHART

Here are some examples of ways to show facts about Class A in a chart.

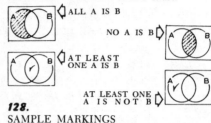

◁ ALL A IS B

NO A IS B ▷ A ⃝ B

◁ AT LEAST
ONE A IS B

AT LEAST ONE ◊
A IS NOT B ◊

128.
SAMPLE MARKINGS

A ▨ B
ⓥ

130.◊
CHART SHOWING
THREE CLASSES

C

When A = our math professors, B = Ph.D's, and C = people who can read French, this chart means that all our math professors are Ph.D's, all Ph.D's read French, and we have at least one math professor. Hence, all our math professors read French, and we have at least one professor who reads French.

northeast shading means, "There is no A that is not B," whereas the northwest-southeast shading means, "There is no B that is not C."

GLYPHS. Small symbols, such as the ⓥ mark in the Venn chart [Fig. 130] and the shapes representing qualities in Fig. 118, can be conveniently grouped under the term *glyphs*. These are widely used in astronomy, logic, electrical-wiring diagrams, proofreading, and music. When a glyph is attached to the rim of a cartouch, it is called an *outrider*. The ones which distinguish the sexes in Fig. 131 are examples.

Form. The form of a chart or diagram may or may not affect its meaning. When it does not, changing the form will often give you a better understanding either of the nature of the drawing or of the subject covered. Thus, the overlapping circles in Fig. 132 seem to constitute a unique form that occurs only in Venn charts. However, as Fig. 134 demonstrates, this is really equivalent to a tabular chart with a specialized arrangement of tabs.

Shifting forms around in this way is excellent training in the art of making and reading charts and diagrams. If you practice it, you will find that even the most uncommon form may turn out to be an old friend in disguise.

Do not take this to mean that the superficial form of a schematic is unimportant—far from it. Venn charts, for example, are

Fig. 134]   No Skill Required   71

used largely for teaching logic. Beginners in that field find it much easier to understand the overlapping circles in Figs. 130 and 132 than to grasp the meaning of a tabular chart like Fig. 134.

Procedure. When in doubt as to the type of schematic you need, note whether there are two sets of interrelated items. If so, a tabular chart is indicated; if not, try some form of web—probably an organization chart. Add arrowheads where (but only where) they have real meaning. Even when the result is not entirely adequate, it will teach you a good deal about the problem in hand. This will usually enable you to select the exact type of drawing you need. Occasions when you must invent an entirely new form are rare.

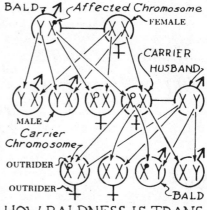

HOW BALDNESS IS TRANS·
MITTED BY HEREDITY

131. DIAGRAM TO FOLLOW ITEMS
THROUGH SEVERAL STAGES

An excellent way to learn the art of making schematics is to choose a problem at random and see what a drawing can do to help. Fig. 125 was made in this way when a friend suggested that drawing might be useful in interpreting a play. I chose *Romeo and Juliet* as an example because I had studied it for years and thought I knew all the answers. Five minutes' work on the chart revealed the striking symmetry in the organization of the characters. This symmetry is certainly an important element in any interpretation of the play, and one that I had never suspected until the chart thrust it under my nose.

VARIATIONS IN FORM

These are all Venn charts for four classes. Although their forms differ greatly, they have the same meaning.

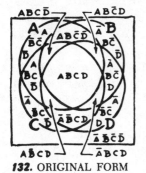

132. ORIGINAL FORM

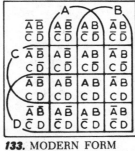

133. MODERN FORM

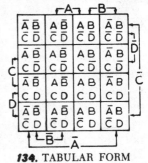

134. TABULAR FORM

4

MAKING EASY ONES
OUT OF HARD ONES

DIAGRAMS ARE EASIER TO
DRAW THAN PICTURES AND
OFTEN MORE EFFECTIVE

135.
PICTURE
OF HEART
AND LUNGS

136.

DIAGRAM SHOWING
HEART AND LUNGS

WE need no skill to draw charts because their value does not depend upon the accuracy of their lines. But practical drawing is not limited to charts. We want to draw pictures of houses, and people, and cows. Pictures require a high degree of accuracy and a correspondingly high degree of skill. What can we do to lower these requirements?

You may not be able to use all the answers given in this chapter until you have had more experience with drawing. Nevertheless, you should know what methods of deskilling exist, so that you will be ready to apply them when opportunities arise.

CAPTIONS, LABELS, NOTES

No self-respecting artist would paint a cow and write under it, "This is a cow." In practical work, however, we not only put a *caption* under the cow, but we *label* the horns, tail, and spigots. When we want to explain something which may not be obvious from the drawing or which cannot be drawn at all, we simply add a *note* [Fig. 136].

The use of captions and labels as substitutes for elaborate drawing turns a picture into a diagram. In extreme cases, it can reduce the need for accuracy to zero and make the diagram merely a collection of labels connected by lines.

Diagrams are much easier to draw than pictures, but this does not mean that they are makeshifts. Actually, they are often better than pictures for practical purposes. Thus, Fig. 135 might enable us to recognize a heart and lungs should we happen to

Fig. 140]   Making Easy Ones Out of Hard Ones   73

find any lying around, but the likelihood of such an encounter hardly justifies drawing a picture. The diagram in Fig. 136, on the other hand, gives a clear idea of what parts are involved and how they function. A student of anatomy could identify every part with the aid of the diagram. If he had nothing to guide him except the picture, he could recognize only the organs that happen to be portrayed clearly.

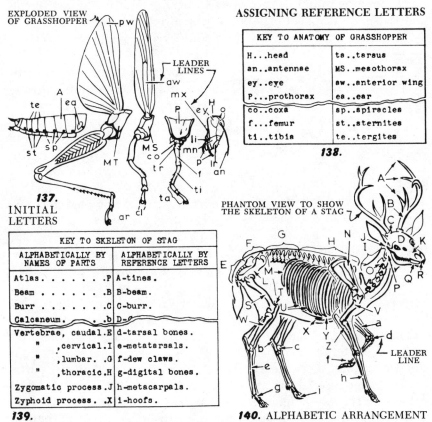

ASSIGNING REFERENCE LETTERS

KEY TO ANATOMY OF GRASSHOPPER	
H...head	ta..tarsus
an..antennae	MS..mesothorax
ey..eye	aw..anterior wing
P...prothorax	ea..ear
co..coxa	sp..spiracles
f...femur	st..sternites
ti..tibia	te..tergites

138.

137. INITIAL LETTERS

PHANTOM VIEW TO SHOW THE SKELETON OF A STAG

KEY TO SKELETON OF STAG	
ALPHABETICALLY BY NAMES OF PARTS	ALPHABETICALLY BY REFERENCE LETTERS
Atlas......P	A-tines.
Beam......B	B-beam.
Burr......C	C-burr.
Calcaneum. ..b	D-∅
Vertebrae, caudal.E	d-tarsal bones.
" ,cervical.I	e-metatarsals.
" ,lumbar. .G	f-dew claws.
" ,thoracic.H	g-digital bones.
Zygomatic process.J	h-metacarpals.
Zyphoid process. .X	i-hoofs.

139.

140. ALPHABETIC ARRANGEMENT

Reference Letters and Numerals. In crowded drawings, like that of the grasshopper in Fig. 137, or in diagrams like Fig. 141 where the parts have no names, we may be forced to use *reference letters* and/or *reference numerals* instead of labels.

When only one type of reference is required, Roman capitals are normally the best choice. If we need more types, we can add Roman lower-case (small) letters, Arabic numerals, or Greek capitals. Greek capitals are conventionally employed in geometry to indicate angles [Fig. 141]. Select Greek letters such as Φ (phi), ϴ (theta), Ψ (psi), Ω (omega), Δ (delta), and Σ (sigma) which cannot be mistaken for Roman capitals.

If references are assigned at random, the drawing is hard to read. This difficulty can be reduced by a wise choice of references, and cases occur where references are actually more helpful than labels.

INITIALS. The parts of the grasshopper in Fig. 137 are designated by the initials of their names. When two or more names have the same initial, I have used either the first two letters or the first two significant letters. Wherever initials are employed, a key should be provided [Fig. 138].

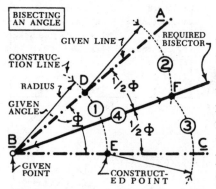

141. **ARRANGEMENT BY SEQUENCE**
Each line is numbered and each point is lettered as it is drawn. Use same radius for Arcs 2 and 3. Arrow heads (◄——►) show that Line 4 is drawn through Points B and F.

INDEXING. Initials are helpful when only a few points are lettered or when the subject is familiar, but they lose much of their value when many points must be marked and many of the names are unknown to those who will see the drawing. Thus, a person with no knowledge of insects might learn from the key [Fig. 138] that "ea" means "ear" and still have to hunt for some time before discovering that a grasshopper's ear is in back of his hind leg. This difficulty may also occur when labels are used.

The drawing of the stag in Fig. 140 minimizes the problem by assigning letters as nearly as possible from left to right and from top to bottom. Because there are more than twenty-six parts, I used lower-case letters after I ran out of capitals. The left-hand column of the key [Fig. 139] lists the parts alphabetically by their names, and thus serves as an index to the illustration. A person who knows nothing about the anatomy of a stag can find, say, "metacarpals" in the key and then locate h in its alphabetic position in the drawing. If I had labeled Fig. 140 instead of lettering it, finding "metacarpals" among the thirty-five labels would be a much slower job.

Diagrams that are to be used extensively should be supplied with two keys—as I have done in Fig. 139. If we know the name of a part and want to find it in the drawing [Fig. 140], the list on the left acts as an index. If we notice a part in the drawing and want to learn its name, we can look up the corresponding reference letter in the list on the right.

Fig. 142]   Making Easy Ones Out of Hard Ones   75

SEQUENCES. In construction diagrams like Fig. 141, we are more interested in following the order in which the lines are drawn than in locating individual parts. This makes it wise to number the lines in sequence and to letter the points alphabetically as they are fixed. The numbers on the lines should be enclosed in cartouches. This method of numbering and lettering diagrams is extremely valuable. We shall use it frequently in later chapters.

DUPLICATION. Many drawings show the same parts in several positions, or they contain parts that are for some reason regarded as duplicates [cow cutout in Fig. 142]. When this occurs, it is convenient to mark all repetitions with the same letter. The different cases can be distinguished like this: A, A' (A *prime*), A'' (A *second*), A''' (A *third*).

Another method is to use subscripts: A, A_1 (A *sub-one*), A_2 (A *sub-two*), . . .

As each letter appears twice in Fig. 142, I could not arrange them in strict alphabetic order. However, I have tried to introduce some system by assigning the plain (unprimed) letters from the cow's head to her tail.

142. USING PRIMED LETTERS TO LABEL DUPLICATE PARTS

LEADER LINES. Labels or references may be put on the parts designated [cow cutout in Fig. 142]. If there is no room on the part, place the label or reference near it and connect it with the part by a *leader line* [Figs. 137 and 140].

A note which applies to an individual part should be placed beside the part and be attached to it by a leader line. If a note must be placed on a part, enclose it in a cartouch to keep it from being interpreted as a label [note on cow's body in Fig. 142]. In this book, I have sometimes distinguished *general notes*—which refer to the drawing as a whole—by printing them in boldface type. In a hand-lettered drawing, however, it is best to set off general notes by placing them in cartouches.

Size Notations. Accuracy in drawing is largely a matter of showing the parts in their true proportions. We can greatly reduce the need for accuracy by marking the sizes of the parts. When this is done, mistakes in proportion are not apt to do harm unless they are large enough to mislead the eye. Marking sizes is called *dimensioning*. Figs. 143–149 illustrate the conventions used.

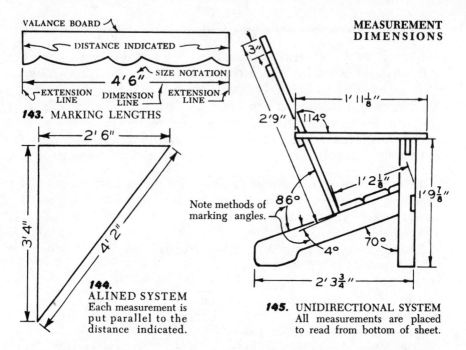

VALANCE BOARD

DISTANCE INDICATED

4′ 6″   SIZE NOTATION

EXTENSION
LINE   DIMENSION
LINE   EXTENSION
LINE

143. MARKING LENGTHS

2′ 6″

3′ 4″

4′ 2″

144.
ALINED SYSTEM
Each measurement is
put parallel to the
distance indicated.

3″

1′ 11⅛″

2′9″   114°

Note methods of
marking angles.

86°

1′ 2⅛″

1′ 9⅞″

4°   70°

2′ 3¾″

145. UNIDIRECTIONAL SYSTEM
All measurements are placed
to read from bottom of sheet.

LENGTHS, WIDTHS, AND THICKNESSES. Feet and inches are shown by the symbols (′) and (″); 2′3¾″ means "two feet three and three-quarter inches," 3′0″ means "three feet," and 0′3″ means "three inches." Machinists often give all dimensions in inches and decimals of an inch. Under this system, the inch symbol is normally omitted so that 31.5 means 2′7½″. When both feet and inches are used, write "one-foot" as 1′0″, not as 12″ or 0′12″.

Meters are commonly abbreviated as "M.," centimeters as "cm.," millimeters as "mm.," microns ($\frac{1}{1000}$ mm.) as "μ," millimicrons ($\frac{1}{1000}$ μ) as "mμ," and angstrom units ($\frac{1}{10}$ mμ) as "λ."

Write 2″ by 4″ as 2″ $\times$ 4″ and 12′0″ by 9′0″ as 12′0″ $\times$ 9′0″. When a measurement is approximate, write it c. 10′0″ or c. 0.5″. The "c" stands for Latin *circum*, which means "about."

Fig. 143 illustrates the normal way of noting lengths. *Extension lines* are drawn at the ends of the distance indicated. They should be perpendicular to the distance and should not touch the object. A *dimension line* is then drawn parallel to the distance indicated, leaving a gap for the size notation. Arrows on the ends of the dimension line just touch the extension lines. The side view of the chair shows various applications of this method [Fig. 145]. Make sure that you understand all of them thoroughly. They are extremely useful in making drawings of your own and also in reading those made by other people.

Length notations may either follow the dimension lines as in the triangle [Fig. 144] or be placed parallel to the bottom of the

Fig. 147]   Making Easy Ones Out of Hard Ones   77

sheet [chair in Fig. 145]. Each method has its advantages, but do not use both in the same drawing.

The sketch of the railing in Fig. 146 shows how two or three measurements can be written in a row and attached to the appropriate part of the structure by a leader line. The apartment plan in Fig. 148 uses a similar method, but places the measurements on the parts themselves and omits leader lines. These methods are needed when the parts are so small that the methods in Fig. 145 would crowd the drawing. When either the method in Fig. 146 or that in Fig. 148 is followed, single measurements may be marked with the aid of extension and dimension lines—as I have done in the sketch of the railing [Fig. 146].

The spacing of symmetrical parts, such as the pickets of the fence in Fig. 147, is usually given from center to center [A]. They are then said to be spaced *on centers*. However, the actual measuring is done as shown in B or C. When a number of parts are evenly spaced, show the size of one space and mark it "o.c." [a, Fig. 146]. This amounts to a note reading, "Space all of these parts at the distance shown on centers."

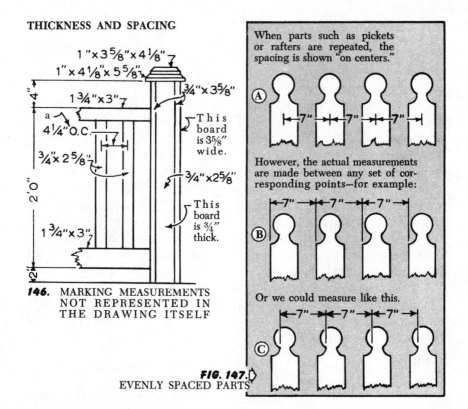

THICKNESS AND SPACING

1"x 3⅝"x 4⅛"
1"x 4⅛"x 5⅝"
1¾"x 3"
4"
a
4¼"O.C.
¾"x 2⅝"
2'0"
1¾"x 3"
2"

¾"x 3⅝"
This board is 3⅝" wide.
¾"x 2⅝"
This board is ¾" thick.

146. MARKING MEASUREMENTS NOT REPRESENTED IN THE DRAWING ITSELF

When parts such as pickets or rafters are repeated, the spacing is shown "on centers."

Ⓐ   ⊢7"⊣ ⊢7"⊣ ⊢7"⊣

However, the actual measurements are made between any set of corresponding points—for example:

Ⓑ   ⊢7"⊣ ⊢7"⊣ ⊢7"⊣

Or we could measure like this.

Ⓒ   ⊢7"⊣ ⊢7"⊣ ⊢7"⊣

FIG. 147.
EVENLY SPACED PARTS

ANGLES AND ARCS. Angles are measured in *degrees* (°). There are 360° in a full circle. Each degree contains sixty *minutes* (60′). Each minute contains sixty *seconds* (60″), but if you draw an angle within 0°10′ of its true value, you are doing well. Write angles less than 1° like this: 0° 25′ 50″. If you omit the zero, the minute- and second-marks may be mistaken for foot- and inch-marks.

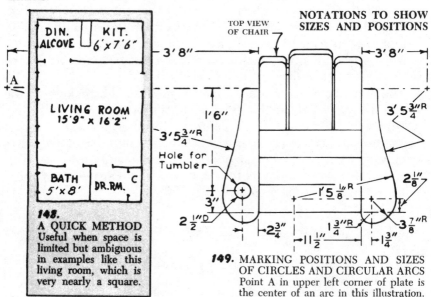

148.
A QUICK METHOD
Useful when space is limited but ambiguous in examples like this living room, which is very nearly a square.

NOTATIONS TO SHOW SIZES AND POSITIONS

149. MARKING POSITIONS AND SIZES OF CIRCLES AND CIRCULAR ARCS
Point A in upper left corner of plate is the center of an arc in this illustration.

When an arc is drawn, both its center and its radius must be indicated [top view of chair in Fig. 149]. Note how the treatment of the arrowheads differs with the lengths of their radii [1′5⅛″, 3⅞″, and 1¾″ arcs, in the lower right-hand corner]. A radius measurement is followed by the abbreviation *R*.

Long radii waste much space on a drawing. Fig. 149 shows two ways of avoiding this. The center for the 3′5¾″ radius on the left is in its true place, but another drawing [apartment plan in Fig. 148] is allowed to extend across the radius and dimension lines. The corresponding radius on the right is shortened by showing it as a symbolic zigzag.

Circles are usually fixed by indicating their centers and radii. For very small circles, however, it is more convenient to show the diameter with a leader line and mark it "D" [lower left-hand corner of chair in Fig. 149].

MEASUREMENT DIMENSIONS VS. SPACE DIMENSIONS. "Dimensions" is an unfortunate term because it has two meanings which are radically different but easily confused. *Measurement dimen-*

Fig. 150]   Making Easy Ones Out of Hard Ones   79

sions represent lengths, like 2′3¾″, or angles, like 70°, and are always numerical. We can show as many measurement dimensions as we wish. Thus, the side view of the chair in Fig. 145 gives six length dimensions and four angular dimensions. Ordinary objects—chairs, elephants, balloons, bedrooms—have three (and only three) *space dimensions* and are therefore said to be *three-dimensional.* The three space dimensions have names: *height, breadth,* and *depth* [chair in Fig. 150].

It is easy to confuse the breadth and depth dimensions. Thus, you may intuitively think of the breadth of a chair as the dimension across the arms and be surprised that I have labeled this "DEPTH" in Fig. 150. The only way to avoid such confusion is to adopt an arbitrary convention, and the most satisfactory convention is the one which labels the dimensions in terms of the drawing. The breadth dimension is the one that seems to run across the paper; the depth dimension is the one which seems to run into the paper. If you draw a man lying on his back with his feet toward you, his height dimension runs from his heels to his toes, his breadth dimension runs across his shoulders, and his depth dimension runs from his feet to his head. Labeling dimensions in terms of the drawing may seem strange at first, but once you become accustomed to it you will find it extremely helpful.

A drawing exists on a flat sheet of paper and can therefore have only two space dimensions: height and breadth. Hence every drawing is really *two-dimensional.* In spite of this, we can represent all three space-dimensions in a drawing—as I have done in Fig. 150. Such a drawing is said to be "three-dimensional" because all three space dimensions are shown. This is very different from a two-dimensional drawing like Fig. 145 which represents only two space dimensions: height and breadth.

Two-dimensional drawings are the orthographic projections mentioned in Chapter 1. We shall use a less pretentious term and call them simply *direct views.*

150.
THE THREE SPACE DIMENSIONS
Each space dimension is perpendicular to the other two. Do not confuse these with measurement dimensions.

SYMBOLS

Symbols do much to make schematics clear and reduce the need for notes. We have already considered the use of symbols in simple, abstract charts and diagrams [pp. 68–70]. Those

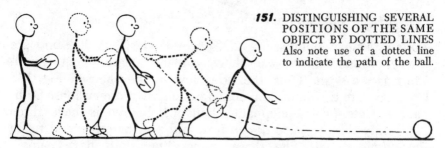

used in more elaborate or more realistic drawings [Figs. 151–165] are not essentially different, but they must be examined in greater detail if we are to obtain the maximum benefit from their use.

Workers in some fields, such as Electricity and Mapping, have developed extensive vocabularies of standardized symbols. In general drawing, however, we usually stick to a few simple forms. This limits our choice, and makes it necessary to give the same symbol different meanings in different drawings.

Lines. We can vary our lines in several ways and assign a separate meaning to each variation.

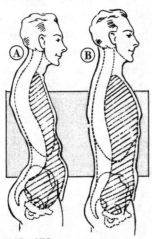

FIG. 152.
SHOWING HIDDEN LINES
Parts normally invisible may be indicated by dotted lines. Note how shading is used to emphasize significant details.

SINGLE, DOUBLE, AND TRIPLE LINES. As the examples in Figs. 117, 122, and 123 show, these are excellent for simple schematics which are not drawn to scale. However, they are of little use in other types of drawing.

LINES OF DIFFERENT WEIGHTS. When a diagram contains two types of elements, we can direct attention to one of them by drawing it with heavier lines. This device was used in Fig. 142 to make the parts of the cow stand out from the lines of the grid. If the elements are of equal importance, drawing one with heavier lines gives it a false emphasis. More than two weights of line are rarely satisfactory.

LINES OF CONTRASTING TYPES. Another thing that distinguishes the cow in Fig. 142 from the grid is the fact that the lines of the cow are irregular curves, whereas those of the grid are straight. The same device is used in maps; roads and boundaries are shown by smooth lines, whereas rivers are indicated by wiggly lines. The principle is carried further in the *phantom view* of the stag

Fig. 154]   Making Easy Ones Out of Hard Ones   81

in Fig. 140, where the skeleton is heavily accented to emphasize it in contrast with the thin, uniform lines that mark the body.

DOTTED LINES. Although the methods just mentioned are useful in many cases, the normal procedure is to represent anything which is not part of the main drawing by dotted lines. Thus, in the bowling diagram [Fig. 151] dotted lines are used to represent alternate positions of the same part. In the posture diagrams [Fig. 152] they reveal hidden parts, and in the soap-box racer [Fig. 153] the internal mechanism is shown by solid lines, and the outer shell is dotted to produce a *phantom view*. Dotted lines are used in many other ways; examples are scattered throughout this book.

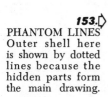

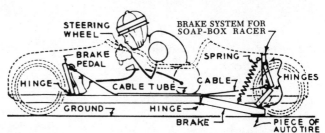

153.
PHANTOM LINES
Outer shell here
is shown by dotted
lines because the
hidden parts form
the main drawing.

BREAKS. We can often save time, trouble, and space by representing a part as though it were broken. Thus, I was able to omit the middle portion of the control board in Fig. 154 by indicating a *break* and connecting the parts with *ditto lines*. These are drawn with short dashes arranged in pairs. The break in this drawing is represented by straight lines alternating with zigzags. That is a conventional symbol used to represent a long break. These devices not only saved space, but made the diagram easier to read and eliminated the chore of adding seventeen more circuits exactly like those shown.

Short breaks are indicated by irregular lines like those in Figs. 155–157. The *cutaway view* of the ventriloquist's dummy in Fig. 155 uses a break to reveal the internal mechanism. This is better than a phantom view when only a small part of the interior is shown and no significant details are omitted from the outer surface.

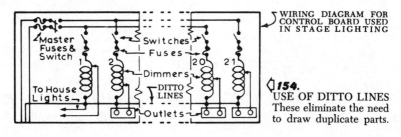

WIRING DIAGRAM FOR
CONTROL BOARD USED
IN STAGE LIGHTING

154.
USE OF DITTO LINES
These eliminate the need
to draw duplicate parts.

The shaded break at A in the handle of Fig. 155 is a convention used to indicate a round, solid rod. However, this gives no information about the nature of the material. The insert [B] illustrates a type of break which announces that the rod is made of wood but which does not show that it is round. Breaks frequently reveal the nature of the material. Compare the lines used for clay in Fig. 156 with those for flannel in Fig. 157.

The conventional break for a hollow pipe is illustrated in Fig. 158. If I had tried to show the whole pipe, I could not have gotten it onto the page without reducing its size. Furthermore, by omitting most of the pipe, the break concentrates attention on the only parts that really matter.

EXPLODED VIEWS. In Fig. 158, the fitting on the left would really be screwed onto the pipe. I have drawn them separately in order to show both the inside and the outside threads. This is an extremely simple example of what is called an *exploded view*. Notice how the dotted *center line* helps to explain the way in which the parts fit together. The grasshopper in Fig. 137 illustrates a more elaborate exploded view.

Most views of this type are complex fixed-line drawings made to show a number of parts and indicate their relations in the completed mechanism. Such views often contain several center lines and would be difficult to understand without them.

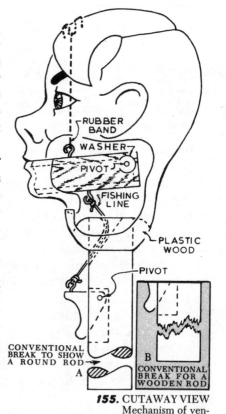

155. CUTAWAY VIEW Mechanism of ventriloquist's dummy.

Shading. Practical drawing is inherently a line process. Indiscriminate shading tends to obscure the meaning of the drawing. Hence, if shading is employed at all, it should be done sparingly and kept simple.

The line shading in the posture diagrams [Fig. 152] emphasizes one element in the drawings. The smooth shading in the

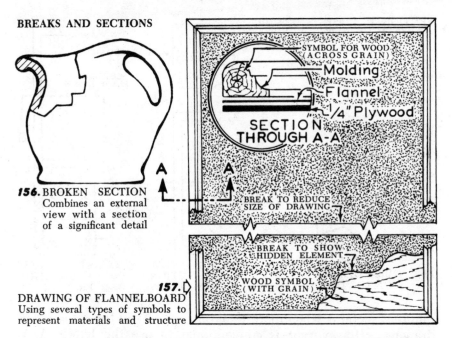

156. BROKEN SECTION
Combines an external
view with a section
of a significant detail

157.
DRAWING OF FLANNELBOARD
Using several types of symbols to
represent materials and structure

background ties the two sketches together. This would indicate
that they deal with the same topic even if they were part of a
plate which contained a dozen other drawings. In the front view
of the flannelboard [Fig. 157], one kind of shading (*stipple*)
represents flannel and other kinds represent wood.

Sections. Shading is conventionally employed to indicate the
cut part in a *section*. This is most clearly illustrated by the
machine part in Figs. 159–161. As the three-dimensional view
shows, the part is supposed to be cut by an imaginary *cutting
plane*. The side view in Fig. 160 represents the location of this
plane by a heavy dotted line, called a *cutting-plane line*. A short
arrow is added at each end of this line and perpendicular to it.
These arrows indicate the direction in which the cut object is
viewed. That is important. The parts behind the cutting plane
are shown in the accompanying section, and the direction in
which we look makes a great difference; compare the section in
Fig. 160 with that in Fig. 161. Letters on the arrows distinguish

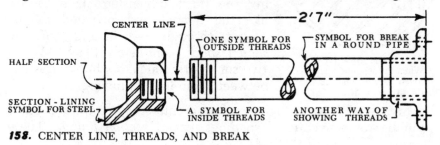

158. CENTER LINE, THREADS, AND BREAK

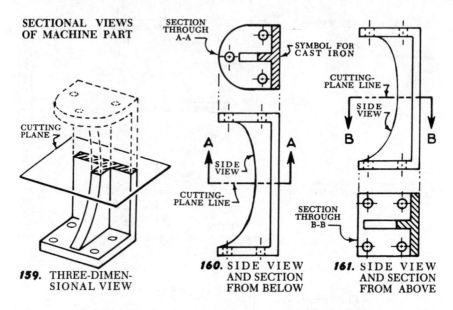

SECTIONAL VIEWS OF MACHINE PART

SECTION THROUGH A–A

SYMBOL FOR CAST IRON

CUTTING PLANE

CUTTING-PLANE LINE

SIDE VIEW

A — A

SIDE VIEW

CUTTING-PLANE LINE

B — B

SECTION THROUGH B-B

159. THREE-DIMEN-SIONAL VIEW

160. SIDE VIEW AND SECTION FROM BELOW

161. SIDE VIEW AND SECTION FROM ABOVE

different sections when more than one appears in the same set of drawings. However, it is conventional to use the letters A–A, even when only one section is given.

HALF SECTIONS AND BROKEN SECTIONS. When an object is symmetrical, we can save time by making a *half section* [left-hand fitting in Fig. 158]. The drawing above the center line shows the outside of the object, and that below the line is a section.

The pitcher in Fig. 156 illustrates how the same principle may be combined with a break to make a *broken section* (or *broken-out section*). This can be used with an unsymmetrical object. It is also helpful when only a small part needs to be sectioned.

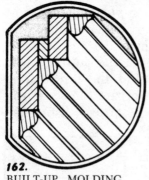

162. BUILT-UP MOLDING
When the sectioned parts touch, section lines slant in different directions.

LINE DIRECTIONS. Section lines normally slant southwest and northeast at 45° to the horizontal. However, when two sectioned parts touch, the lines should slant in different directions. The built-up molding in Fig. 162 illustrates this. It also shows an easy way of indicating the third dimension. Thin pieces, like the flannel and plywood in the section through A–A of Fig. 157, are *shown solid* (completely black). When two such parts touch, a white line is left between them in the drawing.

SECTION LININGS. Engineers and architects have worked out a number of conventional shadings, called *section linings*. These

Fig. 163]   Making Easy Ones Out of Hard Ones   85

not only set off the cut part in the drawing, but also indicate the material from which it is made. The section lining for steel is shown in Fig. 158, that for cast iron in Fig. 160, and that for bronze in Fig. 163. Two linings for wood are given in Fig. 157. One of these runs with the grain, and the other runs across it. They may be used for both sections and exterior views; although this may seem to be a source of confusion, it rarely gives trouble in practice.

As fancy shadings make extra work, many draftsmen use the cast-iron symbol for everything—unless there is a special reason to distinguish one material from another. Thus, I have represented wood in the built-up molding [Fig. 162] and pottery in the pitcher [Fig. 156] by the cast-iron symbol-of-all-work.

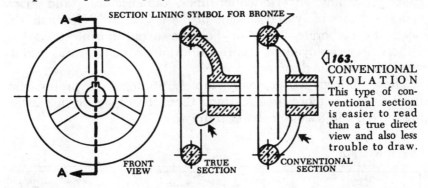

163.
CONVENTIONAL VIOLATION This type of conventional section is easier to read than a true direct view and also less trouble to draw.

SECTION LINING SYMBOL FOR BRONZE

FRONT VIEW   TRUE SECTION   CONVENTIONAL SECTION

CONVENTIONAL VIOLATIONS. Most sections raise no special problems in drawing, but some can be tricky. The hand wheel in Fig. 163 shows a simple example. Devices like this are called *conventional violations,* because they do not give a true direct view of the section. If you have many opportunities to use sections, you will find that conventional violations are not merely valuable short cuts but usually make the drawing clearer—at least to anyone familiar with the conventions.

Unfortunately, these conventions are far from simple. Also, you cannot hope either to read or to make these drawings effectively until you have gained a fair degree of skill in visualizing three-dimensional objects. These difficulties put conventional violations beyond the scope of this book. Nevertheless, the drawing is easy enough; the difficulty lies entirely in visualization. After you have finished Chapter 15, I strongly recommend studying the material on sections and conventional violations in some text on engineering drawing.

Glyphs. In a few fields, such as electricity and mapping, glyphs have become conventionalized; in most other types of drawing, we must invent our own. A glyph may be arbitrary, like those that symbolize individual qualities in the "Scientific Method" diagram [Fig. 118]. However, we should always try to find a design that suggests its meaning. The glyphs in Fig. 164 are almost pictures. Anyone who has some knowledge of electricity, but who had never seen this particular type of diagram, could probably read most of the symbols without the key in Fig. 165.

Special *templates* are available for drawing many conventional glyphs. These are sheets of transparent plastic punched with holes in the shapes of the symbols. Running a pencil around the inside of a hole produces a neat glyph.

Standards. Professional draftsmen have developed standard practices which govern leader lines, dimensioning, and many types and uses of symbols. Some of these standards eliminate the need for elaborate notes or help to avoid misinterpretation. Others are employed to secure uniformity when several people work on the same drawing.

The standards cover many topics. Students of professional drafting spend more time learning them than they do in mastering the techniques of mechanical drawing.

GLYPH SYMBOLS

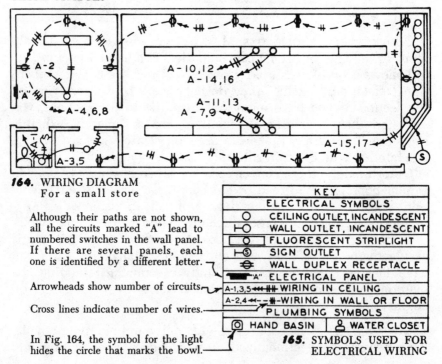

164. WIRING DIAGRAM
For a small store

Although their paths are not shown, all the circuits marked "A" lead to numbered switches in the wall panel. If there are several panels, each one is identified by a different letter.

Arrowheads show number of circuits.

Cross lines indicate number of wires.

In Fig. 164, the symbol for the light hides the circle that marks the bowl.

KEY	
ELECTRICAL SYMBOLS	
O	CEILING OUTLET, INCANDESCENT
⊢O	WALL OUTLET, INCANDESCENT
⊏O⊐	FLUORESCENT STRIPLIGHT
⊢Ⓢ	SIGN OUTLET
⊕	WALL DUPLEX RECEPTACLE
◢█"A"	ELECTRICAL PANEL
A-1,3,5 ⫤⫤⫤	WIRING IN CEILING
A-2,4 ◂◂--⫤	WIRING IN WALL OR FLOOR
PLUMBING SYMBOLS	
⊙ HAND BASIN	⚲ WATER CLOSET

165. SYMBOLS USED FOR
ELECTRICAL WIRING

Fig. 165]   Making Easy Ones Out of Hard Ones   87

Every field has its own requirements. No single standard can meet them all. Practices condemned in one field are required in another. Learning a particular set of standards is a waste of time unless you intend to specialize. On the other hand, if you have any thought of entering a field that imposes professional standards, study a book that gives the conventions in that field and then apply these conventions in every mechanical drawing or sketch that you make. Should you fail to do this, you will develop drawing habits that differ from the standards in your chosen field. Your habits may be no worse and may even be better than the standards, but they will be hard to break later when you must conform to conventional practices.

In preparing the technical illustrations for this book, I have tried to follow the appropriate professional standards as far as possible without introducing details that would require elaborate explanations which have no direct connection with drawing. However, as almost every professional drawing does involve at least one or two such details, my illustrations cannot safely be regarded as models of standard practice. If you do not intend to become a professional, this does no harm. If you plan to become a professional, a few examples here would not be enough to meet your needs.

SIMPLIFICATION

The best practical drawing of any subject is the one which is easiest to read. In most cases, this is also the one which is easiest to make.

Isolation. We can study a set of facts more effectively when we isolate them from all the other facts. That presents no problem in drawing, where we can focus attention on the important facts simply by leaving out everything else. Thus, the shadows and wrinkles in Fig. 166 add no real information. A tracing like that in Fig. 167 eliminates such accidental details and brings out the essentials.

We also employ the principle of isolation when we portray only part of an object and omit the rest. The picture of the heart and lungs in Fig. 135 is an example. This illustration may not appear to be simplified, but think how much more complex it would have been if I had tried to show all the veins and arteries in the body.

We frequently find that the only part of the source in which we are interested is comparatively simple. Anyone can sketch the stick figures and the chair in Fig. 170, but even an equally crude drawing of the whole scene would require far more skill. A partial drawing of this kind is technically known as a *detail*. Do not confuse such drawings with the small items in a drawing, which are also called *details*.

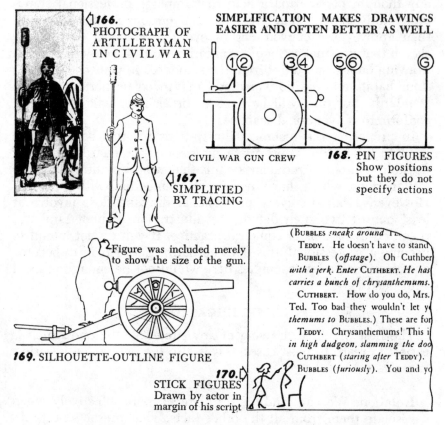

◁166.
PHOTOGRAPH OF
ARTILLERYMAN
IN CIVIL WAR

SIMPLIFICATION MAKES DRAWINGS
EASIER AND OFTEN BETTER AS WELL

CIVIL WAR GUN CREW

168. PIN FIGURES
Show positions
but they do not
specify actions

◁167.
SIMPLIFIED
BY TRACING

Figure was included merely
to show the size of the gun.

169. SILHOUETTE-OUTLINE FIGURE

(BUBBLES *sneaks around*
TEDDY. He doesn't have to stand
BUBBLES (*offstage*). Oh Cuthber
with a jerk. Enter CUTHBERT. *He has*
carries a bunch of chrysanthemums.
CUTHBERT. How do you do, Mrs.
Ted. Too bad they wouldn't let y
themums to BUBBLES.) These are for
TEDDY. Chrysanthemums! This i
in high dudgeon, slamming the doo
CUTHBERT (*staring after* TEDDY).
BUBBLES (*furiously*). You and y

170.◁
STICK FIGURES
Drawn by actor in
margin of his script

GENERALIZATION. In many cases, we make a drawing to illustrate some general principle rather than a particular set of facts. A drawing is generalized when we omit identifying details. Thus, the photograph in Fig. 166 portrays a particular individual. The tracing in Fig. 167 represents any Northern artilleryman. The *pin figures* in Fig. 168 illustrate the positions of any seven-man crew serving a muzzle-loading gun. The silhouette outline in Fig. 169 symbolizes any man.

Every type of material can be generalized in this way. For example, the rectangular cartouch in Fig. 171 is really a map which has been generalized to the point where it becomes a symbol. If the diagram had shown a map of France or the United States, the universal nature of the principle would have been obscured. Also, it would have raised irrelevant questions, such as

Fig. 171]   Making Easy Ones Out of Hard Ones   89

whether the country shown really has a $5,000,000,000 export surplus.

IDENTIFICATION. Simplification works two ways: when we want to generalize, we discard identifying details; when we want to show a particular situation, we select identifying details and omit everything else. Thus, anyone familiar with Civil War uniforms can identify Fig. 167 as a Northern soldier. The ramrod adds the information that he is an artilleryman and the number-one member of his gun crew (see Fig. 168). We can tell the girl in Fig. 170 from the man because she has hair and a skirt; as only two characters are involved, identification is complete. Note that these stick figures also represent the action of the characters at a specific moment in the play, whereas the pin figures in Fig. 168 are more generalized and show only the theoretical positions of the gunners.

A drawing can generalize some elements and identify others. Although the pin figures in Fig. 168 are highly generalized, the position of each crew member is identified by his number and by the letter G (for "Chief Gunner").

Characteristic Views. The ancient Egyptians had a real genius for conveying information through pictures. One of their chief techniques consisted in simplifying their drawings by depicting each object, or part of an object, from the viewpoint that made it easiest to identify [Fig. 172].

The principle of drawing the characteristic view of an object is extremely useful in practical work. Sections are really characteristic views. Conventional violations apply the Egyptian principle to sections, and the rules which govern them are merely rules for selecting that view of each part which is characteristic from the standpoint of engineers and machinists.

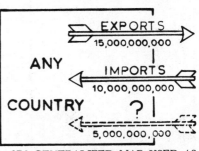

171. GENERALIZED MAP USED AS SYMBOL FOR "ANY COUNTRY" Diagram shows that surplus exports represent a loss unless some real advantage compensates for the deficit indicated by the dotted arrow.

The characteristic view is nearly always some direct view, but the choice of a view differs with the subject. A side view is characteristic of an elephant [C, Fig. 175], though it does not give a clear idea of an airplane [A, Fig. 173] or a house [B, Fig. 174]. The characteristic view of a house is the front, that of an anemone is the top [B, Fig. 176], and that of an airplane is the bottom. In the case of a curving leaf, the characteristic view is the one it would show if spread flat and seen from its face [C, Fig. 176].

A direct view that is not characteristic may be hard to read. If you had never seen an elephant, you might infer from the front view in A, Fig. 175, that the animal has a short snout like a pig. This is not the fault of the drawing; a photograph of this view would produce the same effect.

Oversimplification. We must simplify nature in order to think about it at all. If we simplify by omitting important details, the results may be seriously misleading. The formula for the speed of a falling body is usually given as $s = \sqrt{2 \times 32.174d}$, where s = speed in feet per second and d = the distance through which the body has fallen. This is valid if we remember that it gives the *theoretical* speed of a body *near the earth's surface*, at *latitude 45°*, falling in a *vacuum*. But if we use this formula to compute the speed at which an aviator falling from 20,000 feet with-

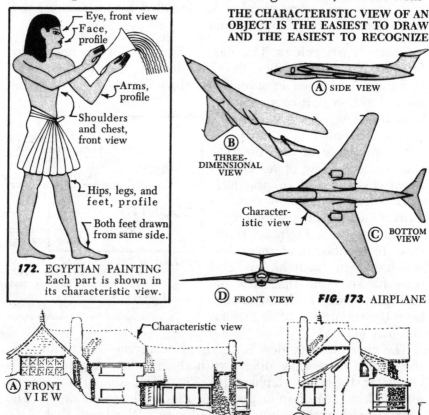

THE CHARACTERISTIC VIEW OF AN OBJECT IS THE EASIEST TO DRAW AND THE EASIEST TO RECOGNIZE

Eye, front view
Face, profile
Arms, profile
Shoulders and chest, front view
Hips, legs, and feet, profile
Both feet drawn from same side.

172. EGYPTIAN PAINTING Each part is shown in its characteristic view.

(A) SIDE VIEW

(B) THREE-DIMENSIONAL VIEW

Characteristic view

(C) BOTTOM VIEW

(D) FRONT VIEW   **FIG. 173.** AIRPLANE

Characteristic view

(A) FRONT VIEW

FIG. 174. RESIDENCE

(B) SIDE VIEW

Fig. 176]   Making Easy Ones Out of Hard Ones   91

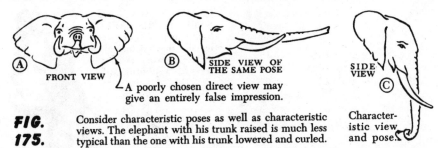

Ⓐ FRONT VIEW

Ⓑ SIDE VIEW OF THE SAME POSE

⎣A poorly chosen direct view may give an entirely false impression.

SIDE VIEW Ⓒ

FIG. 175.   Consider characteristic poses as well as characteristic views. The elephant with his trunk raised is much less typical than the one with his trunk lowered and curled.   Characteristic view and pose.

out a parachute will strike the ground, we get a speed of 1,286,960 feet per second. However, air resistance will cut the actual speed to something between 175 and 340 feet per second. This explains why people have fallen from planes and lived.

Oversimplification is less likely to give trouble in drawing than when it occurs in either language or mathematics. Perhaps the diagrammatic nature of most practical drawings makes the omissions more obvious than when we use words or formulas. Do not let this lull you into a false sense of security. Where oversimplification does occur in a drawing, it can be especially deceptive. Oversimplified graphs, for example, often lead to major errors in thinking.

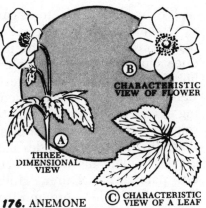

Ⓑ CHARACTERISTIC VIEW OF FLOWER

Ⓐ THREE-DIMENSIONAL VIEW

Ⓒ CHARACTERISTIC VIEW OF A LEAF

176. ANEMONE
We must flatten some objects to get their characteristic views.

Unfortunately, there is not much that you can do about oversimplification except to remember that every practical drawing omits many details and to ask yourself whether any of these details should be taken into account.

5

TECHNIQUES
FOR TRACING

177.
SOURCE

178.
EXACT
TRACING

179.
ADJUSTED
TRACING

A RT teachers tend to regard tracing as a crutch which permits the untalented to produce clumsy copies, but which hobbles creativeness. Architects and designers, on the other hand, look on tracing as a means of escape from the routine stages of drawing. The list of artists who share this attitude includes many of the great Japanese masters and such Western painters as Dürer, Holbein, and Norman Rockwell. Furthermore, most of the world's finest murals were first drawn on paper and then transferred to the wall by pricking holes in a paper pattern. This is essentially a form of tracing.

The gap between the precept of the teachers and the practice of the artists is due chiefly to the fact that the teachers consider tracing as a method of making complete pictures, whereas the artists use it *only as a form of construction.*

TRACING AS TRANSLATION

Strictly speaking, it is impossible to trace a photograph. Instead, we translate a picture in light and shade into a drawing in line.

Adjustments. An exact tracing of a photograph is likely to seem as far from the original as a literal translation of a passage in a foreign language. The shapely siren in Fig. 177 loses much of her allure when the exact tracing in Fig. 178 brings out every flaw in her figure. In Fig. 179, I have rounded the arm and calves,

Fig. 184]   Techniques for Tracing   93

trimmed the waist and hips, and lengthened the leg below the knee. These adjustments are needed to compensate for the difference in effect between a photograph and a line drawing. After you gain a little experience, your eye will tell you what changes are needed and you will make them almost automatically.

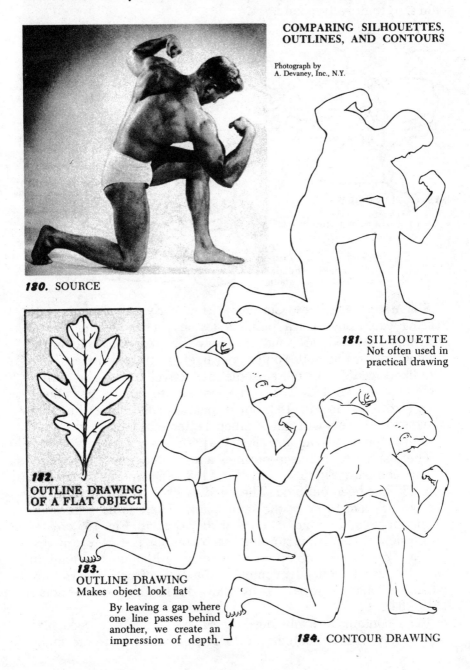

COMPARING SILHOUETTES, OUTLINES, AND CONTOURS

Photograph by
A. Devaney, Inc., N.Y.

180. SOURCE

181. SILHOUETTE
Not often used in practical drawing

182.
OUTLINE DRAWING OF A FLAT OBJECT

183.
OUTLINE DRAWING
Makes object look flat

By leaving a gap where one line passes behind another, we create an impression of depth.

184. CONTOUR DRAWING

Look on adjustments as little lessons in freehand sketching. They provide you with exercise-problems that are usually easy to solve because they involve only minor points of the total drawing. By solving these, you train your eyes and hand to deal with the larger and more difficult problems that you will meet when you start to draw freehand.

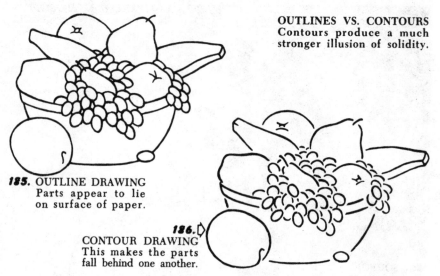

OUTLINES VS. CONTOURS
Contours produce a much stronger illusion of solidity.

185. OUTLINE DRAWING
Parts appear to lie on surface of paper.

186. CONTOUR DRAWING
This makes the parts fall behind one another.

Silhouettes, Outlines, Contours. Your early experiments with tracing can also furnish painless lessons in the techniques of drawing. Figs. 181, 183, and 184 show three ways of tracing the photograph in Fig. 180. You are not likely to trace a mere *silhouette* like Fig. 181, but most people instinctively adopt the *outline* technique of Fig. 183. This is a good way to draw a flat object, such as the leaf in Fig. 182, but it makes a solid object look like a paper doll. You will get a much better effect of solidity and weight if you draw *contours* [Fig. 184].

The distinction between outlines and contours may be clearer if you compare Fig. 185 with Fig. 186. Each piece of fruit in Fig. 185 has been outlined. The effect is like a jigsaw puzzle; all the pieces seem to lie in the same plane. There is no suggestion of roundness and no indication that they overlap. Fig. 186 creates an illusion of depth by stopping each contour just before it disappears behind the object in front of it. Although the lines in Fig. 186 are technically contours, the full effect appears only when the masses interlock—as they do in the human figure [Fig. 184].

Some contours are obvious; others are difficult to recognize —especially from a photograph. Moreover, when there are many

Fig. 189]   Techniques for Tracing   95

small contours, drawing them all makes the picture seem fussy. Only experience can teach you to see subtle contours and to decide which should be shown and which should be ignored. If you form the habit of looking for contours whenever you trace a construction or make a drawing, you will soon find that they give no trouble.

ACCENTS SUGGEST SOLIDITY

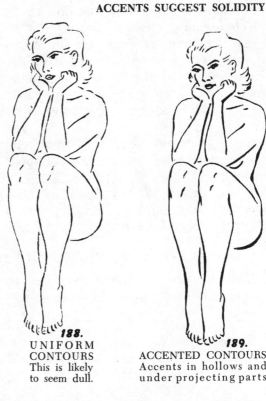

187.
SOURCE FOR TRACING
The use of light and shade in this drawing does not add any real information.

188.
UNIFORM
CONTOURS
This is likely
to seem dull.

189.
ACCENTED CONTOURS
Accents in hollows and under projecting parts

Accents. Beginners tend to draw lines of uniform weight [Fig. 188]. Such lines can be highly effective in the hands of an expert, but few people master the use of uniform lines without years of study. On the other hand, you can get surprisingly good results on your first attempt by drawing accented lines [Fig. 189]. These greatly increase the impression of depth and weight. Note also that a drawing with accented lines is a more accurate translation of an original in light and shade than is a tracing done with uniform lines. Fig. 188 follows the forms of Fig. 187 but completely misses its spirit. Fig. 189 comes much closer to reproducing the effect of the original.

The easiest procedure for learning to handle accents is to begin by tracing faint-line contours like those in Fig. 188 from sources which interest you. Then add accents wherever they appear to be needed. This method permits you to concentrate on the problems of using accents without wasting time wondering where to draw the lines themselves.

There are several ways of arranging accents. The one illustrated in Fig. 189 is the easiest to learn and the most widely applicable. Essentially, it consists in accenting hollows and the undersides of curves. Such accents suggest shadows and make the object seem rounder.

This method will get you started, but do not devote much thought to it; concentrate on getting the lines in the right places. Experiment with the interesting techniques that you find in your sources, but avoid cultivating any particular one. All you can do consciously is to strive for consistency; avoid accenting some lines on one system and others on another. Your technique will develop of its own accord if you give it a chance. It will then be really *your* technique, perfectly adapted to your needs and your personality.

If you master contours and accents by tracing, you will not have to worry about elementary problems of technique when you take up freehand drawing.

SPECIAL METHODS AND MATERIALS

This section contains suggestions which will make tracing much more useful and widen the range of subjects that you can trace.

Transferring. Tracing paper is comparatively flimsy. Also, a tracing cannot be read clearly unless it is placed on a white, opaque surface. Transferring the tracing to ordinary paper overcomes both limitations.

If the tracing has been made with a fairly soft pencil, it can be transferred by laying it face down on a sheet of opaque paper and rubbing the back of the tracing with the bowl of a spoon. Although this reverses the drawing, that may not be objectionable.

Other methods of transferring do not reverse the drawing, but they do involve retracing. This is rarely serious if the transfer is made when the tracing is at the faint-line stage. Most such tracings can be transferred very quickly.

The simplest procedure is to attach the final sheet to the original with Stik-tacks and hold it against a windowpane while you retrace it. Another method is to make the ordinary paper temporarily transparent by moistening it with rubbing alcohol or rub-

Fig. 191]   Techniques for Tracing   97

ber-cement thinner. The original tracing can then be retraced on this paper without difficulty. A fourth way consists in placing *artist's carbon paper* over the opaque paper and laying the original on top of that. You can then transfer the drawing by going over it with a hard pencil. Typewriter carbon is unsatisfactory as it leaves greasy marks. If artist's carbon is not available, you can make a substitute by rubbing one side of a sheet of ordinary paper with a soft pencil or by rubbing pencil on the back of the tracing itself.

No matter how carefully a tracing is transferred, it will never be more than a faint-line construction. It must be adjusted and then strengthened by redrawing. If you omit these steps, you cannot hope to produce satisfactory results.

Tracing on Acetate. Where details are important, tracing paper may blur them so badly that accurate drawing becomes impossible. This is especially troublesome when working from newspaper photographs. In such cases, use *tracing acetate*, which is like the clear acetate described in the text at p. 42 but has its surface roughened to take pencil.

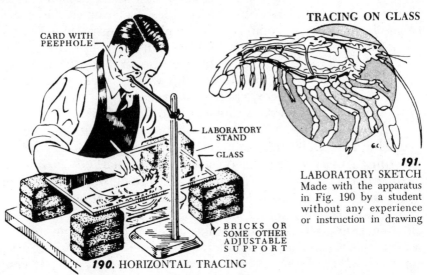

TRACING ON GLASS

CARD WITH PEEPHOLE

LABORATORY STAND

GLASS

BRICKS OR SOME OTHER ADJUSTABLE SUPPORT

190. HORIZONTAL TRACING

191.
LABORATORY SKETCH
Made with the apparatus in Fig. 190 by a student without any experience or instruction in drawing

Tracing on Glass. By tracing on glass instead of on paper, we can work from three-dimensional sources. Fig. 190 shows a simple arrangement that takes all the drudgery out of laboratory drawing. This method saves time for the expert and enables even the least talented to make accurate sketches. Instead of struggling with problems of drawing, the student is free to concentrate on observing the specimen.

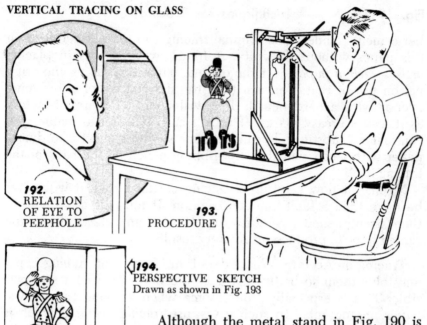

192.
RELATION
OF EYE TO
PEEPHOLE

193.
PROCEDURE

◁**194.**
PERSPECTIVE SKETCH
Drawn as shown in Fig. 193

Although the metal stand in Fig. 190 is convenient, a wooden substitute could easily be built. The arm holding the card need not be adjustable. Determine the most comfortable height by experiment and screw or nail the arm to the upright.

The vertical set-up in Fig. 193 is more elaborate but still within reach of the most inexperienced carpenter. It provides an easy way to draw portraits, flowers, and landscapes.

Ordinary pencils do not mark glass. *China-marker* pencils work but make lines that are too broad for most drawings. Many *felt-tipped* pens work well on glass. Those marked *fineline* or *razor point* are adequate for nearly all tracing purposes. When you need hairlines, use India ink in an artist's steel pen.

You may have to hold your pen upside down to keep the ink flowing [Fig. 193]. This may take practice before you get the knack, but it is not really difficult. Some pens will work upside down, but the only one I have found will not mark glass. If you do much tracing on glass, you will be wise to experiment with every new type of pen you can find.

A tracing on glass must be transferred to paper before it can be used. The arrangement in Fig. 190 can double as a device for transferring tracings. If a drawing has been made on the glass, lay a sheet of notebook paper over it and place an electric light under the glass. The lines of the drawing will be visible through the paper. When the transfer is complete, the ink can be washed

Fig. 194]   Techniques for Tracing   99

off the glass with soap and water. Drawings in china-marker pencil can also be removed in this way, though rubbing alcohol is more efficient. If the original drawing is on tracing paper or acetate, lay it on the glass, cover it with a sheet of ordinary paper, and proceed to retrace the drawing on this.

TRACING FIXED-LINE DRAWINGS

From the standpoint of tracing, fixed-line drawings (including charts, and mechanical drawings like those in Fig. 195) are essentially different from the free-line type that we have been discussing. Although it is almost impossible to make an exact copy of a free-line source by direct tracing, anyone can trace a fixed-line drawing so accurately that the duplicate is identical with the original. In spite of this, the best way to get a replica of a fixed-line drawing done on tracing paper is to have a *blueprint* or a *whiteprint* made. Pencil drawings made on any paper can be duplicated on an office copier if the lines are dark and sharp. A copier in *perfect* condition will produce black lines that look like ink, and which can be used to illustrate a printed pamphlet or book.

Drawings as Experimental Models. A fixed-line drawing that is worth tracing is usually an original design. Creative design almost always involves experiment, and drawing is the simplest way to provide models on which to test our ideas.

Step 1, Fig. 195, is my first model for a vertical tracing frame. As soon as I drew it, I realized that putting the diagonal braces in front would interfere with the freedom of my right hand while drawing. My second model [Step 2] shows the braces in back. When I studied this arrangement, I saw that braces at the rear would cut off the view of anything seen through the lower corners of the glass. I therefore tried again, restoring the left brace to the front and substituting an iron corner plate for the brace on the right.

We often sketch experimental lines and abandon them only to find later that they deserve further study. If they have been erased, they are gone forever. When the experiments are as simple as the positions of the braces in a tracing frame, we can usually remember them. But when they are more complex, an attempt to reconstruct them from memory may be a frustrating if not a hopeless task.

For this reason, "Trace, don't erase" is a maxim with many architects and designers. Instead of erasing the braces in Steps 1 and 2, I traced the other lines on fresh paper. This enabled me to keep my earlier experiments for future reference. It did not

TRACING FIXED-LINE DRAWINGS

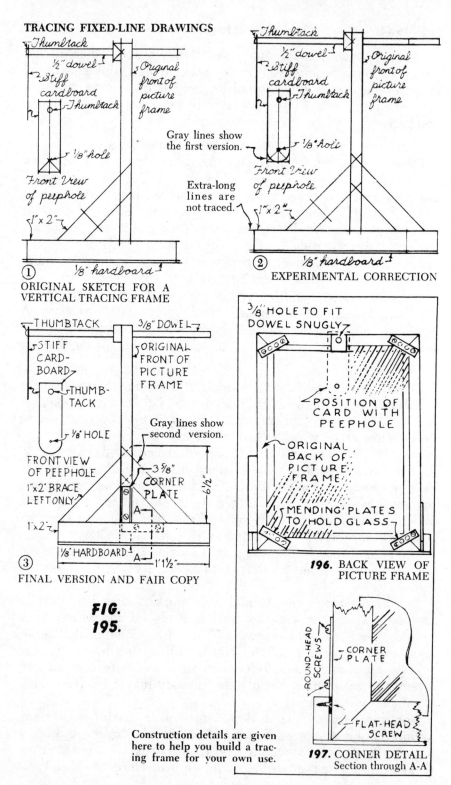

Thumbtack
½" dowel
Stiff cardboard
Thumbtack
⅛" hole
Original front of picture frame

Front View of peephole

1"x 2"

① ⅛" hardboard
ORIGINAL SKETCH FOR A VERTICAL TRACING FRAME

Gray lines show the first version.

Extra-long lines are not traced.

Thumbtack
½" dowel
Stiff cardboard
Thumbtack
⅛" hole
Original front of picture frame

Front View of peephole

1"x 2"

② ⅛" hardboard
EXPERIMENTAL CORRECTION

THUMBTACK   ⅜" DOWEL
STIFF CARD-BOARD
THUMB-TACK
⅛" HOLE
ORIGINAL FRONT OF PICTURE FRAME

Gray lines show second version.

3 ⅝" CORNER PLATE
6½"

FRONT VIEW OF PEEPHOLE
1"x2" BRACE LEFT ONLY
A
1"x2"
③ ⅛" HARDBOARD
A   1'1½"
FINAL VERSION AND FAIR COPY

FIG. 195.

⅜" HOLE TO FIT DOWEL SNUGLY

POSITION OF CARD WITH PEEPHOLE

ORIGINAL BACK OF PICTURE FRAME

MENDING PLATES TO HOLD GLASS

196. BACK VIEW OF PICTURE FRAME

ROUND-HEAD SCREWS
CORNER PLATE
FLAT-HEAD SCREW

197. CORNER DETAIL
Section through A-A

Construction details are given here to help you build a tracing frame for your own use.

Fig. 197]   Techniques for Tracing   101

waste time because tracing is so quick that we can trace half-a-dozen lines with less effort than we could erase one.

"Trace, don't erase," applies only to experiments and not to straightforward mistakes. Also, no one would trace an elaborate drawing to save a few lines of an experiment that failed. The rule is sound, nevertheless, and one that you should certainly follow in most cases.

Fair Copies. Even when no experiments are involved, any attempt to produce a fair copy in a first draft is rarely worth while. Pencil lines smudge unless we take pains to avoid it. As lines cannot be measured before they are drawn, we seldom make them exactly the right length. If they are too short, they must be extended. This wastes time and may leave ugly joints. Expert draftsmen avoid such difficulties by deliberately making their lines extra long at first. After the details have been worked out, it is neater—and often easier—to trace the whole drawing than to erase all the unwanted extensions.

When you do succeed in producing a neat first draft, you have probably done so by resigning yourself to omitting some desirable but not absolutely necessary improvements. Moreover, if you make a single bad mistake, or if you change your mind about one part of the design (as I did about the braces in the tracing frame), you will have to trace a fair copy anyway. In that case, your effort to keep the draft neat will have proved futile.

Finally, if the drawing is important, you should check it line by line. But checking takes almost as long as tracing a fair copy. Hence, any time spent in keeping the draft neat is largely wasted —even when you are completely successful.

TRACING AS A LEARNING TOOL

The use of tracing on paper as a learning aid is by no means confined to tracing illustrations for research notes, making quick copies of maps, and sketching biological specimens. Tracing will help you to learn in almost any situation where you have, or can find, a picture or diagram as a source.

Interpreting Complex Material. Intricate diagrams like Fig. 198 are difficult to follow by eye. A diagram that seems hopelessly tangled to the beginner may appear simple to the expert, but even the expert finds some diagrams too complex to be readily understood. Tracing eliminates much of this difficulty. It enables us to break down the most involved diagram into a series of simple lines.

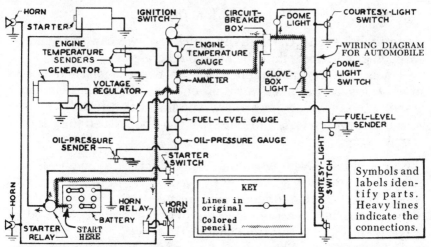

198. HOW TRACING CAN BE USED TO UNRAVEL COMPLEX DIAGRAMS

Lay tracing paper over the source. Start at some point that you understand [battery in Fig. 198]. Follow any line with a colored pencil to keep track of the part that you have covered. Where the line branches, mark one branch with an arrow and follow the other. When you come to the end of the line, go back to the first arrow and follow the line to which it points.

If your diagram is exceptionally elaborate, trace one part with a red pencil. Then switch to some other color. This makes each part, in effect, an uncomplicated diagram that can be followed without trouble.

This half was covered with tracing paper. The parts were then outlined in pencil.

INTERPRETING DETAILS OF AN OBSCURE PHOTOGRAPH

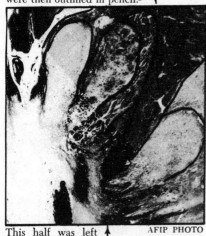

This half was left bare to show source. AFIP PHOTO

199. OUTLINING PARTS OF A COMPLEX ILLUSTRATION

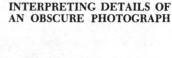
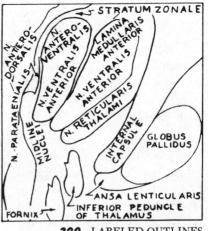

200. LABELED OUTLINES ON TRACING PAPER

Fig. 204]   Techniques for Tracing   103

Fields as far from each other as Biology and Air Reconnaissance require the interpretation of photographs like that in Fig. 199, where details appear at first sight to be mere shapeless blobs. If you lay acetate over such a photograph and outline each form, you bring out the important elements and get rid of those that are irrelevant. This simplifies the problem of identifying and interpreting the various parts. It also aids memorization.

When a picture like Fig. 199 is examined by eye, items that seem to have no meaning are easily overlooked. Tracing calls especial attention to these obscure forms; their lack of clear outlines makes them difficult to trace, and this automatically forces us to think about them.

Interpretative tracing is the very reverse of slavish copying. Never trace a line unless you either know what it means or clearly recognize it as a problem that requires further study.

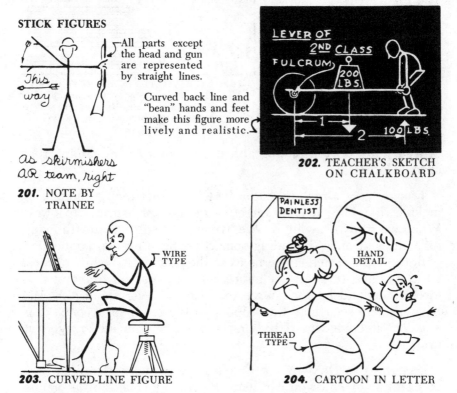

STICK FIGURES

This way

All parts except the head and gun are represented by straight lines.

Curved back line and "bean" hands and feet make this figure more lively and realistic.

as skirmishers as team, right

201. NOTE BY TRAINEE

LEVER OF 2ND CLASS
FULCRUM
200 LBS.
1
2   100 LBS.

202. TEACHER'S SKETCH ON CHALKBOARD

WIRE TYPE

203. CURVED-LINE FIGURE

PAINLESS DENTIST
HAND DETAIL
THREAD TYPE

204. CARTOON IN LETTER

Labeled Outlines as Notes. Outlining a photograph serves primarily as a mental tool. It will have fulfilled its purpose when your interpretation of the picture is complete. Although the drawing itself is really a by-product, labeling the parts turns it into a valuable note [Fig. 200]. This can be kept, either for its own sake

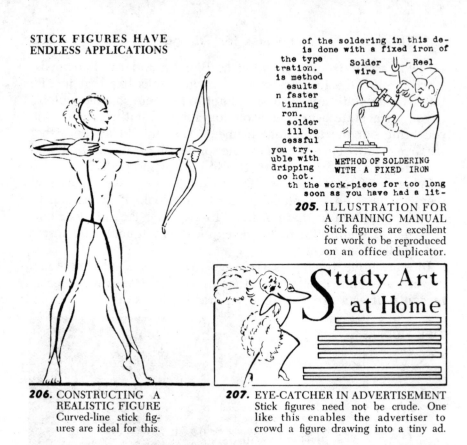

of the soldering in this de-
is done with a fixed iron of

the type
t ration.
is method
esults
n faster
tinning
ron.
solder
ill be
cessful
you try.
uble with
dripping
oo hot.

Solder
wire

Reel

METHOD OF SOLDERING
WITH A FIXED IRON

th the wcrk-piece for too long
soon as you have had a lit-

205. ILLUSTRATION FOR
A TRAINING MANUAL
Stick figures are excellent
for work to be reproduced
on an office duplicator.

Study Art
at Home

206. CONSTRUCTING A
REALISTIC FIGURE
Curved-line stick fig-
ures are ideal for this.

207. EYE-CATCHER IN ADVERTISEMENT
Stick figures need not be crude. One
like this enables the advertiser to
crowd a figure drawing into a tiny ad.

or as a guide to the photograph if you want to re-examine that
at some later time.

Tracing as a Drawing Tutor. Tracing is not only a method of
making drawings; it is an effective method of learning to draw.
When we study drawing by eye, we are forced to deal with many
difficulties at once—including some that have no real connection
with the topic which concerns us at the moment. When we trace,
we can concentrate all our efforts on the aspect of drawing that
interests us and let the source take care of everything else. We
have already seen how this applies to the study of accents; it is
equally effective when studying any other element or type of
drawing.

LEARNING TO DRAW STICK FIGURES. Let us take stick figures as
an example of how you can learn by tracing. These little people
are as useful as they are fascinating. They are fun to draw, they
catch the eye, they serve as technical notes [Fig. 201], as cartoons
[Figs. 203 and 204], and as illustrations for training manuals
[Fig. 205]. They also provide ideal constructions for drawing
realistic figures [Fig. 206].

Fig. 210]   Techniques for Tracing   105

Stick figures look easy to draw, but I tried for years without achieving any that were not hopelessly crude. One day, while I was simplifying a map by tracing, it occurred to me that a stick figure is also a form of simplification. This suggested studying stick figures by using realistic figures as constructions over which the stick figures could be traced.

My first attempt [Step 1, Fig. 208] taught me that the trouble was largely in the hip- and shoulder-lines. A few more experimental tracings revealed that I had been getting the shoulder line too high and the hip line too low (corrected in Step 2).

I next discovered that in drawing stick figures I had been careless about the way shoulder- and hip-lines slant (see the girl in Fig. 20). When I corrected this, I found that I had an acceptable stick figure [Step 3, Fig. 208].

These *matchstick-type* stick figures will do for most practical purposes. Curving the back line, as in Fig. 202, often adds life. *Wire-type* figures, in which all the lines are curved, are especially interesting [Figs. 203 and 209]. They may even be decorative [Fig. 207]. The simpler ones are no harder to draw than the

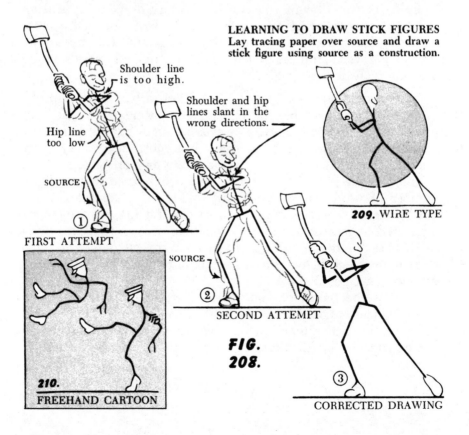

LEARNING TO DRAW STICK FIGURES
Lay tracing paper over source and draw a stick figure using source as a construction.

Shoulder line is too high.

Hip line too low

Shoulder and hip lines slant in the wrong directions.

SOURCE

① FIRST ATTEMPT

209. WIRE TYPE

SOURCE

②
SECOND ATTEMPT

FIG. 208.

210. FREEHAND CARTOON

③ CORRECTED DRAWING

matchstick type. I made Fig. 209 by laying tracing paper over Step 3, Fig. 208, and experimenting until I was satisfied with the result. After a few such "exercises," I had no further difficulty; I could draw a satisfactory stick figure by tracing from a well-posed source. Better still, I found that—without further study—I could sketch passable stick figures freehand [Fig. 210].

Thread-type figures like those in Fig. 204 are also worth investigating, especially when you want to show clothing. Their proportions can be far from realistic, and their hands give no trouble at all.

Although tracing is helpful, there is no reason to deny yourself the benefit of any other assistance you can get. A study of Figs. 211–216 will teach you a little about anatomy and a good deal about how stick-figure lines—straight or curved—are related both to the body and to the underlying skeleton.

A comparison of Figs. 201–210 with Figs. 211–216 reveals the important fact that it is much easier to make figures interesting when they show action than when they merely stand erect. This is especially true of stick figures; Figs. 212, 214, and 216 are hopelessly dull. If you begin your study of figure drawing by tracing stick figures from sources in violent action, you will almost automatically learn to create interesting poses and will avoid the tendency toward stiffness that troubles most people who start by drawing realistic figures.

LEARNING TO RENDER DETAILS. A lobster, a box, or a map can be pictured recognizably by drawing its outline. Such things as fur, drapery, and the hands and eyes of small figures cannot be adequately represented by outlines but must be portrayed by some method that is either more elaborate or more subtle.

Any of these things can be indicated or *rendered* in an infinite number of ways. Thus, each hand in Fig. 217 illustrates a different method of rendering. For practical drawing, we are chiefly interested in shorthand methods that will express the thing with the fewest number of strokes. If you have trouble depicting some particular object or material, use tracing to study the techniques used by other people.

Thus, if the hands of your stick figures seem difficult, trace many typical hands. Do not trace the whole figure. That wastes time and distracts attention from the subject of hands. Such tracing will teach you that two or three strokes may be enough if

DIAGRAMS ILLUSTRATING RELATION OF ▷
STICK FIGURES TO BODY AND SKELETON
Observe that stick figure does not follow either
the skeleton or the outlines of the body exactly.

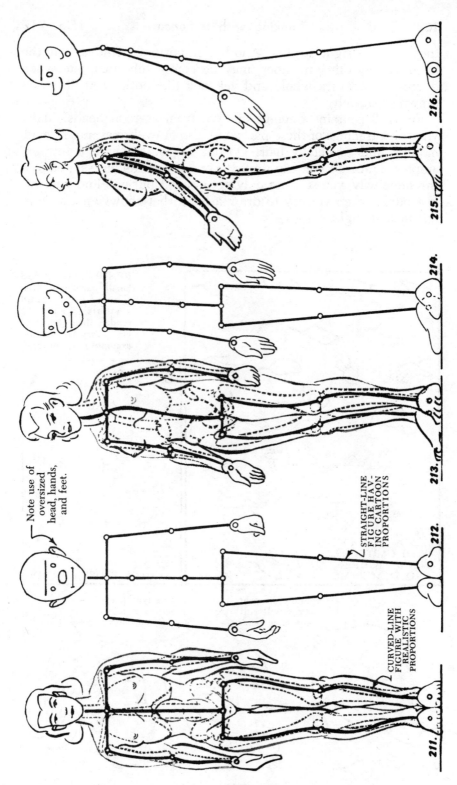

Note use of oversized head, hands, and feet.

STRAIGHT-LINE FIGURE HAVING CARTOON PROPORTIONS

CURVED-LINE FIGURE WITH REALISTIC PROPORTIONS

211. 212. 213. 214. 215. 216.

107

they are the right strokes. Another important point is that the hand, or any other member, may be completely adequate when drawn as part of a whole and yet look like nothing at all when drawn separately.

Fig. 218 contains tracings of eyes from cartoon heads. Make your own tracings of these parts and also of eyebrows, noses, ears, mouths, and especially hair. Do not be content with a few examples. Trace all you can find. If you always render, say, ears in the same way, you will not only get in a rut but will find yourself in trouble when you try to draw a head that shows an ear from an unusual angle.

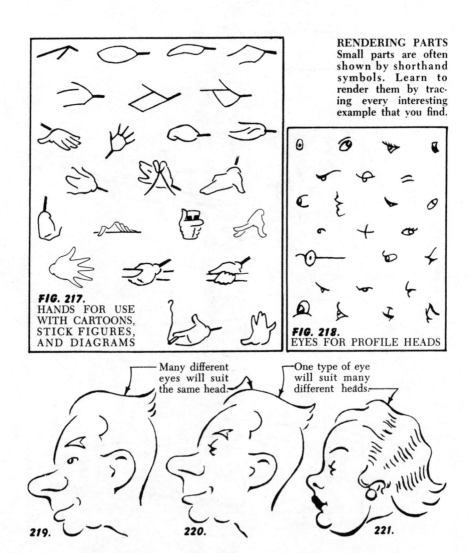

RENDERING PARTS
Small parts are often shown by shorthand symbols. Learn to render them by tracing every interesting example that you find.

FIG. 217.
HANDS FOR USE WITH CARTOONS, STICK FIGURES, AND DIAGRAMS

FIG. 218.
EYES FOR PROFILE HEADS

Many different eyes will suit the same head.

One type of eye will suit many different heads.

219.   220.   221.

6

CREATIVE TRACING

222.
Every schoolboy
knows this one.

WHEN we invent a gadget or design a costume, we create something new. No source for the whole can exist. Nevertheless, even the most original design is produced by rearranging old material. We can follow the same principle in our drawing by tracing from several different sources, or by tracing most of the lines and then adding an original part—much as a schoolboy draws a mustache on a poster.

If you lack skill in freehand drawing, creative tracing will open a whole new world for you. It substitutes ingenuity for skill and permits anyone to make an adequate drawing of anything for which he can obtain suitable sources. Admittedly, finding sources sometimes presents major difficulties. They must be the right size and viewed from the correct angle.

When the source is satisfactory except for its size, you can obtain a photograph or photostat of it and then have this reduced or enlarged to the size needed. If you cannot find a picture that shows your subject from the desired angle, a posed photograph may be the answer. I am a poor hand with a camera, and most of my snapshots are technically atrocious. But as long as they are clear enough to be traced, they serve my needs.

The problem of finding suitable sources is not entirely a liability. If creative tracing were always easy, there would be little motive for learning to sketch freehand. Actually, creative tracing is just easy enough to get you over any real difficulty and just hard enough to provide an incentive for mastering freehand drawing. It is a tool, not a crutch.

REARRANGEMENT

To produce Fig. 223, I first drew the tube on tracing paper. I then laid another sheet over this and drew the jar, making it

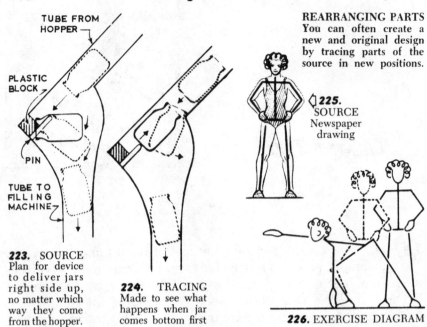

TUBE FROM HOPPER

PLASTIC BLOCK

PIN

TUBE TO FILLING MACHINE

223. SOURCE Plan for device to deliver jars right side up, no matter which way they come from the hopper.

224. TRACING Made to see what happens when jar comes bottom first

REARRANGING PARTS You can often create a new and original design by tracing parts of the source in new positions.

◁**225.** SOURCE Newspaper drawing

226. EXERCISE DIAGRAM

just the right size to fit the tube. Next, I put the drawing of the jar under the drawing of the tube and re-traced the jar in the four different positions shown. Fig. 224 was then traced from Fig. 223 by shifting the paper to bring the jars into their proper positions. This is both quicker and more accurate than making the drawings separately on opaque paper. The same process can be applied to a wide range of subjects [Figs. 225–236].

Adjustment. Although nearly all the parts of Fig. 226 were traced from their respective sources, the head, hand, and right foot of the bending figure had to be drawn freehand. Do not forget that such adjustments are miniature drawing lessons. You

REARRANGING PROFILE POSES

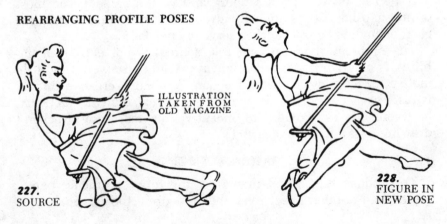

ILLUSTRATION TAKEN FROM OLD MAGAZINE

227. SOURCE

228. FIGURE IN NEW POSE

Fig. 233]   Creative Tracing   111

may not always be satisfied with your results, but you will always learn enough to pay for your trouble.

As the heads in Figs. 44 and 45 demonstrate, we can make extensive alterations while tracing. We then treat the source as a rough construction, which fixes the general proportions of the tracing but which permits us to vary details at will.

Draw piano and stool on tracing paper and place it over the template.

STICK FIGURES FROM TEMPLATES
Drawing a figure in any profile position by tracing template in Fig. 216.

Use a compass to draw an arc through which knee can move. 3

2 Trace foot.

229.

4 Trace body in its position on the piano stool.

230.

Trace thigh. 7

5 Place pencil on the pivot point of hip.

231.

6 Paper pivoted to bring knee on arc.

8 Move paper to put knee here and ankle here.

9 Trace shin.

232.

233.
Trace other parts from template in same way. Remove faint-line construction from source, correct errors, and redraw with firm lines (a curved-line version is shown in Fig. 203).

Pivoting. Rearranging the parts of a human figure to show it in a new position is fairly simple if the figure is in strict profile [Figs. 227 and 228]. Otherwise, the process may not work at all. Even with profile figures, fixing the exact points at which the

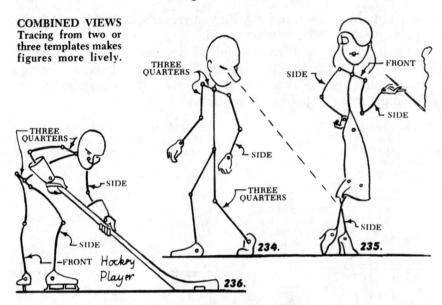

COMBINED VIEWS
Tracing from two or
three templates makes
figures more lively.

THREE QUARTERS

SIDE

FRONT

SIDE

THREE QUARTERS

SIDE

THREE QUARTERS

SIDE

THREE QUARTERS

SIDE

FRONT   Hockey Player

234.

235.

236.

parts pivot sometimes gives trouble. With stick figures, however, the locations of the pivot points are obvious, and this makes drawing new positions extremely easy. Figs. 229–233 show how the pivoting method is used to trace a stick figure from the template in Fig. 216.

Experiment with profile positions first. After you have mastered these, apply the Egyptian principle by combining front, three-quarter, and profile positions in the same drawing [Figs. 234–236]. Adding *properties* (usually shortened to *props*) like the skates, gloves, and hockey stick will increase the interest of your figures.

When heads, hands, or feet must be shown from viewpoints not included in the templates, you can usually find sources to trace (and adapt) by the methods used to draw the heads in Figs. 44 and 45. Finding sources that are exactly the right size may take a little time. However, cartoon figures often exaggerate the head, hands, and feet in relation to the body. As the exact amount of exaggeration is unimportant, you will have less trouble finding sources for these parts in cartoon figures than you will for those in which the proportions must be realistic. Another way to provide hands for your pivoted figures is to choose one of the simplified hands in Fig. 217 and adapt it to your needs.

Tracing stick figures from templates is far from difficult, but it is by no means push-button drawing. It can teach you much about figure proportions and still more about posing your figures effectively. Even after you acquire a fairly high degree of skill

Fig. 237]   Creative Tracing   113

at sketching figures, you may want to fall back on template-tracing when you need to depict an unusual position and have no source to serve as a guide.

Foreshortening. Any part of the body appears shorter when it is placed at an angle to the observer. This effect is called *foreshortening*. It presents a major problem when dealing with realistic figures, but causes little difficulty in drawing stick figures.

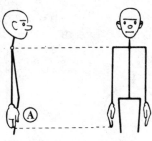

Fig. 237 illustrates the principle. The man in the side views swings his arm directly forward. As he does so, the arm is foreshortened in the front views. Note that the length changes more rapidly as the arm is raised. The difference between C and D is much greater than that between A and B. By imagining a side view, you can compute the amount of foreshortening in the corresponding front view easily and accurately.

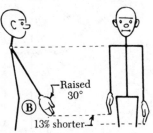

The problem becomes more complex when the arm is raised to the front and to the side at the same time [Figs. 238 and 239]. Fortunately, you rarely need to work out the exact foreshortening. In most cases you can follow the procedure explained in Fig. 240. Even if you make a fairly bad mistake, the arm will not look *out of drawing* but will merely appear to be in a different position.

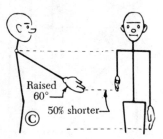

Reversal. Turning the tracing paper over reverses the drawing. This is an extremely useful device, especially when we want to make a person or animal face in the opposite direction from the source [fencers in Fig. 242]. In many cases, reversal is all that is needed. However, as this also exchanges the right and left sides, a number of adjustments may be required. Thus, I not only moved the sword arm of the reversed fencer in Fig. 242 but had to redraw his head, hands, and left foot as well.

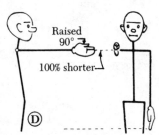

FIG. 237.
SIMPLE FORESHORTENING
Raising arm in side view makes it shorter in the front view.

With a little ingenuity, we can often produce a drawing by reversal that would be much more difficult if made freehand. For example, the mirror in Fig. 244 appears concave only because of the way the shading is shaped. Drawing this requires either a trained eye or a knowledge of advanced construction. However,

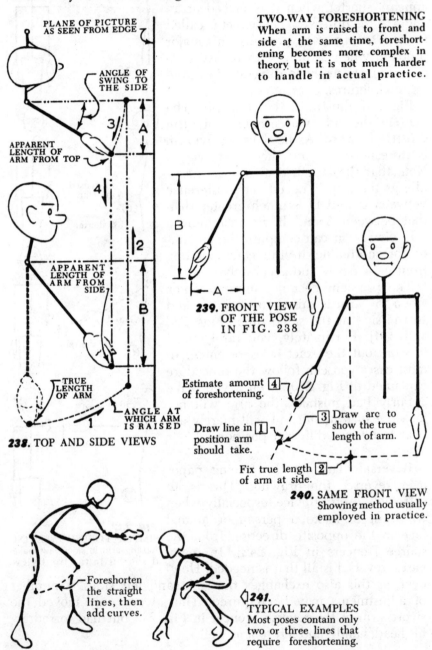

TWO-WAY FORESHORTENING
When arm is raised to front and side at the same time, foreshortening becomes more complex in theory but it is not much harder to handle in actual practice.

PLANE OF PICTURE AS SEEN FROM EDGE

ANGLE OF SWING TO THE SIDE

APPARENT LENGTH OF ARM FROM TOP

APPARENT LENGTH OF ARM FROM SIDE

TRUE LENGTH OF ARM

ANGLE AT WHICH ARM IS RAISED

238. TOP AND SIDE VIEWS

239. FRONT VIEW OF THE POSE IN FIG. 238

Estimate amount 4 of foreshortening.

Draw line in 1 position arm should take.

3 Draw arc to show the true length of arm.

Fix true length 2 of arm at side.

240. SAME FRONT VIEW
Showing method usually employed in practice.

1 Foreshorten the straight lines, then add curves.

241.
TYPICAL EXAMPLES
Most poses contain only two or three lines that require foreshortening.

Fig. 244]   Creative Tracing   115

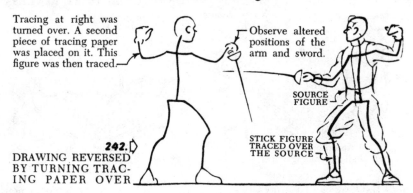

Tracing at right was turned over. A second piece of tracing paper was placed on it. This figure was then traced.—

Observe altered positions of the arm and sword.

SOURCE FIGURE

STICK FIGURE TRACED OVER THE SOURCE

242.
DRAWING REVERSED BY TURNING TRAC- ING PAPER OVER

tracing it from the convex high light in the source is easy, and reversing the paper makes the mirror seem concave.

SYMMETRY. Reversal is almost essential when drawing a sym- metrical object, such as a vase, or a symmetrical pattern of any kind. The tracings in Fig. 245 illustrate its use on a slightly more complex subject—a portrait of a live box turtle. Turtles are re- garded as lethargic, but my model lumbered off at such a rate that I had to sketch him almost on the fly. Under these conditions, drawing half a turtle was much easier than drawing a whole one. By making use of reversal, half was all I needed.

Turtles are especially reluctant to pose for bottom views [Fig. 247]. Here again, reversal made matters easier for both artist and model.

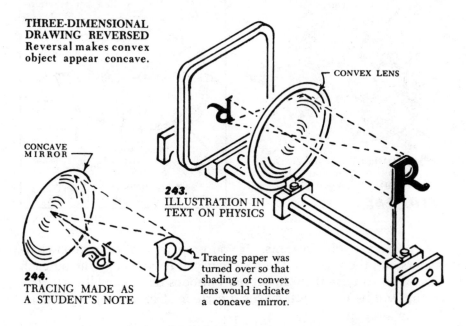

THREE-DIMENSIONAL DRAWING REVERSED
Reversal makes convex object appear concave.

CONVEX LENS

CONCAVE MIRROR

243.
ILLUSTRATION IN TEXT ON PHYSICS

244.
TRACING MADE AS A STUDENT'S NOTE

Tracing paper was turned over so that shading of convex lens would indicate a concave mirror.

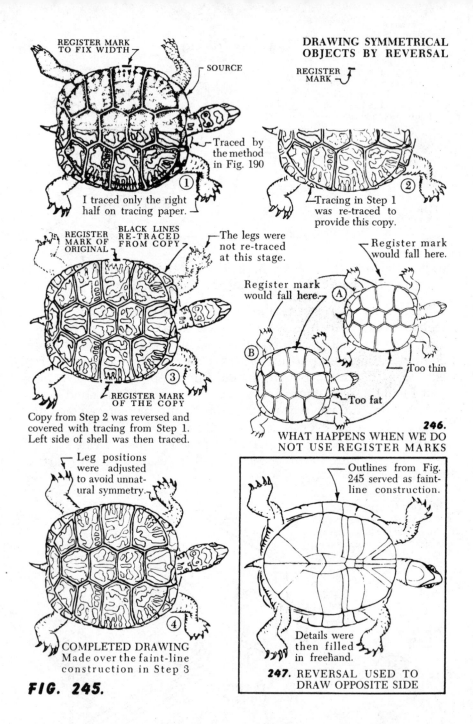

REGISTER MARK
TO FIX WIDTH

SOURCE

REGISTER
MARK

Traced by
the method
in Fig. 190

I traced only the right
half on tracing paper.

①

②

Tracing in Step 1
was re-traced to
provide this copy.

REGISTER
MARK OF
ORIGINAL

BLACK LINES
RE-TRACED
FROM COPY

The legs were
not re-traced
at this stage.

Register mark
would fall here.

Register mark
would fall here.

Ⓐ

Ⓑ

Too thin

Too fat

③

REGISTER MARK
OF THE COPY

Copy from Step 2 was reversed and
covered with tracing from Step 1.
Left side of shell was then traced.

246.
WHAT HAPPENS WHEN WE DO
NOT USE REGISTER MARKS

Leg positions
were adjusted
to avoid unnat-
ural symmetry.

Outlines from Fig.
245 served as faint-
line construction.

④

COMPLETED DRAWING
Made over the faint-line
construction in Step 3

Details were
then filled
in freehand.

247. REVERSAL USED TO
DRAW OPPOSITE SIDE

FIG. 245.

FLANNELBOARD "DRAMAS." If you prepare a set of cartoon characters and then reverse them so that you have a copy facing each
way, you can use them to act out episodes on a flannelboard. The
result will be midway between a cartoon strip and a puppet play.

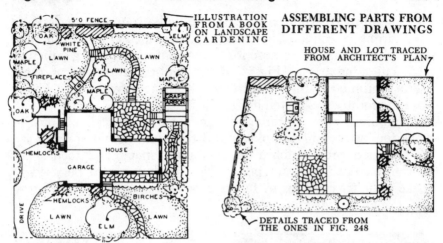

ILLUSTRATION FROM A BOOK ON LANDSCAPE GARDENING

ASSEMBLING PARTS FROM DIFFERENT DRAWINGS

HOUSE AND LOT TRACED FROM ARCHITECT'S PLAN

DETAILS TRACED FROM THE ONES IN FIG. 248

248. SOURCE   **249.** ORIGINAL DESIGN

This sort of thing grows dull if carried to any length, but a brief example adds interest to any talk.

COMBINATIONS

The house and lot of the landscape design shown in Fig. 249 were traced from the architect's plan, and the details were traced from Fig. 248. This idea of combining parts taken from different sources can be used in many ways and often saves much time.

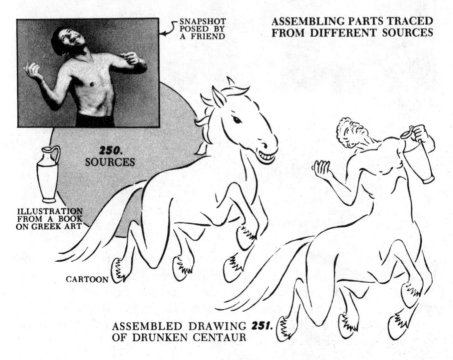

SNAPSHOT POSED BY A FRIEND

ASSEMBLING PARTS TRACED FROM DIFFERENT SOURCES

250. SOURCES

ILLUSTRATION FROM A BOOK ON GREEK ART

CARTOON

ASSEMBLED DRAWING **251.** OF DRUNKEN CENTAUR

Assembling. It would not be easy to find a source for a drawing of a drunken centaur, but there is no difficulty in persuading some obliging friend to pose for a snapshot or in finding a picture of a galloping horse [Fig. 250]. Traced constructions of these were combined with a third taken from a drawing of a Greek vase to produce the sketch in Fig. 251.

Combining parts of different sizes produces excellent illustrations for instruction pamphlets and training manuals [Fig. 253]. The cartoon effect catches the eye, saves space, and focuses attention on the important points. This trick can also be used to make ordinary cartoons by taking a head from one realistic figure and a smaller body from another.

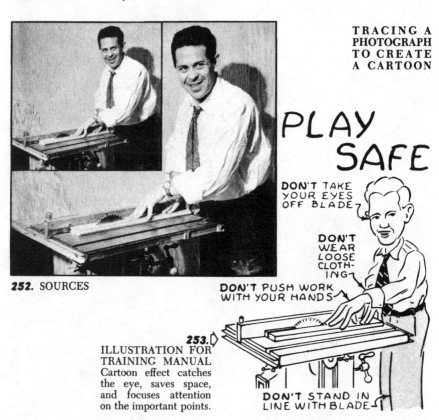

TRACING A
PHOTOGRAPH
TO CREATE
A CARTOON

PLAY
SAFE

DON'T TAKE
YOUR EYES
OFF BLADE

DON'T
WEAR
LOOSE
CLOTH-
ING

DON'T PUSH WORK
WITH YOUR HANDS

DON'T STAND IN
LINE WITH BLADE

252. SOURCES

253.
ILLUSTRATION FOR
TRAINING MANUAL
Cartoon effect catches
the eye, saves space,
and focuses attention
on the important points.

Additions. Fig. 255 shows a diagram made by tracing the difficult parts of a drawing and adding a few freehand changes. We have already seen how such additions can be used to create original heads from newspaper cartoons [Figs. 44 and 45]. A slight variation of this technique provides a valuable type of training doodle [Figs. 256 and 257].

Fig. 256]   Creative Tracing   119

Beginners usually find difficulty in representing facial expressions. You can quickly master this by tracing a series of heads with their eyes and lips in different positions [Fig. 256]. In your early doodles, do not try to produce a particular mood, such as gaiety or anger. Simply alter the expression and note the result. By changing the hair, forehead, nose, and chin of each successive doodle, you can learn to create heads for different characters [Fig. 257].

When you work in this way you cannot fail; every head will have some expression and some character. Hogarth, Rowlandson, and Daumier all trained themselves by doodling on this principle to make what Andrew Loomis, the artist and writer, calls "happen heads."

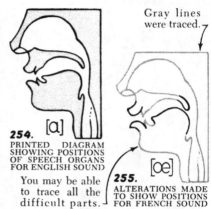

Gray lines were traced.

254. [ɑ] PRINTED DIAGRAM SHOWING POSITIONS OF SPEECH ORGANS FOR ENGLISH SOUND

You may be able to trace all the difficult parts.

255. [œ] ALTERATIONS MADE TO SHOW POSITIONS FOR FRENCH SOUND

ADDING PARTS FREEHAND
Difficult drawings become easy when you trace part of a picture and adapt it to your own needs with freehand additions.

Combining Methods. Any number of these methods can be used in a single drawing. I began the costume sketch in Fig. 258 by taking a posed snapshot and tracing a faint-line construction for the figure from that. I then improved on my model by slimming the waist and hips and lengthening the legs. This gave me a firm basis. Once that was established, I could not go far wrong.

You will need a fair amount of experience before you can safely tackle so much freehand drawing. However, I have chosen the example to demonstrate that creating any sketch over a traced

FIG. 256. DOODLE METHOD OF LEARNING TO VARY EXPRESSIONS
Each head was drawn by laying tracing paper over the one before it and changing the positions of the eyes, eyebrows, and lips.

construction requires only a tenth as much skill as making a sketch of equal quality entirely freehand. If I had known this when I studied costume design, I would have gotten much better grades—and saved myself many hours of hard work.

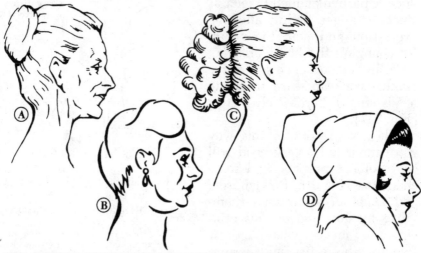

257. DOODLE METHOD OF LEARNING TO CREATE CHARACTER
This is the technique of Fig. 256, but the basic shapes of the features are changed instead of merely altering their expressions.

Progressive Tracing. Tracing may be useful even when the only sources are your own memory and imagination. I began the sketch in Fig. 259 by drawing the chair [Step 1]. If I had then drawn the boy and failed to get him right, I would have needed to redraw the chair. By covering the chair with tracing paper and drawing the boy on that [Step 2], I could throw away any mistakes and still keep the chair. When I had completed the boy to my satisfaction, I added another sheet of tracing paper and drew the girl on the boy's lap [Step 3]. I then transferred all three drawings to the same sheet. That gave me a faint-line construction over which I redrew Step 4. Notice that this is essentially another application of the experimental tracing method illustrated in Fig. 195.

Corrections. The same principle can be applied in making corrections. Treat the faulty version [Step 1, Fig. 260] as a construction by covering it with tracing paper and drawing the correction on this [Step 2]. If your first attempt does not succeed, you can try again as often as you like by using a new sheet—or a new part of a sheet—of tracing paper each time. When your construction satisfies you, erase the faulty lines of the original, transfer the improved version as a construction, and redraw it in its proper

Fig. 258]　　　　　Creative Tracing　　　　　121

place [Step 3]. One erasure will seldom spoil a drawing; two or more are likely to do so no matter how carefully they are carried out.

The value of this procedure is not confined to minor corrections. We can remake a whole drawing in this way. Furthermore, we can repeat the process as often as we like without producing a wooden, worked-over appearance. The French painter, Degas, traced and retraced his ballet girls and race horses many times.

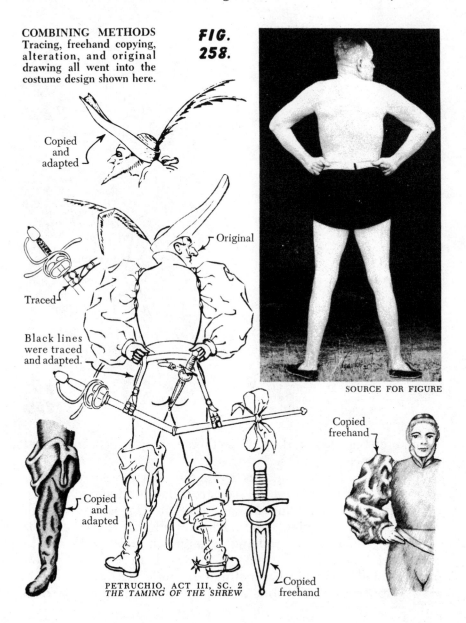

COMBINING METHODS
Tracing, freehand copying, alteration, and original drawing all went into the costume design shown here.

FIG. 258.

Copied and adapted

Original

Traced

Black lines were traced and adapted.

SOURCE FOR FIGURE

Copied freehand

Copied and adapted

Copied freehand

PETRUCHIO, ACT III, SC. 2
THE TAMING OF THE SHREW

Copied freehand

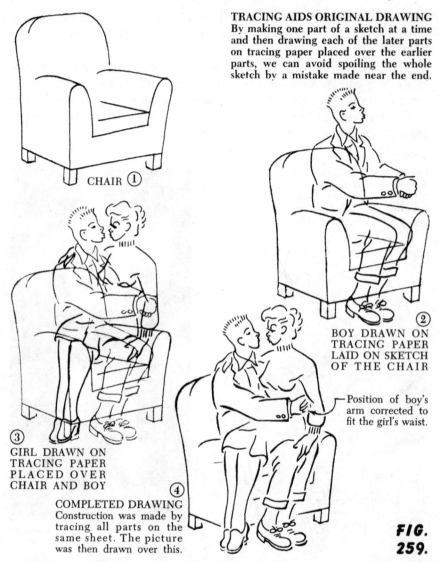

CHAIR ①

TRACING AIDS ORIGINAL DRAWING
By making one part of a sketch at a time and then drawing each of the later parts on tracing paper placed over the earlier parts, we can avoid spoiling the whole sketch by a mistake made near the end.

BOY DRAWN ON TRACING PAPER LAID ON SKETCH OF THE CHAIR ②

—Position of boy's arm corrected to fit the girl's waist.

GIRL DRAWN ON TRACING PAPER PLACED OVER CHAIR AND BOY ③

COMPLETED DRAWING ④
Construction was made by tracing all parts on the same sheet. The picture was then drawn over this.

FIG. 259.

In spite of that, his works look as though they had been dashed off at high speed from life.

The secret of retaining this freshness depends on *invariably* treating the faulty version as a construction and doing your very best to make every tracing an improvement. This is easy enough when you are correcting some obvious fault, but it may call for real effort when you are redoing an entire drawing and come to some part that you feel cannot be bettered. In such cases, you must remind yourself that nothing is quite perfect. There is always opportunity for subtle improvements. You do not need to

Fig. 260]   **Creative Tracing**   **123**

find improvements in order to keep your drawing fresh: the important thing is to make an honest search for them. Woodenness in a drawing is not a sign of a mechanical technique. It is a reflection of a wooden mind.

CORRECTIONS MADE
ON TRACING PAPER

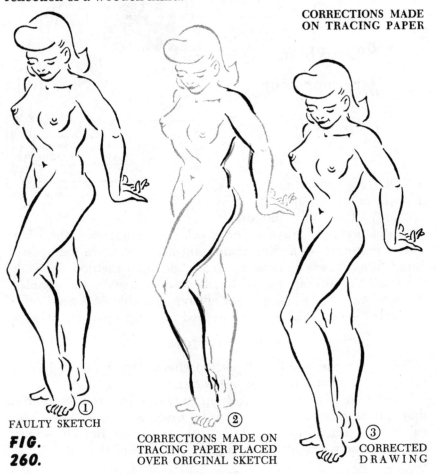

FAULTY SKETCH

**FIG.
260.**

CORRECTIONS MADE ON
TRACING PAPER PLACED
OVER ORIGINAL SKETCH

CORRECTED
DRAWING

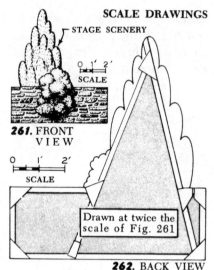

STAGE SCENERY

SCALE

261. FRONT VIEW

SCALE

Drawn at twice the scale of Fig. 261

262. BACK VIEW

7

PROPORTION,

MEASUREMENT,

ALINEMENT

JUDGING proportions by eye requires skill. In fact, it is probably the only important phase of practical drawing for which skill is indispensable. This puts a premium on finding easier and more accurate methods of fixing proportions. Tracing provides one such method; it establishes all proportions automatically and does it in the simplest possible way. But tracing is not always available. We need other methods. Some of these are described in the present chapter.

PROPORTION

Before we can handle proportion effectively, we must have a clear idea of what it is and how it works.

Proportion is a size relationship between any two quantities that can be compared. John may be twice as rich as Sam. This oak may be three times as old as that apple tree. But no proportion exists between John's wealth and the age of the oak.

Scale Ratio. In practical drawing, we are chiefly concerned with proportions of length. A drawing in which every length is reduced or enlarged in the same proportion is called a *scale drawing.* Thus, Fig. 261 shows both a piece of stage scenery and a *scale,* which is really a picture of a ruler reduced in the same proportion as the main drawing. We can use this scale to measure any length in the drawing. If the work has been done properly, the measurements of the drawing correspond exactly to those of the actual piece of scenery.

When a drawing is made *to scale,* there is always a fixed, numerical *scale ratio* between the lengths in the source and the lengths in the drawing. Every length in the real piece of scenery

Fig. 262]   Proportion, Measurement, Alinement   125

is ninety-six times the corresponding length in Fig. 261 and forty-eight times the corresponding length in Fig. 262. The term "scale ratio" is often shortened to "scale," but remember that a ratio is always numerical and do not confuse it with the scale in Fig. 261, which is a calibrated line.

Scale ratios may be written as 1 : 96 or 1 : 48. In this case, the first number represents the drawing and the second represents the actual object. Another method is to express a ratio as a fraction—$\frac{1}{96}$ or $\frac{1}{48}$. The most common method, however, and the only one suited to mechanical drawing, is to write scale ratios as equations. Thus, the scale ratio of Fig. 262 is $\frac{1}{4}'' = 1'0''$. As the right-hand side of the equation is always one unit, we may abbreviate this and speak of a "quarter-inch scale." But note that the ratio here is not 1 : 4 but 1 : 48.

When a small object is enlarged, the scale ratio may be written 3 : 1, $\times 3$, $3'' = 1''$, or 3 cm. = 1 cm. All four terms refer to the same ratio; in any drawing where 3 cm. equals 1 cm., $3''$ will equal $1''$.

Length, Area, Volume. Ordinarily, the term "scale ratio" applies only to lengths. Do not let the length ratio confuse you when you deal with areas or volumes. There is a great difference, as Figs. 263–265 demonstrate.

The corresponding areas in any drawings are in proportion to the squares of any pair of corresponding lengths. Thus, a square $1''$ on a side has an area of 1 square inch, a square $2''$ on a side has an area of 4 square inches ($2^2 = 2 \times 2 = 4$), and one $3''$ on a side has an area of 9 square inches ($3^2 = 3 \times 3 = 9$). This is equally true of irregular shapes. Fig. 262 is twice as wide as Fig. 261, and its area is exactly four times as great.

The volume varies as the cube of the length. If a model of a dinosaur is $3''$ long and the real dinosaur was $60'0''$ long, the dinosaur was 240 times as long as the model and 240^3 or 13,824,000 times as bulky.

When you have drawings photostated, or engraved for printing, it is important to know that people who do this work normally think in terms of length. If you tell them that you want a drawing reduced one-half, they will reduce it to one-quarter of its area. Furthermore, they usually think in terms of ratios rather than reduction. An order for a 20% reduction is likely to produce an engraving that is only one-fifth the height of the original. The safest procedure is to specify one dimension and say "make this so many inches wide (or high)." Do not specify both width and height; one automatically controls the other.

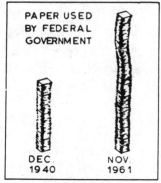

263. HEIGHT CHART BASED
ON A HEIGHT SCALE
A chart like this one will
convey the true meaning.

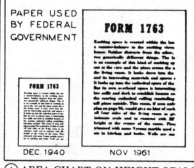

(A) AREA CHART ON HEIGHT SCALE
This makes the areas proportional
to the *squares* of the data. Such
charts can be seriously misleading.

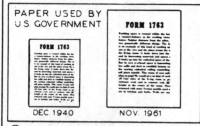

(B) AREA CHART ON AREA SCALE
This chart is theoretically correct.
However, it makes the larger area
appear too small in proportion.

FIG. 264.

AREA VARIES AS SQUARE OF LENGTH
VOLUME VARIES AS CUBE OF LENGTH

The eye cannot compare areas or volumes
accurately. Pictorial charts should be based
on heights, like Fig. 263, or on lengths. If
they show either areas or volumes, they are
apt to mislead those who try to read them.

(A) VOLUME CHART BASED
ON A HEIGHT SCALE
Volumes are in proportion
to the cubes of the data.

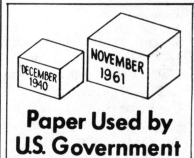

(B) VOLUME CHART BASED
ON AN AREA SCALE
Volumes in proportion to
the squares of the data.

(C) VOLUME CHART BASED
ON A VOLUME SCALE
Volumes are in proportion
to the data, but the chart
creates a false impression.

FIG. 265.

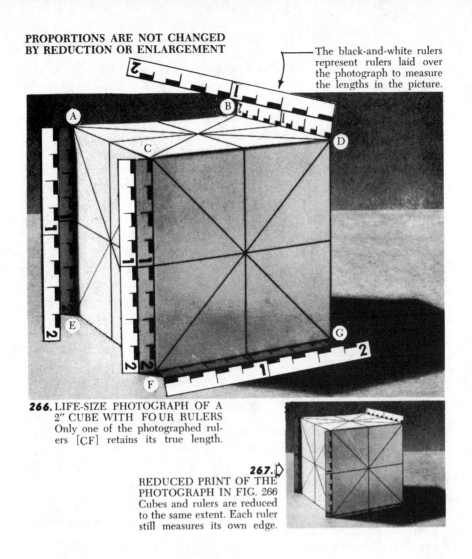

The black-and-white rulers represent rulers laid over the photograph to measure the lengths in the picture.

266. LIFE-SIZE PHOTOGRAPH OF A 2″ CUBE WITH FOUR RULERS
Only one of the photographed rulers [CF] retains its true length.

267. ▷
REDUCED PRINT OF THE PHOTOGRAPH IN FIG. 266
Cubes and rulers are reduced to the same extent. Each ruler still measures its own edge.

Distortion. It is not possible to make a completely true scale drawing which represents all three dimensions. Some measurements will always be distorted. This can be confusing if you are not prepared for it.

LENGTHS. A photograph is essentially a machine-made *perspective* drawing. Any rule that applies to the lines of a photograph will also be true of a technically correct perspective drawing. Fig. 266 is as near as we can come to a *full-scale* (life-size) photograph of a 2″ cube. Although every edge of the source measures 2″, only CF does this in Fig. 266. AE is less than 1¾″ long, and BD is only $^{15}/_{16}$″. Furthermore, lines that seem to run into the picture change their scale ratios as they recede. The far inch of FG, for example, measures $\frac{1}{16}$″ less than the near inch.

127

ANGLES. Distortion affects angles as well as lengths. All the edges of a real cube are perpendicular to each other, but none of the edge-lines in Fig. 266 meet at 90°. ABD is 162°, whereas BDC measures only 20°.

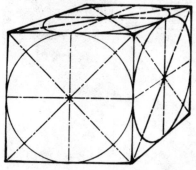

268. DISTORTION DOES NOT CHANGE INTERSECTIONS OR POINTS OF TANGENCY

CHANGE OF SCALE. When we photograph or draw a three-dimensional object, we introduce distortion. But changing the scale of a photograph or drawing does not increase the amount of distortion, no matter how great the change may be. Fig. 267 is two-fifths the scale of Fig. 266. This means that every line in Fig. 267 is exactly two-fifths the length of the corresponding line in Fig. 266, but there is no other difference between the two pictures.

A change of scale does not affect the sizes of the angles. ABD is 162° in both photographs, and BDC is 20°.

INTERSECTIONS AND TANGENTS. The cube in Fig. 268 demonstrates that distortion does not affect intersections. The front face duplicates the source; the top and side faces are badly distorted. Nevertheless, *whenever three or more lines meet at one point in the source, the corresponding lines meet at one point in the drawing.*

This rule is universal. It applies to the most extreme form of distortion. It even applies where the distortion is completely unsystematic—as it is in a large-headed cartoon like Fig. 253.

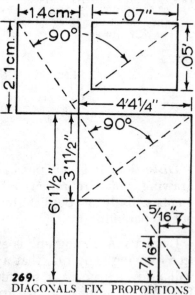

269. DIAGONALS FIX PROPORTIONS

The rule of intersections is a great help in construction. If three lines intersect at a point in the source, and if we can fix the point where two of them meet in the drawing, we can be sure that the third line will also pass through this point. The rule applies to curved lines as well as straight ones.

Fig. 270]   Proportion, Measurement, Alinement   129

Another important rule is that *points of tangency are not affected by distortion*. Thus, the circle on the front of the cube in Fig. 268 is tangent to the enclosing square at the points where the square is cut by its center lines. On the other two faces, the circles become ellipses, and the squares are lopsided diamonds. In spite of this, the ellipses are tangent to the diamonds at points where the diamonds are cut by the lines that correspond to the center lines of the front.

Do not think of distortion as a fault. It is inevitable in three-dimensional drawing, and we often employ it deliberately to emphasize some part of an illustration or to create a comic effect in a cartoon. Distortion is like fire—useful when controlled, but bad if it gets out of hand.

Diagonals. The fact that angles remain constant without regard to the scale of the drawing means that if one rectangle has its sides parallel to another and they share a common diagonal, their sides have the same ratio [Fig. 269]. This is also true when the diagonals are parallel or perpendicular. The same rule applies to right triangles in which the sides of one are in line with, perpendicular to, or parallel to the sides of the other. We can use this principle to construct proportions even when the scale ratio is unknown. The method of dividing a line into proportional segments with a ruler [Fig. 27] is an example.

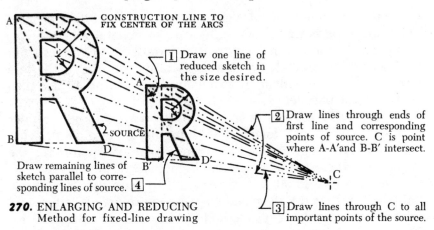

CONSTRUCTION LINE TO FIX CENTER OF THE ARCS

[1] Draw one line of reduced sketch in the size desired.

[2] Draw lines through ends of first line and corresponding points of source. C is point where A-A'and B-B' intersect.

Draw remaining lines of sketch parallel to corresponding lines of source. [4]

[3] Draw lines through C to all important points of the source.

270. ENLARGING AND REDUCING
Method for fixed-line drawing

Enlarging and Reducing. Figs. 270 and 271 show how the diagonal principle can be used to enlarge or reduce drawings. The *fan method* [Fig. 270] is practical only for simple fixed-line subjects. The *rectangle method* [Fig. 271] is extremely flexible and can be applied to any drawing no matter how complex. It allows us to make many subdivisions in an area, such as a head,

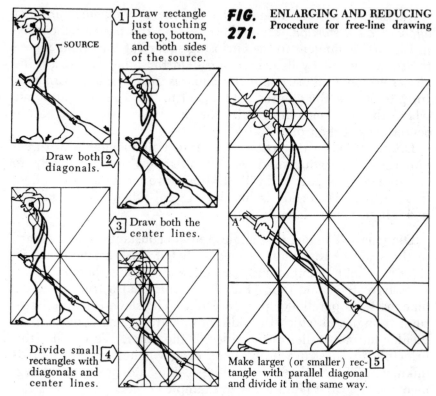

FIG. 271. ENLARGING AND REDUCING
Procedure for free-line drawing

SOURCE

1 Draw rectangle just touching the top, bottom, and both sides of the source.

2 Draw both diagonals.

3 Draw both the center lines.

4 Divide small rectangles with diagonals and center lines.

5 Make larger (or smaller) rectangle with parallel diagonal and divide it in the same way.

where there is much detail. On the other hand, we do not need to subdivide parts that show little detail or none at all.

Any straight line in the copy will be parallel to the corresponding line in the original. I was able to draw the line of the gun barrel in the enlargement by fixing the single point A′ and then ruling the line parallel to the one in the source.

The rectangle method is more satisfactory for most purposes than the conventional device of *squaring off* the original drawing and then laying out a grid of smaller or larger squares for the copy. Nevertheless, the squaring-off method is better for cases like the kiva in Fig. 90, where we want to keep the grid simple and where we need to designate squares by reference letters and numbers. The squaring-off method can also be recommended for painting theatrical scenery, where it is easy to make an error in placing the diagonal at the correct angle and where such an error might seriously distort the design.

Ability to enlarge and reduce drawings is especially helpful in connection with creative tracing as it eliminates the necessity of finding sources that are exactly the right size. Also, by enlarging or reducing the stick-figure templates in Figs. 211–216, you can

Fig. 272]   Proportion, Measurement, Alinement   131

make new templates in any size you like. This will enable you to trace large stick-figures for posters or small ones for cartoons in private letters.

272. ARCHITECT'S TRIANGULAR SCALE RULE

MEASUREMENT

By measuring the lines in a source and then making a construction which represents these lines by their scale-ratio equivalents, we fix the proportions of our drawing accurately without having to estimate them by eye. Where such measurements can be made, they eliminate the need for skill in fixed-line drawing and reduce it to a minimum in free-line drawing.

Lengths. If the source is a real object, we can measure it with a steel tape or a ruler. When we make an original design for a mechanical device, some measurements are fixed by the specifications and we choose the rest arbitrarily. Most of the measurements for the vertical tracing frame in Fig. 195 were set by the size of a picture frame that I happened to have and by the sizes of wood in my workshop. The remaining measurements were governed by my ideas on how large the parts should be to serve their functions.

Scale Rules. Once the measurements are known, the next problem is to reproduce them on paper at the desired scale ratio. We can do this with an ordinary ruler. At a scale ratio of $\frac{1}{2}'' = 1'0''$, for example, a length of $3'6''$ will be represented by a line $1\frac{3}{4}''$ long and one $4'9''$ by a line $2\frac{3}{8}''$ long.

Although this method works, it involves much mental arithmetic. Also, such dimensions as $1'11\frac{1}{2}''$ and $2'4\frac{3}{4}''$ cannot be measured accurately. Both difficulties are avoided by the use of *scale rules*. These are essentially rulers made to fit particular ratios. Thus, if a rule has a scale of $\frac{1}{2}'' = 1'0''$, the foot-divisions will be $\frac{1}{2}''$ apart, and the inch-divisions will be $\frac{1}{24}''$ apart.

Fig. 272 shows an *architect's triangular scale rule* which is also used for many types of engineering work. This rule has six faces. One of them is graduated in inches and sixteenths like an ordinary ruler. Each of the other five faces bears two scales as follows: $\frac{1}{8}''(=1'0'')$ and $\frac{1}{4}''$; $\frac{1}{2}''$ and $1''$; $\frac{3}{32}''$ and $\frac{3}{16}''$; $\frac{3}{8}''$ and $\frac{3}{4}''$; $1\frac{1}{2}''$ and $3''$. Another type of rule has scales of $10'$, $20'$, $30'$, $40'$, $50'$, and $60'$ to the inch. This type of rule is used in civil engineering and is called an *engineer's scale rule*. The *architect's flat scale rule* shown in Fig. 273 has four faces with two scales each: $\frac{1}{8}''$ and $\frac{1}{4}''$; $\frac{1}{2}''$ and $1''$; $\frac{3}{8}''$ and $\frac{3}{4}''$; $1\frac{1}{2}''$ and $3''$.

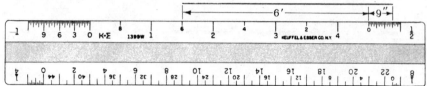

273. MAKING A MEASUREMENT WITH AN ARCHITECT'S FLAT SCALE RULE

Architect's scale rules are graduated in a way that is extremely convenient in practice, but which may be confusing until you learn how to read them. As you can see from Fig. 273, only the end divisions are calibrated in inches, and the numbers run in both directions. One set of these numbers represents the larger scale and the other the smaller scale. Thus, the $1''$ scale runs from left to right, and the $\frac{1}{2}''$ scale runs from right to left. Fig. 273 illustrates the method of making a measurement of $6'9''$ with the $\frac{1}{2}''$ scale.

The process of measuring a length that has already been fixed is called *scaling*. The procedure (shown in Fig. 274) is slightly different from that used to fix a length, but it should not give you any trouble—especially if you try it with an actual scale rule that you can slide back and forth.

In spite of their name, ordinary scale rules should not be employed for ruling lines as this may damage the face of the rule. Draw the line with a ruler or straightedge. Then measure along it with the rule.

SCALING LENGTHS ALREADY FIXED   *FIG. 274.*

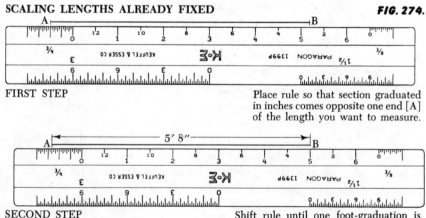

FIRST STEP

Place rule so that section graduated in inches comes opposite one end [A] of the length you want to measure.

SECOND STEP

Shift rule until one foot-graduation is exactly opposite other end [B] of length. Length can now be read from the scale.

Fig. 277]   Proportion, Measurement, Alinement   **133**

Dividers. As Figs. 276–277 show, *dividers* are used to repeat the same measurements several times in a drawing. The example in Fig. 276 is a flight of steps, but dividers are equally convenient when drawing frameworks—such as those used for stage scenery —in which many of the members have the same width.

Dividers are also handy when we want to make one line in some simple proportion to another. Fig. 277 demonstrates how to divide AB in half and then make AC as long as three of these halves. This technique is more accurate than the one in Fig. 27.

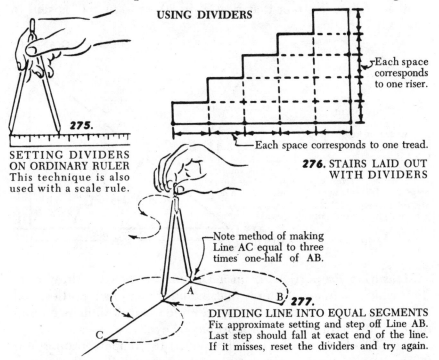

USING DIVIDERS

275.

SETTING DIVIDERS
ON ORDINARY RULER
This technique is also
used with a scale rule.

┌Each space
corresponds
to one riser.

└Each space corresponds to one tread.

276. STAIRS LAID OUT
WITH DIVIDERS

─Note method of making
Line AC equal to three
times one-half of AB.

277.
DIVIDING LINE INTO EQUAL SEGMENTS
Fix approximate setting and step off Line AB.
Last step should fall at exact end of the line.
If it misses, reset the dividers and try again.

Measuring Angles. We can measure an angle either with a *protractor* [Fig. 278] or by its *run* and *rise,* as shown in Fig. 279. The sizes of the run and the rise are often given by the source.

If we divide the rise by the run, arithmetically, we get the *tangent ratio.* This term is usually abbreviated to "tangent" or "tan," but do not confuse tangent ratios with the tangents that are lines touching circles. Tables of tangent ratios are printed in all books on trigonometry and in most mathematical reference works. With their aid, you can find the angle in degrees and minutes that corresponds to any tangent ratio. Using such a table does not require any knowledge of trigonometry.

In Fig. 279, the tangent ratio $1\frac{9}{16}'' \div 1\frac{7}{8}'' = 0.8333$. This corresponds almost exactly to the angle 39° 48′ 20″. As the size of the angle does not change with the size of the drawing, we would have the same tangent ratio (and the same angle) if the run were 6″ and the rise were 5″. The ratio of the rise to the run is often called the *slope*. Thus the line in Fig. 279 has a slope of 5 in 6. Unfortunately, there is no fixed convention as to whether the rise or the run is given first; some people might say that Fig. 279 has a slope of 6 in 5 or 6 to 5. The only safe method of specification is to say that the slope has a rise of 5 for a run of 6. Street and road *grades* are specified in tangent ratios expressed as percentages. Thus, a street that rises 1′ in 20′ or 5′ in 100′ is said to have a 5% grade.

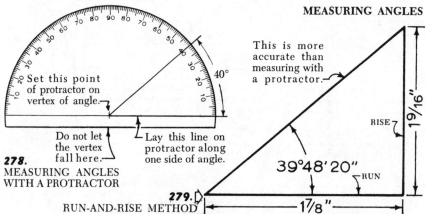

MEASURING ANGLES

Set this point of protractor on vertex of angle.

40°

Do not let the vertex fall here.

Lay this line on protractor along one side of angle.

278.
MEASURING ANGLES
WITH A PROTRACTOR

This is more accurate than measuring with a protractor.

RISE

19/16″

39°48′20″

RUN

279.
RUN-AND-RISE METHOD

1⅞″

Measuring Proportions from a Distance. When we draw from *life* (which is an artist's term that includes dead fish, bottles, and machinery), the methods in Figs. 280–283 can do much to eliminate the need for judging proportions by eye.

Fig. 280 illustrates the use of a pencil to compare proportions in the source. This is the traditional method followed by most artists, but a ruler is more convenient for the purpose. Thus, OR in Fig. 282 is one-sixth of BR. It would be difficult to measure this proportion accurately with a pencil, but even with an ordinary opaque ruler it can be seen at a glance. With a squared, transparent ruler, like that shown, we can compare a whole array of proportions at once. When measuring with a ruler, do not hold it at arm's length but keep it fairly close to the eye. Move it back and forth until marks on the ruler cover important points on the source.

ALINEMENT

Making constructions for free-line drawings depends largely upon finding imaginary lines that fix a number of points in the

MAKING MEASUREMENTS
AND ALINING POINTS
FOR FREEHAND DRAWING

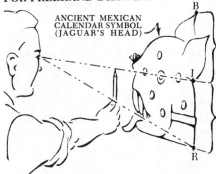

ANCIENT MEXICAN
CALENDAR SYMBOL
(JAGUAR'S HEAD)

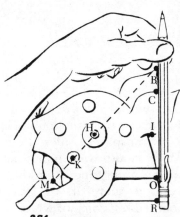

280. MEASURING WITH A PENCIL
Hold the pencil at arm's length and sight one point [I] over tip. Bring thumb in line with Point R. Then, move the pencil upward and note that BI exactly equals IR.

281.
PENCIL AS ALINING TOOL
Let the pencil hang free like a plum bob. In this case, B, C, O, and R lie on the same vertical line. Oblique alinements, such as BHKM, can be checked by holding the pencil on a slant.

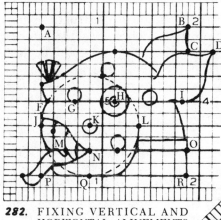

ABRP is a square with center H. JK = KL, KQ = 1/3 BR. BC = BD = KN = MN = NQ = OR = 1/2 KQ. F, G, H, and J are on a horizontal line, and K, N, and Q are on a vertical line.

282. FIXING VERTICAL AND HORIZONTAL ALINEMENTS

283. ◗
OBLIQUE MEASUREMENTS
Fig. 282 suggests that there may be a construction circle (dotted line) with center K, and radius KQ equal to 4 spaces. By tipping the rule, we see that KE also equals 4 spaces. Tipping the rule at a different angle would show that FK is the same length. These measurements prove that Points F, E, L, Q, and J all lie on the circle.

drawing. If we can determine that these lines are vertical or horizontal, so much the better.

Determining Alinements from a Distance. Fig. 281 shows how we can use a pencil to learn what points on the right of our source are in the same vertical line. In this case, we find that B, C, O, and R are in line, but that the bottom of the left ear [I] is a little to the left of the line. With this information, we can draw a construction line to fix the first four points exactly. We can also fix I with a high degree of accuracy by placing it slightly to the left of our construction line.

A transparent ruler is a much better alining device [Fig. 282]. With its aid, we can find horizontal and vertical construction lines at the same time. In addition to the two alinements noted in the caption, there are at least six others which fix points that are marked but some of which are not lettered.

Square and Circular Shapes. Finding imaginary squares and circles that fit the source is a great help in construction. A squared transparent ruler makes this easy. In Fig. 282, for example, there is a square that passes through J, L, and Q, and has one corner at P. The center of this square is at K, which is also the center of the spot on the jaguar's cheek.

This particular square is of little value for construction; but wherever there is a square there must be a circle. Fig. 283 shows how to test whether important points lie on this circle. The test demonstrates that the circle fixes point E and the upper lip as well. This makes it a welcome construction aid in drawing the jaguar's head.

Measurement and alinement have enabled us to fix fourteen points in the source exactly and eight others approximately. This is more than enough to let us make a construction framework on which we can base our drawing.

The method of assigning reference letters in Figs. 280–283 is worth noting. Each letter is assigned to the same point in all four drawings. This means skipping letters in a drawing whenever a point is not lettered, but that is less confusing than indicating the same point by different letters in the same set of drawings.

8

FIXED-LINE CONSTRUCTION

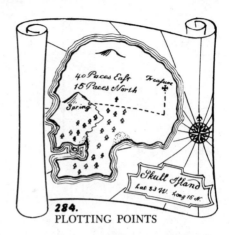

284.
PLOTTING POINTS

I F you ever read a pirate story, you know how to start at one point and locate another with no guide except a set of distances and directions. This is all that fixed-line construction amounts to, whether we use it to represent mechanical objects or to sketch the grids and webs on which free-line drawings are based.

A complex drawing, such as the plan for a factory, is made by applying a few simple processes over and over again. Although the whole job may require many steps, no one step is any more difficult than constructing the route to the treasure on the map in Fig. 284.

PARALLELS AND PERPENDICULARS

Most fixed-line constructions are based on parallels and perpendiculars. For this type of construction, we need a *point of origin* (spring in our pirate map), and two base lines—one for each space-dimension represented in the drawing. These space lines are called *axes*. The *breadth axis* of the map is the line running east and west through the spring, and the *height axis* is an imaginary line running north and south.

Fixing Lines. We saw in Chapter 1 that two points are required to fix a line. But when we work from an origin and axes, we can fix a line parallel to either axis by making only one measurement [Figs. 285 and 286]. A line parallel to one axis is perpendicular to the other.

The axis method of locating lines and points in a drawing combines the principles of construction illustrated in Figs. 9 and 10 with the scale principle described in Chapter 7. If you have already learned to apply these principles, the next few pages are merely a review and extension of your present knowledge.

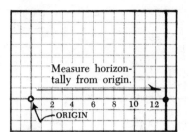

Measure horizontally from origin.

ORIGIN

285. FIXING VERTICAL LINE

These methods are basic in most forms of construction.

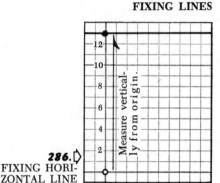

Measure vertically from origin.

286. FIXING HORIZONTAL LINE

Squared paper facilitates fixed-line construction by furnishing us with a ready-made grid. For rough sketches, we do not even need to make measurements; we can simply count squares. This is the normal procedure in drawing graphs. It can also be put to use in making mechanical sketches, as the design for a desk in Fig. 28 demonstrates.

Square-counting is fairly accurate when we deal with half- or quarter-squares, but decimal fractions cannot be represented with any great degree of precision. This is sometimes a handicap in graphing, where the data often contain figures such as 7.2 and 9.3. With noncumulative data, minor deviations from accuracy may create noticeable distortions of the graph, and we must be careful not to let this mislead us.

Plotting Points. As the road map in Fig. 10 illustrates, we can fix any point if we can draw two lines which intersect at that point. When we use the axis method of construction, we need not actually draw the intersecting lines but can use measurements

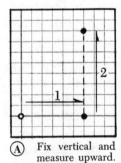

Ⓐ   Fix vertical and measure upward.

These all achieve the same result, but one may be more convenient than the others.

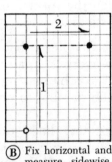

Ⓑ   Fix horizontal and measure sidewise.

FIG. 287.

THREE METHODS FOR LOCATING A POINT (6, 8)

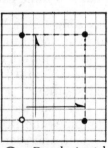

Ⓒ   Draw horizontal and vertical to fix intersection.

Fig. 291]   Fixed-Line Construction   139

instead. Two measurements are required to locate a point that is not on an axis. Fig. 287 shows three methods of doing this. Fixing points is called *plotting*. The same term is sometimes used for the procedure of fixing lines, especially those that appear in graphs.

Where the measurements of a point are written (as they are in the caption of Fig. 287), they are conventionally placed in parentheses with the horizontal measurement first. Thus, "(6,8)" means "6 spaces to the right and 8 spaces upward."

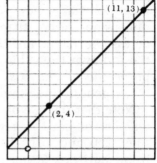

288. LOCATING AN OBLIQUE LINE
Fix two points and then draw the line through them.

Oblique Lines. A line which is not parallel to either axis is described as oblique. Such lines can be located on a run-and-rise basis by plotting two points [Fig. 288]. Note that these points need not be at the beginning and end of the line.

POINT	CUMULATIVE		NONCUMULATIVE	
	RUN	RISE	RUN	RISE
A	0.00	0.00	0.00	0.00
B	37.35	9.11	37.35	9.11
C	61.23	22.21	23.88	13.10
D	75.50	36.38	14.27	14.17
E	106.50	48.45	31.00	12.07

289. TABLE LISTING MEASUREMENTS

FIXED- AND SHIFTING-ORIGINS

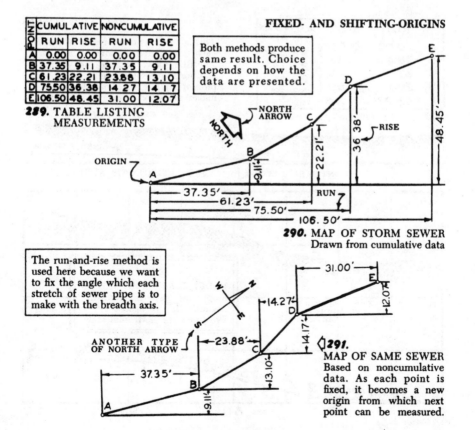

Both methods produce same result. Choice depends on how the data are presented.

290. MAP OF STORM SEWER
Drawn from cumulative data

The run-and-rise method is used here because we want to fix the angle which each stretch of sewer pipe is to make with the breadth axis.

ANOTHER TYPE OF NORTH ARROW

291.
MAP OF SAME SEWER
Based on noncumulative data. As each point is fixed, it becomes a new origin from which next point can be measured.

Shifting Origin. When the data are cumulative, we can use the method in Fig. 288 to produce drawings like Fig. 290. With non-cumulative data, however, it is more convenient to treat each fixed point as a new "origin" and to think of the axes as space dimensions rather than as actual lines [Fig. 291]. Lines drawn across the paper are then said to be *on the breadth axis,* and those drawn from the bottom to the top of the sheet are said to be *on the height axis.* Thinking in terms of axes is particularly convenient in three-dimensional drawing.

Note that the rise of an angle is measured along the height axis whether or not this represents a vertical line in space. Thus, in Figs. 290 and 291, the rises are measured along lines running from southeast to northwest. In Figs. 293 and 294, on the other hand, the rises represent lines which are really vertical in space. At first, you may be confused when the direction of a line on paper differs from the actual direction of the corresponding line in the source. However, once you become accustomed to the idea, you will make the necessary mental adjustment automatically.

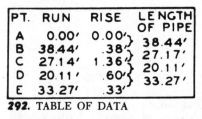

PT.	RUN	RISE	LENGTH OF PIPE
A	0.00'	0.00'	38.44'
B	38.44'	.38'	27.17'
C	27.14'	1.36'	20.11'
D	20.11'	.60'	33.27'
E	33.27'	.33'	

292. TABLE OF DATA

USING TWO SCALES

This is an "Egyptian" section in which each run of pipe is shown in its characteristic view. Because the vertical- and horizontal-scales are the same, the pipe appears to be almost level. That makes the slopes difficult to visualize.

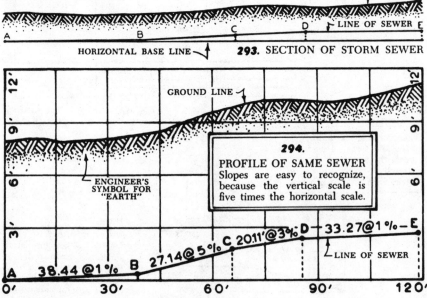

293. SECTION OF STORM SEWER

294.

PROFILE OF SAME SEWER
Slopes are easy to recognize, because the vertical scale is five times the horizontal scale.

Fig. 297]   Fixed-Line Construction   141

Using Two Scale Ratios. If the measurements in one direction are much smaller than those in the other, we can visualize the facts better by employing a different scale ratio for each axis [Fig. 294]. Engineers call this type of drawing a *profile*.

POSITIVE AND NEGATIVE MEASUREMENTS

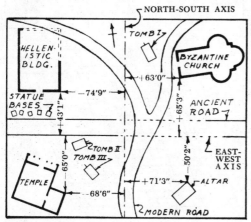

295. ARCHEOLOGICAL MAP
Based on positive and
negative measurements

DATA FROM ACCURACY TEST ON REVERSIBLE TACHOMETER			
COUNTER-CLOCKWISE		CLOCKWISE	
RPM	ERROR %	RPM	ERROR %
100	-18.6	100	-20.0
450	-13.4	300	-16.1
650	- 6.5	700	- 5.2
850	- 1.4	1200	+ 1.6
1050	+ 1.8	1800	+ 5.0
1350	+ 5.0	2350	+ 5.1
2000	+ 5.1	2800	+ 5.2
2500	+ 5.2	3200	+ 6.1
3000	+ 5.1	3500	+ 6.2
3500	+ 5.7	3700	+ 6.3
4000	+ 6.1	4000	+ 6.7

296. TABLE OF DATA
FOR THE GRAPH
SHOWN BELOW

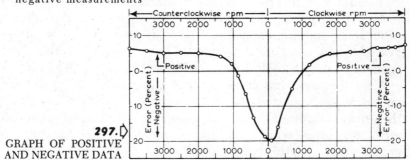

297.
GRAPH OF POSITIVE
AND NEGATIVE DATA

Positive and Negative Measurements. When mapping an area for archeological work [Fig. 295], the axes are normally placed in the middle of the area to be surveyed. This saves time by eliminating the need for long measurements. However, measurements must then be made in four directions instead of only two. The extra directions may mislead us unless we distinguish them by some convention. The standard method is to treat measurements made upward or to the right as *positive* and those made downward or to the left as *negative*.

CARTESIAN CO-ORDINATES. Graphs like that in Fig. 297 are drawn on the same principles as the map in Fig. 295. The pairs

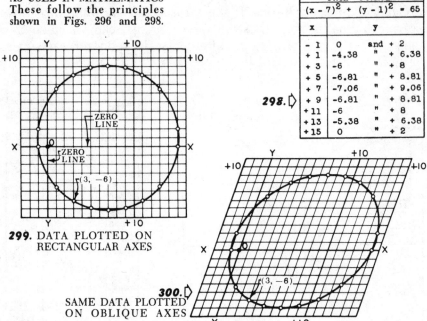

CARTESIAN CO-ORDINATES
AS USED IN MATHEMATICS
These follow the principles
shown in Figs. 296 and 298.

298.

DATA COMPUTED FROM FORMULA		
$(x - 7)^2 + (y - 1)^2 = 65$		
x	y	
− 1	0	and + 2
+ 1	−4.38	" + 6.38
+ 3	−6	" + 8
+ 5	−6.81	" + 8.81
+ 7	−7.06	" + 9.06
+ 9	−6.81	" + 8.81
+ 11	−6	" + 8
+ 13	−5.38	" + 6.38
+ 15	0	" + 2

299. DATA PLOTTED ON
RECTANGULAR AXES

300.
SAME DATA PLOTTED
ON OBLIQUE AXES

of measurements corresponding to each point are called *Cartesian co-ordinates*, after the French mathematician René Descartes.

Anyone following the behavior of the stock market normally plots the point for each day's sales as soon as the returns are available. In most cases, however, we compile all the data at once and arrange them in a table like that in Fig. 296.

After the table has been prepared, the point for each pair of co-ordinates is plotted just like those in the map. The curve is then drawn through the points, either freehand or with the aid of a *French curve* (which is a kind of curved ruler). Squared paper greatly facilitates this type of drawing.

The same procedure was used to plot the circle in Fig. 299, but here the co-ordinates in the table were computed from the mathematical formula. This demands enough knowledge of algebra to solve the equation involved.

To compute the table, we let x in the formula equal -1. Then, $(-1-7)^2 + (y-1)^2 = 65$, and $y^2 = 2y$. Therefore, $y = 0$ or 2. This tells us that there will be two y values—and two points—for each value of x. We can then let $x = 0, 1, 2$, and so on, and determine the corresponding values of y in each case. It is not always necessary to calculate points for each unit; in the example, I have used two-unit intervals.

Mathematicians call the height axis the *Y-axis* and the breadth axis the *X-axis*. Their intersection is the origin, which is usually

142

Fig. 303]   Fixed-Line Construction   143

marked "0." Values of y are measured parallel to the Y-axis, and values of x are measured parallel to the X-axis.

OBLIQUE AXES. It is ordinarily convenient to make the axes perpendicular to each other, but oblique axes can be used [Fig. 300]. In this case, y-values are still plotted parallel to the Y-axis, though they can no longer be measured in a direction perpendicular to the X-axis. Curves drawn on oblique axes are distorted; the circle in Fig. 299 has now become an ellipse.

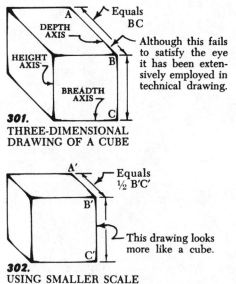

301.
THREE-DIMENSIONAL
DRAWING OF A CUBE

302.
USING SMALLER SCALE
ON THE DEPTH AXIS

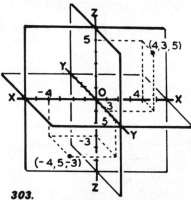

SUPPLYING A THIRD AXIS FOR
THREE-DIMENSIONAL DRAWING

303.
AXES FOR THREE-DIMENSIONAL
RECTANGULAR CO-ORDINATES
AS EMPLOYED IN MATHEMATICS
Note the letters assigned to each axis
and conventions by which positive and
negative co-ordinates are indicated.

Three-Dimensional Drawing. When we show the third dimension, we need a third axis. This is called the *depth axis* [Fig. 301]. It must be oblique; we cannot draw three lines perpendicular to each other on a flat sheet of paper.

If we use the same scale for all three axes, a drawing of a cube looks like Fig. 301. Although the eye refuses to accept this as a cube, the method of drawing is perfectly practical; military engineers used it for centuries. Fortunately, we need not confine ourselves to one scale. The eye is much better satisfied by drawings like Figs. 302 and 303, which use a smaller scale for lines on the depth axis.

Mathematicians call the third axis the Z-*axis*. They have established a convention of representing it as vertical, so that it becomes the height axis [Fig. 303]. Under this convention, the Y-axis becomes the depth axis. A convention which gives the Y-axis one position in two-dimensional drawing and thinking and a different position in three dimensions strikes me as unfortunate, but I have never heard a mathematician complain.

Normally, only individual points, straight lines, and planes are plotted on three axes. Computers, however, can now draw extremely complex three-dimensional surfaces. Although you cannot do this yourself, you should be able to read one intelligently if you find it in a magazine or a book.

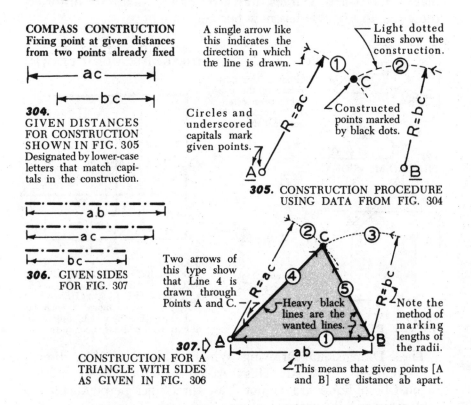

COMPASS CONSTRUCTION
Fixing point at given distances from two points already fixed

304.
GIVEN DISTANCES FOR CONSTRUCTION SHOWN IN FIG. 305 Designated by lower-case letters that match capitals in the construction.

306. GIVEN SIDES FOR FIG. 307

A single arrow like this indicates the direction in which the line is drawn.

Circles and underscored capitals mark given points.

Two arrows of this type show that Line 4 is drawn through Points A and C.

Heavy black lines are the wanted lines.

307. CONSTRUCTION FOR A TRIANGLE WITH SIDES AS GIVEN IN FIG. 306

Light dotted lines show the construction.

Constructed points marked by black dots.

305. CONSTRUCTION PROCEDURE USING DATA FROM FIG. 304

Note the method of marking lengths of the radii.

This means that given points [A and B] are distance ab apart.

CONSTRUCTIONS INVOLVING CURVES

Constructions made with a compass are almost as useful as those based on parallels and perpendiculars.

Fig. 305 illustrates the method of finding a wanted point [C] at given distances ac and bc from two given points [A and B]. A point or line is said to be "given" when it is either provided by the problem or chosen to satisfy the situation.

The second basic method of compass construction is diagrammed in Fig. 308. It locates the wanted point [B] on the given line at the given distance [ab] from Point A. This procedure was used to draw the hexagon in Fig. 309. Here, the line on which the points are fixed is not straight but is a circle. Arcs with radii

Fig. 309]   Fixed-Line Construction   145

equal to AB were drawn with centers at A and B. The intersection of these arcs fixes the center [C], and this made it possible to draw the circle. That intersects Arc 2 at D. From this point on, each corner is fixed by an arc with its center at the previous point. This is another application of the shifting-origin principle illustrated in Fig. 291.

Although construction lines are necessary, they tend to clutter a drawing. In complex cases, the construction lines may develop into a maze that makes the drawing unreadable. We can minimize this tendency by marking only those parts of construction lines that are needed to fix the points. This is illustrated in Figs. 308 and 309. I have drawn the whole lines in order to explain the construction. In your own work, however, you should omit those parts of the lines that are shown in gray and draw only those shown in black. Notice that some lines are reduced to mere *ticks* less than ⅛″ in length.

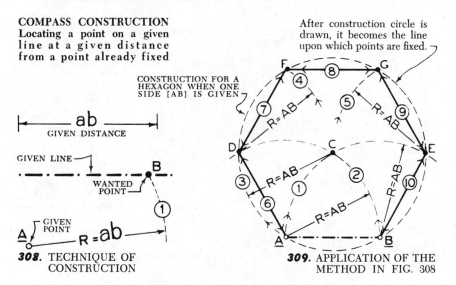

COMPASS CONSTRUCTION
Locating a point on a given line at a given distance from a point already fixed

After construction circle is drawn, it becomes the line upon which points are fixed.

CONSTRUCTION FOR A HEXAGON WHEN ONE SIDE [AB] IS GIVEN

308. TECHNIQUE OF CONSTRUCTION

309. APPLICATION OF THE METHOD IN FIG. 308

Construction Diagrams. The constructions in Figs. 305–325 are useful in so many ways that you may want to memorize them. Moreover, by studying these examples you will become familiar with the methods of construction and learn to solve problems that arise in your own drawing. Many more constructions can be found in other books, and you may invent some yourself. You cannot commit all of these to memory, but it will pay you to make notes of every one. The ability to find the right construction when you need it saves much time. It also enables you to fix points accurately where you would otherwise need to guess.

USEFUL CONSTRUCTIONS MADE WITH A COMPASS

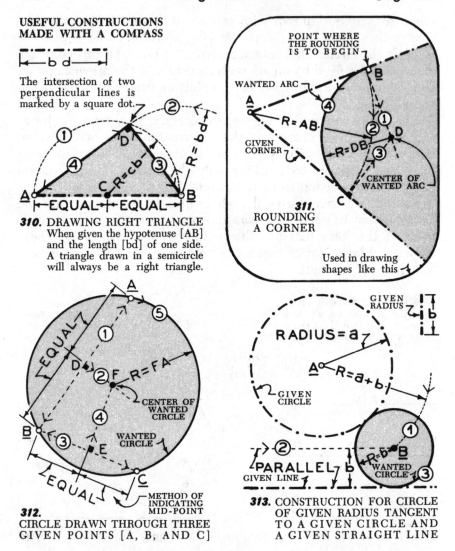

The intersection of two perpendicular lines is marked by a square dot.

310. DRAWING RIGHT TRIANGLE
When given the hypotenuse [AB] and the length [bd] of one side. A triangle drawn in a semicircle will always be a right triangle.

311. ROUNDING A CORNER

Used in drawing shapes like this

312. CIRCLE DRAWN THROUGH THREE GIVEN POINTS [A, B, AND C]

313. CONSTRUCTION FOR CIRCLE OF GIVEN RADIUS TANGENT TO A GIVEN CIRCLE AND A GIVEN STRAIGHT LINE

The usual procedure for making notes of constructions is to draw the diagram and then explain it, step by step, in writing. A much more convenient method is to use conventional symbols that make the diagram explain itself. The examples given here illustrate how this can be done.

As I am limited to black ink, I have used dotted lines of different weights. Your notes will be easier to draw and to read if you use blue pencil for the given lines and points, graphite pencil for the construction lines and points, and red pencil for the wanted lines and points.

Fig. 316]　　　Fixed-Line Construction　　　147

These construction diagrams also provide you with exercises in reading technical drawings. Study the illustrations line by line. The numbers show the order in which the lines are drawn, and the arrow conventions in Figs. 314–316 explain how the position of each line is fixed. Points are lettered in alphabetical order as they are plotted. Learn to recognize the other symbols and note the various ways in which each one is used.

ARROW CONVENTIONS

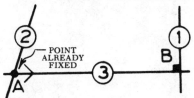

314. Arrow shows that Line 3 is drawn from Point A. Square dot shows that Line 3 is drawn perpendicular to Line 1. Line 3 establishes the position of Point B on Line 1.

If you have already developed some skill in visualization, reading the diagrams should not prove difficult. If it gives you trouble, you can be sure that you need just this sort of exercise before you can hope to either read or make drawings fluently. In case you cannot read a diagram "in your head," cover it with tracing paper and trace the lines in numerical order (see Fig. 198).

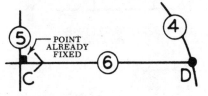

315. Arrow shows that Line 6 is drawn from Point C. Square dot shows that Line 6 is perpendicular to Line 5 at C. Line 6 fixes the position of Point D on Line 4.

After you have studied my diagrams, go through your high-school geometry book and make notes of every construction you find. You can complete all of these exercises in two or three hours. They will teach you more about fixed-line construction than many people know after completing a college course in engineering drawing.

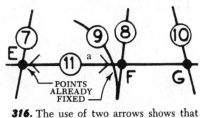

316. The use of two arrows shows that Line 11 is drawn through Points E and F to fix Point G on Line 10. The arrows refer to the nearest dotted points. For example, the arrow marked "a" refers to Point F although Line 9 lies between them.

Ellipses. Next to straight lines and circles, ellipses and elliptical arcs are by far the most useful construction elements. Circles in three-dimensional drawings usually appear as ellipses, and the ellipse itself forms a basic shape for constructing many biological and mechanical subjects. The constructions in Figs. 317–320 show how to draw neat ellipses with a ruler and a French curve or a compass. Figs. 321–324 will prove helpful when you start learning to draw ellipses freehand.

ELLIPSE AXES. An ellipse has two axes, *long* and *short* [Fig. 318]. These are always perpendicular to each other. They may be parallel to the height- and breadth-axes of the drawing as they are in Fig. 317. However, this is by no means a rule; ellipse axes often run in different directions from those of the drawing.

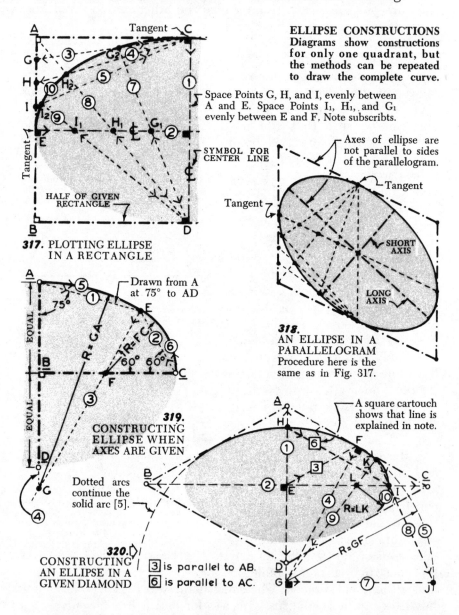

ELLIPSE CONSTRUCTIONS
Diagrams show constructions for only one quadrant, but the methods can be repeated to draw the complete curve.

Space Points G, H, and I, evenly between A and E. Space Points I₁, H₁, and G₁ evenly between E and F. Note subscribts.

SYMBOL FOR CENTER LINE

HALF OF GIVEN RECTANGLE

Tangent

317. PLOTTING ELLIPSE IN A RECTANGLE

Axes of ellipse are not parallel to sides of the parallelogram.

Tangent

Tangent

SHORT AXIS

LONG AXIS

318.
AN ELLIPSE IN A PARALLELOGRAM
Procedure here is the same as in Fig. 317.

Drawn from A at 75° to AD

EQUAL

EQUAL

R=CA

75°

R=FC

60° 60°

319.
CONSTRUCTING ELLIPSE WHEN AXES ARE GIVEN

Dotted arcs continue the solid arc [5].

A square cartouch shows that line is explained in note.

R=LK

R=GF

320.
CONSTRUCTING AN ELLIPSE IN A GIVEN DIAMOND

3 is parallel to AB.
6 is parallel to AC.

APPROXIMATE ELLIPSES. Ellipses are sometimes drawn with special instruments called *ellipsographs*, but these are both ex-

FREEHAND ELLIPSES

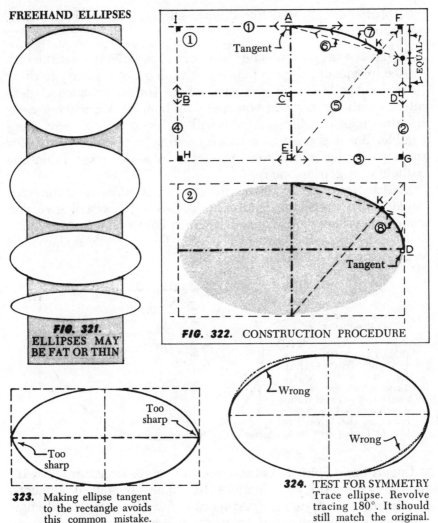

FIG. 321.
ELLIPSES MAY
BE FAT OR THIN

FIG. 322. CONSTRUCTION PROCEDURE

323. Making ellipse tangent
to the rectangle avoids
this common mistake.

324. TEST FOR SYMMETRY
Trace ellipse. Revolve
tracing 180°. It should
still match the original.

pensive and inconvenient. A more handy device is the *ellipse template,* which is a sheet of transparent plastic similar to those used for drawing glyphs but punched with elliptical openings. Unfortunately, each ellipse requires a different opening, and the range of manufactured templates is limited as to both sizes and shapes.

When neither an ellipsograph nor a suitable template is available, we can construct points and then draw the ellipse through these points with a French curve [Figs. 317 and 318]. Less accurate, but quicker ellipses can be produced by using a compass to draw four circular arcs [Figs. 319 and 320]. These compass methods are excellent when the short axis is more than half the length of the long axis. For thinner ellipses, the method in Fig. 317 is much better.

FREEHAND ELLIPSES. The lack of a completely satisfactory device for making ellipses puts a premium on your ability to draw them freehand. This is one case where formal practice is definitely worth the effort. If you spend an hour or two making careful drawings of ellipses, they will never give you any more trouble. But if you attempt an ellipse only when you need it for some particular application, you can draw them for a lifetime without ever getting one right.

Start by looking at a coin or the rim of a tumbler from different angles. Then trace the ellipses in Fig. 321. That will give you some idea of how the shapes vary. Next, construct a few for yourself by the method shown in Fig. 322. This is really a simplified version of the construction in Fig. 317.

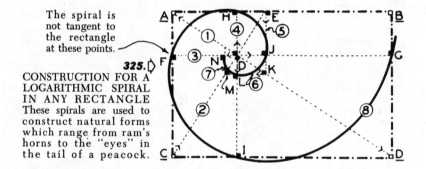

The spiral is not tangent to the rectangle at these points.

325.
CONSTRUCTION FOR A LOGARITHMIC SPIRAL IN ANY RECTANGLE
These spirals are used to construct natural forms which range from ram's horns to the "eyes" in the tail of a peacock.

Logarithmic Spirals. As these are the curves of natural growth, they make useful constructions for many biological subjects. Man-made objects as far apart as cams used in mechanical engineering and the volutes of Ionic capitals on a Greek temple are also based on *logarithmic spirals*.

Fig. 325 illustrates an easy way to construct a logarithmic spiral. Each *quadrant* (quarter) approximates a quadrant of an ellipse so closely that the difference cannot be detected by eye. If you have learned to draw ellipses, you will have no trouble in learning to draw fairly accurate logarithmic spirals with the aid of this construction.

Patterns. In some fields, the same pattern is constructed over and over again but with different measurements in each case. The dressmaker's pattern in Fig. 327 is a typical example.

The customer's measurements are normally recorded on an order blank rather than in a table like Fig. 326, but the effect is the same. Each entry in the table corresponds to a measurement or a radius in the drawing, and every measurement must be known (or estimated) before the pattern can be constructed. Note that the radius HI of Arc 12 is marked with capitals to indicate that it is to be taken from the drawing itself and not from the table of data.

If you make construction diagrams like these, all the material in an elaborate book on pattern-drafting can be condensed into a few pages of notes.

VARIABLE PATTERNS
Each individual pattern must be redrawn to fit different measurements.

Distances between capitals in pattern correspond to the lower-case letters in table.

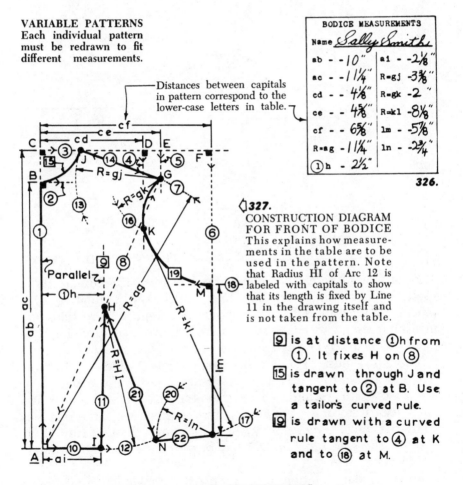

BODICE MEASUREMENTS

Name *Sally Smith*

ab - -	$-10''$	a1 -	$-2\frac{1}{8}''$
ac - -	$-1\frac{1}{4}''$	R=gj	$-3\frac{3}{8}''$
cd - -	$4\frac{1}{8}''$	R=gk	$-2''$
ce - -	$4\frac{5}{8}''$	R=kl	$-8\frac{1}{8}''$
cf - -	$6\frac{5}{8}''$	lm -	$-5\frac{7}{8}''$
R=ag -	$1\frac{1}{4}''$	ln -	$-2\frac{3}{4}''$
①h -	$2\frac{1}{2}''$		

326.

◁**327.**
CONSTRUCTION DIAGRAM FOR FRONT OF BODICE
This explains how measurements in the table are to be used in the pattern. Note that Radius HI of Arc 12 is labeled with capitals to show that its length is fixed by Line 11 in the drawing itself and is not taken from the table.

⑨ is at distance ①h from ①. It fixes H on ⑧

⑮ is drawn through J and tangent to ② at B. Use a tailor's curved rule.

⑲ is drawn with a curved rule tangent to ④ at K and to ⑱ at M.

WEB CONSTRUCTIONS

A point in a web construction is normally fixed by its distance and direction from some other point. We have already used this method in the road map [Fig. 10]. However, when we employ it in more complex constructions, we must adopt a few conventions

similar to those which determine whether Cartesian co-ordinates
are positive or negative. Several different sets of conventions are
possible, but they all produce the same results.

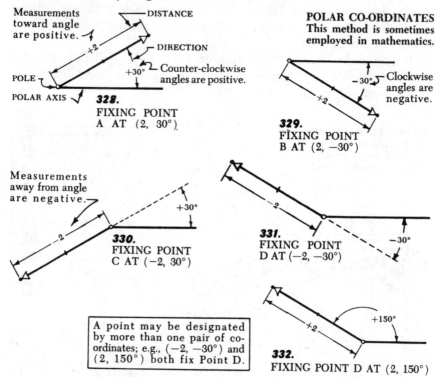

**Measurements
toward angle
are positive.**

DISTANCE

DIRECTION

POLE

POLAR AXIS

+2

+30°

Counter-clockwise
angles are positive.

328.
FIXING POINT
A AT (2, 30°)

POLAR CO-ORDINATES
This method is sometimes
employed in mathematics.

−30°

+2

Clockwise
angles are
negative.

329.
FIXING POINT
B AT (2, −30°)

**Measurements
away from angle
are negative.**

−2

+30°

330.
FIXING POINT
C AT (−2, 30°)

−2

−30°

331.
FIXING POINT
D AT (−2, −30°)

A point may be designated
by more than one pair of co-
ordinates; e.g., (−2, −30°) and
(2, 150°) both fix Point D.

+2

+150°

332.
FIXING POINT D AT (2, 150°)

Polar Co-ordinates. The conventions in Figs. 328–332 are those
used by mathematicians. The data are always cumulative. Distances are measured from the *pole,* and angular directions are
measured from the *polar axis.* Such distances and directions are
known as *polar co-ordinates.*

The drawings explain the conventions which determine
whether a co-ordinate is positive or negative. These conventions
are used with formulas like that for the logarithmic spiral
(Φ = logarithm of r), where Φ is the angle and r is the distance
from the pole. Angles may measure more than a full circle
(360°); the spiral in Fig. 325 has been drawn through an angle
of 545°.

Solving polar equations often involves a knowledge of advanced
mathematics. However, if you can solve such an equation and
prepare a table similar to that in Fig. 298, plotting the corresponding curve is no more difficult than plotting from Cartesian
co-ordinates—except for the fact that measuring angles is fussier
than measuring lengths.

Surveying. The surveys in Figs. 333 and 334 were drawn on the polar principle, but with different conventions. Survey data are always noncumulative, and both lengths and angles are always positive. The base line (polar axis) runs north and south. Angles are measured east or west of north or south. Under these conventions, angles greater than 90° are not needed.

You can compare the two systems by noting that under the surveyor's conventions, Line BC in Fig. 334 is 70.00′ long and runs 85° 9′ 40″ to the east of a north-south line (surveyors call this "South 85° 9′ 40″ East"). Under the mathematical conventions, if you treat Point B as the pole and think of the polar axis as running east and west, the co-ordinates of Point C will be (70.00′, –4°50′20″).

**CONSTRUCTIONS BASED ON
DISTANCES AND DIRECTIONS**

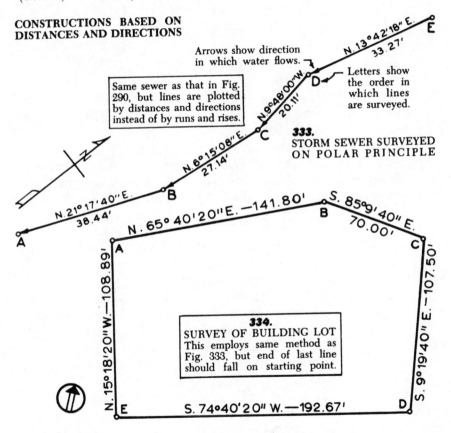

Arrows show direction in which water flows.

Same sewer as that in Fig. 290, but lines are plotted by distances and directions instead of by runs and rises.

Letters show the order in which lines are surveyed.

333.
STORM SEWER SURVEYED
ON POLAR PRINCIPLE

N. 13°42′18″ E. 33.27′

N.9°48′00″W. 20.11′

N. 8°15′08″ E. 27.14′

N. 21°17′40″ E. 38.44′

N. 65° 40′20″ E. —141.80′

S. 85°9′40″ E. 70.00′

N. 15°18′20″ W. —108.89′

S. 9°19′40″ E. —107.50′

334.
SURVEY OF BUILDING LOT
This employs same method as Fig. 333, but end of last line should fall on starting point.

S. 74°40′20″ W. —192.67′

9

CONSTRUCTIONS

FOR FREE-LINE

DRAWINGS

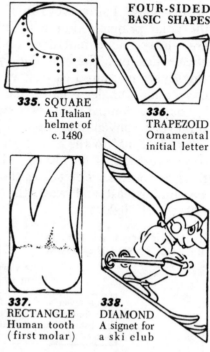

335. SQUARE
An Italian
helmet of
c. 1480

336.
TRAPEZOID
Ornamental
initial letter

337.
RECTANGLE
Human tooth
(first molar)

338.
DIAMOND
A signet for
a ski club

EVEN the most irregular object will fit some simple geometrical shape. The shape should touch the main lines of the object but need not enclose projecting parts [Fig. 335]. If we determine the basic geometrical shape for any particular source and draw this shape as a construction, we fix the proportions of the drawing and also provide ourselves with useful guide lines by which the positions and forms of individual details may be determined.

GRID CONSTRUCTIONS

Any object can be drawn in a rectangle, but some other shape may fit better. Although choosing a basic shape will probably seem difficult at first, experience makes it easy.

The exact number of possible basic shapes depends on how we classify shapes. One person may regard all triangles as a single shape. Another will divide them into several types (see examples on next page). In any case, the number of basic shapes is small. Memorize them and experiment with each one by trying to find objects which fit it.

Curved shapes like those in Figs. 347–349 are particularly helpful in drawing natural forms. They can also be used when sketching streamlined mechanical devices that range from airplanes to vacuum cleaners.

Combining Shapes. Simple shapes may be combined in various ways to produce more complex shapes which will fit the subject better or to make a grid which will fix points within the main

Fig. 346]   Constructions for Free-Line Drawing   155

shape. The principal types of combination are shown in Figs. 350–355.

Deviations. A construction need not fit the source precisely. Thus, in Fig. 350, it is almost as easy to fix Cape Horn a little south and west of Point A as to draw it exactly at the point. Keep your constructions simple and take care of deviations by eye.

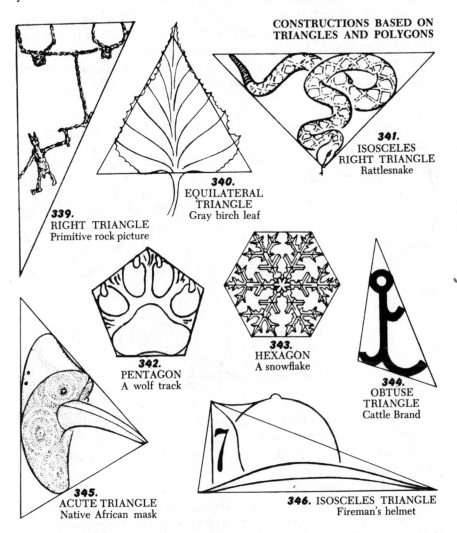

CONSTRUCTIONS BASED ON
TRIANGLES AND POLYGONS

341.
ISOSCELES
RIGHT TRIANGLE
Rattlesnake

340.
EQUILATERAL
TRIANGLE
Gray birch leaf

339.
RIGHT TRIANGLE
Primitive rock picture

343.
HEXAGON
A snowflake

342.
PENTAGON
A wolf track

344.
OBTUSE
TRIANGLE
Cattle Brand

345.
ACUTE TRIANGLE
Native African mask

346. ISOSCELES TRIANGLE
Fireman's helmet

Making the Drawing Match the Construction. Whenever we have no reason to copy a source exactly, it may be better to ignore minor irregularities and adapt the drawing to the construction. This simplifies the drawing and therefore makes it clearer. Furthermore, it usually improves the design.

The design factor is worth noting. When we deliberately set out to create a formal design, we are apt to get the best results by making the drawing fit the construction—even though this involves some distortion. When I designed the little skier in Fig. 338, I used the diamond to determine the length of his nose, the size and angle of his cap, the curve of his scarf, the positions of his poles, and the length of his skis.

I do not suggest that every sketch becomes a pleasing design when forced into a geometrical shape. All I claim is that when you are not trying to achieve complete accuracy or to bring out some irregularity in your source, adjusting your drawing to fit the construction is more likely to improve it than to make it worse.

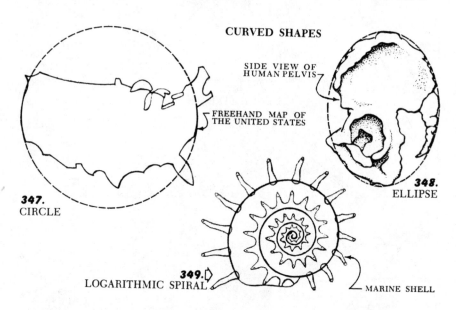

CURVED SHAPES

SIDE VIEW OF
HUMAN PELVIS

FREEHAND MAP OF
THE UNITED STATES

347.
CIRCLE

348.
ELLIPSE

349.
LOGARITHMIC SPIRAL

MARINE SHELL

Memorizing Constructions. If you have occasion to repeat the same drawing over and over again, work out a construction and memorize it. The maps in Figs. 347 and 350 illustrate what can be done along this line.

The use of memorized constructions is largely confined to drawings made for notes or to explain points in lectures. As speed is normally more important than accuracy for these purposes, both construction and drawing should be kept extremely simple.

Locating Details by Construction. The examples already given will probably meet most of your needs. However, when some particular drawing taxes your skill, or when you want to be especially accurate, you can carry construction much further.

Fig. 355]   Constructions for Free-Line Drawing   157

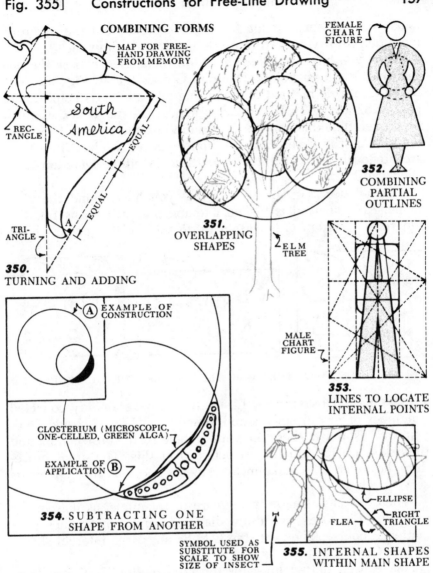

COMBINING FORMS

MAP FOR FREE-HAND DRAWING FROM MEMORY

South America

REC-TANGLE

TRI-ANGLE

EQUAL

EQUAL

EQUAL

A

350.
TURNING AND ADDING

351.
OVERLAPPING
SHAPES

ELM
TREE

FEMALE
CHART
FIGURE

352.
COMBINING
PARTIAL
OUTLINES

MALE
CHART
FIGURE

353.
LINES TO LOCATE
INTERNAL POINTS

A EXAMPLE OF
CONSTRUCTION

CLOSTERIUM (MICROSCOPIC,
ONE-CELLED, GREEN ALGA)

EXAMPLE OF B
APPLICATION

354. SUBTRACTING ONE
SHAPE FROM ANOTHER

SYMBOL USED AS
SUBSTITUTE FOR
SCALE TO SHOW
SIZE OF INSECT

FLEA

ELLIPSE

RIGHT
TRIANGLE

355. INTERNAL SHAPES
WITHIN MAIN SHAPE

Choosing Basic Shapes. If you recognize a definite shape (such as a triangle or a circle) in your source, you should probably use it as your basic shape. In any case, you can always fall back on a rectangular shape. You may even prefer a rectangle because it permits you to fix details by drawing diagonals and center lines. This is often an important advantage. Thus, the dotted line in Diagram A, Fig. 356, shows that the jaguar's head could be constructed in half of an upright ellipse. Nevertheless, the square in Diagram C will fix many more points. The half-ellipse would make a better construction for a quick sketch, but the square is more helpful if you need to make an accurate drawing.

When you have a choice of several rectangles, choose the one that fixes the most points. Diagram C does this in Fig. 356. The transparent-rule method of measuring and alining is helpful here [Figs. 282 and 283]. If you can visualize the diagonals, so much the better. The diagonals in Diagram C fix the center of the eye, the spot on the cheek, and the upper end of the jaw line. They are obviously more helpful than those in either Diagram A or Diagram B.

It is not necessary to be sure that you have found the ideal shape. All you need is to find a shape that will be useful. The square in Diagram C is certain to do this for the jaguar's head.

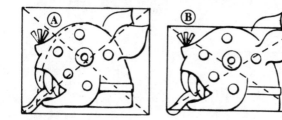 

FIG. 356. SELECTING   THE   BASIC   RECTANGLE   FOR A CONSTRUCTION

PRINCIPAL CONSTRUCTION LINES. If you have already collected a number of measurements and alinements [Figs. 282 and 283], you can establish these in your geometrical construction and then sketch a faint-line construction over this. The usual procedure, however, is to make measurements and look for alinements as we go along.

When our basic shape is a square or rectangle, as it is in the example [Fig. 358], we draw diagonals and center lines as a matter of course. The next step is to fix any large internal shape, such as Circle 10.

I have used dotted lines for the construction, but very faint pencil lines are more satisfactory in practice. Whenever you locate part of the subject, indicate it with heavier (but still faint) lines. I have done this with several lines in Figs. 358 and 359.

If the only measuring and alining tool available is a pencil, the work will be more difficult and less exact—and you may not be able to find so many construction lines. Even in that case, however, you should have no real trouble in making a construction which is adequate for most purposes.

LOCATING MINOR DETAILS. Fig. 359 demonstrates that we can use construction to fix almost every point in a drawing. You will

Basic shape is a square.

357. SOURCE

358. CONSTRUCTION

KEY

STRAIGHT LINES – – – – –
CIRCULAR ARCS ————
ELLIPTICAL ARCS — · · — · · ··
FREE LINES ···················

359. CONSTRUCTION EXTENDED TO INCLUDE MINOR DETAILS

360. GEOMETRICAL LINES IN THE DRAWING ITSELF

rarely need to go to such lengths. But if you have difficulty with some part of your faint-line construction, you may want to locate a few key points in the trouble area.

Geometrical Lines in the Drawing. No matter how far you carry the actual construction, there will always be lines that must be added freehand. This is easier when you visualize the lines in geometrical terms instead of regarding them as irregular forms [Fig. 360]. Nothing is gained by carrying this to extremes. I could have visualized the tips of the teeth as semicircles; actually I merely rounded them off.

As you acquire skill, you will have less and less need to analyze lines geometrically. Nevertheless, thinking of them in this way is a real help while you are learning. It lets you use your brain instead of depending entirely on your eye, and it will do much to strengthen your powers of visualization.

Microscopic Subjects. Expert microscopists take advantage of the fact that we have binocular vision. Place enough magazines beside the instrument to bring the top of the pile about 10″ below the level of the eyepiece. Lay your drawing paper on this. Look in the microscope with your left eye and look at the paper and your pencil with your right eye. If you do *not* focus on either one, your mind will combine the source and the tip of the pencil into a single image. You can then trace the source as though you were working on tracing paper laid over a photograph. This sort of

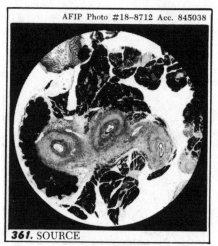

AFIP Photo #18–8712 Acc. 845038

361. SOURCE

Compare shaded details in Steps 1 and 2 with the corresponding areas in the source [Fig. 361].

FIG. 362.

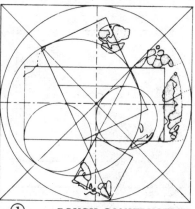

DRAWING WITH MICROSCOPE
All proportions, alinements, and shapes must be estimated by eye.

① ROUGH CONSTRUCTION
Begin with a circle to represent field of microscope. Add square, diagonals, and center lines. Then draw geometric shapes to fix main elements of sketch.

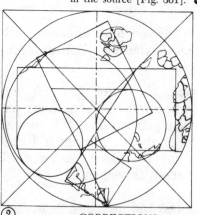

② CORRECTIONS
Compare rough construction with source and make corrections. This is easier when the drawing shows only simple shapes and there are no details to mislead the eye.

CONSTRUCTION IN STEP 2

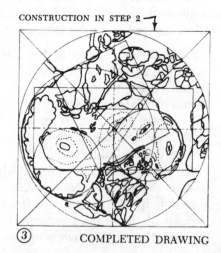

③ COMPLETED DRAWING

Fig. 364]   Constructions for Free-Line Drawings   161

tracing requires a definite knack. If you cannot master it, or if you use a microscope only on rare occasions, you can fall back on construction [Fig. 362].

After the internal shapes have been constructed, you will find that they act as a check on each other. When one shape is too large, another will be crowded; when one is too small, those around it will have too much room. This makes blunders stand out, as you can see by comparing Step 1, Fig. 362, with Fig. 361. The mistakes have been corrected in Step 2, Fig. 362. Once these steps are completed, adding details gives little trouble [Step 3].

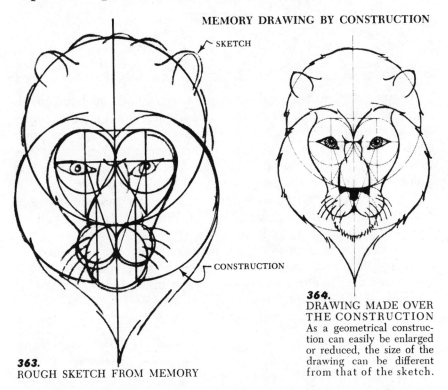

MEMORY DRAWING BY CONSTRUCTION

SKETCH

CONSTRUCTION

363.
ROUGH SKETCH FROM MEMORY

364.
DRAWING MADE OVER THE CONSTRUCTION
As a geometrical construction can easily be enlarged or reduced, the size of the drawing can be different from that of the sketch.

Construction from Memory. The difficulty in drawing from memory is that we rarely recall all the facts we need. Construction here serves as a memory aid. When I drew the lion's head in Figs. 363 and 364, I began by making a crude sketch. This was far from accurate, but it enabled me to visualize the problem. I then placed tracing paper over my sketch and worked out a construction to fix the proportions.

Ordinarily, the sizes and positions of the forms would be located by eye, but I have established these geometrically to demonstrate that a rigidly mechanical construction can be made

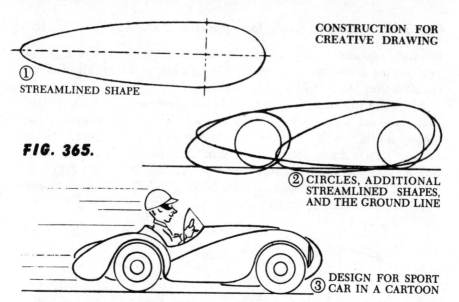

① STREAMLINED SHAPE

FIG. 365.

② CIRCLES, ADDITIONAL
STREAMLINED SHAPES,
AND THE GROUND LINE

③ DESIGN FOR SPORT
CAR IN A CARTOON

to fit even the most irregular natural forms. You can learn much about construction by working out how each line in the example was drawn. The eye circles and the jaw circle all have the same radius. Take this as given and draw the construction without making any measurements. The trick lies chiefly in locating the points that are used as centers for the circles and arcs.

Fig. 364 shows the finished head drawn over the construction. I do not know what a zoologist would think of this, but I believe that anyone can recognize it as a lion.

The success of a memory construction obviously depends on how complete and accurate your memory is. If you have only a vague recollection of the source, you cannot hope to draw it correctly. Even in such cases, you will do much better with construction than you could without it.

Construction for Design. When we want to design something new, construction not only aids drawing but does much to improve the design itself. I know nothing about sports cars, but a book of photographs informed me that many of them are composed of streamlined ovals made up of two half-ellipses [Step 1, Fig. 365]. With this as a basis, the rest was easy. I had to experiment with ovals of various sizes and shapes before I found ones that would fit together and please the eye. Nevertheless, the fact that I succeeded in producing a fairly satisfactory cartoon with no previous knowledge of sports cars shows how far construction can carry us. Of course, if I had wanted to design an actual car, I would have required a wide background of engineering experience. But when we merely wish to design a drawing, a few data and a knowledge of construction are all we need.

Fig. 368]   Constructions for Free-Line Drawings   163

Learning Construction. The quickest way to learn construction is by laying tracing paper over a picture and experimenting with various shapes and lines. Use ruler, compass, and dividers freely. When the construction is complete, place the tracing paper on a white sheet and make your final drawing over the construction —using the source as a model. You will gain a clearer idea of what you are doing if you sketch the construction in colored pencil and employ lead pencil for the drawing itself. I get a good deal of fun out of this sort of construction, and I know of nothing that can do more to improve your skill in drawing.

GRIDS VS. WEBS FOR FIGURE CONSTRUCTION

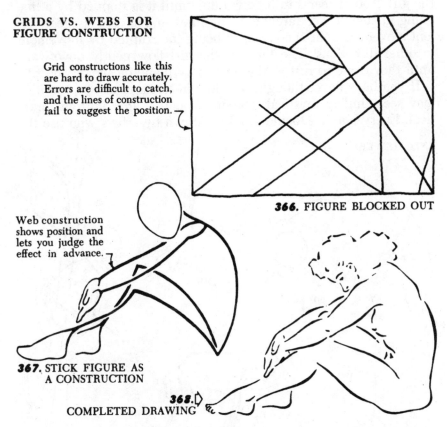

Grid constructions like this are hard to draw accurately. Errors are difficult to catch, and the lines of construction fail to suggest the position.

366. FIGURE BLOCKED OUT

Web construction shows position and lets you judge the effect in advance.

367. STICK FIGURE AS A CONSTRUCTION

368. COMPLETED DRAWING

WEB CONSTRUCTIONS

Grid constructions are best suited to objects that are fairly compact. Branching forms, such as human figures, animals, and trees can be constructed more effectively on webs.

Human Figures. Many artists *block out* a figure with a grid like that in Fig. 366. Unfortunately, this gives no hint as to the nature of the object. Blocking out is difficult to do accurately because even major mistakes in proportion are easily overlooked. Its most serious fault, however, is the fact that it fails to show the *action* of the figure.

"Action," in this sense, is a technical term used by artists to describe the feeling of movement suggested by the lines themselves. It does not imply that the object is shown in motion. A pine tree has action, but this is entirely different from the action of a weeping willow. The girl in Fig. 368 also has action although she is completely relaxed. Even the grid in Fig. 366 has action. Unfortunately, this action bears no resemblance to the action of the girl. Action seems to follow a line until it is stopped by a line going in some other direction. The lines in Fig. 366 suggest violent movement that is constantly being interrupted by movement in other directions. The lines of the girl flow gently downward until they come to rest at the imaginary plane on which she sits.

If you have never thought of a line in terms of action, the idea may seem highly mystical. I assure you that it is entirely practical. Every line in Donald Duck is drawn by artists who use the

ANIMAL WEBS

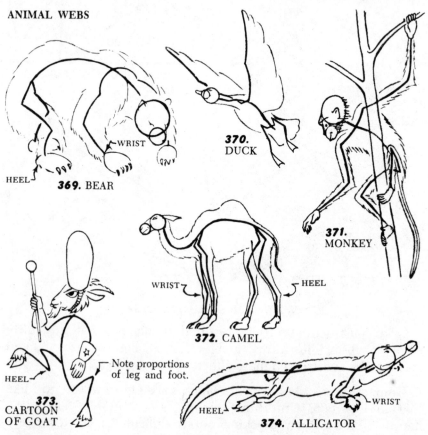

WRIST

HEEL

369. BEAR

370. DUCK

371. MONKEY

WRIST

HEEL

372. CAMEL

HEEL

— Note proportions of leg and foot.

373. CARTOON OF GOAT

HEEL

WRIST

374. ALLIGATOR

Fig. 377]   Constructions for Free-Line Drawings   165

idea of action in the same matter-of-fact way that a bookkeeper uses the idea of addition.

The stick figure in Fig. 367 is a web. It is not open to any of the objections that can be urged against the grid and is a much better type of construction for use in figure drawing. The action of Fig. 367 cannot be identical with that of Fig. 368 because any change in a line necessarily changes the action. Nevertheless, the action of the two figures is so much alike that Fig. 367 is an excellent basic construction for Fig. 368.

At first, you may find that the advantages of webs are offset by the fact that drawing a web normally requires more experience than drawing a grid. Webs have no geometrical shape to serve as a guide. The points between which the lines run are not clearly marked in the source but must be visualized mentally. Also, many webs include curved lines. As these curves are often subtle, you are not likely to get them exactly right until you have had some experience in sketching webs. This is one reason why I recommend studying stick-figure drawing by means of tracing.

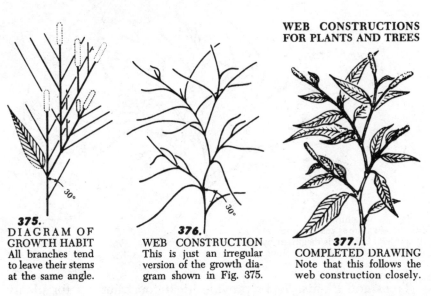

WEB CONSTRUCTIONS FOR PLANTS AND TREES

375.
DIAGRAM OF GROWTH HABIT
All branches tend to leave their stems at the same angle.

376.
WEB CONSTRUCTION
This is just an irregular version of the growth diagram shown in Fig. 375.

377.
COMPLETED DRAWING
Note that this follows the web construction closely.

Animals. Any four-limbed animal can be constructed around the standard web shown in Figs. 369–374. The construction for an alligator has different proportions from that for a camel; the curves in the camel's spine are more pronounced, and its limbs do not make such sharp angles. In spite of these differences, the general structure of the web is the same in both cases.

Study animal webs with the aid of tracing. Choose profile poses for your first experiments. Any position that shows the animal from an angle presents problems that will become easier to handle after you have studied three-dimensional drawing.

Pay especial attention to the proportions of the legs. In alligators, bears, and elephants, the leg is drawn with two lines, and the foot is roughly oval. In camels, horses, cats, and goats, the animal walks on its toes. This brings the "heel" and "wrist" a third of the way up the leg or even higher. Three lines must be used, and the hind legs have a characteristic "Z" shape.

Adding the head, hands, and feet turns a human-figure web into a stick figure—which is a drawing in its own right. Unfortunately, this does not apply to animal webs except in the case of monkeys. Humanized cartoon animals, however, make excellent stick figures if the hind legs are given the shape appropriate to the animal [goat in Fig. 373]. Note that the forelegs are treated like human arms.

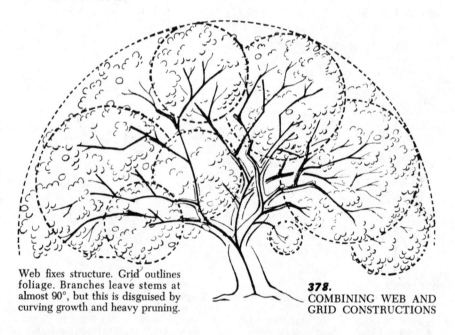

Web fixes structure. Grid outlines foliage. Branches leave stems at almost 90°, but this is disguised by curving growth and heavy pruning.

378.
COMBINING WEB AND GRID CONSTRUCTIONS

Trees and Plants. Webs provide ideal constructions for plants and trees because they bring out the characteristic growth habits of the species. The same pattern is repeated over and over again from the stem or trunk to the tips of the leaves [Fig. 375]. The branch angle tends to be regular for any given species. This regularity is obscured when we sketch from life; some angles are warped by accidents of growth, and many of them may be disguised by the effects of perspective. In spite of this, if you once work out the growth pattern of a plant or tree, you will find that

Fig. 379]   Constructions for Free-Line Drawings   167

it is a great help in drawing a construction web [Fig. 376]. After the web has been drawn, you should not have much difficulty in drawing the plant or tree itself [Fig. 377].

When sketching plants and trees, it is usually convenient to construct both a web and a grid [Fig. 378]. The grid fixes the over-all shape, and the web provides a skeleton for the branches. Unless you get both shape and skeleton right, the drawing is likely to seem formless and will not resemble the source.

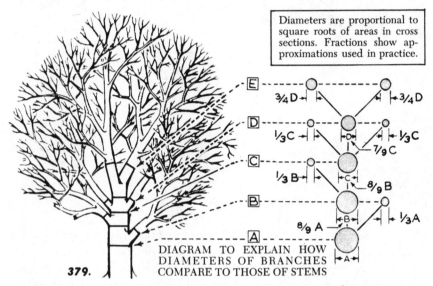

Diameters are proportional to square roots of areas in cross sections. Fractions show approximations used in practice.

DIAGRAM TO EXPLAIN HOW DIAMETERS OF BRANCHES COMPARE TO THOSE OF STEMS

379.

Fig. 379 illustrates an easy method of estimating the thicknesses of the various branches. The combined thickness of all the parts is approximately uniform from the ground to the tips of the twigs. However, the tree is three-dimensional, and we draw it in two dimensions. This means that the thickness of any part is proportional to the square root of its area in cross section.

Calculating square roots is laborious, but you can approximate the results by a few rules of thumb. When a stem splits into two equal branches, each branch is roughly three-quarters the width of the stem [Level E in Fig. 379]. When there are two small branches, each one-third the width of the stem below the crotch, the stem above the crotch will be seven-ninths the width of the lower stem [Level D]. After a little practice with these rules, you will learn to apply them without thinking.

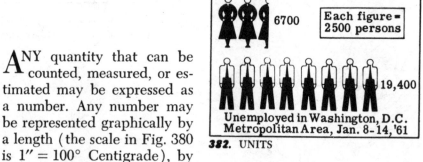

10

VISUALIZING NUMERICAL DATA

380. LENGTH   **381.** ANGLES

6700   Each figure = 2500 persons

19,400

Unemployed in Washington, D.C. Metropolitan Area, Jan. 8-14, '61

382. UNITS

ANY quantity that can be counted, measured, or estimated may be expressed as a number. Any number may be represented graphically by a length (the scale in Fig. 380 is $1'' = 100°$ Centigrade), by an angle (in Fig. 381, $360° = 12$ hours or 60 minutes), or by a set of glyphs (each figure in Fig. 382 represents 2500 persons). We can also represent numbers by areas. This should be avoided when possible as it is apt to be misleading (see charts showing quantities of paper on p. 126), but it is sometimes necessary.

DATAGRAMS

The graphic representation of numbers is employed primarily to translate numerical tables into charts, graphs, and statistical maps—collectively known as *datagrams*.

Uses. Numerical tables compress large, and even enormous, amounts of data into a small space. Datagrams go further and provide a bird's-eye view of these data. They permit the observer to take in the situation at a glance instead of having to dig out the facts, number by number, from a table. That is a major virtue. The datagram catches the eye and invites inspection, whereas few people will study a table if they can avoid it. More important still, the clarity of a datagram brings out many facts which a numerical table conceals. This is so true that most scientists and economists regard datagrams as essential tools for thought. If you translate the numerical tables you meet in your work into datagrams, you will gain new insight from nearly every one.

Fig. 382]   Visualizing Numerical Data   169

Rendering. Drawing datagrams presents no problem unless you want to get fancy and make *pictograms* like Fig. 382. Rough and semifinished charts and graphs can be sketched quickly on squared paper. The best way to make datagrams for display is to use the special *statistical tape* sold for the purpose. This is similar to cellophane tape but comes in a wide range of widths and colors.

Limitations. Unfortunately, these advantages are partially off-set by a serious weakness. The self-correcting tendency that is characteristic of most drawings is virtually lacking in datagrams. If Fig. 382 had shown 19,400 unemployed women against 6700 unemployed men, the error might be sufficiently gross to suggest that something was wrong. However, mistakes small enough to be plausible are rarely disclosed by a chart. Graphs like Fig. 297 may be more revealing. Presumably, the true curve for a tachometer is smooth. Ours shows a jog at 3200 clockwise rpm. Even such a minor inaccuracy is immediately obvious from the curve, but it would have gone unnoticed in a careful study of the table in Fig. 296. Nevertheless, such cases are exceptions. Under ordinary circumstances, a mistake that escapes notice in the table will not be revealed by the datagram. Furthermore, if a table is incorrectly translated, the datagram may introduce serious mistakes of its own. Datagrams are wonderful tools, but we cannot afford to take them for granted.

This lack of a self-correcting tendency need not be judged too harshly. Datagrams may suffer by comparison with other types of practical drawing, but they are at least as effective on that score as either language or mathematics. However, datagrams do have one fault which is all their own. Their apparent simplicity is deceptive. Although they look easy to read, this is an illusion. It is easy to read what they say, but we must interpret their statements before we can learn what they mean.

The pictogram in Fig. 382 seems obvious; 19,400 men and 6700 women in the Washington area were unemployed during the week of January 8th, 1961. However, the local papers for that period carried 75,559 lines of help-wanted ads and only 2847 lines of situations-wanted ads. This suggests that the demand for labor greatly exceeded the supply and raises a suspicion that "unemployed" really means "receiving relief." If so, the figures in the pictogram should be corrected by subtracting all those who were on relief to avoid work and by adding those who tried unsuccessfully to obtain jobs but were being supported by friends or relatives.

Even if "unemployed" really means "unable to obtain work," we still need a practical test to distinguish the loafers from the unfortunates. We must also have some adequate means of knowing whether the clerks who collected the data actually applied the test in a competent and conscientious manner.

This is only the beginning. The whole group of items covered by a set of statistics is called the *population*, regardless of whether these items are people, sunspots, or cases of erysipelas. When a population is large, it is rarely practical to count every item, and statisticians often rely on a *sample*. Books on statistics devote long chapters to the dangers and difficulties of sampling. Their conclusions can be summed up in three sentences: Under favorable conditions, sampling is an invaluable tool. Under unfavorable conditions, its value ranges from "better than nothing" to "highly deceptive." Under any conditions, it should be done and evaluated only by an expert.

The risk of being misled is much larger in the datagrams that you read than in those you make for yourself—especially if you collect your own data. Thus, you can hardly go wrong with an *achievement chart* like Fig. 383.

SEPT . 27	OCT . 4	OCT . 11	OCT . 18	NOV . 1	NOV . 8
76	165		100	128	79
76		241	341	469	548

383. AN ACHIEVEMENT CHART TO KEEP RECORD OF WORK ACCOMPLISHED
Light lines show the work done during each period. Heavy lines show work completed to date. The entries may represent items turned out by a factory that has a quota of 100 articles per week, the value of the orders secured by a sales force, or the pages of a student's outside reading. When quotas are fixed, each space equals 100% of the quota for the period. When quotas are not fixed, each space acts as a scale unit representing some convenient round number of items—such as 5, 50, 100, or 1000.

The *range chart* in Fig. 384 is another example of a datagram which is both useful and foolproof. Like organization charts, range charts can be used to survey a subject before starting a formal study of it. I chose History of Music as an example because it is a field about which I know almost nothing. My "research" consisted in turning to "Music" in the *Encyclopaedia Britannica*. There I found a page showing portraits of twenty famous composers. The captions supplied their names, nationalities, and dates. The job took less than an hour. In spite of this, it gave me a bird's-eye view of the whole subject. If I had continued my studies, I would have added more composers to the chart as I went along. This would have furnished a clear picture of how the new facts fitted in with the previous ones, and it

Fig. 384]   Visualizing Numerical Data   171

would have provided an automatic review of everything that I had already learned. If you survey any new subject with a range chart before you begin to study it and then correct the chart whenever you acquire new information, you will find that you learn twice as much with half the effort.

As range- and organization-charts present the same facts from different angles, it often pays to make both. Range charts are not restricted to chronological material. They can be used to survey any field in which the individual items have definite ranges on some numerical scale.

There is no sure test to distinguish a safe datagram from a graphic booby trap like Fig. 382, but the following rules are reliable as far as they go:

1. Remember that a datagram does not represent facts; it represents a numerical table—which may or may not represent facts.

2. Be sure you know the definitions of the population and of any classes into which it may be divided.

3. Be sure you know what tests were used to apply these definitions; satisfy yourself that the tests were adequate, and that they were applied in an effective manner.

4. Learn whether the data represent a full count or a sample; if they represent a sample, view them with suspicion unless an expert in the field can give you assurance that the sampling technique was valid.

5. If the data have been subjected to any statistical treatment, such as taking averages, be sure you know what the treatment was and what effect it has had.

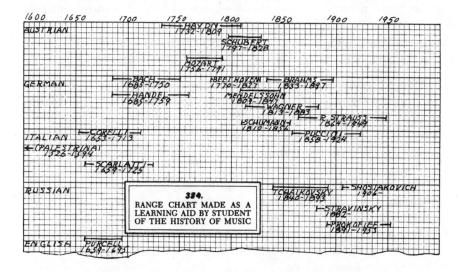

384.
RANGE CHART MADE AS A
LEARNING AID BY STUDENT
OF THE HISTORY OF MUSIC

6. The more you learn about statistics the less risk you run of being misled by a statistical datagram.

I have tried to make my explanations as simple as possible. But if I made the explanations simpler than the facts, I would do you more harm than good. The interpretation of datagrams is not easy and can never be made so. If you are not prepared to study the subject carefully, you may skip this chapter and the next without missing anything you need to understand the rest of the book. But, in that case, do not put much weight on your interpretation of any datagrams you meet in textbooks or periodicals.

TYPES OF NUMERICAL DATA

At least 90 percent of all data suitable for presentation in datagrams can be divided into three main classes. Each class has special types of datagrams which are particularly adapted to bringing out the nature of that class of data.

Types of Numerical Data—A. One-Scale Data

When a table shows only one set of numerical data, there can be only one scale [Fig. 386]. If the tabs form a list but *not* a sequence, the items can be arranged in any order. The proper way to represent such data is with a *bar chart* [Fig. 386] or a *columnar chart* [Fig. 387]. There is no real difference between these types. The choice depends partly on convenience; long tabs fit better on a bar chart. Natural symbolism should also be considered: columns suggest thermometers and are appropriate for charting temperatures; bars are better fitted to represent such things as speeds and distances.

In their normal forms, these charts are used almost entirely for communication and have little value as aids to thought. But observe that achievement charts and range charts are essentially specialized bar charts, and both are excellent working tools.

Chart Layout. *Bars and columns duplicate the data and are not substitutes for them.* Every word and number in the table should appear on the chart; compare Figs. 385 and 386. We may, however, make formal changes. Thus, the table in Fig. 385 gives the items in millions of dollars, whereas Fig. 386 shows a scale of billions.

The scale should always be plainly marked along the margins, but only the major divisions are represented by lines across the chart. Minor scale divisions are indicated by ticks [Fig. 386].

The sole function of a bar- or columnar-chart is to present a table in visual form. If the zero line is omitted [Fig. 388] or if

Fig. 389]   Visualizing Numerical Data   173

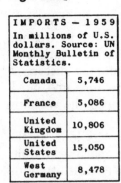

IMPORTS — 1959 In millions of U.S. dollars. Source: UN Monthly Bulletin of Statistics.	
Canada	5,746
France	5,086
United Kingdom	10,806
United States	15,050
West Germany	8,478

385. TABLE WITH BUT A SINGLE DATA COLUMN The title of the table also serves as the tab for the data column.

BAR AND COLUMNAR CHARTS
These serve the same purposes. However, bars run horizontally, whereas columns run vertically.

NOTE

TABS   Billions of U.S.A. dollars   SCALE
          0   5   10   15

United States 15.05
United Kingdom ...... 10.81   BARS
West Germany .... 8.48   DATA
Canada ..... 5.75   TITLE
France ... 5.09   IMPORTS·1959
                    TICKS

0   5   10   15
Source: UN Monthly Bulletin of Statistics

386. CORRECTLY DRAWN BAR CHART

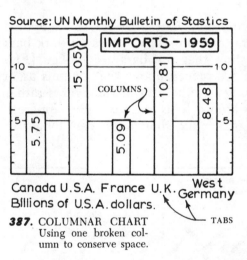

Source: UN Monthly Bulletin of Stastics

IMPORTS — 1959

COLUMNS

Canada U.S.A. France U.K. West Germany
Billions of U.S.A. dollars.

387. COLUMNAR CHART
Using one broken column to conserve space.   TABS

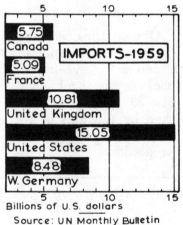

IMPORTS-1959

5.75 Canada
5.09 France
10.81 United Kingdom
15.05 United States
8.48 W. Germany

5   10   15
Billions of U.S. dollars
Source: UN Monthly Bulletin of Statistics

388. FAULTY BAR CHART
Zero line omitted, data placed on breaks in bars.

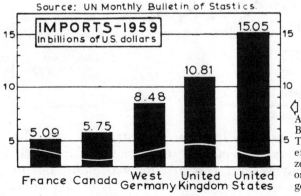

Source: UN Monthly Bulletin of Stastics.

IMPORTS-1959
In billions of U.S. dollars

5.09   5.75   8.48   10.81   15.05

France Canada West Germany United Kingdom United States

389.
A CHART SHOWING BROKEN COLUMNS This creates the same effect as omitting the zero line. Putting data on tops of columns suggests false proportions.

the bars or columns are broken [Fig. 389], the chart completely fails to serve this function. On the contrary, the visual impression suggests a different set of facts by exaggerating the variations between the items. Note that breaking the columns distorts a chart to exactly the same degree as omitting the zero line. Such charts warn us that they are meaningless if we heed the warning and misleading if we fail to heed it.

When one bar or column is more than twice as long as the next longest, it may be broken. This either saves space or permits us to use a larger scale. The mere fact of the break calls attention to the unusual length. On the other hand, when the longest bar or column is less than twice the length of the second one, the use of a break creates an exaggerated impression of length and is therefore misleading. This is the case in Fig. 387.

Some published charts have no scale at all. That may not be proof of an attempt to deceive. But if you put faith in such a chart, you deserve what you get.

Optical Illusions. Avoid anything that may create an optical illusion. For example, placing data in white spaces on dark bars deceives the eye by suggesting that the bars are broken [Fig. 388]. Again, if tabs or data are placed above the columns as in Fig. 389, the eye tends to judge by the tops of the figures rather than by the tops of the columns. This increases the apparent length of each column and makes the short ones seem longer in proportion.

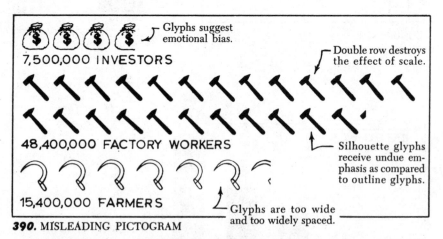

390. MISLEADING PICTOGRAM

Pictograms. These are really bar charts decorated to catch the eye. Any attempt to make them more than that is illegitimate. Theoretically, each glyph represents a number of units. But in practice, what matters is the length of the row. Do not try to be more accurate than half a glyph. Although each glyph in Fig. 382 represents 2500 persons, 6700 women are represented by 2½ glyphs, not by 2.68 glyphs.

All glyphs should be the same width, and they should aline vertically as well as horizontally. The use of broad glyphs or wide spacing to extend a row raises grave suspicion of dishonesty ["Farmers" in Fig. 390].

Arranging glyphs in a double row to represent an exceptionally large item makes it impossible for the eye to compare items. It, therefore, defeats the purpose of the chart. About all we can read from Fig. 390 is that there are a lot more factory workers than there are investors and farmers combined.

Beware of glyphs that may bias the observer. Using money bags for "Investors," hammers for "Factory Workers," and sickles for "Farmers" may lead some observers to regard investors as rich and greedy and cause others to think of factory workers and

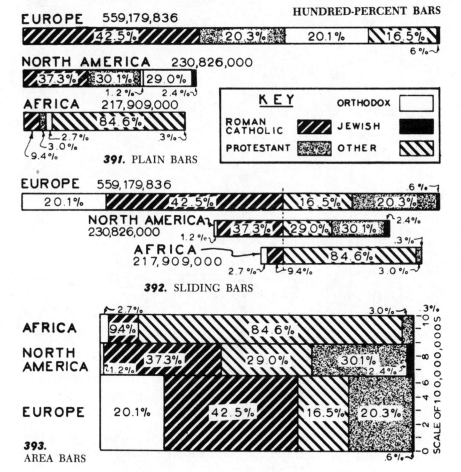

HUNDRED-PERCENT BARS

EUROPE   559,179,836

42.5%   20.3%   20.1%   16.5%   6%

NORTH AMERICA   230,826,000

37.3%   30.1%   29.0%   1.2%   2.4%

AFRICA   217,909,000

2.7%   84.6%   3%   3.0%   9.4%

KEY

ROMAN CATHOLIC   JEWISH   PROTESTANT   OTHER   ORTHODOX

391. PLAIN BARS

EUROPE   559,179,836   .6%

20.1%   42.5%   16.5%   20.3%

NORTH AMERICA   230,826,000   1.2%   37.3%   29.0%   30.1%   2.4%

AFRICA   217,909,000   .3%   84.6%   2.7%   9.4%   3.0%

392. SLIDING BARS

AFRICA   2.7%   9.4%   84.6%   3.0%   .3%

NORTH AMERICA   1.2%   37.3%   29.0%   30.1%   2.4%

EUROPE   20.1%   42.5%   16.5%   20.3%   .6%

SCALE OF 100,000,000s

393. AREA BARS

farmers as tools cf Communism. Even if you sincerely believe such ideas yourself, you have no right to insinuate them into a chart that pretends to represent statistics.

Hundred-Percent Bars. In Fig. 391, the length of each bar represents the size of its population, and the classes within the population are shown as percentages of the length.

Sliding bars, like those in Fig. 392, make comparison easier. The two largest classes are placed at the middle of each bar, and the bars are alined on the vertical line between these classes.

The *area bars* in Fig. 393 are all the same width, which represents 100 percent. Differences in the sizes of the populations are shown by the heights of the bars. Although this produces an area scale, it is not misleading; we judge percentages by the width scale and totals by the height scale.

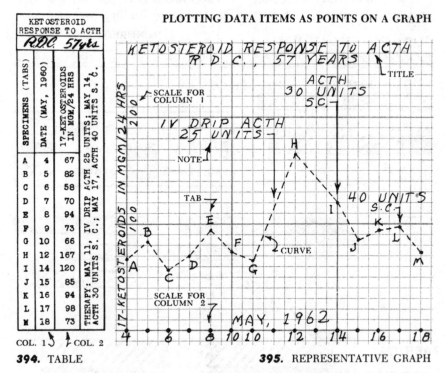

PLOTTING DATA ITEMS AS POINTS ON A GRAPH

SPECIMENS (TABS)	DATE (MAY, 1960)	17-KETOSTEROIDS IN MGM/24 HRS
A	4	67
B	5	82
C	6	58
D	7	70
E	8	94
F	9	73
G	10	66
H	12	167
I	14	120
J	15	85
K	16	94
L	17	98
M	18	73

KETOSTEROID RESPONSE TO ACTH

THERAPY: MAY 11, IV DRIP ACTH 25 UNITS; MAY 17, ACTH 40 UNITS S. C.; MAY 14, ACTH 30 UNITS S. C.

COL. 1 } COL. 2

394. TABLE   **395.** REPRESENTATIVE GRAPH

TYPES OF NUMERICAL DATA—B. TWO-SCALE DATA

When a table contains two sets of numerical data, and each item in one set corresponds to an item in the other set, the most effective form of datagram is normally a graph.

Plotting Points. As our table contains two columns, we let one axis of the graph represent a scale for one set of numbers and

Fig. 395]   Visualizing Numerical Data   177

the other axis represent a scale for the other. We then plot our points just as we did in Fig. 297.

The fact that you can make a graph is not proof that you understand it. I translated the table in Fig. 394 into the graph in Fig. 395 without difficulty, but I was working entirely with the numbers in the data columns. I have no idea what some of these numbers mean. I know that ACTH is a drug, and I suspect that MGM is an abbreviation for "milligrams" and not for "Metro-Goldwyn-Mayer." However, I cannot even guess what 17-keto-steroids are or whether they are good or bad. My ignorance on these points will not in itself make the graph invalid; a doctor who could understand the table might find the graph illuminating. But the graph can have no meaning for anyone who does not understand the table on which it is based. Also, there is a very real chance that I have misunderstood the data so badly that the graph is meaningless or sadly misleading. I turned this table into a graph to show that it could be done blindly, but it is not a safe thing to do under ordinary circumstances.

Tabs. The tabs at the heads of the data columns in the table become the names of the scales in the graph. The tab for each pair of items becomes the name of a plotted point. Ordinarily, these tabs are mere reference letters or numbers which would add nothing to the graph and which are therefore omitted. However, even reference tabs can be worth indicating. If we want to discuss Fig. 395, it is more convenient to speak of "Point H" than to say, "the peak on May 12th." The graph in Fig. 395 is supplemented by notes showing the doses of ACTH administered to the patient. Pertinent notes of this sort make a graph easier to read.

Scales. Both columns of data for the circle in Fig. 299 represent lengths, and the same scale is used for both vertical and horizontal axes. In most graphs, however, each scale represents a different quantity; the horizontal scale may show days and the vertical scale may show "17-ketosteroids in mgm/24 hrs," or one scale may indicate height in feet and the other the speed of a falling body.

As there is no inherent relation between such distinct quantities, we are free to choose any scales we like. Nevertheless, we should select scales that neither exaggerate the fluctuations nor minimize them. There is no rule here; the choice depends on the nature of the data. Figs. 396–400 illustrate this. If the peak at Point H is exceptionally high, we may want to stress this by increasing the vertical scale [Fig. 397] or shortening the hori-

HOW SCALES AFFECT SHAPE OF CURVE

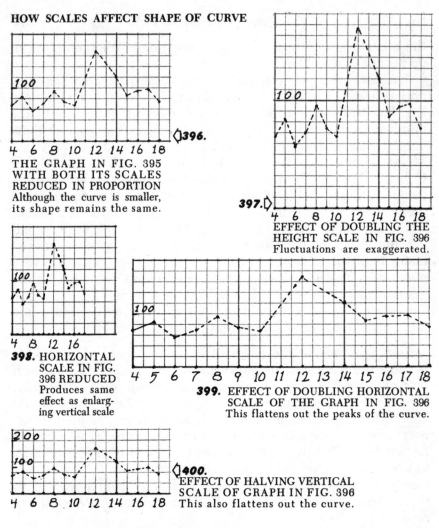

◊**396.**

THE GRAPH IN FIG. 395
WITH BOTH ITS SCALES
REDUCED IN PROPORTION
Although the curve is smaller,
its shape remains the same.

397.◊

EFFECT OF DOUBLING THE
HEIGHT SCALE IN FIG. 396
Fluctuations are exaggerated.

398. HORIZONTAL
SCALE IN FIG.
396 REDUCED
Produces same
effect as enlarg-
ing vertical scale

399. EFFECT OF DOUBLING HORIZONTAL
SCALE OF THE GRAPH IN FIG. 396
This flattens out the peaks of the curve.

◊**400.**
EFFECT OF HALVING VERTICAL
SCALE OF GRAPH IN FIG. 396
This also flattens out the curve.

zontal scale [Fig. 398]. Both methods have the same effect, except
that increasing a scale makes the whole graph larger. Conversely,
if the high peak is well within the normal range, we should avoid
stressing it. We can handle this by increasing the horizontal scale
[Fig. 399] or decreasing the vertical scale [Fig. 400].

Scales are shown by numbers along the borders of the graph.
Scale ratios like "1″ = 4 days" or "1″ = 5 17-ketosteroids in
mgm/24 hrs" need not be indicated.

UNITS VS. CONTINUITIES. When we deal with quantities such as
men and money, the data always represent definite numbers; we
cannot have 27.3 men or $2.736. This type of data is said to be
integral, which means "without fractions." In the case of money,
the units are cents; we can have fractional dollars, but not fractional cents.

Fig. 400]   Visualizing Numerical Data   179

On the other hand, quantities such as averages and lengths provide *continuous* data; we can have an average of 27.3 men or a height of 2.736419+″. In collecting data or preparing datagrams, make a point of noting whether the data are integral or continuous. You are not likely to confuse the two types. But if you do, the result may be seriously misleading.

BROKEN SCALES. Although a scale has no gaps, what constitutes a gap depends on circumstances. Anyone graphing a football game would be interested only in playing time and would omit time out and intermissions from the time scale.

ZERO LINES. These need not always be included in a graph and may not be significant. There is no reason to show the beginning of the Christian era on a graph of conditions from 1940 to 1960. Nevertheless, where the zero point is significant, its omission is as misleading as it would be on a bar chart. In Fig. 395, May 4th is an arbitrary starting point and not a true zero. It is merely the day when the physician began to record his data. On the other hand, there is presumably such a thing as "0 17-ketosteroids in mgm/24 hrs." If so, the vertical scale should show a zero line, or the graph will give a false picture of the facts.

Points and Curves. When points representing each data item in the table have been plotted, we normally draw a line through them [Fig. 402]. This line is called a *curve* even though it may actually be straight or zigzag.

The points are based on the data in the table. If the table is correct and the points are accurately plotted, they will represent the facts. The curve, on the other hand, is something added to the data while the graph is drawn. *An infinite number of curves can pass through the plotted points, and any one of them will satisfy the data in the table.* The curves in Figs. 402–404 differ greatly, but all of them fit the points indicated by Fig. 401.

The dotted zigzag in Fig. 402 is the curve best suited to experimental and economic data. It is noncommittal and does not pretend to be more than an approximation. That is why I used this type of curve in my ACTH graph. Suppose, however, that Column A in Fig. 401 represents minutes and that Column B gives readings from the speedometer of a car. A recording device attached to the speedometer would have drawn a curve like that in Fig. 403, but the plotted points do not enable us to construct such a curve even approximately. Again, for all I know, a patient's ketosteroid response to ACTH may vary widely from minute to

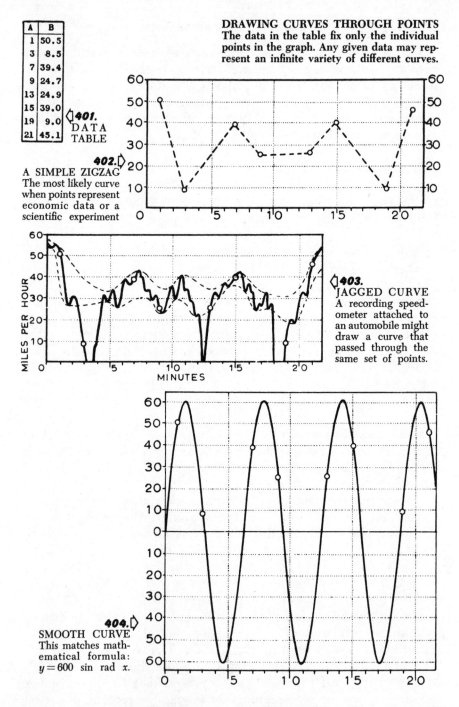

A	B
1	50.5
3	8.5
7	39.4
9	24.7
13	24.9
15	39.0
19	9.0
21	45.1

DRAWING CURVES THROUGH POINTS
The data in the table fix only the individual points in the graph. Any given data may represent an infinite variety of different curves.

◁**401.**
DATA TABLE

402.▷
A SIMPLE ZIGZAG
The most likely curve when points represent economic data or a scientific experiment

◁**403.**
JAGGED CURVE
A recording speedometer attached to an automobile might draw a curve that passed through the same set of points.

MILES PER HOUR

MINUTES

404.▷
SMOOTH CURVE
This matches mathematical formula:
$y = 600 \sin \operatorname{rad} x$.

minute. If so, the curve in my graph [Fig. 395] is deceptive and the data in the table are not much better.

At first glance a fluctuating curve like that in Fig. 403 may seem too irregular to provide much information, even when we

180

Fig. 405]   **Visualizing Numerical Data**   **181**

have enough data to draw one. Nevertheless, if you study it carefully, you will see that a speedometer curve of this type can tell you a great deal about the psychology of the driver and the kind of traffic he met. Such study is facilitated by drawing a dotted line through the peaks and another through the valleys of the graph (omitting stops).

Again, the data in Fig. 401 may have been computed from a mathematical formula. This happens to be the true interpretation. The formula is $y = 600 \sin x$, where x is an angle expressed in *radians*. One radian = 57°.30 (57° 17′ 45″). That may seem like an awkward unit, but it is convenient in some fields. Fig. 404 shows the curve corresponding to this formula.

Data taken from a laboratory experiment or from speedometer readings would not be likely to match a mathematical formula exactly. Approximate matches, on the other hand, occur frequently. Anyone foolish enough to draw a graph with no information except the table in Fig. 401 would be almost certain to produce the curve in Fig. 402. Under such circumstances, this would be entirely unwarranted. We cannot even guess at the nature of the curve without knowing something about the nature of the data.

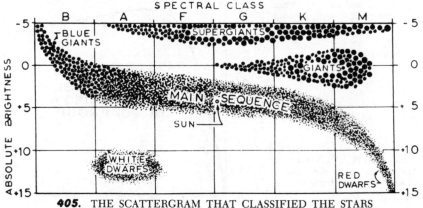

405. THE SCATTERGRAM THAT CLASSIFIED THE STARS

This schematic was made to illustrate the principle of a Russel Chart. A real Russel chart is much more elaborate and accurate. Each star is plotted as an independent point. No curve can be drawn through such points, but they form distinct areas. When Russel made his first chart, he found that the stars in each area belonged to a separate type.

Scattergrams. The absolute-brightness scale in Fig. 405 is calibrated to show star magnitudes which give the brightest stars the smallest numbers. The spectral classes (B, A, F, and so on) also form a scale, although that was not recognized when the letters were assigned. This *scattergram* led to a major breakthrough in astronomy and demonstrates that a graph does not need a curve to be useful. It represents each star by a point and reveals the important fact that stars fall into definite groups, corresponding to different areas of the scattergram.

TREND LINES

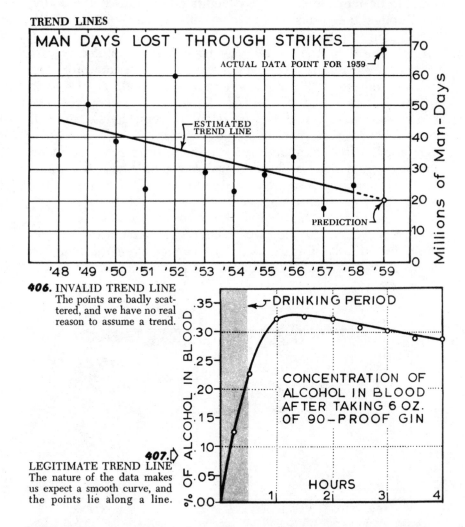

MAN DAYS LOST THROUGH STRIKES

ACTUAL DATA POINT FOR 1959

ESTIMATED
TREND LINE

PREDICTION

Millions of Man-Days

'48 '49 '50 '51 '52 '53 '54 '55 '56 '57 '58 '59

406. INVALID TREND LINE
The points are badly scattered, and we have no real reason to assume a trend.

407. LEGITIMATE TREND LINE
The nature of the data makes us expect a smooth curve, and the points lie along a line.

DRINKING PERIOD

CONCENTRATION OF
ALCOHOL IN BLOOD
AFTER TAKING 6 OZ.
OF 90-PROOF GIN

% OF ALCOHOL IN BLOOD

HOURS
1   2   3   4

Trend Lines. When the points are somewhat scattered but seem to indicate a trend, we are tempted to represent this by a *trend line*. Thus, an economist studying the data on strikes [Fig. 406] might have assumed in 1958 that, in spite of wide fluctuations, there was a definite tendency for strikes to decrease in severity. He might then have drawn a trend line like that in Fig. 406. This, however, would have been unjustified. The trend line would have predicted a decrease, or at most a mild rise, for 1959. Actually, that turned out to be the worst year in a decade.

Fig. 407]   Visualizing Numerical Data   183

Nevertheless, when the points on the graph form a narrow band, as they do in Fig. 407, we may draw a trend line through the center of the band and feel reasonably sure that the line has a meaning. Even in such cases, the line should not be regarded as a statement of fact but merely as a hypothesis. It is to be interpreted as saying, "This batch of data suggests that the factors under consideration obey some law approximately like the one indicated by this trend line."

Never disguise a trend line as a true curve by drawing the line and then erasing the plotted points.

Interpolation and Extrapolation. When the data represent a smooth curve, we can draw the curve and then *interpolate* values between the plotted points with some degree of assurance. Fig. 408 was based on a table giving the speed of an automobile at intervals of one second. The height of the curve at any point shows the speed of the car in feet per second or miles per hour at that point (1 mph = 1.466 feet per second). The data indicate that the car is accelerating as rapidly as possible. Hence, we are justified in assuming that the curve is smooth. On this assumption, we can measure the height of the curve at 2.5 seconds [Point A] and make an estimate of approximately 34.2 feet per second (23.3 miles per hour) for the speed of the car at that time.

If our data stop at 10 seconds, we may continue the curve to 11 seconds and measure the height of the curve at that point [C]. This process is called *extrapolation*. It is much less certain than interpolation. If the car was making 29.5 feet per second at 2 seconds and 38.5 feet per second at 3 seconds, 34.2 feet per second at 2.5 seconds cannot be far wrong. But if we extrapolate and find the speed of 84.0 feet per second at 11 seconds, we neglect the possibility that the driver may have slammed on his brakes or run into a cow.

Neither interpolation nor extrapolation can be relied on unless we have reason to believe that our data represent a smooth curve; it would be meaningless to apply either process to a case like Fig. 403 where the curve fluctuates. Even with a smooth curve, any attempt to predict the future by extrapolation must be used with caution. When the extension of the curve is short, the process is fairly safe. In fact, science, engineering, and business could not be carried on without it. However, as the extension increases, the reliability of extrapolation diminishes rapidly. If a merchant has sales data through March, he may predict his April sales with fair certainty. But an attempt to predict October sales may be little better than an informed guess.

Rate of Change. The rate at which data are changing at any given point is shown by the slope of a tangent to the curve at that point. Thus, the height of the curve at Point A in Fig. 408 represents the speed of the car at 2.5 seconds. But if we want to know the acceleration at that moment, we must draw the tangent. This has a rise of 36 feet per second for a run of 4 seconds, or 9 feet per second for a run of 1 second. We interpret this as an acceleration of 9 feet per second per second.

Cumulative and Noncumulative Data. The curve in Fig. 408 represents noncumulative data. The height of the curve at any

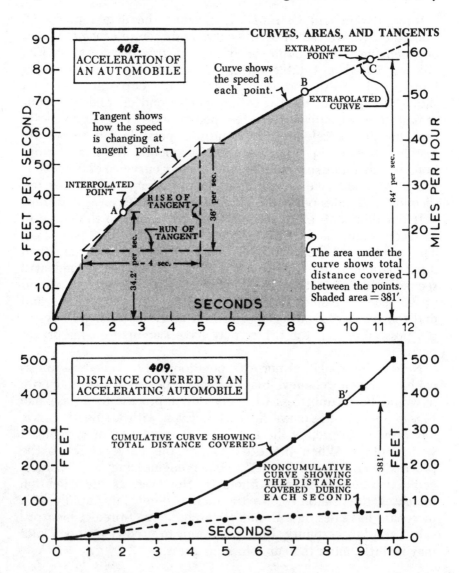

Fig. 409]   Visualizing Numerical Data   185

point shows the speed of the car at that instant, but it tells us nothing about how far the car has traveled. On the other hand, the area under the curve is cumulative. It represents the total distance traveled but gives no information about the speed. Thus, the shaded area under the curve to the left of Point B corresponds to 381' covered between 0 and 8.5 seconds.

Although the area in Fig. 408 shows the distance covered, this is unsatisfactory from a graphic standpoint because the eye is incapable of comparing areas accurately. I therefore made a numerical computation of the distance covered in each second and plotted the corresponding points [black circles in Fig. 409]. The dotted curve through these points represents noncumulative data. Finally, I added the distance covered in each second to the total distance already covered. This gave me the heights marked by the small squares. The solid curve through these squares shows cumulative data. The height of this curve at Point B' is numerically equal to the shaded area to the left of Point B in Fig. 408. This would be true of any pair of corresponding points on the two curves.

In Fig. 409, the curves are the only things that count. The areas under the curves have no meaning.

These curves deserve careful study. If you do not understand the principles illustrated, you are apt to mistake a length for a quantity—even in a graph that you draw yourself.

Adding and Subtracting Curves. We can divide a play into scenes marked by the entrance or exit of a character. The horizontal axis in Fig. 410 represents a sequence of such scenes in a one-act play. The number of male characters in each scene is shown by the light squares and the number of female characters by the dark squares. We could have plotted the sexes on separate datagrams, but by adding them together we get the total number of characters in each scene.

These data are noncumulative; we cannot add the characters in Scene A to those in Scene B. But if Fig. 410 represented passengers boarding buses at a particular station during a certain period, the data could be used cumulatively. We could then say that the 24 buses picked up 65 men and 59 women, or a total of 124 passengers.

Fig. 412 illustrates how curves can be added and subtracted. The "Green" and "Violet" curves represent the relative amounts of light energy at various wave lengths thrown onto a white surface by spotlights shining through sheets of colored glass. The scale shows relative energy rather than the actual strength of the light. The actual strength changes with the distance of the surface from the spotlights, whereas the relative energy is independent of this.

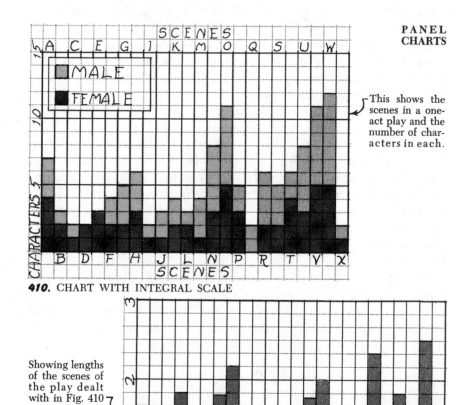

PANEL CHARTS

This shows the scenes in a one-act play and the number of characters in each.

410. CHART WITH INTEGRAL SCALE

Showing lengths of the scenes of the play dealt with in Fig. 410

411. CHART WITH CONTINUOUS SCALE

At 550 mμ in Fig. 412, the "Green" curve shows 241 units, and the "Violet" curve shows 166 units. Hence, the "Total" curve must show $241 + 166 = 407$ units. If we know the "Total" curve and the "Green" curve, we can reverse this process to find the "Violet" curve by subtraction.

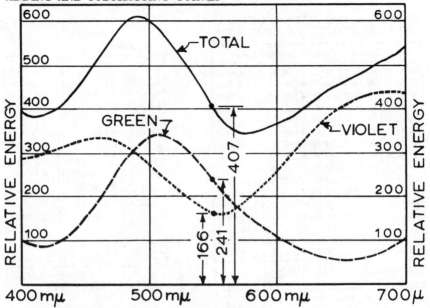

412. GRAPH SHOWING RELATIVE QUANTITIES
The amount of light at every visible wavelength
cast on a surface by each of two colored spotlights, and the effect produced by combining them

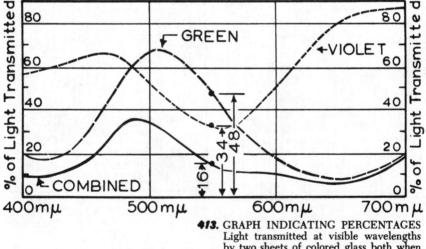

413. GRAPH INDICATING PERCENTAGES
Light transmitted at visible wavelengths
by two sheets of colored glass both when
taken separately and when superimposed.

When the data represent percentages, a different process is
required. The "Green" curve in Fig. 413 shows the percentage of
light transmitted at each wave length by a sheet of green glass,
and the "Violet" curve shows the corresponding percentage for
a sheet of violet glass. If you place both sheets together over the
same spotlight, the result can be found by multiplying percent-

RETABULATING SCALE-SEQUENCE DATA AND PLOTTING STEP CHARTS

HEIGHTS IN INCHES OF 80 DRAFTEES				
AA 67.0	AQ 70.1	BG 71.2	BW 69.3	CM 66.3
AB 68.1	AR 71.3	BH 67.6	BX 63.7	CN 69.4
AC 69.0	AS 65.0	BI 68.2	BY 70.2	CO 64.9
AD 69.5	AT 66.5	BJ 65.2	BZ 68.7	CP 67.6
AE 72.0	AU 68.0	BK 70.6	CA 70.8	CQ 70.4
AF 61.7	AV 70.1	BL 62.3	CB 69.0	CR 68.4
AG 73.5	AW 67.8	BM 75.9	CC 68.4	CS 69.1
AH 68.9	AX 66.0	BN 66.4	CD 65.9	CT 71.1
AI 69.2	AY 67.3	BO 69.5	CE 68.6	CU 68.3
AJ 69.9	AZ 71.7	BP 64.6	CF 68.2	CV 70.5
AK 68.7	BA 72.6	BQ 69.6	CG 67.5	CW 63.2
AL 72.1	BB 68.5	BR 67.4	CH 71.6	CX 70.2
AM 67.9	BC 70.7	BS 66.7	CI 66.9	CY 68.8
AN 72.9	BD 67.9	BT 65.6	CJ 74.6	CZ 71.6
AO 64.1	BE 73.8	BU 70.9	CK 66.2	DA 72.8
AP 69.8	BF 75.2	BV 71.4	CL 73.9	DB 69.7

414. TABLE OF RAW DATA

PERCENTAGE
FREQUENCY
TALLY MARKS

	#	%
61.0–61.9 I	1	1.2
62.0–62.9 I	1	1.2
63.0–63.9 II	2	2.5
64.0–64.9 III	3	3.7
65.0–65.9 IIII	4	5.0
66.0–66.9 IIIIII	7	8.8
67.0–67.9 IIII IIII	9	11.3
68.0–68.9 IIII IIII III	13	16.3
69.0–69.9 IIII IIII II	12	15.0
70.0–70.9 IIII IIII	10	12.5
71.0–71.9 IIII II	7	8.8
72.0–72.9 IIII	5	6.3
73.0–73.9 III	3	3.7
74.0–74.9 I	1	1.2
75.0–75.9 II	2	2.5
TOTALS	80	100.0

CLASS TABS

415. A WORK SHEET USED TO RETABULATE DATA

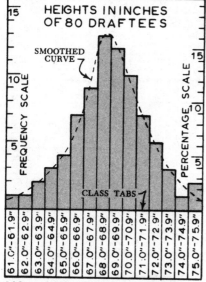

416. A STEP CHART BASED ON EVENLY SPACED CLASSES

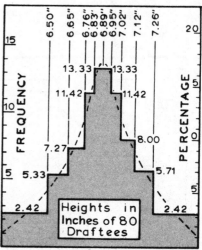

417. STEP CHART IN WHICH EACH CLASS CONTAINS 10% OF THE SAMPLE

ages. Thus, at 550 mμ, the green glass transmits 48 percent of the light, and the violet glass transmits 34 percent. Both glasses together will transmit only .48 × .34 = 16 percent.

Although the curves have the same shapes in both graphs, there is an important difference in the scales. The scale in Fig. 412 is arbitrary; any numbering could have been used as long as the relations of the lines to each other was unchanged. In Fig. 413, on the contrary, any change in the scale would falsify the graph.

Fig. 417]   Visualizing Numerical Data   189

A glass that transmits 24 percent of the light at 550 mμ is very different from one that transmits 48 percent.

Types of Numerical Data—C. Scale-Sequence Data

Bar-chart data have only one scale, and the arrangement of the items is arbitrary. We now come to types of data which also have only one scale, but which require arranging the items in definite sequences. This is often confused with two-scale data and plotted to imitate a graph—a practice which can be seriously misleading. The only way to avoid that is to form a clear idea of the distinction between a scale and a sequence. The study required is well worth while because scale-sequence data appear frequently in both science and business.

Primary Data. When there is only one column of data but this must be arranged in a definite sequence, it can be most clearly shown by a *panel chart* like those in Figs. 410 and 411.

Fig. 410 indicates the number of characters in each scene of a one-act play. As we cannot have 0.7 characters, the vertical axis represents an integral scale where 1 unit = 1 character. Fig. 411, on the other hand, shows the length of each scene, and its vertical axis represents a continuous scale of time.

In both examples, the horizontal axis is *not* a scale but merely a sequence of separate items arranged in a definite order. Each segment stands for one scene, and the segments are all the same length whether the scenes are long or short.

The panels should be separated by vertical lines. The height of the data in each column is marked by a heavy, horizontal line. The area below these lines must be shaded, or the chart will be hard to read. When two kinds of data can be lumped together, they can be shown on a single chart like Fig. 410. However, any attempt to treat three or more types in this way is likely to result in confusion. Place the proper tab at the bottom of each panel and mark the scale along one or both side borders.

Retabulated Data. The table in Fig. 414 lists the heights of 80 men. The tabs are arbitrary letter symbols used instead of the names of the men.

We could translate this into a panel chart with one panel for each man and a vertical height scale. However, the result would not have much significance. A more useful plan is to divide the heights into classes, say from 61.0″ to 61.9″, 62.0″ to 62.9″, and so on. If we then retabulate the data and count the number of men in each class, we get new data that may yield valuable information.

Fig. 415 illustrates the procedure. Column 1 gives the tabs of the new table. Note that these are numbers (in this case heights) and not names or letters. Column 2 contains the *tally marks* used to facilitate counting. Column 3 shows the number of men in each class, and Column 4 converts these numbers into percentages of the whole.

Fig. 416 shows how the data in Fig. 415 can be plotted on a *step chart*. The vertical scale does not represent heights but is either a *frequency scale* showing the number of men in each height-class, or a percentage scale showing the percentage of the sample in each height-class. Frequency- and percentage-scales are interchangeable. We can use whichever one interests us, or we can use both—as I have done in the example.

Step charts are always cumulative. The area under the step-line represents the total number, or the total percentage, of all items in the sample. When we deal with percentages, the area must equal 100 percent.

CLASS LIMITS. The data in Fig. 414 give the heights of draftees to the nearest 0.1″. If we set our class limits at 61.0″ to 61.9″, 62.0″ to 62.9″, and so on, where do we put a man who measures 61.94″? Obviously, he belongs in the 61.0″ to 61.9″ class. This means that when we use 61.0″ to 61.9″, 62.0″ to 62.9″, and so on as class tabs, the actual *class boundaries* are 60.95″ to 61.95″, 61.95″ to 62.95″, and so on.

If a man appears to measure exactly 61.95″, he may be put in either the first or the second class. This is an arbitrary decision by the person who does the measuring. Such cases are normally rare, and errors due to classifying them arbitrarily tend to cancel out.

However, situations arise where we may suspect that the number of borderline cases is large enough to demand serious consideration. For example, data showing sales in a store may be classified by prices such as $0.00 to $9.99, and $10.00 to $19.99. This suggests that the average in each class will be about $5.00, $15.00, and so on. But stores tend to charge prices like $9.98 and $19.95. They almost never charge $10.02 or $20.05. Hence, the average price that is actually charged may be almost $5.00 higher than the apparent average indicated by the chart.

UNEQUAL SPACING. Data are sometimes tabulated in a way that makes each class contain the same number of items. We might, for example, be told that the shortest 10 percent of the men in

Fig. 418] Visualizing Numerical Data 191

Fig. 414 ranges from 61.7″ to 65.0″, the next 10 percent from 65.2″ to 66.5″, and so on. This would cause unequal spacing along the horizontal axis of our chart.

We can handle such data by treating the horizontal axis as a scale, but this scale is used *only* to determine the width of the classes and not to plot points on the chart. We then compute the height of each step by dividing the number of items in a class by the width of the class. In our example, each class contains 8 men. As the first class ranges from 61.7″ to 65.0″, it is 3.3″ wide. Hence, the first step must be 8 ÷ 3.3 or 2.42 units high [Fig. 417].

Note that equal spacing makes any frequency scale integral; something is wrong if our data show 2.42 men. Unequal spacing, on the other hand, makes the corresponding scale continuous, and fractional numbers are to be expected.

SMOOTHING STEP CHARTS. If we used half-inch intervals for our classes instead of the one-inch intervals in Fig. 416, the step line would be smoother. But if we used smaller and smaller intervals, the line would grow more and more irregular and would finally cease to have any definite form. Although we could correct this by collecting more data, the line would not turn into a smooth curve unless the classes were infinitely small and the population infinitely large. In that case, the horizontal axis would be a true scale and the chart would be a graph.

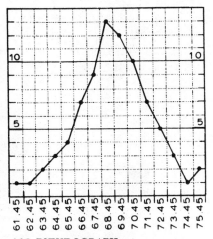

418. PSEUDOGRAPH
This is really the step chart in Fig. 416 disguised to resemble a graph. It is misleading and no easier to draw.

When we want to study the theory behind our data, a curve may supply a clearer picture than a step chart. By drawing a smooth curve which passes approximately through the midpoints of each step, we get a graph which shows what an infinite population would be like *if our actual data are taken from a truly representative sample* [Fig. 416]. As this is always questionable, it is wise to use a solid line for the steps and a dotted line for the curve. The step line then marks the known data, and the curve gives the theoretical assumption derived from it. Note that although the spacing in Fig. 416 is even and that in Fig. 417 is uneven, both charts show approximately the same curve.

Data in Disguise. Columnar charts, panel charts, step charts, and graphs can be (and often are) used interchangeably. However, this is poor practice. A good datagram should not only represent the numbers in the data table clearly; it should avoid any misleading suggestions about the nature of the data themselves. A columnar chart suggests independent items; we can rearrange them, add more, or take some away without affecting the validity of the chart. Panel charts indicate that the items are independent in size but form a definite sequence; any change in the order or the number of panels in Fig. 410 would make the chart false—or at least incomplete. Step charts represent a population or a sample. We can enlarge or reduce the sample, and we can control the width of the steps. Nevertheless, we cannot legitimately change the order or height of a step. A graph implies two scales and should not be used in cases like Fig. 416 where the data have only one scale. Note how much the curve of the *pseudograph* in Fig. 418 differs from the dotted curves in Figs. 416 and 417.

If you understand the nature of the data, you should have no difficulty in selecting the appropriate type of datagram; if you do not understand the nature of the data, you have no business drawing any datagram at all.

2.9% TO OUR STOCKHOLDERS

53.9% FOR MATERIALS AND OTHER COSTS

38.1% TO OUR EMPLOYEES

5.1% FOR TAXES

WHERE THE U.S. STEEL DOLLAR GOES

419. 100% PIE CHART

11

MORE USES FOR ABSTRACT SCALES

THE principles explained in Chapter 10 can be applied and combined in endless ways. The examples given here are worth mastering for their own sakes, but the real purpose of this chapter is to demonstrate that almost any type of numerical data becomes clearer when it is translated into graphic terms.

CIRCULAR FORMS

Pie charts like Fig. 419 resemble hundred-percent bars, except that the scale is based on angles instead of on lengths. The circular form makes the hundred-percent nature of the chart obvious and catches the eye better than bars. It is, however, less satisfactory for purposes of comparison.

Partial Pie Charts. Although 360° always represents 100 percent in any one pie chart, we may need several such charts in cases like Fig. 420 where the data cannot be totaled. Each circle in this illustration represents a different number of women, and those who die unmarried after fifty appear in all four charts. Hence, we cannot add the percentages together and need four separate charts to present them graphically.

Circular Graphs. Automatic recording devices often draw graphs on cardboard disks. The angular scale normally represents time; the quantity being measured is shown by the distance of the curve from the center of the disk. Such graphs are less satisfactory than the rectangular variety. They are used only because they simplify the recording mechanism.

In a case like Fig. 421, on the other hand, the circular form was chosen because it is the best way to express the idea involved. This drawing represents the amount of light emitted in different directions by an electric bulb of the type used in spotlights. Note that most of the light shines either forward toward the lens or backward toward the reflector, and that comparatively little light is wasted at the sides. The angles in this drawing do not represent a scale but are shown in their own right; an angle of 30° from the main axis is an angle of 30° from the main axis and nothing else. Distances from the center, however, do constitute a scale. In our example, the scale is 1″ = 1500 candle power.

420. PARTIAL PIE CHARTS

Cycle Datagrams. Fig. 422 has no scale at all. It simply shows the angular distances from the vertical at which the spark occurs and the valves open and close. Nevertheless, a similar datagram could be made showing planting and harvest times of various crops in relation to the year. We should then have an angular scale of 360° = 12 months.

An understanding of the various ways in which such forms can be used will prepare you to invent new schematics for handling

CIRCULAR FORMS

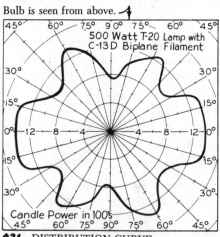

421. DISTRIBUTION CURVE
Showing amounts of light emitted in different directions by a lamp designed for theatrical spotlights

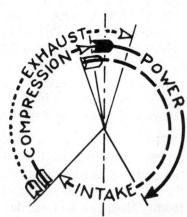

422. CYCLE DIAGRAM
Made to explain the operation of a four-cycle gasoline engine

unusual problems. It will also keep you from interpreting something as a scale where none exists or from failing to recognize a scale that is the key to a datagram.

THREE-FACTOR FORMS

Ordinary graphs provide only two scales. Simple, mathematical diagrams may be drawn on a set of three-dimensional axes like those in Fig. 303. But if we tried to show the curve of a graph in this way, it would be almost impossible to visualize the result. There are, however, methods of charting three, and even four, factors. Some of these are too complex for anyone but the specialist, but others are worth investigating.

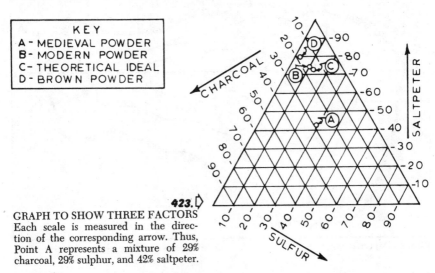

KEY
A – MEDIEVAL POWDER
B – MODERN POWDER
C – THEORETICAL IDEAL
D – BROWN POWDER

423.
GRAPH TO SHOW THREE FACTORS
Each scale is measured in the direction of the corresponding arrow. Thus, Point A represents a mixture of 29% charcoal, 29% sulphur, and 42% saltpeter.

Triangular Graphs. When our three factors are percentages and always add up to 100 percent, we can plot them on a *triangular graph* like the one in Fig. 423. Moreover, if we plot the point that corresponds to two of the factors, it will automatically correspond to the third. We can therefore use the graph as a computing device.

Contour Lines. Ordinary maps represent two space dimensions, breadth and depth. When we wish to represent heights above sea level, we draw *contour lines* [Fig. 424]. With a *contour interval* of 10', each contour line shows where the shore line would be if the sea rose 10' higher.

We draw a contour line by fixing a number of points at the same level and then connecting these points with the line. The same principle is applied in drawing weather maps, but here the third dimension is not a dimension of height but one of temperature or barometric pressure. Hence, each line is drawn through points where the temperature or the pressure is constant. Do not confuse contour lines with the contours used in ordinary free-line drawing (see man in Fig. 184 and fruit in Fig. 186).

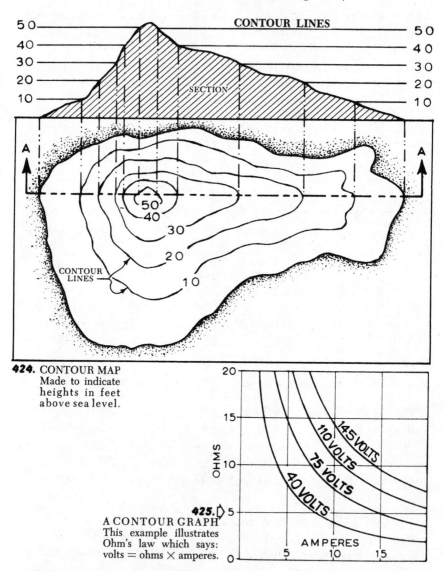

424. CONTOUR MAP
Made to indicate heights in feet above sea level.

425. ◇
A CONTOUR GRAPH
This example illustrates Ohm's law which says: volts = ohms × amperes.

The contour principle is not limited to maps. It can be used in any datagram where the main drawing represents two dimensions, and we want to show a third. Fig. 425 employs contour lines to illustrate Ohm's law in electricity (volts = ohms × am-

Fig. 428]   More Uses for Abstract Scales   197

peres). The vertical axis represents ohms, and the horizontal axis represents amperes. The contour lines here pass through the points of constant voltage just as those in Fig. 424 pass through the points of equal height.

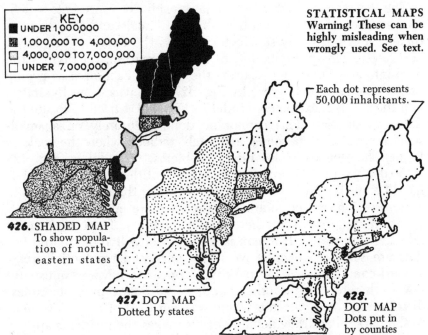

KEY
■ UNDER 1,000,000
▨ 1,000,000 TO 4,000,000
☐ 4,000,000 TO 7,000,000
☐ UNDER 7,000,000

STATISTICAL MAPS
Warning! These can be highly misleading when wrongly used. See text.

Each dot represents 50,000 inhabitants.

426. SHADED MAP
To show population of northeastern states

427. DOT MAP
Dotted by states

428. DOT MAP
Dots put in by counties

Data Maps. Maps are sometimes shaded like that in Fig. 426. This is a good way to show which states went Republican or Democratic, or which states provide a death penalty. However, shading is a poor substitute for a scale. In Fig. 426, for example, the "scale" does not take areas into account. This makes Rhode Island and the District of Columbia seem thinly populated. Moreover, the graduations of shading are not even. The first step is 1,000,000, the next two 3,000,000 each, and the last is 7,000,000. Furthermore, the shading implies that the difference between Massachusetts and Pennsylvania corresponds to that between Virginia and New Jersey, whereas it is actually four times as great. If we attempt to correct these faults by letting each step correspond to 3,600,000 inhabitants, we throw nine states into the bottom class and leave only New York for the top class.

This particular map also errs by using the darkest shading to indicate the smallest population. Such shading is inconsistent with the average reader's assumption that "dark" symbolizes "many." Any failure to comply with the reader's intuitive ideas about symbols is apt to confuse him.

The misleading nature of shading is obvious in a population map. But in one showing (say) the number of public schools, or the number of homicides during a particular year, it can create a completely false impression.

The dot method in Fig. 427, where each dot represents a definite number of items, avoids problems of scale and area. Nevertheless, it is not really satisfactory unless the dots can be placed accurately. This presents difficulties. The map maker divides the map into areas and then scatters the dots for each area as evenly as possible over that area. In Fig. 427, this was done by states, and the result is extremely crude. In Fig. 428, I tried to locate the dots by counties. This cannot be done accurately on a small-scale map, and it becomes extremely tedious when the scale is large. The dot-scale also raises problems. One dot in Fig. 428 = 50,000 people. Vermont is therefore entitled to 8 dots, but it has 14 counties. No matter how you arrange the dots, they create an impression that large areas of the state are uninhabited.

City maps present another type of difficulty. Data are usually tabulated by wards. If a map is made to show live births and the dots are scattered evenly over both park and residential areas, a ward containing a large park will appear to have an unusually low birth rate. On the other hand, if the dots represent crimes, distributing them over the whole ward instead of confining them to the park where they actually occur makes the residents appear as criminals although they may actually be victims.

COMPARISON DATAGRAMS

Perhaps the most valuable characteristic of datagrams is the fact that they enable us to compare two sets of facts at a glance.

Operation Datagrams. If we divide a datagram into zones and decide to take different actions depending on the zone into which a point falls, we have an *operation chart*. The example in Fig. 429 is a simple type called a *control chart*. This shows that a manufactured product is supposed to weigh no more than 16.30 ounces and not less than 15.70 ounces. We draw horizontal *take-action lines* slightly inside these points and draw *warning lines* between the take-action lines. Whenever a sample is examined, its weight is plotted on the chart. If the dots stay within the warning lines, we are safe in assuming that the process is under control. If a dot slips past a warning line, or if several dots bunch near the line [A], we take samples more frequently. If the dots wander back toward the ideal line, we can relax [C]. If they continue to move farther away [B] and slip past the take-action

Fig. 429]   More Uses for Abstract Scales   199

line, we abandon sampling and inspect each individual item. What further action is taken depends on the situation, but it normally involves some type of trouble-shooting. This is an over-simplified account of the control process. For a more detailed but not too technical version see *Facts from Figures*, by M. J. Moroney.

Fig. 429 is essentially a panel chart and not a scattergram. The vertical axis represents a scale, but the horizontal axis shows a sequence; each space corresponds to one of the samples whether or not the samples are taken at regular intervals. For some purposes, however, it would be desirable to make the horizontal axis a time scale. The dot for each sample would then be plotted above the corresponding time, and the drawing would be a scattergram. Such an arrangement would show instantly whether or not the inspector had taken samples at regular intervals. Also, if the weights of the samples tended to rise or fall, the scattergram would indicate the rate of change.

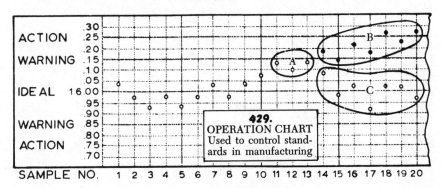

429.
OPERATION CHART
Used to control standards in manufacturing

Interlocking Graphs. Sometimes our interest is not in the comparative heights of points or curves but in the places where curves intersect. The graph in Fig. 430, which illustrates the economic law of diminishing returns, is especially interesting. The three sets of points marked by vertical lines indicate three entirely different relationships between the curves. On the other hand, the points where the average- and marginal-curves cross the total-output curve have no significance.

The law of diminishing returns offers a fine example of the difference between continuous and integral data. Fig. 430 shows ideal curves which represent continuous data. In practice, however, the input is ordinarily integral—we add men in one-man units to a labor gang or buses in one-bus units to a bus line. When we compute the marginal output in such cases and plot the result, we get a step chart like Fig. 416 and not a true curve.

If our input data are in pints, we can draw step charts for either pints or quarts. However, if we try to generalize our data by drawing a smooth curve through the midpoint of each step as we did for Fig. 416, the pint-curve will differ from the quart-curve—and neither will match the theoretical marginal-output curve shown in Fig. 430. This represents the shape that our step chart would have if we could measure the marginal output from minute increases in input.

The ideal curve in Fig. 430 was plotted from data computed by the formula $I = aM - bM^2$, where I is the input at any point, M is the marginal output at that point, and a and b are *parameters* which vary with the quantities being measured. Any change in these parameters will produce different curves. Nevertheless, their general shapes and their relations to each other will be the same.

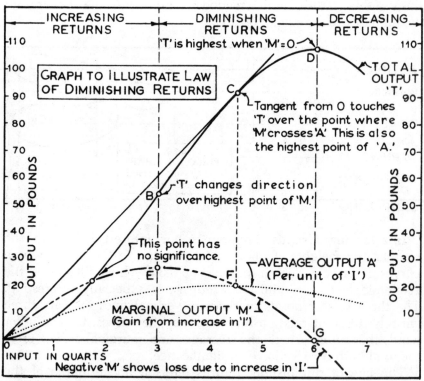

430. INTERRELATED LINES AND CURVES

Ideal Curves vs. Actual Curves. Graphs are not confined to data which can be expressed in exact numbers. They can show any quantity, however abstract, that may be regarded as rising or falling. Thus, the audience-interest in a play should move in

Fig. 431]   More Uses for Abstract Scales   **201**

waves, and each wave should be higher than the one before it. The dotted line in Fig. 431 shows an ideal curve for a particular one-act play. The solid line represents the rise and fall of interest that is estimated from a rough draft of the text. Whenever a noticeable gap appears between the curves, the script probably needs to be revised. Any competent playwright or director should be able to make a fairly accurate estimate of the relative rise and fall, even though he could not tell whether there would be enough interest in the play as a whole to satisfy an audience.

The principle of comparing ideal and actual curves can be applied to many types of planning. An engineer comparing the performance of a motor with some theoretical ideal might calculate his ideal curve mathematically and base his actual curve on elaborate tests. Nevertheless, his mental process while making the comparison would be much like the playwright's.

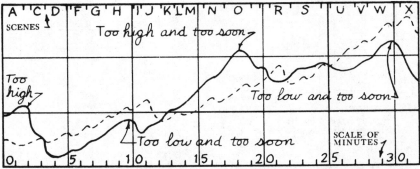

431.   IDEAL CURVE COMPARED WITH ONE BASED ON ACTUAL DATA
The dotted line represents the theoretical ideal rise and fall of interest for this one-act play. The solid line shows estimated interest curve for a preliminary draft of the script. Gaps between the two curves call attention to scenes that need revision.

Large Values vs. Small Values. Businessmen often want to compare small figures with large ones. Thus, they may compare the records of one branch office with those for the rest of the firm. Scientists may need to know how closely the behavior of a small sample matches that of a large one. Ordinary graphs or panel charts like Fig. 432 are not well suited to this purpose. The lines are too far apart, and the fluctuations in the lower line seem flat by comparison with those in the upper one. The relation between the two sets of data is much clearer in Fig. 433, where the data for Branch "B" were *weighted*. As the total sales for Branch "B" were 1/11.7 of the total for the other branches, I multiplied each item for Branch "B" by 11.7 to get the heights of the panels representing the branch in Fig. 433. Note that this *compound panel chart* carries two scales, one for Branch "B" and one for the totals of the other branches.

Weighting may be much more elaborate than this. Statisticians sometimes assign a different *weight* to each item in the data. That sort of treatment should be attempted only by the expert and then only with utmost caution.

Another device for comparing large and small quantities is to convert our data into percentages. Thus, in Fig. 432 the total sales of Branch "B" were $166,802, and its January sales of $12,498 were 7.5 percent of this. The total sales for the other branches were $1,951,560, and the January sales of $142,103 were 7.2 percent of this. We can then make a compound panel chart like Fig. 433. In that case, there will be only one scale—and this will show percentages, not dollars.

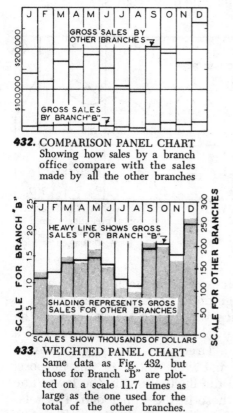

432. COMPARISON PANEL CHART
Showing how sales by a branch office compare with the sales made by all the other branches

433. WEIGHTED PANEL CHART
Same data as Fig. 432, but those for Branch "B" are plotted on a scale 11.7 times as large as the one used for the total of the other branches.

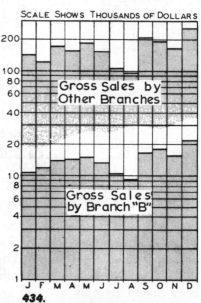

COMPARING LARGE AND SMALL VALUES

434.
PANEL CHART ON RATIO PAPER
Using a logarithmic vertical scale makes rises and falls proportional, even though Branch "B" is shown at the bottom of the chart and the other branches appear at the top.

Special Rulings. A third method of comparing large and small values is to plot the curves on *ratio paper* [Fig. 434]. This has a uniform horizontal scale but uses a *logarithmic scale* on the vertical axis. A logarithmic scale substitutes the logarithm of a

Fig. 436]   More Uses for Abstract Scales   **203**

number for the number itself. The zero line on a logarithmic scale is at minus infinity. Hence, it cannot appear on the graph, and there can be no minus values.

You can use a logarithmic scale without understanding logarithms. The only problem comes in assigning numbers to the divisions of the scale. The printed ratio paper over which Fig. 434 was drawn was divided into three *cycles,* each of which was numbered from "1" to "9." The second cycle represents values which are ten times those of the first, and the third represents values which are a hundred times those of the first. We can let the lowest "1" represent "1" or "1 multiplied or divided by 10, 100, and so on." My data for Fig. 434 ranged from $9103 to $254,987. I therefore labeled the "1" of the first cycle "$1000." The "1" of the second cycle then became $10,000, and that of the third cycle $100,000. This brought the highest item ($254,987) well within the third cycle. In a scientific graph with a three-cycle logarithmic scale, the lowest "1" might represent 1 mm. The next "1" would then equal 1 cm. (10 mm.). The next would equal 10 cm. (100 mm.), and the limit of the scale would be 1 M. (1000 mm.). Again, we could let the lowest "1" represent ".0001." The next would then stand for ".001," and the third for ".01."

When the data for Fig. 432 are plotted on ratio paper, we still get high and low curves. In this case, however, the fluctuations in each set of panels is in proportion to the data for those curves and weighting is unnecessary.

Another characteristic of ratio paper often proves useful. In dealing with data that cover a wide range, we may want to show

MORE USES FOR RATIO PAPER

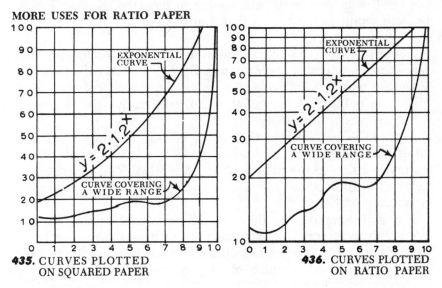

435. CURVES PLOTTED ON SQUARED PAPER

436. CURVES PLOTTED ON RATIO PAPER

even minor fluctuations in the small values but still leave room
on a graph for high peaks. As Fig. 436 demonstrates, we can draw
a curve on ratio paper that makes the rise from 11 to 12 plainly
visible but also lets us show a rise from 11 to 94 on the same
2″ graph. The advantage of this becomes clear when we compare it with the same data plotted on squared paper in Fig.
435.

A third property of ratio paper is that it represents any curve
of the formula $y = a \times b^x$ as a straight line. Such *exponential
curves* are common in some fields. Plotting two points on ratio
paper and drawing the curve accurately with a ruler [Fig. 436]
is much easier than plotting a number of points on uniformly
ruled paper and drawing the curve more or less inaccurately with
a French curve [Fig. 435].

Other special rulings are available. If you draw many graphs,
it will pay you to investigate these. But do not use them for
graphs that are intended to be read by laymen. Anyone who is
not familiar with special scales is likely to find them both confusing and misleading.

GRAPHIC COMPUTATION

When we scale a line on a working drawing instead of computing its length by arithmetic, we are making a graphic computation. The same thing is true when we interpolate a value from
a graph by measuring the height of the curve at a particular
point.

More complex methods are used in some technical fields. I have
neither the space nor the knowledge to describe these at length,
but you should at least know that they exist.

Vectors. Lines drawn on the polar co-ordinate system may
represent numbers by their lengths. Such lines are called *vectors*.
They are widely used by engineers to calculate the forces oper-
ating at a point. Problems of this kind constantly arise in designing structures or machinery.

Figs. 437–439 illustrate the use of vectors to study the forces
affecting an airplane in flight. In Fig. 437 these vectors are shown
in their relation to the plane and to each other. This arrangement
helps us to understand the situation but does not permit graphic
computation.

Fig. 438 demonstrates the graphic method of adding vectors.
We take the vectors in any convenient order and draw each one
from the tip of the one preceding it. When this has been done,
a line joining the beginning of the first vector to the tip of the

Fig. 439] More Uses for Abstract Scales **205**

last will show both the direction and the force (on a scale of length) of the combined effect of all the other vectors. This line is called the *resultant*. We can add as many vectors as we like in this way.

The resultant usually represents the force that the engineer must overcome. In Fig. 438 it is the total drag on the airplane. But what really interests the engineer is the thrust required to counteract that drag. This thrust equals the drag in force (length of line) but is applied in the opposite direction [Fig. 439]. Vector diagrams are usually drawn in this way, partly because they give the answer the engineer actually wants but chiefly because they help to avoid mistakes. In Fig. 439 all the arrows follow each other; if one is reversed, something is wrong. On the other hand, if we made our diagram like Fig. 438, the resultant would always point

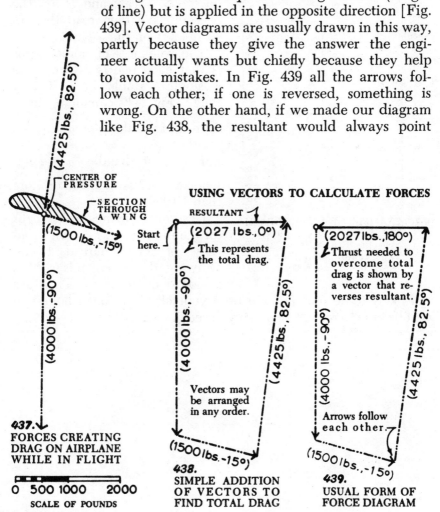

USING VECTORS TO CALCULATE FORCES

CENTER OF PRESSURE

SECTION THROUGH A WING

(4425 lbs., 82.5°)

(1500 lbs., -15°)

Start here.

RESULTANT

(2027 lbs., 0°)
This represents the total drag.

(2027 lbs., 180°)
Thrust needed to overcome total drag is shown by a vector that reverses resultant.

(4000 lbs., -90°)

(4000 lbs., -90°)

(4425 lbs., 82.5°)

(4000 lbs., -90°)

(4425 lbs., 82.5°)

Vectors may be arranged in any order.

Arrows follow each other.

437.
FORCES CREATING DRAG ON AIRPLANE WHILE IN FLIGHT

0 500 1000 2000
SCALE OF POUNDS

(1500 lbs. -15°)
438.
SIMPLE ADDITION OF VECTORS TO FIND TOTAL DRAG

(1500 lbs., -15°)
439.
USUAL FORM OF FORCE DIAGRAM

"backward." This does not matter when we are dealing with only three or four vectors. However, when we work with complex diagrams, we need a simple rule to keep us from pointing a vector in the wrong direction. The follow-my-leader rule serves this purpose, but it requires us to use the reverse of the resultant instead of the resultant itself.

Nomographs. These are a kind of graphic slide rule [Fig. 440]. They enable anyone to make the computations for a formula like that shown by simply laying a ruler on the proper points of two scales and reading the result on the third. In the example, the ruler is placed between 6000 on the Σx^2 scale and 15 on the N scale. We then read the answer (20) on the σ scale.

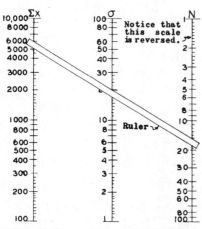

The weakness of nomographs is that each one is restricted to a single formula in a limited range. Fig. 440 cannot be used with a formula like $y = \sqrt{\dfrac{x^2}{N}}$, nor can it handle $\sigma = \sqrt{\dfrac{\Sigma x^2}{N}}$ when Σx^2 is less than 100 or more than 10,000.

4.40. EXAMPLE OF A NOMOGRAPH
This is used for computation from the formula $\sigma = \sqrt{\Sigma x^2/N}$. Thus, reading along the ruler shows that $\sigma = \sqrt{6000/15} = 20$.

Designing nomographs calls for familiarity with a wide variety of mathematical forms. Drawing them demands a high standard of accuracy. They are not likely to become popular do-it-yourself items, but I hope you will be able to recognize one if you see it.

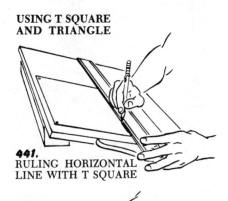

12

MECHANICAL AIDS

441.
RULING HORIZONTAL
LINE WITH T SQUARE

442.
RULING A VERTICAL
WITH A TRIANGLE

YOU have no doubt discovered by this time that, except when we can construct by tracing, nearly every drawing involves many straight lines—and that most of these are parallels and perpendiculars. We can draw parallels and perpendiculars with squared paper or a squared ruler, but the purchase of a few more mechanical aids will make the process easier, quicker, and much more accurate.

EQUIPMENT AND METHODS

The basic equipment consists of a drawing board with a straight edge on the left, a *T square*, a *45° triangle*, and a *30°–60° triangle*.

T Square and Triangles. Horizontal and vertical lines are drawn by the methods shown above. When your paper is much smaller than the board, place it near the left-hand edge. Even the best T square is slightly flexible. The right-hand end may sag a little and produce lines that are not parallel.

Press the T square firmly against the left-hand edge of the board at all times [Fig. 441]. If it is even slightly loose, the lines will not be parallel. You may have trouble remembering to do this at first, but after a little experience it becomes second nature.

Put your pencil on the point through which the line is to pass. Slide the T square gently upward until it touches the lead. Never set the T square by eye and then place the pencil against it. If you do, the slightest change in the way you hold your pencil will make the line too high or too low. The same thing may happen if your

207

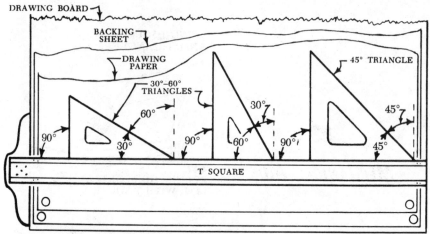

443. ANGLES DRAWN WITH ONE STOCK TRIANGLE

pencil is sharpened so that the point is not in the exact center of the lead. Placing the pencil first and moving the T square up to it automatically eliminates both sources of error.

The T square can be turned upside down and used as a long straightedge for drawing oblique lines. Do not use it for vertical lines. The edges of your board are probably not exactly perpendicular to each other. If they are crooked, verticals drawn with a T square will also be crooked.

Rule vertical lines with one of your triangles [Fig. 442]. Let the triangle rest on the upper edge of the T square. Place your pencil on a point that will fix the line, and slide the triangle until it touches the pencil. The left hand then holds the T square firmly against the edge of the board and at the same time keeps the triangle tight against the T square. This is not hard to do, but it is easy to forget until experience makes it habitual. The vertical

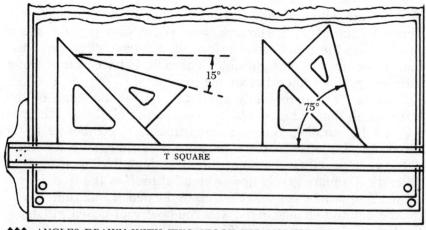

444. ANGLES DRAWN WITH TWO STOCK TRIANGLES

Fig. 447]   Mechanical Aids   209

side of the triangle should be on your left, so that you reach across the triangle to draw. This keeps your right hand from smudging the paper.

Figs. 443 and 444 show how to rule lines at the *stock angles* of 15°, 30°, 45°, 60°, and 75°. Any of these can be drawn by fixing a single point and ruling the line through that.

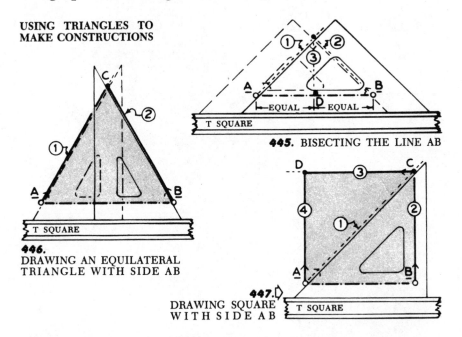

USING TRIANGLES TO MAKE CONSTRUCTIONS

445. BISECTING THE LINE AB

446.
DRAWING AN EQUILATERAL TRIANGLE WITH SIDE AB

447.
DRAWING SQUARE WITH SIDE AB

Triangle Constructions. Books on geometry give constructions which employ only a straightedge and a compass. Many of the same forms can be constructed with the aid of standard triangles as illustrated in Figs. 445–449. If you have any trouble with these, follow the diagrams on a drawing board with an actual T square and triangles. In Fig. 448, for example, Lines 2 and 5 are ruled with the T square, Lines 1, 3, and 6 are drawn with the triangle turned as shown, and Lines 4 and 7 are drawn with the triangle reversed. The straightedge-and-compass methods are theoretically exact, but the triangle methods are easier, quicker, and at least as accurate in actual practice.

Oblique Lines. A line that is not at a stock angle must be fixed either with a protractor or by using the run-and-rise method to plot points. A triangle is then employed as a straightedge to draw the line through the points. Once an oblique line has been fixed, we can rule parallels or perpendiculars to it with the aid of two triangles, as illustrated in Figs. 450 and 451.

The two-triangle method is also used to draw tangents to a circle [Fig. 452]. If the line must be tangent to a specific point [P] on the circle, set a side of one triangle [Position a, dotted outline] on this point and the center [C]. Slide this triangle until the other side passes through the point [Position b, solid outline]. The tangent can then be ruled.

**TRIANGLE CONSTRUCTIONS
FOR HEXAGON AND OCTAGON**

Note that Center A
is given in both of
these constructions.

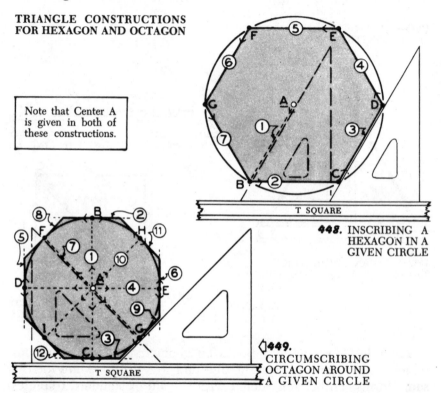

T SQUARE

448. INSCRIBING A
HEXAGON IN A
GIVEN CIRCLE

449.
CIRCUMSCRIBING
OCTAGON AROUND
A GIVEN CIRCLE

T SQUARE

If the tangent is to pass through a point [Q] outside the circle, begin by placing one side of the triangle so that it lies on the point and just touches the circumference [Position b, solid outline]. Mark the point of tangency [P]. The first setting will probably be slightly inaccurate. Check it by sliding the triangle until the other side lies on Point P [Position a]. This side should then touch the center [C]. If it fails to do so, correct the mark for the point of tangency and try again. You will rarely need to make more than one such correction.

An adjustable triangle [Fig. 453] eliminates the need for the two-triangle method. It also acts as a protractor which enables us to set angles with an accuracy of about a quarter of a degree. After one line is placed, we can draw parallels and perpendiculars to it without resetting the triangle.

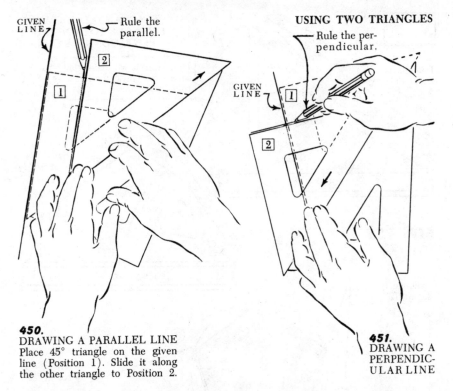

GIVEN LINE — Rule the parallel.

2

1

USING TWO TRIANGLES

— Rule the perpendicular.

GIVEN LINE

1

2

450.
DRAWING A PARALLEL LINE
Place 45° triangle on the given line (Position 1). Slide it along the other triangle to Position 2.

451.
DRAWING A PERPENDIC-ULAR LINE

French Curves. When straight lines are ruled and circles are drawn with a compass, a freehand curve seems painfully crude by comparison. For this reason, noncircular curves in finished mechanical drawings should be ruled with a French curve [Fig. 454].

To use such a curve, plot points on the wanted line. Draw a faint construction line through these points. Place the curve along the line, finding the best fit that you can [Step 1]. Rule part of the line, but stop short of the point where the French curve departs from the line. Shift the French curve until it fits the next section of the line, making it overlap the part already ruled [Step 2]. This is a slow

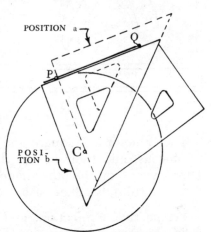

POSITION a

Q

P

POSITION b

C

452. DRAWING TANGENT EITHER AT A POINT [P] ON THE CIRCLE OR FROM A POINT [Q] OUTSIDE THE CIRCLE; SEE TEXT P. 210

process. However, it is the only way to draw irregular curves that are really smooth and accurate. *Flexible rulers* are sold for this purpose, but I have never found them satisfactory.

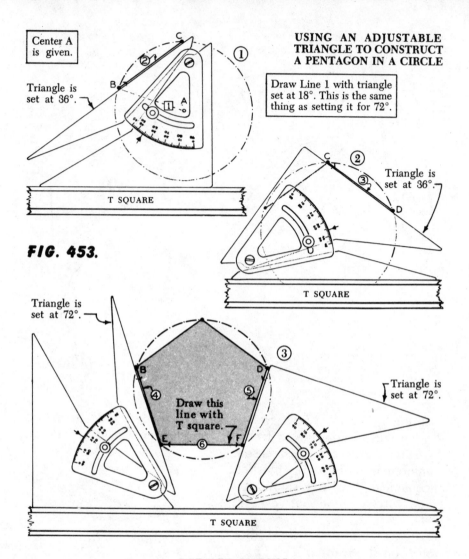

Center A is given.

Triangle is set at 36°.

Draw Line 1 with triangle set at 18°. This is the same thing as setting it for 72°.

T SQUARE

FIG. 453.

Triangle is set at 36°.

T SQUARE

Triangle is set at 72°.

Draw this line with T square.

Triangle is set at 72°.

T SQUARE

DIRECT VIEWS

The value of a T square and triangles in preparing datagrams is obvious, and their use in this field requires no explanation. Direct views, on the other hand, require further study before we can take full advantage of our drafting instruments.

Perspective, Projection, and Construction. When we trace a solid object on a glass plate [Fig. 455], the *projecting rays* converge at the eye. This reduces the drawing in size, but the change is not uniform—the far parts of the object are reduced more than those which are nearer.

It is easy to trace such a perspective drawing on a glass plate. However, when we try to construct one from a set of measurements, the task becomes tedious. Also, if we attempt to measure

Fig. 454]   Mechanical Aids   213

the lines of a completed perspective, we must go through an elaborate procedure to correct the distortion.

If we could create parallel projecting rays and cause them to trace a drawing on an imaginary *picture plane,* the result would be a direct view and the distortion would disappear—except in oblique planes like the roof in Fig. 456.

These illustrations demonstrate that both perspectives and direct views can be produced by *projection.* The effect of perspective is created by *conical projection,* where the rays fit roughly into a cone with its apex at the eye of the observer. Parallel rays produce effects known as *parallel projections.* Direct views are the simplest examples of these. Perspective has a name of its own; we shall therefore take advantage of this to use the term "projection" as an abbreviation for "parallel projection."

In construction, we draw lines that are either part of the picture itself or form a skeleton on which the picture can be sketched; none of these lines connects the picture with its source. In projection, we project rays from the source onto the picture plane. My diagrams show the rays as dotted lines, but this is merely a device to aid visualization. The rays themselves are imaginary and touch the picture only at their ends.

Construction is essentially a method for achieving the results of projection by more convenient means. However, although drawings can be made more easily by construction, they can be understood more completely if we think in terms of projection. This may seem like a roundabout approach, but experience

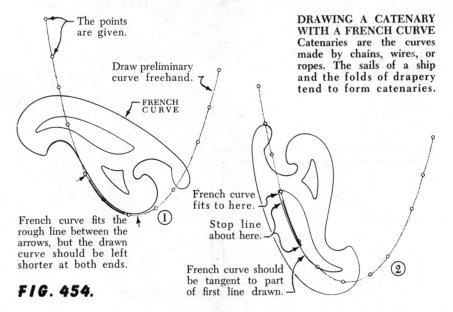

The points are given.

Draw preliminary curve freehand.

FRENCH CURVE

French curve fits the rough line between the arrows, but the drawn curve should be left shorter at both ends.

FIG. 454.

French curve fits to here.

Stop line about here.

French curve should be tangent to part of first line drawn.

DRAWING A CATENARY WITH A FRENCH CURVE
Catenaries are the curves made by chains, wires, or ropes. The sails of a ship and the folds of drapery tend to form catenaries.

①

②

proves it to be sound. Once you learn to think in terms of projection, you will find that many things about drawing which originally seemed arbitrary or meaningless suddenly become clear. Better still, problems that appeared hopeless before can be solved at a glance. I cannot stress this too strongly. Construction is a valuable tool, but *projection is the master key to an understanding of the meaning and methods of drawing.*

Basic Views. Figs. 457–459 demonstrate how thinking in terms of projection helps us to visualize the relations of the six basic, direct views to the source and to each other. Fig. 457 shows how these views would look if they were projected onto the faces of

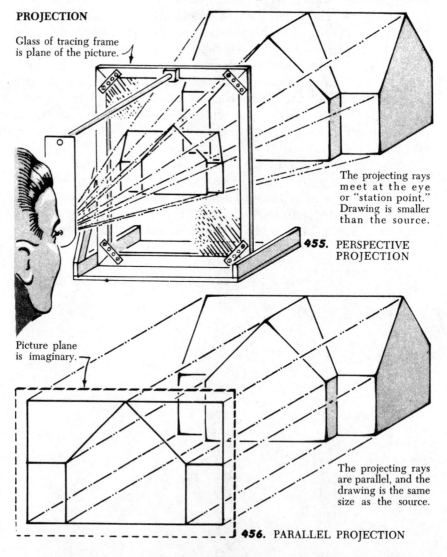

PROJECTION

Glass of tracing frame is plane of the picture.

The projecting rays meet at the eye or "station point." Drawing is smaller than the source.

455. PERSPECTIVE PROJECTION

Picture plane is imaginary.

The projecting rays are parallel, and the drawing is the same size as the source.

456. PARALLEL PROJECTION

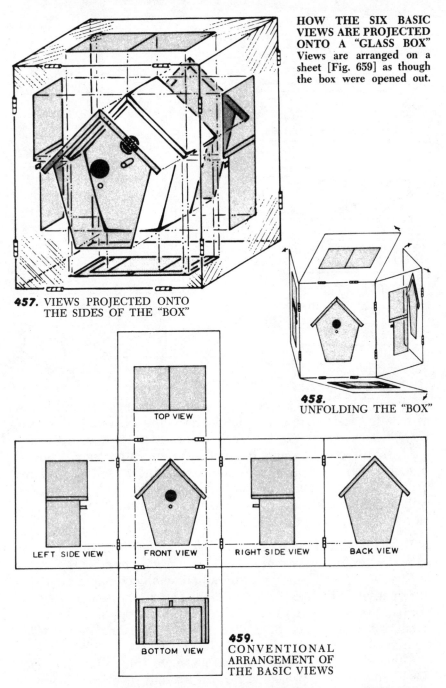

HOW THE SIX BASIC
VIEWS ARE PROJECTED
ONTO A "GLASS BOX"
Views are arranged on a
sheet [Fig. 659] as though
the box were opened out.

457. VIEWS PROJECTED ONTO
THE SIDES OF THE "BOX"

TOP VIEW

458.
UNFOLDING THE "BOX"

LEFT SIDE VIEW   FRONT VIEW   RIGHT SIDE VIEW   BACK VIEW

BOTTOM VIEW

459.
CONVENTIONAL
ARRANGEMENT OF
THE BASIC VIEWS

an imaginary glass box with hinged sides. If we open this box out
flat, the six views can all be seen at once [Fig. 459].

Observe that this glass-box principle controls the arrangement
of the views on the sheet [Fig. 459]. The top view is directly
above the front view, and the bottom view is directly below it.

215

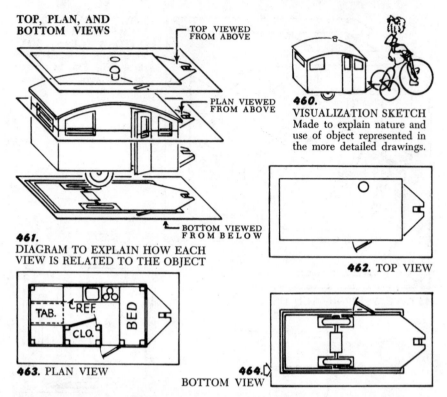

TOP VIEWED
FROM ABOVE

PLAN VIEWED
FROM ABOVE

460.
VISUALIZATION SKETCH
Made to explain nature and
use of object represented in
the more detailed drawings.

BOTTOM VIEWED
FROM BELOW

461.
DIAGRAM TO EXPLAIN HOW EACH
VIEW IS RELATED TO THE OBJECT

462. TOP VIEW

TAB. REF. CLO. BED

463. PLAN VIEW

464.
BOTTOM VIEW

Back- and side-views are on a level with the front view and follow
a definite order. Drawings should normally be grouped in this
way, just as words are arranged alphabetically in a dictionary.

All six direct views may be needed to give a complete concep-
tion of an irregular object. Architectural subjects will also require
a number of sections and perhaps many detailed drawings as
well. For most purposes, however, the top-, front-, and one side-
view will contain all the information we need.

Top-, Plan-, and Bottom-Views. The value of thinking in terms
of projection emerges more clearly when we consider the trailer
in Figs. 460–464. The top view of a hollow object may not be very
informative [Fig. 462]. A *plan view* (often shortened to *plan*)
normally tells us much more [Fig. 463]. The top view shows the
outside, whereas the plan is a section revealing the interior
arrangement.

Although the plan and the bottom views both show the floor,
the bottom view is projected downward and seen from below so
that it is reversed in comparison to the top and plan views. This
explains why the door is below the plan in Fig. 463 but is above
the bottom view in Fig. 464. This can be confusing if you think
in terms of construction. But when you think in terms of projection, everything becomes clear.

Fig. 464]   Mechanical Aids   **217**

The little sketch in Fig. 460 is a device that could profitably be used more often in practical drawing. It is not strictly necessary, but at one glance it tells the reader that the trailer is a toy, indicates its approximate size, and shows how it is to be used. Such a sketch also makes it easier to visualize the individual views.

Sections. The plan of the trailer in Fig. 463 is a typical section. Everything behind (in this case, below) the cutting plane is projected by parallel rays onto the picture plane. Conventional violations get their name from the fact that they disobey some laws of parallel projection. It will pay you to turn back to the conventional violation in Fig. 163 and note how the drawing departs from the true projection in the same figure.

Applied Projection. Projection is much more than a theory. Three-dimensional diagrams, like those in Figs. 455 and 456, are of little use except as illustrations in a book on drawing. But the methods of two-dimensional projection provide many short cuts, and they enable us to handle problems that would otherwise be insoluble.

CONVENTIONS. Construction and projection are often employed in the same drawing. We therefore need special conventions to distinguish projecting rays from construction lines. In your own notes, you should use a colored pencil (say brown or purple) for rays. However, as I am confined to black, I have represented the rays by lines in which a dash alternates with two dots [Fig. 465]. The direction of each ray is shown by a half-headed arrow. Numbers placed on these arrows indicate the order in which the rays are drawn.

As each point is projected by a set of rays, and as *all the sets are drawn on exactly the same principle*, I have chosen one set as a typical example and shown this by a heavy, dotted line. For your own notes, you need draw only the typical rays and can omit the rest.

Projection is normally used where we make at least two views of the same source. Hence, each point appears two or more times in a set of drawings. I have lettered the points in the first drawing and used the same letters with subscripts for the corresponding points in the succeeding drawings. Thus, in the birdhouse [Fig. 465] Points A_1, A_2, and A_3 represent various projections of Point A.

A drawing of the source is really a collection of given lines. I found it more confusing than helpful to indicate these by dotted lines as I did in the construction diagrams. I have, therefore,

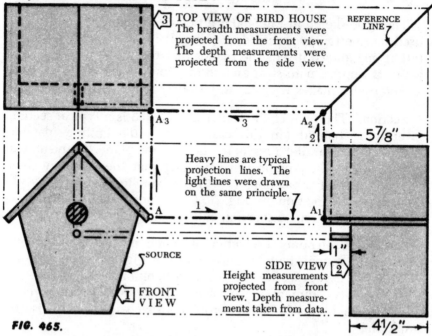

3 TOP VIEW OF BIRD HOUSE
The breadth measurements were
projected from the front view.
The depth measurements were
projected from the side view.

REFERENCE
LINE

Heavy lines are typical
projection lines. The
light lines were drawn
on the same principle.

SOURCE

1 FRONT
VIEW

SIDE VIEW 2
Height measurements
projected from front
view. Depth measure-
ments taken from data.

FIG. 465.

been forced to be content with designating the source by a label. In your own notes, you will find it convenient to draw the source with a pencil of the same color that you use for given lines in construction diagrams.

Ticks. Although the rays must be drawn in projection diagrams to show the procedure, in actual practice we omit most of each ray and make only a small tick to mark where the ray fixes a point on a line or on another ray.

Reference Lines. We often need to make rays turn a corner without changing their distances from each other. Fig. 465 shows how to do this with the aid of a *reference line*. The reference line can be placed at any convenient location on the sheet. Draw it at half the angle through which the rays are to be bent. Thus, turning the rays 90° calls for a reference line at 45°.

Projection by Tracing. If we want to draw the individual views of an object on separate sheets, we can do so by a combination of projection and tracing [Figs. 466 and 467]. As this requires visualizing the object in two or three views at once, it may seem like a sure way to confuse yourself. However, after you become used to the idea you will find that it is a labor-saving device of major importance. Furthermore, practice with it will prepare you for more advanced types of projection where the ability to visualize two or three views at the same time is essential.

Fig. 467]   Mechanical Aids   219

The procedure is almost identical with that shown in Fig. 465. The front view [gray lines in Fig. 466] is drawn first and is then used as the source. Tracing paper is placed over this. The horizontal lines of the side view are ruled through the corresponding points of the front view. Widths are assumed (or taken from data) and measured to fix the verticals.

Another sheet of tracing paper is now placed over the side view [Fig. 467]. This permits both the front and side views to be seen. A reference line is drawn at 45°. The position of the reference line affects the vertical position of the top view but is otherwise unimportant. The top view can now be traced without making further measurements. The reference line is used only to turn the verticals of the side view into the horizontals of the top view. The verticals in the top view are drawn directly through the corresponding points on the front view.

You will find that tracing your own projections is easier than reading mine. With mine, you must puzzle out the purpose of each line before you can understand it. With your own, you know the meaning of the line before you even think of drawing it.

PROJECTION BY TRACING

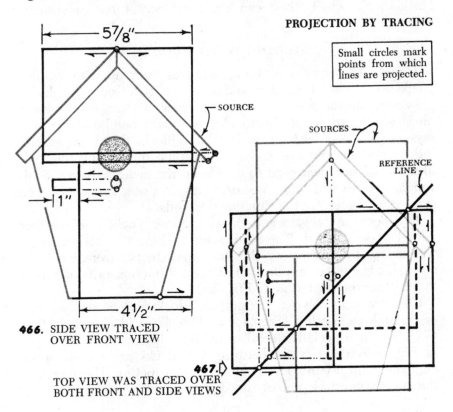

Small circles mark points from which lines are projected.

SOURCE

SOURCES

REFERENCE LINE

466. SIDE VIEW TRACED OVER FRONT VIEW

467. TOP VIEW WAS TRACED OVER BOTH FRONT AND SIDE VIEWS

13

ADDING THE
THIRD DIMENSION

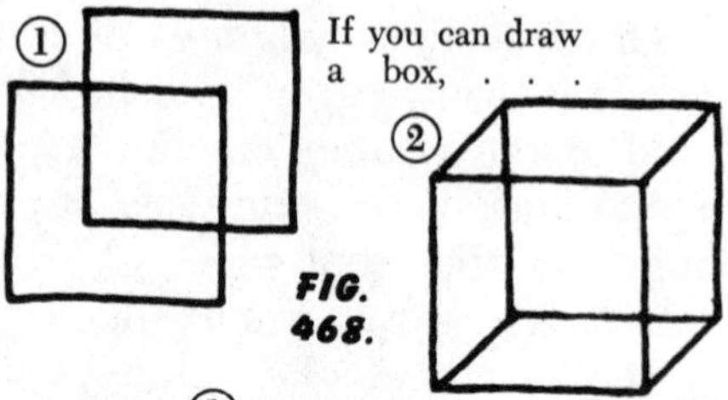

If you can draw a box, . . .

FIG. 468.

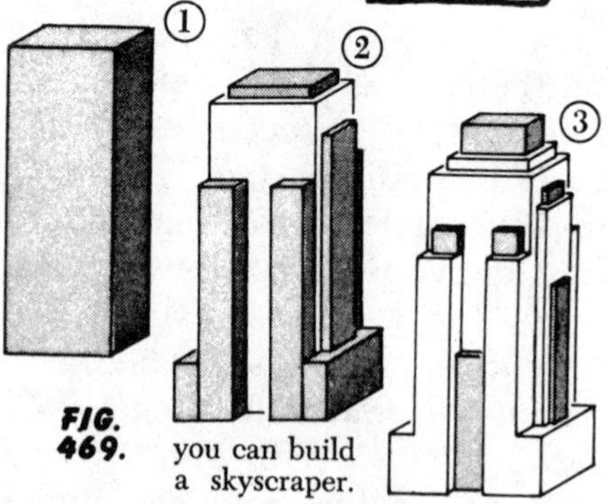

FIG. 469.

you can build a skyscraper.

THE drawing in Fig. 468 is a symbol of lost opportunities. Most children are taught this trick of sketching a box, but few of them are ever told that the box contains a set of graphic building blocks with which they can construct any three-dimensional object.

BUILDING WITH BLOCKS

The skyscraper shown in Fig. 469 was built up with graphic blocks exactly as a child would have built it from toy blocks. However, anyone working with toy blocks is hampered by the physical limitations of the blocks; he could not build this toy skyscraper unless he happened to have blocks that were exactly the right sizes. We can make our graphic blocks any sizes we like. We do not even need to decide on the measurements in advance; we can wait until we are ready to use a block and then make it whatever size the situation demands.

Toy blocks are always added, but graphic blocks can be either added or subtracted. The sign letter in Fig. 470, for example, was drawn by subtracting the four small blocks from the large one. This is another application of the subtraction principle used to construct the closterium in Fig. 354.

Unlike wooden blocks, our graphic blocks can be pushed into or through each other [fireplace in Fig. 471 and church in Fig. 472]. This is especially useful in modern design. The skyscraper in Fig. 469 seems crude because the blocks are merely stuck onto the central core. The church is much better. The fact that the blocks interlock makes the design an integral unit.

Fig. 472]   Adding the Third Dimension   221

Three-Dimensional Constructions. The value of graphic blocks is by no means limited to fixed-line construction. We can build up a set of blocks for an irregular object like the fireplace in Fig. 471 and then use this construction as a framework on which to sketch the actual drawing.

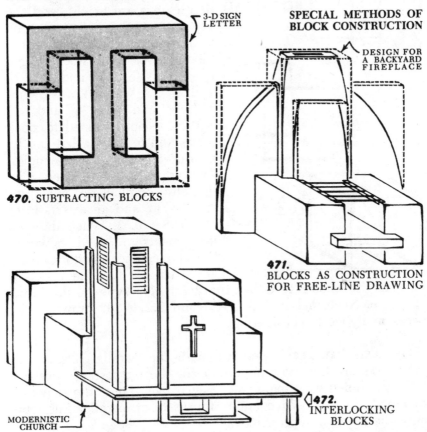

3-D SIGN LETTER

SPECIAL METHODS OF BLOCK CONSTRUCTION

DESIGN FOR A BACKYARD FIREPLACE

470. SUBTRACTING BLOCKS

471.
BLOCKS AS CONSTRUCTION FOR FREE-LINE DRAWING

472.
INTERLOCKING BLOCKS

MODERNISTIC CHURCH

Axes. The technical name for the box trick is *oblique drawing.* Every rectangular block has twelve edges [Figs. 473–475]. The four edges on each axis belong to the same *parallel set. All lines that are parallel in the source must be parallel in the drawing and must be drawn to the same scale.*

Angles and Scales. In oblique drawing, the height and breadth lines are both drawn to the same scale and are perpendicular to each other, just as they are in the source. There is no fixed rule for the depth lines. In Fig. 473, the depth lines are drawn at two-thirds of the scale used for the height and breadth lines. This produces a 3:3:2 *axis ratio,* which can be measured by any one of four pairs of stock scales: $1\frac{1}{2}''$ ($= 1'0''$) and $1''$

$(= 1'0'')$; $\frac{3}{4}''$ and $\frac{1}{2}''$; $\frac{3}{8}''$ and $\frac{1}{4}''$; $\frac{3}{16}''$ and $\frac{1}{8}''$. When the axis ratio is 3:3:2, the depth lines are usually drawn at 30° to the horizontal [Fig. 475].

AXES

473. LINES ON THE HEIGHT AXIS

474. LINES ON THE BREADTH AXIS

475. LINES ON THE DEPTH AXIS

30°

Another common arrangement is shown in Fig. 468. Here, the depth lines are at 45°, and the axis ratio is 2:2:1. This can be measured with any one of the following pairs of stock scales: $3''$ and $1\frac{1}{2}''$; $1\frac{1}{2}''$ and $\frac{3}{4}''$; $1''$ and $\frac{1}{2}''$; $\frac{3}{4}''$ and $\frac{3}{8}''$; $\frac{1}{2}''$ and $\frac{1}{4}''$; $\frac{3}{8}''$ and $\frac{3}{16}''$; $\frac{1}{4}''$ and $\frac{1}{8}''$. We are not confined to stock scales and to angles that can be measured with stock triangles. An offhand sketch may accidentally employ an angle of, say, 36°30′ and an axis ratio of 1 : 0.98 : 0.53. When drawing instruments are used, however, the convenience of stock scales and triangles has the effect of limiting the choice to either the 2:2:1, 45° type or the 3:3:2, 30° type. Nevertheless, 3:3:2, 45° and 2:2:1, 30° drawings are occasionally worth considering.

OFF-AXIS PARALLEL SETS. Although the parallel sets on the main axes are the most important for the purpose of construction, we can use as many sets as we like. Thus, the deuce of diamonds in Fig. 476 contains four sets of parallel lines, but only the set that represents the long edges of the card are on an axis (depth) in my drawing.

Off-axis sets obey the same rules as on-axis sets: all lines that are parallel in the source are parallel in the drawing, and all lines in the same set are drawn to the same scale. When an off-axis set is parallel to the picture plane [short edges of deuce in Fig. 476], the lines are measured by the scale used for the

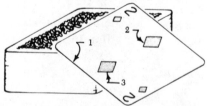

476. OFF-AXIS PARALLEL SETS
This illustration shows three parallel sets of lines besides those on axes of the drawing.

height- and breadth-axes. Unfortunately, the scales of other off-axis sets, such as the edges of the diamonds on the card, are

Fig. 478]   Adding the Third Dimension   223

almost never stock scales. In spite of this, the principle is useful.
As soon as I had established one side of a large diamond in
Fig. 476, I knew that the three lines parallel to it in both large
diamonds were the same length.
We can also apply the principle
when we want to make one line
in proportion to another. Dividers
are useful here [Fig. 277].

CHOOSING AXES. Some distortion
is inevitable in oblique drawing,
but it can be minimized by placing
the longest measurement of the
source on either the height- or
the breadth-axis. The severe distortion in Fig. 477 is due to the
fact that the length of the table is
on the depth axis and its width is
on the breadth axis. Turning the
table to bring the length onto the
breadth axis produces a much better effect [Fig. 478].

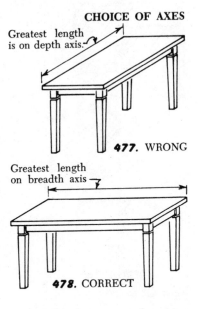

CHOICE OF AXES

Greatest length
is on depth axis.

477. WRONG

Greatest length
on breadth axis

478. CORRECT

Do not use the terms "length" and "width" for axes; they are
apt to cause confusion. Also, remember that depth is a horizontal
dimension and not a vertical one as it is when we speak of the
"depth" of the sea.

Planes. The twelve edges of a block outline six planes. These
also form three parallel sets called *height-breadth planes, height-
depth planes,* and *breadth-depth planes* after the axes to which
they belong [Figs. 479–481].
A parallel set may contain any number of planes. In a cutaway view of a skyscraper, for example, all the floors would be
horizontal and hence they would all be breadth-depth planes.
We can draw as many parallel sets as the source requires.
Thus, an oblique drawing of the residence in Fig. 174 would
be constructed on two sets of planes for the walls, one for the
porch floor, and four for the roof. The slight curves in the walls
and roof would then be drawn over this construction.
We shall use the term *axial planes* for those which belong to
one of the main parallel sets. Those which are off axis, like the
roof planes in Fig. 174 or the deuce of diamonds in Fig. 476, will
be called *oblique planes.*

Solid Blocks vs. Hollow Blocks. We can use our blocks to construct hollow objects as well as solid ones [police diagram in Fig. 482]. The only difference is that we omit the lines of the front and draw those of the back instead. Whether the block is solid or hollow, we can show only three faces in their correct positions. When we want to show more, we must either make two drawings or open out the other three faces—as I have done with the police diagram.

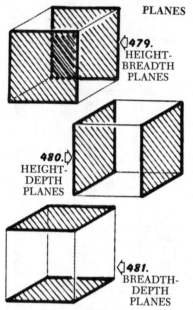

PLANES

479. HEIGHT-BREADTH PLANES

480. HEIGHT-DEPTH PLANES

481. BREADTH-DEPTH PLANES

Viewpoints. The effect of distortion in an oblique drawing is at a minimum when the apparent viewpoint corresponds to the actual viewpoint. Thus, the police diagram in Fig. 482 is easy to visualize because it is at the bottom of a left-hand page, and we are looking down into it from the right. If it were at the top of a right-hand page, it might have seemed meaningless until you had given it some study.

As we rarely see objects from below, a drawing that shows something from above is fairly easy to visualize. This is true even

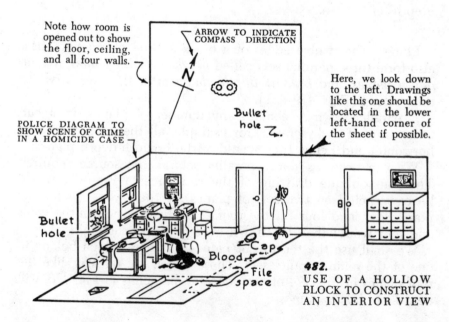

Note how room is opened out to show the floor, ceiling, and all four walls.

ARROW TO INDICATE COMPASS DIRECTION

N

Bullet hole

Here, we look down to the left. Drawings like this one should be located in the lower left-hand corner of the sheet if possible.

POLICE DIAGRAM TO SHOW SCENE OF CRIME IN A HOMICIDE CASE

Bullet hole

Cap

Blood

File space

482. USE OF A HOLLOW BLOCK TO CONSTRUCT AN INTERIOR VIEW

Fig. 484]   Adding the Third Dimension   225

when the drawing is placed at the top of the page so that we actually look up toward it. You probably had no trouble with the block in Fig. 479. In fact, you may not have noticed that you were looking up at the drawing but looking down on the block.

When, however, a drawing presents an unusual view, try to place it on the sheet so that the actual viewpoint corresponds to the apparent viewpoint. The ceiling in Fig. 483, for example, was drawn as though we were looking up at it from the left; the fact that it is in the upper right-hand corner of a right-hand page means that we really do see it from this angle.

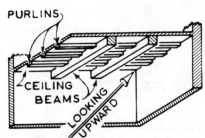

483. POSITION AND VIEWPOINT
As this illustration shows the upper right-hand corner of a room, it is easiest to visualize when placed in the upper right-hand corner of the sheet.

Fig. 484 illustrates what may happen if this rule is ignored—especially when both the object and the viewpoint are unfamiliar. Anyone able to read this sketch at first glance can congratulate himself on his powers of visualization. Nevertheless, it is an accurate drawing showing the interior of a doghouse. The right and rear walls are removed, and we look upward from the right. Placing this illustration in the upper left-hand corner of a left-hand page would have made it much easier to recognize. Should you still have trouble in making sense of it, try holding it a little above your line of vision and about 6″ to the left of your nose.

Devices That Emphasize the Third Dimension. There are several ways to help an observer visualize a drawing as a three-dimensional object. These devices are especially useful where we cannot control the observer's viewpoint. When I made the illustrations for this book, I did not know whether any particular drawing would fall on a left-hand or a right-hand page. This meant that I could not tell if it

484. DRAWING IN BAD POSITION
This was drawn from the lower right, but it is placed so that you see it from the upper left.

would be better to make the depth lines slant up to the right or to the left. Whenever I guessed wrong, I had to either remake the drawing or take a chance on your being able to read it in spite of its poor position. The tables in Figs. 477 and 478 would have seemed less distorted if their depth lines had slanted up to the left.

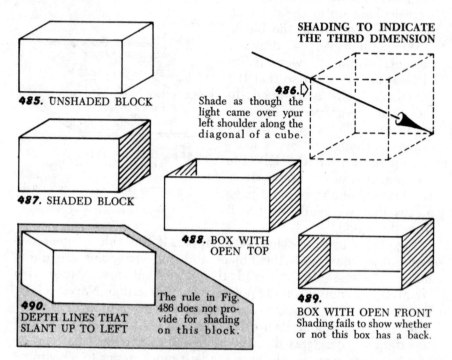

SHADING TO INDICATE THE THIRD DIMENSION

485. UNSHADED BLOCK

486. Shade as though the light came over your left shoulder along the diagonal of a cube.

487. SHADED BLOCK

488. BOX WITH OPEN TOP

490. DEPTH LINES THAT SLANT UP TO LEFT

The rule in Fig. 486 does not provide for shading on this block.

489. BOX WITH OPEN FRONT
Shading fails to show whether or not this box has a back.

SHADING. The easiest way to bring out the third dimension is to shade the drawing as though it were illuminated by light shining over the observer's left shoulder along the diagonal of a cube [Fig. 486]. Fig. 487 is shaded in this way and leaves no doubt that it represents a solid block.

The convention of showing the light as coming from the left is so thoroughly established that light which appears to come from the right is likely to make raised portions of the drawing seem like hollows. This effect appears even in photographs. If you turn the coin in Step 3, Fig. 35, upside down, it may look like the die from which the coin was stamped. Note that the rule requiring the light to come over the left shoulder does not permit a block to be shaded when the depth lines slant upward to the left [Fig. 490].

If Fig. 488 were not shaded, the lines alone would show that it represents a box with no top. In that case, however, the reader might not be able to recognize the object at a glance (compare the line drawing in Fig. 485). By shading Fig. 488, I was able to make the nature and position of the box obvious. The shading in Fig. 489 is less satisfactory. It tells us that this box lacks a front but gives no information about its back. I could have made this point clear by adding *cast shadows* [Figs. 491 and 492].

Shading is placed on those parts of an object that are turned away from the light; a cast shadow is thrown by an object either onto another part of itself or onto some other object. In practical drawing, shading is usually conventional and gives no trouble. Deciding where cast shadows will fall is also fairly easy, unless we need to be absolutely correct [cross in Fig. 493]. It can then involve complications which carry us beyond the scope of this book.

Figs. 494 and 495 illustrate a special type of arbitrary shading that enables the draftsman to show whether or not an open box has a back. This trick is useful when the drawing is one of a group, and the others employ conventional shading like that in Fig. 489 but ignore shadows. Figs. 494 and 495 also demonstrate that, unlike ordinary shading, these types are effective when the depth lines slant upward to the left.

SHADING VS. CAST SHADOWS

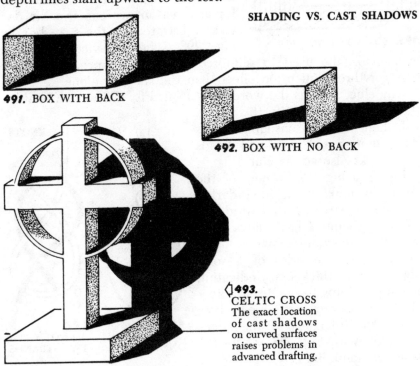

491. BOX WITH BACK

492. BOX WITH NO BACK

◁**493.**
CELTIC CROSS
The exact location of cast shadows on curved surfaces raises problems in advanced drafting.

KNOTS. These present special problems. If only one strand is involved, the simplest procedure is to draw a single line and break it whenever one part crosses behind another [Fig. 496].

Mark the loose end with a dot to distinguish it from the main rope or "standing part." This is important; many reliable knots become treacherous if the standing part and end are reversed.

ARBITRARY SHADING
This does not represent either light or texture. It merely distinguishes one surface from another.

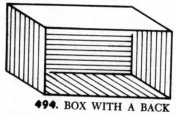

494. BOX WITH A BACK

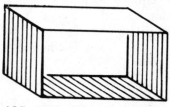

495. BOX WITH NO BACK

When two strands are joined, avoid confusion by making one black and one white [Fig. 497]. Wherever the white strand crosses itself, blacken the rear part for a short distance on either side of the crossing [Point B]. Reverse this process where the black strand crosses itself [Point C]. Blacken the end of the white strand [Point A] and leave the end of the black strand white [Point D].

OTHER METHODS OF EMPHASIZING THE THIRD DIMENSION. Where shading is impractical or undesirable for any reason, we can use the devices illustrated by the soap box in Fig. 498. These devices may, of course, also be used to reinforce shading and produce a still stronger three-dimension effect than the shading alone.

Any clue, such as the word "SOAP" in Fig. 498, which enables the observer to identify the object, will help him to visualize it as three-dimensional. The nail heads and cracks also act as clues.

Emphasizing the corners of the object by making the lines darker or thicker stresses the third dimension, though I have never been able to understand why.

Whenever the sides of a solid object have thickness, indicating the edges helps to create an effect of depth. Compare the soap box, where the thickness of the edges is shown, with Fig. 488, where the edges are mere lines.

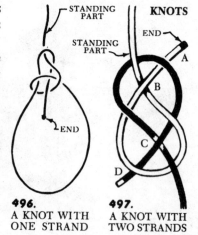

496.
A KNOT WITH ONE STRAND

497.
A KNOT WITH TWO STRANDS

Finally, our old friend the trick of stopping lines just before they disappear behind other lines can be used with great effect. In the soap box, only the lines of the rear left-hand corner and

Fig. 500]   Adding the Third Dimension   229

the crack between the back boards stop in this way, but these play a real part in making the box seem hollow.

OFF-AXIS FORMS

Blocks provide a basis for three-dimensional drawing, but we need other solid forms when we want to sketch such objects as pup tents and church steeples.

Wedges and Pyramids. Many man-made objects and some natural ones fit into wedge shapes. Fig. 499 illustrates how we can construct a wedge of any proportions in any position by combining two blocks and drawing diagonals.

498. DEVICES TO EMPHASIZE THE THREE-DIMENSIONAL EFFECT These may also be used to reduce the difficulty of visualizing the object when the picture is placed in a poor position on the sheet.

The pyramid in Fig. 500 is constructed on the same principle as the wedges except that it requires four blocks instead of two.

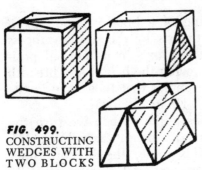

FIG. 499. CONSTRUCTING WEDGES WITH TWO BLOCKS

Off-Axis Lines. When a single line lies in one of the axis planes, we can locate it by constructing a block and then drawing the line as a diagonal to one face [Fig. 501]. All the lines in this example have slopes with a rise of 9 for a run of 7. If we want a line with a different slope, we have only to use the proper proportions in drawing the block.

Where we do not know the slope of a line, but do know its length and the angle it makes with the horizontal, we can compute the slope graphically by making an *auxiliary drawing* [Fig. 502]. Auxiliary drawings solve many problems, especially those that arise in making three-dimensional drawings of complex objects.

500. CONSTRUCTING PYRAMID WITH FOUR BLOCKS

When a slanting line is not in one of the axial planes, we can construct a block and then draw the line between diagonally opposite corners [Fig. 503]. Note that whereas a slanting line in one face of a block can be drawn from only two measurements, a line like that in Fig. 503 requires three measurements (7, 8, and 9).

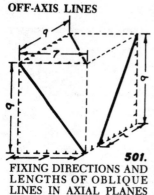

501.
FIXING DIRECTIONS AND LENGTHS OF OBLIQUE LINES IN AXIAL PLANES

One of the limitations of three-dimensional drawing is that isolated off-axis lines are hard to visualize. We can get around this by drawing a block to indicate the positions and scales of the axis lines, as I did in Figs. 501 and 503. Fortunately, the difficulty does not arise when off-axis lines occur in a fairly realistic drawing like the schoolhouse in Fig. 504.

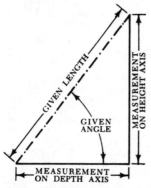

502. AUXILIARY DRAWING
Made to determine the slope of a line when its length and its angle with the horizontal are given.

Tip, Turn, and Tilt. Oblique drawing is easy as long as the main lines of the object can be placed on the axes. However, this is not always possible. Thus, the whole point of Fig. 505 depends on the fact that the books slant in different directions.

A drawing of a book can be *tipped* on its depth axis by the simple process of keeping this axis in its normal position and showing the height and breadth lines at the angles that they have in the source [Vol. III in Fig. 505].

Difficulties appear when we *turn* the block about its height axis [Vol. II]. When this is done, the breadth lines are foreshortened and thrown off axis. The depth lines are also thrown off axis, but they are lengthened instead of being shortened. We must therefore draw two sets of lines having angles and lengths that cannot be fixed directly. In all such cases, the answer lies in referring these lines to on-axis construction lines which can be drawn and measured with ease. This is done by making one or more auxiliary drawings.

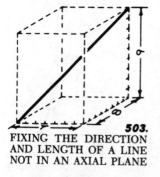

503.
FIXING THE DIRECTION AND LENGTH OF A LINE NOT IN AN AXIAL PLANE

The auxiliary drawing needed to turn Vol. II is a top view [Fig. 506]. The measurements of the book are known or assumed. The thickness is represented by a, and the length from front to back is b. The angle of turn is also known or assumed.

Fig. 504]   Adding the Third Dimension   231

With these data, we can easily draw Fig. 506. This fixes the breadth measurements e and f and the depth measurements c and d. Fig. 507 shows how this can be used to construct an oblique drawing of Vol. II. Note that the new measurements found in the auxiliary drawing become given measurements in the three-dimensional construction. All the oblique drawings in this plate have an axis ratio of 2:2:1 and a depth axis set at 30°.

504. APPLICATIONS OF OFF-AXIS CONSTRUCTIONS
The roof is a wedge. The steeple is two pyramids. Ladders A and C are constructed either as wedges or by the method in Fig. 501. Ladders B and D are constructed by the off-axis method shown in Fig. 503.

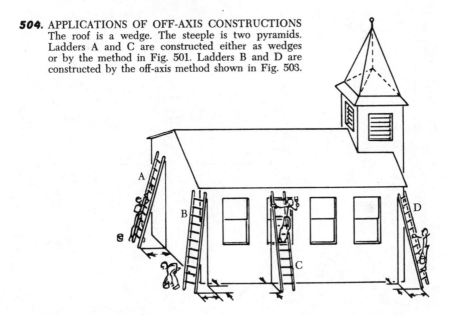

Study Figs. 506 and 507 carefully until you are sure you understand how each line is drawn and what purpose it serves. The difficulty of this study will depend entirely on how far you have developed your ability to visualize lines in three dimensions. If you can handle this sort of visualization, you will be able to read Figs. 506 and 507 almost at a glance. If your powers of visualization are weak, you may have to mull over the illustrations for some time before you can make anything out of them. Should they give you trouble, do not lose heart. Understanding normally comes with a rush. At one moment, the drawing is a meaningless maze of lines; the next moment it is so clear that you cannot imagine why you had trouble with it.

Even if you are not yet prepared to read Figs. 506 and 507, you may nevertheless achieve an offhand sketch of Vol. II. Try it anyway. Make the breadth lines a little shorter than those for Vol. I, and let them slant slightly. Lengthen the depth lines a trifle and draw them at a somewhat smaller angle than 30°. If

you succeed with this, come back to Figs. 506 and 507 and try
to construct an accurate drawing of Vol. II with the aid of my
auxiliary plan [Fig. 506].

Books are ideal objects for practice-doodling when you study
three-dimensional drawing. They are almost as easy as blocks, but
they have enough detail to hold your interest and to present you
with a few minor problems as well.

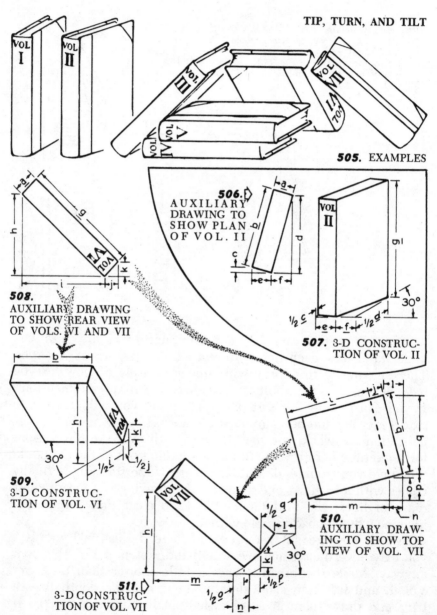

TIP, TURN, AND TILT

505. EXAMPLES

506. AUXILIARY DRAWING TO SHOW PLAN OF VOL. II

507. 3-D CONSTRUCTION OF VOL. II

508. AUXILIARY DRAWING TO SHOW REAR VIEW OF VOLS. VI AND VII

509. 3-D CONSTRUCTION OF VOL. VI

510. AUXILIARY DRAWING TO SHOW TOP VIEW OF VOL. VII

511. 3-D CONSTRUCTION OF VOL. VII

Fig. 511]   Adding the Third Dimension   233

When you have mastered the use of an auxiliary top view in turning a book, study the method of *tilting* Vol. VI on its breadth axis as illustrated in Figs. 508 and 509. Fig. 508 is a direct view of this volume, and g represents its known or assumed height when erect. Measurements on the height axis in the drawing are marked h and k. Depth measurements are represented by i and j. Once these are determined, we can use them to construct the oblique drawing in Fig. 509. If you really understand Figs. 506 and 507, Vol. VI should give you no trouble.

Vol. VII is entirely off axis; it is tipped, turned, and tilted at the same time. I have simplified matters by giving it the same tilt as Vol. VI. Hence, Fig. 508 doubles as a rear view of Vol. II. In this case, however, we also need a top view [Fig. 510]. Measurements i and j become oblique lines in this view. Measurements o, p, and q represent depths, and l, m, and n are breadths. Fig. 511 shows how these can be combined with heights from Fig. 508 to construct the off-axis block. You may find this process difficult to visualize, even though you had no trouble with Figs. 507 and 509. If so, you need more practice in three-dimensional visualization. Stick at it until you get it. When you can read every line in Fig. 511, you will have taken a big step toward mastery of three-dimensional drawing.

SHORT CUTS

The block approach aids visualization because it lets us build a drawing by adding one block at a time. It is also a good way to construct drawings of rectangular objects. However, after you gain skill, you will often prefer to follow one of the more direct methods given below.

Draw As You Go. When you have learned to visualize in three dimensions, you can construct oblique drawings a line at a time —just as you would normally make a direct view. Fig. 512 shows the sequence in which I drew the lines of a loudspeaker cabinet. Many other sequences would have been possible.

The first step is to establish the axes of the sketch by drawing three lines from one corner [the lines from Corner A in Step 1]. The depth scale is then chosen, and the length of the line on the depth axis is measured or estimated [Line 1]; this fixes Point B.

The remaining lines may then be added in any order, subject to the following rules: (1) A line must start at a point already established (Line 4 could not be drawn until Line 1 had been

placed and Point B had been fixed by measuring from Point A).
(2) If the line is on an axis, it must be parallel to the proper
axis and measured by the scale for that axis (Line 5 is parallel
to the depth axis and measured by the depth scale). (3) If a
line is off axis, it must be plotted by the run-and-rise method or
drawn between two points previously fixed (Line 11 in Step 2
runs between Points C and D).

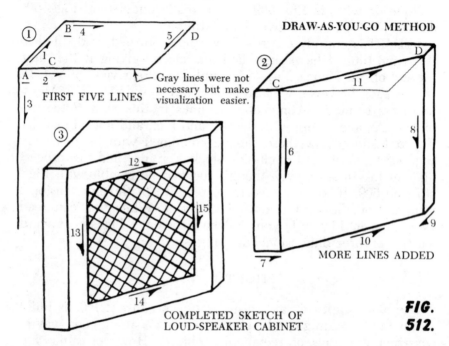

DRAW-AS-YOU-GO METHOD

① FIRST FIVE LINES

Gray lines were not
necessary but make
visualization easier.

② MORE LINES ADDED

③ COMPLETED SKETCH OF
LOUD-SPEAKER CABINET

**FIG.
512.**

Working from Direct Views. When we already have a plan
of the object, we can easily transform it into an oblique drawing
by the method used for the stage setting in Fig. 513. This trick
is a real time-saver for scene designers, architects, interior dec-
orators, and engineers. Archeologists will also find it useful in
working out reconstructions. Note the use of a 3:3:2 axis ratio
in these drawings. This slightly exaggerates the effect of height,
but it gives a better view of the walls than we could achieve with
a 2:2:1 ratio.

The advertising cutout of the toy soldier in Fig. 514 was
drawn on the same principle, except that I started with a front
view instead of a plan. The curves and irregularities in the source
are handled by tracing and do not add to the difficulties of making a three-dimensional drawing. This example is really a more
elaborate version of the method used in Fig. 162 to suggest the
third dimension in drawing a built-up molding.

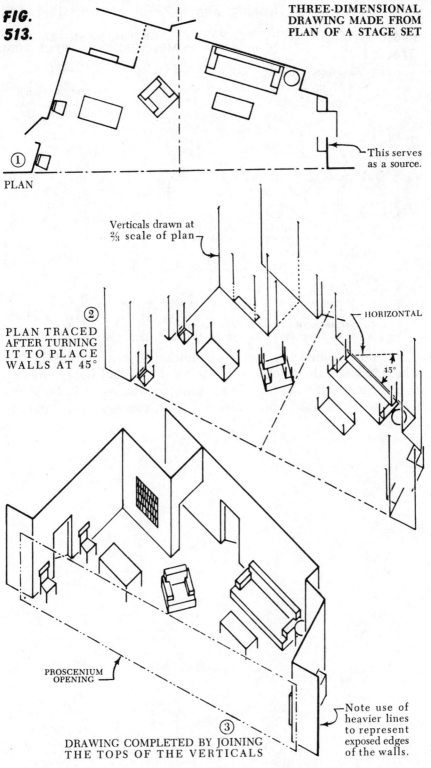

FIG. 513.

THREE-DIMENSIONAL
DRAWING MADE FROM
PLAN OF A STAGE SET

This serves
as a source.

① PLAN

Verticals drawn at
⅔ scale of plan

HORIZONTAL

② PLAN TRACED
AFTER TURNING
IT TO PLACE
WALLS AT 45°

45°

PROSCENIUM
OPENING

Note use of
heavier lines
to represent
exposed edges
of the walls.

③ DRAWING COMPLETED BY JOINING
THE TOPS OF THE VERTICALS

235

FIG. 514.

MAKING A THREE-DIMENSIONAL DRAW-
ING FROM A VERTICAL DIRECT VIEW

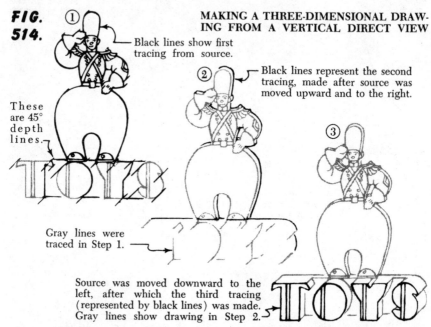

Black lines show first tracing from source.

Black lines represent the second tracing, made after source was moved upward and to the right.

These are 45° depth lines.

Gray lines were traced in Step 1.

Source was moved downward to the left, after which the third tracing (represented by black lines) was made. Gray lines show drawing in Step 2.

The only technical point worth noting is that the depth lines which indicate the thickness of the soldier extend backward (up to the right) whereas the depth lines for the word "TOYS" extend both backward and forward (up to the right and down to the left).

14

CONTROLLING DISTORTION

515. ISOMETRIC
(1:1:1)

1
1
1

30° 30°

3 3
4

516. APPROXIMATE
4:3:3
DIMETRIC

15° 15°

517. APPROXIMATE
4:4:3
DIMETRIC

3 4
4

30° 15°

N O three-dimensional drawing can eliminate distortion
entirely. Nevertheless, by choosing the right procedure, we gain
a fair degree of control over both
the kind and amount of distortion.

Perspective drawing satisfies
the eye but is *metrically dis-
torted.* It provides no direct way of measuring lengths and angles.
This is a serious weakness in drawing done for practical purposes. Oblique drawing, on the other hand, has a minimum of
metrical distortion, but the fact that receding planes appear to
be warped means that they suffer from severe *optical distortion.*

Fortunately, oblique drawing is only one of several methods
collectively known as *axial drawing.* The others tip the breadth
axis as well as the depth axis [Figs. 515–517]. This introduces
some distortion on the height-breadth planes but greatly reduces
that on the other two sets of axial planes. These types have long
Greek names. Do not let that frighten you. Pure water would
sound poisonous if you heard it called "dihydrogen monoxide."

Except for changes in the angles and the axis ratios, the other
types employ the exact procedure used in oblique drawing. They
are equally easy as long as the source is limited to straight lines.
Problems do arise when the source contains circles, but these are
not difficult to handle when you know the tricks.

STRAIGHT-LINE DRAWINGS

The new types of axial drawing can be made with a wide
range of axis ratios. However, the only ones that deserve serious

consideration are those which permit the use of stock scales. This limits us to five ratios: 1:1:1 (shown in Fig. 515 and called *"isometric"* because all three axes are measured with the same scale); 4:3:3; 4:4:3; 3:3:2; and 2:2:1.

The last four ratios require two scales each and can theoretically be used for *dimetric drawings*. However, the 3:3:2 and 2:2:1 ratios are not really satisfactory except for oblique drawings (which are actually dimetric, but which are never called by that name). In practice, therefore, the term "dimetric" is confined to drawings made on either the 4:3:3 ratio [Fig. 516] or the 4:4:3 ratio [Fig. 517]. Both types can be drawn with any one of the following pairs of stock scales: 1″ (=1′0″) and ¾″ (= 1′0″); ½″ and ⅜″; ¼″ and ¾″.

Axial drawings with three different scales are called *"trimetric."* These offer no advantages and cannot be measured with stock scales. The nearest we can come is a 4:3:2 ratio (using 1″, ¾″, and ½″ scales) or a 6:4:3 (using ¾″, ½″, and ⅜″ scales). Both of these create so much optical distortion that they are worthless.

We would also like to rule our axis lines with standard triangles. This restricts us to angles of 15° and 30°. You will find that 45° angles are satisfactory only for oblique drawing, and we normally have no reason to set an axis at an angle larger than this.

Isometric Drawing. Because isometric has an axis ratio of 1:1:1 and needs only one scale, we can choose any scale we like instead of being restricted to particular scales as we are with oblique and dimetric drawing.

Both the breadth- and the depth-axis in isometric make angles of 30° with the horizontal [Fig. 515]. As these axes are symmetrical, it does not matter which one we call "breadth" and which one we call "depth." However, if one axis-measurement in the source is longer than the other, it is convenient to follow the practice used in oblique drawing and regard the longer measurement as the breadth axis.

Dimetric Drawing. We saw in Chapter 12 that direct views are constructions made to imitate parallel projections. This is equally true of axial drawings. Isometric drawings are theoretically perfect imitations of projections, except that it is unusual to make a drawing at the exact scale of the projection. On the other hand, the two dimetric types described here are only approximate projections. The discrepancies are negligible in straight-line work. In fact, I used these types for years before I discovered that they were theoretically inaccurate. True dimetrics cannot be drawn with standard triangles.

4:3:3, 15°–15° Dimetric. The height axis in this type is measured by the larger scale and the other two axes by the smaller scale [Fig. 516]. The breadth- and depth-axes are set at 15° from the horizontal. The tracing box in Fig. 518 is a good example of an object which is adapted to this type of representation.

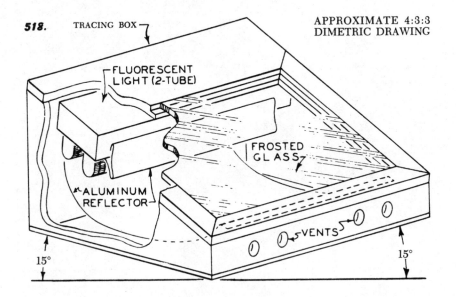

4:4:3, 15°–30° Dimetric. Here, the height- and breadth-axes are measured by the larger scale and the depth axis by the smaller one [Fig. 517]. The breadth axis is set at 15° and the depth axis at 30° from the horizontal.

I find that I have slighted this type of drawing in making the illustrations for this book, but do not underestimate it on that account. It is probably the most generally satisfactory type to use when the source does not contain curves.

Viewpoints. By restricting ourselves to four types of axial drawing we limit the number of available viewpoints. Fortunately, these are distributed in a way that meets every normal need [Fig. 519].

When all the important details are on one set of parallel planes, make an oblique drawing [stage set in Fig. 513 and toy soldier in Fig. 514]. The work goes quickly, and the parts that matter are not distorted either optically or metrically.

4:3:3 DIMETRIC

4:4:3 DIMETRIC

4:3:3 DIMETRIC

4:4:3 DIMETRIC

ISOMETRIC

4:4:3 DIMETRIC

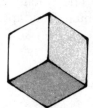

4:3:3 DIMETRIC

FIG. 519.
VIEWPOINTS AVAILABLE
FOR THREE-DIMENSIONAL
DRAWINGS PLANNED TO
FIT STANDARD SCALES

4:3:3 DIMETRIC

The unshaded cubes
represent viewpoints
which are not likely
to satisfy the eye.
— o —
Viewpoints provided
by oblique drawings
correspond roughly
to the ones given
for 4:4:3 dimetric.

4:4:3 DIMETRIC

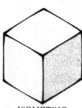

ISOMETRIC

4:4:3 DIMETRIC

4:3:3 DIMETRIC

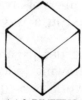

4:4:3 DIMETRIC

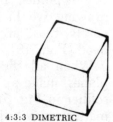

4:3:3 DIMETRIC

Fig. 521]   Controlling Distortion   241

If the chief elements are best shown by a front or a side view but the other two aspects are also of interest, use the 4:4:3 ratio [Fig. 517].

Where both front and side views are important but the top contains few details, make a 4:3:3 drawing [Fig. 516]. Fig. 518 is a special case; the tracing surface slants and takes advantage of both front and top views.

Isometric should be used when all three aspects of the source deserve the same consideration, but this is rarely the case. Normally, the interesting features are confined to one aspect or at most two. Isometric divides attention equally and therefore fails to emphasize the chief elements of the source. Also, as only two positions are possible [Fig. 519], and as all angles and scales are equal, isometric tends to be monotonous—especially in a project that involves many three-dimensional drawings.

ELLIPSES

Circles on the height-breadth planes of an oblique drawing are not distorted, but all other circles in axial drawing are represented by ellipses. In order to draw these ellipses, we must understand the laws that govern their positions and shapes.

The Tangent Law. We have already seen that when a circle in the source is tangent to a line, it is represented in the drawing by a circle or ellipse which is tangent to the corresponding point of the line in the drawing [Fig. 268]. This *tangent law* is especially important in dealing with metrical distortion.

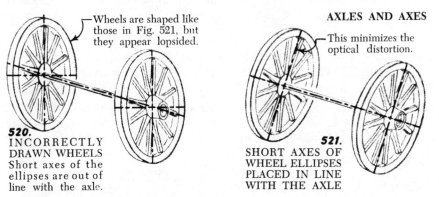

—Wheels are shaped like those in Fig. 521, but they appear lopsided.

AXLES AND AXES

—This minimizes the optical distortion.

520.
INCORRECTLY
DRAWN WHEELS
Short axes of the
ellipses are out of
line with the axle.

521.
SHORT AXES OF
WHEEL ELLIPSES
PLACED IN LINE
WITH THE AXLE

The Short-Axis Law. If an ellipse in the drawing represents a wheel in the source, placing the short axis of the ellipse in line with the axle of the wheel reduces optical distortion to a minimum [Figs. 520 and 521]. This is the *short-axis law*. It is chiefly concerned with optical distortion.

The bicycle in Fig. 522 shows further applications of the short-axis principle. Turning the wheels in different directions tips their axle lines at different angles. The short axes of the ellipses must therefore be tipped at the corresponding angles.

Although the principle is most readily grasped by thinking in terms of wheels and axles, the law itself is completely general.

522.
WHEELS ON DIFFERENT AXES
The short-axis rule applies, no matter which way the axle slants.

Hence, we can state it in this form: *When a circle appears as an ellipse in a drawing, the short axis of the ellipse should be parallel to a perpendicular to the plane of the circle.*

The easiest way to understand this is to visualize the circle as lying on one face of an imaginary cube [mouth of bucket in Fig. 523]. The short axis of the ellipse should then be parallel to the lines that lie on the third axis of the cube. Note that when a circle lies in a horizontal plane, the short axis of the corresponding ellipse must be vertical. However, when the circle is vertical, the short axis of the ellipse is not normally horizontal.

If a drawing obeys this law, we can tip it at any angle without increasing the distortion. Thus, the picture of the bucket in Fig. 524 duplicates that in Fig. 523. In order to lay the bucket on its side, I simply tipped Fig. 523 until the line representing the left side of the bucket was horizontal.

The Long-Axis Law. If circles are drawn on the faces of an axial cube and are tangent to its edges, all their long axes are the same length. This means that, in any given drawing, the long axes of all ellipses lying on axial planes are drawn to the same scale regardless of their size. As that is never one of the axial scales, the long axes cannot be measured directly. In spite of this, the law is well worth remembering; it suggests useful short cuts in many situations.

In axial drawing, the long axis of an ellipse always passes through the center of the circle and is perpendicular to the short axis [Fig. 523].

Axial vs. Perspective Ellipses. In strict theory, perspective ellipses do not obey the short-axis law. Nevertheless, artists usually follow the law when drawing perspectives—as I have done with the bucket in Fig. 525. This is much simpler than plot-

Fig. 525]   Controlling Distortion   243

ting a theoretically correct ellipse, and the effect is usually more pleasing to the eye.

Even when we take advantage of this simplification, ellipses give far more trouble in perspective than they do in axial drawing. The axial view of a wedding cake in Fig. 526 is definitely better for practical purposes than the perspective of the same cake in Fig. 527. The axial view may show slightly more optical distortion than the perspective, but it suffers far less from metrical distortion. Furthermore, the axial drawing was much easier to make; all of its ellipses have the same shape, but the shapes of the perspective ellipses vary widely. Also, perspective ellipses above the *horizon* (eye level) curve up in front, whereas those below the horizon curve down.

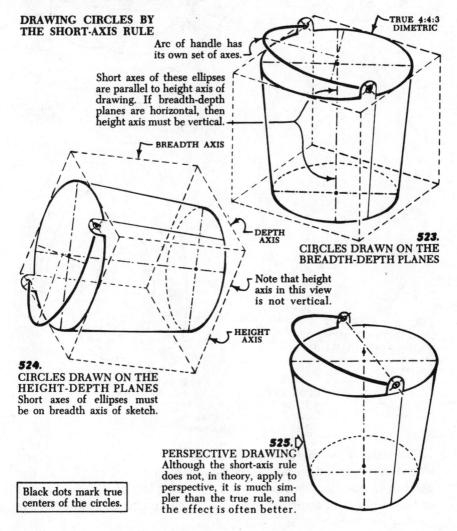

DRAWING CIRCLES BY THE SHORT-AXIS RULE

TRUE 4:4:3 DIMETRIC

Arc of handle has its own set of axes.

Short axes of these ellipses are parallel to height axis of drawing. If breadth-depth planes are horizontal, then height axis must be vertical.

BREADTH AXIS

DEPTH AXIS

523.
CIRCLES DRAWN ON THE BREADTH-DEPTH PLANES

Note that height axis in this view is not vertical.

HEIGHT AXIS

524.
CIRCLES DRAWN ON THE HEIGHT-DEPTH PLANES
Short axes of ellipses must be on breadth axis of sketch.

Black dots mark true centers of the circles.

525.
PERSPECTIVE DRAWING
Although the short-axis rule does not, in theory, apply to perspective, it is much simpler than the true rule, and the effect is often better.

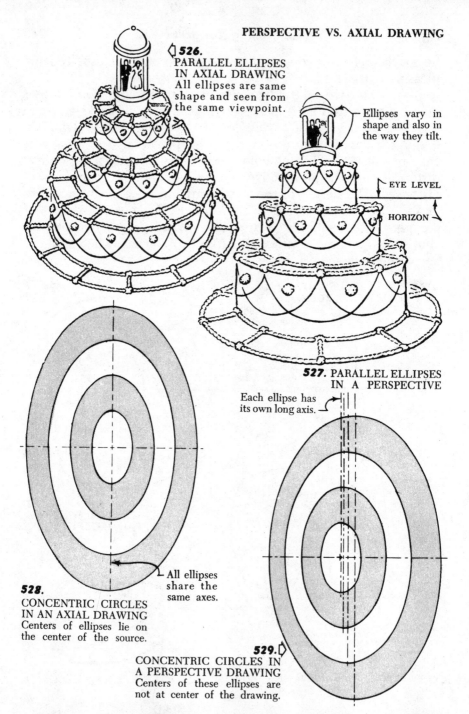

526.
PARALLEL ELLIPSES
IN AXIAL DRAWING
All ellipses are same
shape and seen from
the same viewpoint.

Ellipses vary in
shape and also in
the way they tilt.

EYE LEVEL

HORIZON

527. PARALLEL ELLIPSES
IN A PERSPECTIVE

Each ellipse has
its own long axis.

All ellipses
share the
same axes.

528.
CONCENTRIC CIRCLES
IN AN AXIAL DRAWING
Centers of ellipses lie on
the center of the source.

529.
CONCENTRIC CIRCLES IN
A PERSPECTIVE DRAWING
Centers of these ellipses are
not at center of the drawing.

The axial view of the target in Fig. 528 took less than a third
as much time to make as the perspective view in Fig. 529. In the
axial drawing, the centers of all the ellipses fall at the true center
of the target, and their long axes all lie along the same line. In the

perspective view, every ellipse has its own center, and none of these are at the center of the target. Each long axis lies on a separate line, and there is no simple way to determine where any of them should fall or how long it should be.

Perspective does have some advantages. For example, Fig. 529 shows clearly that the left-hand side of the target is nearer to the

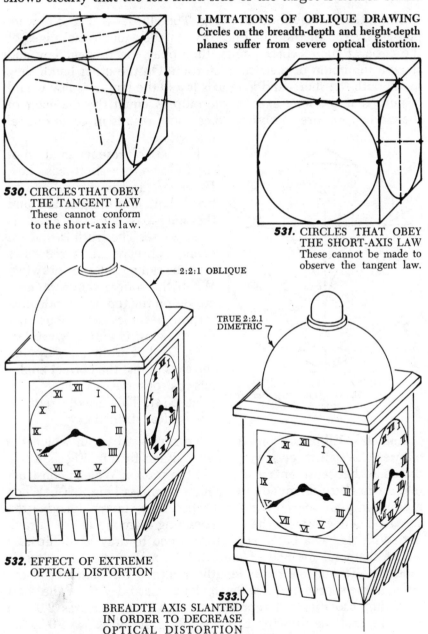

LIMITATIONS OF OBLIQUE DRAWING
Circles on the breadth-depth and height-depth planes suffer from severe optical distortion.

530. CIRCLES THAT OBEY THE TANGENT LAW
These cannot conform to the short-axis law.

531. CIRCLES THAT OBEY THE SHORT-AXIS LAW
These cannot be made to observe the tangent law.

2:2:1 OBLIQUE

TRUE 2:2:1 DIMETRIC

532. EFFECT OF EXTREME OPTICAL DISTORTION

533. BREADTH AXIS SLANTED IN ORDER TO DECREASE OPTICAL DISTORTION observer than the right-hand side. In the axial drawing [Fig. 528] we cannot tell which side is nearer and which is farther away. For practical purposes, however, such advantages are heavily outweighed by the fact that perspective drawings are far harder to make and require much more time, and their parts cannot be scaled directly.

Limitations of Oblique Drawing. The ellipses in Fig. 530 were plotted by the method in Fig. 318. As they touch the edges of the cube at their center points, they obey the tangent law and show a minimum of metrical distortion. On the other hand, they break both the short- and long-axis laws (the long-axis law would require that the long axes of the ellipses equal the diameter of the circle). Failure to observe these laws results in acute optical distortion.

534. ISOMETRIC ELLIPSES
Showing difference between isometric and ellipse axes

Fig. 531 represents an attempt to follow the short-axis law. However, as this forced me to break both the tangent law and the long-axis law, the effect is even worse. The truth is that we cannot observe all three laws in the same oblique drawing. When the source shows tangent curves on the top or the side, distortion becomes so serious that the drawing is almost worthless [Fig. 532]. Fortunately, tipping the axes at just the correct angles lets us observe all three laws [Fig. 533]. This greatly reduces the optical distortion.

Isometric Ellipses. Isometric is the simplest case in which the ellipses obey all three laws perfectly. Each face in Fig. 534 is a diamond that represents a square in the source. We can construct ellipses in these diamonds by using a compass [Fig. 320]. When a circle in your source is not inscribed in a square, imagine the square. Then, construct the corresponding diamond in your drawing. With this as a basis, you can proceed to draw the ellipse.

The diamond method of construction makes the axes slightly too short. To find their true lengths, multiply the diameter of the circle in the source by 1.225 for the long axis and .707 for the short axis. Suppose Fig. 534 represnts a cube that measures 2′9″ on an edge, and the drawing is made to a scale of ⅜″ = 1′0″. The circles will be 2′9″ in diameter, but the long axis of the ellipses that represent these circles must be 2′9″ × 1.225 = c. 3′4½″ when measured with a ⅜″ scale. Similarly, the short axes must measure 2′9″ × .707 = c. 1′11⅜″. The illustration may not show exactly these measurements because distortions are inevitable in printing.

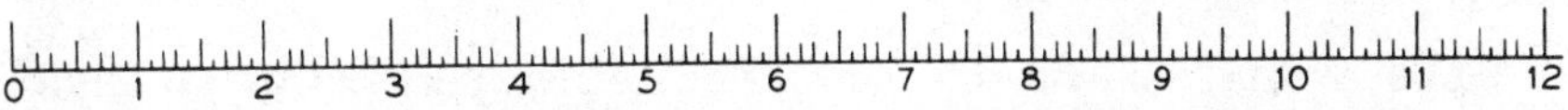

535. A SCALE FOR CONVERTING SCALE FEET-AND-INCHES INTO UNITS THAT CAN BE MORE EASILY HANDLED BY ARITHMETIC

The decimal scale in Fig. 535 provides a way to avoid the trouble of multiplying feet, inches, and fractions. Place your scale rule against this decimal scale and measure the diameter. With a scale of ⅜″ = 1′0″, you will find that 2′9″ = c. 3.13. This figure is used only for computation and has no other meaning. When we multiply by the factors in the preceding paragraph, we get 3.13 × 1.225 = c. 3.83, and 3.13 × .707 = c. 2.21. Place your scale rule beside the decimal scale again. You will find that 3.83 on the decimal scale equals c. 3′4½″ on the ⅜″ = 1′0″ scale, and that 2.21 on the decimal scale equals c. 1′11⅜″ on the ⅜″ = 1′0″ scale. This procedure may appear complex. But if you work out a few examples, you will find it quite easy. It works with any foot-and-inch scale.

		Axis Ratio	4:3:3	4:4:3
		Angle of Breadth Axis	15°	15°
		Angle of Depth Axis	15°	30°
E l l i p s e s		Length of Long Axis	1.03	1.13
	Height-Breadth	Shape-Angle	40° or 45°	50°
		Tip-Angle	19°	17°30′
		Short Axis	.70	.86
	Height-Depth	Shape-Angle	40° or 45°	30°
		Tip-Angle	19°	37°30′
		Short Axis	.70	.59
	Breadth-Depth	Shape-Angle	15°	20°
		Tip-Angle	0°	0°
		Short Axis	.27	.43

DATA FOR APPROXIMATE DIMETRIC DRAWINGS CONSTRUCTED WITH 45° and 30°–60° TRIANGLES

Once the axes have been fixed, we can use the method in Fig. 319 to construct the ellipses with a compass. This is no more accurate than the diamond method, but the axis lengths are correct, which is sometimes important. If we want really accurate ellipses, we must use either an ellipsograph or an ellipse template.

Ellipse Templates. These not only improve the accuracy of our work but save a great deal of time. In fact, we can make an isometric ellipse with a template almost as quickly as we can draw a straight line with a ruler. In order to take full advantage of ellipse templates we must know the conventions used to specify their shapes and sizes.

ELLIPSE SHAPES. The shape of an ellipse is specified by an angle. Think of the ellipse as a tilted circle; the apparent angle of tilt above the horizontal is the angle of the ellipse. Thus, a 15° ellipse is thin, and a 60° ellipse is thick. The angle has nothing to do either with the size of the ellipse or with the position of the ellipse in the drawing. All ellipses on the axial planes of any isometric drawing are 35°16′ ellipses [Fig. 534].

ELLIPSE SIZES. The size of an ellipse is usually specified by giving the length of its long axis. However, some template manufacturers treat isometric ellipses as a special case and specify their sizes by giving the diameter of the corresponding circle. For example, an edge of the cube in Fig. 534 measures approximately 1″. Hence, the "circles" must be c. 1″ in diameter, and we would use a 1″ template to draw the ellipses. An ellipse marked 1″ by the diameter method has a long axis that actually measures $1'' \times 1.225 = 1^{15}\!/_{64}''$.

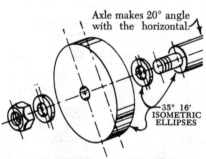

Axle makes 20° angle with the horizontal.

—35° 16′ ISOMETRIC ELLIPSES

536. EXPLODED VIEW OF A WHEEL AND AXLE Based on ellipse axes

AXIS MARKS. Most templates carry marks indicating the axis lines of the ellipse. To use such a template, we rule construction lines for the axes in the drawing [A, Fig. 534]. The template is laid on the drawing with the marks matching these lines. Running a pencil around the opening in the template produces the ellipse.

Some isometric templates are marked with the isometric axes [B, Fig. 534]. If these are in addition to the marks for the ellipse axes, this is a desirable feature. But when only the isometric axes are marked, the template is inconvenient to use.

The exploded view in Fig. 536 illustrates the desirability of having the ellipse axes marked. I started with the center line. I then placed a dot at the center of each ellipse and ruled perpendicular construction lines through these, using two triangles by the method in Fig. 451. This was all the construction required.

Fig. 538]   Controlling Distortion   249

If I had been forced to use templates marked only with the isometric axes, I should have had to locate the center line and set
the points as before. I would then have needed to draw two
construction lines through each point, one at 40° and one at 80°
to the horizontal. Furthermore, the work would have required
greater accuracy; small diagonal errors show up more than do
those which are parallel or perpendicular to the center line.

Note that the center line in Fig. 536 is at 20° rather than at
30°. The drawing is not, strictly speaking, isometric. But this did
not keep me from getting adequate results with isometric ellipses.
Fig. 528 shows only two dimensions and hence has no "axle." This
explains why I was able to make the short axis horizontal and still
avoid serious distortion. I could not have done that if the target
had been painted on one face of a cube.

Satisfactory isometric templates are made in a wide range of
sizes. Unfortunately, the range of templates that can be used for
dimetric drawing is limited, and none of them are precisely the
right shape. This is a major handicap. When a drawing must
contain many wheels, gears, pipes, or other circular forms, the
ability to use templates freely is so advantageous that it out-
weighs all other considerations. Isometric, therefore, is the only
satisfactory choice for such drawings.

TANGENT ELLIPSES IN
APPROXIMATE DIMETRIC

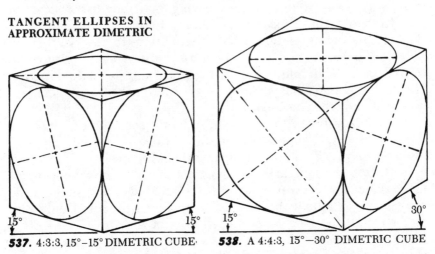

537. 4:3:3, 15°–15° DIMETRIC CUBE   **538.** A 4:4:3, 15°—30° DIMETRIC CUBE

Dimetric Ellipses. An ellipse on a breadth-depth plane of a
4:3:3, 15°-15° dimetric drawing obeys both the tangent law and
the short-axis law [Fig. 537]. With this exception, neither of our
two types of approximate dimetric permit us to observe both laws
at the same time. We can, however, come close enough for most
purposes if we understand a few principles.

TANGENT ELLIPSES. When a circle in the source is tangent to one or more straight lines or to another circle, we should obey the tangent law but can ignore the short-axis law. Fig. 537 illustrates this for a 4:3:3 cube and Fig. 538 does the same thing for a 4:4:3 cube. All of the ellipses in these drawings were plotted by the method in Fig. 318 except the one on the height-breadth axis in Fig. 538, which was constructed with a compass by the method in Fig. 320.

The plotting process is simplified when you know the angles that the short axes make with the horizontal. The table on p. 247 gives these as *tip angles*. You need a protractor or an adjustable triangle to place the axes accurately. Remember that both short- and long-axes pass through the center of the parallelogram that represents the face of the cube.

A 15° ellipse fits the breadth-depth plane of a 4:3:3, 15°-15° cube; it is a pure coincidence that this happens to equal the angle of the breadth- and the depth-axes. No templates are made that fit the other planes of dimetric drawing well enough to be used for making tangent ellipses.

FREE ELLIPSES. When a circle in the source has no tangent, we can always provide one in the drawing by ruling a construction line. In theory, the ellipse corresponding to the circle should obey the tangent law in relation to this line. Failure to observe the law increases both the optical and metrical distortion. Fortunately, this effect is negligible in our two types of approximate dimetric. Hence, if an ellipse has no tangent, we can ignore the tangent law but must obey the short-axis law.

Fig. 539 illustrates the procedure. Draw construction lines for the ellipse axes. Compute the lengths of the axes, using data from the table on p. 247 and the decimal scale in Fig. 535.

In theory, the long-axis law does not apply strictly to approximate dimetrics. However, as the discrepancies are slight, it is convenient to follow the law. I have, therefore, listed only one factor for all the long axes in each type of dimetric. The factors for the short axes vary with the axis plane. In true 4:4:3 dimetric, ellipses on the breadth-depth planes would match those on the height-depth planes. In 4:4:3, 15°–30° dimetric, on the other hand, breadth-depth ellipses are decidedly slimmer.

Note that all measurements, including those of the breadth-depth ellipses, are measured with the scale of the *height* axis. No principle is involved here; I computed all factors on the basis of the height scale in order to keep the table simple.

DIMETRIC TEMPLATES. Although no templates are made in the proper shapes for dimetric ellipses, we can take liberties with the shapes when the ellipses have no tangents. The table on p. 247 lists the best shapes, but we can substitute others without materially increasing the apparent optical distortion. Figs. 540 and 542 show how far we can get away from the best shapes and still avoid serious optical distortion. This is worth knowing. If you do

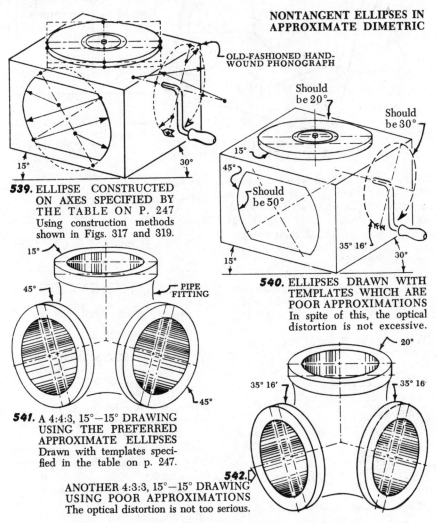

NONTANGENT ELLIPSES IN APPROXIMATE DIMETRIC

OLD-FASHIONED HAND-WOUND PHONOGRAPH

539. ELLIPSE CONSTRUCTED ON AXES SPECIFIED BY THE TABLE ON P. 247
Using construction methods shown in Figs. 317 and 319.

PIPE FITTING

540. ELLIPSES DRAWN WITH TEMPLATES WHICH ARE POOR APPROXIMATIONS
In spite of this, the optical distortion is not excessive.

541. A 4:4:3, 15°—15° DRAWING USING THE PREFERRED APPROXIMATE ELLIPSES
Drawn with templates specified in the table on p. 247.

542. ANOTHER 4:3:3, 15°—15° DRAWING USING POOR APPROXIMATIONS
The optical distortion is not too serious.

not have a template of the right size and the proper shape, you may be able to substitute an ellipse of another shape that will do almost as well.

After the axis lengths have been fixed in the drawing, we can use the compass method in Fig. 319 to construct height-breadth

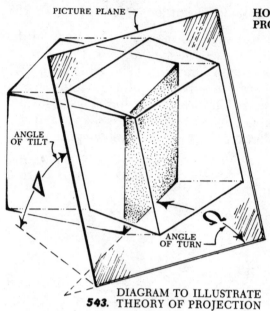

ANGLE
OF TILT

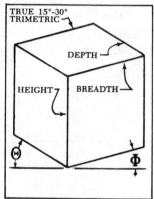

TRUE 15°-30°
TRIMETRIC

DEPTH

HEIGHT

BREADTH

Φ

ANGLE
OF TURN

543. DIAGRAM TO ILLUSTRATE
THEORY OF PROJECTION

544. DIRECT VIEW OF
PICTURE PLANE
Somewhat reduced

A cube, each edge of which measures 1 unit, is turned through Angle Ω in relation to the picture plane which is tilted at Angle Δ [Fig. 543]. If this cube is projected onto the picture plane, the result will be a drawing like Fig. 544.

Let H, B, and D represent the foreshortened edges of the cube in the drawing. Then, $H^2 + B^2 + D^2 = 2$.

When Angles Ω and Δ are given:

$\tan \Phi = \sin \Delta \tan \Omega$,

and $\tan \Theta = \dfrac{\sin \Delta}{\tan \Omega}$.

Example:

Let $\Delta = 27°56'$ and $\Omega = 32°2'$.
$\tan \Phi = .4684 \times .6256 = .293$,
$\Phi = 16°20'$.

$\tan \Theta = \dfrac{.4684}{.6256} = .749$, $\Theta = 36°50'$.

When Angles Ω and Θ are given,

$\Psi = 90° - (\Phi + \Theta)$.

Then, $H = \sqrt{1 - \tan \Phi \tan \Theta}$,
$B = \sqrt{1 - \tan \Phi \tan \Psi}$,
$D = \sqrt{1 - \tan \Theta \tan \Psi}$,
$\cos \Delta = H$,
$\cos \Omega = B \cos \Theta$.

Example:

Let $\Phi = 16°20'$ and $\Theta = 36°50'$.

Then, $\Psi = 36°50'$.

$B = H = \sqrt{1 - .2931 \times .7490}$

$= \sqrt{.7805} = .8835$,

$D = \sqrt{.1 - .7490 \times .7490}$

$= \sqrt{.4390} = .6626$,

$\cos \Delta = .8835$, $\Delta = 27°56'$,

$\cos \Omega = .8835 \times .9596 = .8478$,

$\Omega = 32°2'$.

**When an axis ratio (such as 4:4:3)
is given,** assign the letters h, b, and d to the numbers in the ratio. The smallest number always represents the depth axis and should be called "d"; e.g., $h = 4$, $b = 4$, $d = 3$. To convert these into the foreshortened lengths H, B, and D, apply the following formulas:

$\dfrac{h^2 + b^2 + d^2}{2} = u^2$, where u is a figure that will disappear in later computations.

$\dfrac{h^2}{u^2} = H^2$, $\dfrac{b^2}{u^2} = B^2$, $\dfrac{d^2}{u^2} = D^2$.

Example: $\dfrac{4^2 + 4^2 + 3^2}{2} = u^2 = 20.5.$

$\dfrac{4^2}{20.5} = H^2 = .7805,$

$\dfrac{4^2}{20.5} = B^2 = .7805,$

$\dfrac{3^2}{20.5} = D^2 = .4390.$

Check: $.7805 + .7805 + .4390 = 2.$
Apply the following formulas to find Φ and θ:

$$\sqrt{\dfrac{H^2 + B^2 - D^2}{2H^2B^2}} = \cos \Phi,$$

$$\sqrt{\dfrac{H^2 + D^2 - B^2}{2H^2D^2}} = \cos \theta.$$

Example:

$$\sqrt{\dfrac{.7805 + .7805 - .4390}{2 \times .7805 \times .7805}} = .9596,$$

$\cos \Phi = .9596, \ \Phi = 16°20'.$

$$\sqrt{\dfrac{.7805 + .4390 - .7805}{2 \times .7805 \times .4390}} = .8004,$$

$\cos \theta = .8004, \ \theta = 36°50'.$

The shape of an ellipse is specified by its angle (see text p. 248).

sin of ellipse angle
$= \dfrac{\text{short axis of ellipse}}{\text{long axis of ellipse}},$
cos angle of ellipses on height-breadth planes $= H,$
cos angle of ellipses on height-depth planes $= B,$
cos angle of ellipses on breadth-depth planes $= D.$

In a cube with ellipses on the three visible faces, the long axes of these ellipses are all the same length and $= m = \dfrac{u}{h}.$

Example: In a 4:4:3 cube, $u^2 = 20.5,$ $u = 4.528,$ and $h = 4.$

Then, $m = \dfrac{4.528}{4} = 1.132.$

If a height edge of the cube *in the drawing* measures 1″, the long axes of all three tangent ellipses will measure 1.32″ (approximately 1$\frac{5}{16}$″).

Use the following formulas to find the lengths of the short axes of the ellipses in proportion to a height edge of the cube:

$$f = \sqrt{\dfrac{h^2 + b^2 - d^2}{2h^2}},$$

$$s = \sqrt{\dfrac{h^2 + d^2 - b^2}{2h^2}},$$

$$t = \sqrt{\dfrac{b^2 + d^2 - h^2}{2h^2}}.$$

Examples: Isometric, $f = s = t$

$$= \sqrt{\dfrac{1^2 + 1^2 - 1^2}{2 \times 1^2}} = \sqrt{\dfrac{1}{2}} = .707.$$

4:3:3 $\quad f = s$

$$= \sqrt{\dfrac{4^2 + 3^2 - 3^2}{2 \times 4^2}} = \sqrt{\dfrac{1}{2}} = .707.$$

4:4:3 $\quad s = t$

$$= \sqrt{\dfrac{4^2 + 3^2 - 4^2}{2 \times 4^2}} = \sqrt{\dfrac{9}{32}} = .530.$$

REFERENCE TABLE OF ELEMENTS IN TRUE AXIAL PROJECTIONS		Ref.	OBLIQUE	ISO-METRIC	DIMETRIC	
Axis Ratio			2:2:1 or 3:3:2	1:1:1	4:3:3	4:4:3
Angle of Breadth Axis		Φ	0°	30°	13°38′	16°20′
Angle of Depth Axis		θ	30° or 45°	30°	13°38′	36°50′
Ellipses	Length of Long Axis	m	Circle with a diameter equal to a height edge	1.225	1.031	1.132
	Height-Breadth Shape-Angle			35°16′	43°19′	48°30′
	Height-Breadth Short Axis	f		.707	.707	.848
	Height-Depth Shape-Angle		None	35°16′	43°19′	27°56′
	Height-Depth Short Axis	s		.707	.707	.530
	Breadth-Depth Shape-Angle			35°16′	14°1′	27°56′
	Breadth-Depth Short Axis	t		.707	.250	.530

and height-depth ellipses. This method is not suited to ellipses as thin as those on the breadth-depth planes. These must be plotted by the method in Fig. 417.

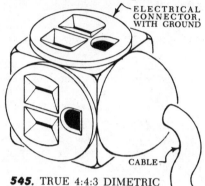

ELECTRICAL CONNECTOR, WITH GROUND

CABLE

545. TRUE 4:4:3 DIMETRIC

PROJECTION AND
AXIAL DRAWING

In oblique projection, the picture plane is parallel to the main plane of the source, just as it is in Fig. 456. The rays, however, strike the picture plane at an angle. In true isometric and dimetric projection, the source is turned at an angle to the picture plane [Ω in Fig. 543] and the plane is tilted at another angle [Δ]. The rays are then projected perpendicular to the picture plane. When these conditions are met, distortion is minimized and the projection obeys the tangent law and both axis laws.

We can reduce this type of projection to algebraic formulas. These may then be used to compute the true axis angles and ellipse shapes for any axis ratio. Once these are known, it is easy to imitate a projection by construction. The formulas need not alarm the antimathematical reader. I have worked out all the answers he needs and placed them in the table on p. 253. If anyone does want to use the formulas, they are in the note that accompanies the table.

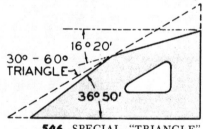

16°20'

30° – 60°
TRIANGLE

36°50'

546. SPECIAL "TRIANGLE"
For drawing true dimetrics with a 4:4:3 axis ratio.

Angles and Axis Ratios. When we apply our formulas to the 1:1:1 ratio of isometric, we find that the breadth- and depth-axes should be set at 30°. This corresponds to the rule we have already been following. But when the formulas are used with the 4:3:3 ratio, they set the axes at 13°38′ instead of 15°. This difference is almost negligible. The discrepancies for the 4:4:3 dimetric, however, are large enough to take seriously. Here, the breadth axis should be set at 16°20′ and the depth axis at 36°50′. We can rule lines at any of these angles with the aid of an adjustable triangle.

The additional trouble involved in using an adjustable triangle is hardly justified in the case of 4:3:3 dimetrics. The discrepancy is small, drawings of this type are comparatively rare, and few of them show tangent ellipses.

The 4:4:3 axis ratio is another matter. This is an extremely useful type of drawing, and the sources often include one or two tangent arcs or circles. The electrical connector in Fig. 545 is a good example. An isometric drawing would have been perfectly symmetrical and therefore rather dull. Also, the top and the front faces of the connector are identical; a 4:4:3 dimetric gives a clear view of one face, and the fact that it gives poor views of the others does no harm. An isometric would give equally poor views of all three.

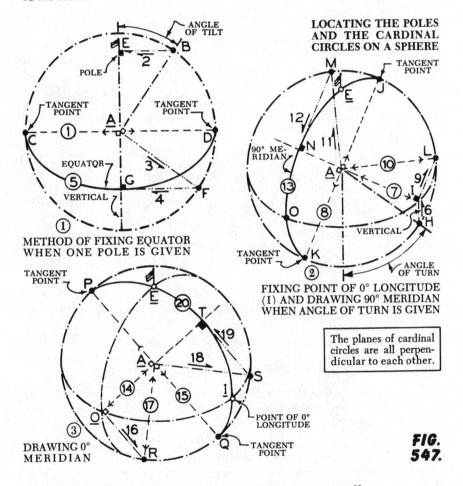

METHOD OF FIXING EQUATOR
WHEN ONE POLE IS GIVEN

LOCATING THE POLES
AND THE CARDINAL
CIRCLES ON A SPHERE

FIXING POINT OF 0° LONGITUDE
(I) AND DRAWING 90° MERIDIAN
WHEN ANGLE OF TURN IS GIVEN

The planes of cardinal circles are all perpendicular to each other.

DRAWING 0°
MERIDIAN

**FIG.
547.**

If you make many dimetrics of this type, it will pay you to provide yourself with a special "triangle" like that in Fig. 546. This can easily be cut on a circular saw from a standard 30°–60° triangle.

It may interest you to see what happens if we start with the breadth- and depth-axes at 15°. This calls for an axis ratio of

4 : 3.0392 : 3.0392, which cannot be used with stock scales. Setting the breadth axis at 15° and the depth axis at 30° and applying our formulas gives a trimetric ratio of 4 : 3.624 : 2.829 [Fig. 544]. Neither of these ratios is convenient for practical use.

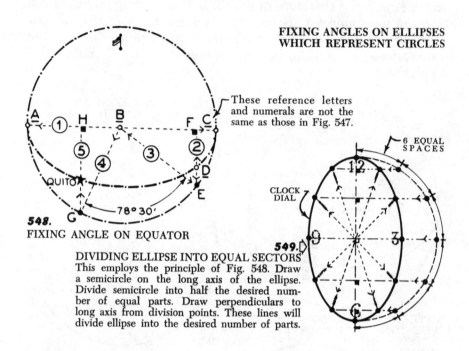

**FIXING ANGLES ON ELLIPSES
WHICH REPRESENT CIRCLES**

These reference letters and numerals are not the same as those in Fig. 547.

6 EQUAL SPACES

CLOCK DIAL

548.
FIXING ANGLE ON EQUATOR

549.
DIVIDING ELLIPSE INTO EQUAL SECTORS
This employs the principle of Fig. 548. Draw a semicircle on the long axis of the ellipse. Divide semicircle into half the desired number of equal parts. Draw perpendiculars to long axis from division points. These lines will divide ellipse into the desired number of parts.

Circles on Spheres. A sphere in the source is always represented by a circle in axial drawing. When we need to draw ellipses for the equator and meridians on a sphere, we can start with a cube, construct a plane for each ellipse, and then plot the ellipses on the planes. This, however, is a laborious process—especially when we want to tilt and turn the sphere at specified angles.

Useful short cuts that permit us to draw the ellipses directly and accurately, no matter how the sphere is tilted and turned, are shown in Fig. 547. These methods are based on the short- and long-axis laws, plus the fact that *the ends of the ellipses are always tangent to the circle which represents the sphere.*

The diagrams in Fig. 547 require a little study, but once you have grasped the procedure, you will be able to draw ellipses at any desired angle on a sphere with greater ease than you can draw them on the faces of a dimetric cube.

Fig. 548 shows how to locate a point on the equator at any given angle from another point. The same principle can be used to fix a point on a meridian at any given latitude.

Fig. 550]   Controlling Distortion   **257**

An extension of this principle is used to divide an ellipse into parts that represent equal angles in the source [Fig. 549]. The spokes of the wheel and the ribs of the umbrella for the hot-dog cart in Fig. 550 show other applications of the method.

OFFHAND SKETCHING IN THREE DIMENSIONS

Once you understand the principles, the ability to make three-dimensional drawings depends upon your power of visualization. Begin with simple, straight-line objects; use drafting instruments and measure each line. When you can do this with all four of the common axial types, try objects that combine straight lines and curves. This experience will almost certainly increase your skill in visualization to a point where you find yourself making offhand sketches as a matter of course.

Except for the obvious difference between web constructions, like the trapeze performers in Figs. 551 and 552, and block con-

structions [Figs. 553 and 554], all axial drawings are made on the same principle. If you can construct a boat, you can construct an octopus, an airplane, or a bull fiddle. However, one or two tricks of the trade are worth noting.

Tilting Axes. I drew the boat in Fig. 554 on an even keel with the height axis vertical and used approximately a 4:4:3 ratio. I then turned my paper to raise the stern of the boat and drew the sawhorse. If I had sketched the sawhorse first and then tried to construct the boat on the same axes as the horse, every line of the construction would have been off axis, and the work would have required far higher powers of visualization.

550.
EXAMPLE SHOWING APPLICATION OF METHODS IN FIGS. 547–549

Cylinders and Circles. You cannot hope to get either the angles or the measurements exactly right in offhand drawing. This tends to cause distortion when the source involves cylinders and circles. However, you can compensate for the distortion almost auto-

matically by basing your construction on the short-axis law
[Fig. 555].

Draw the "axles" of all wheels, cylinders, and disks. This fixes
the direction of the short axes. The lengths of these axes must be
estimated by eye, but the distances between their centers can be

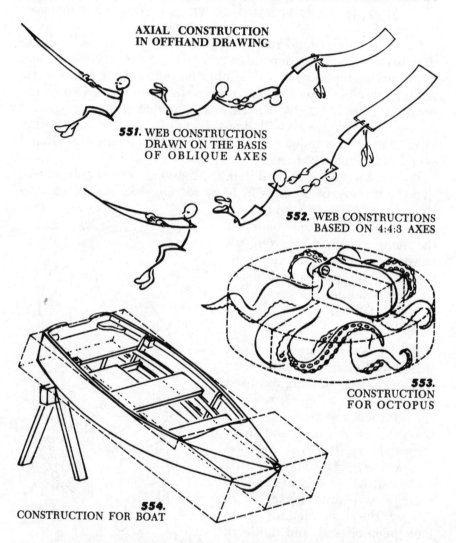

**AXIAL CONSTRUCTION
IN OFFHAND DRAWING**

551. WEB CONSTRUCTIONS
DRAWN ON THE BASIS
OF OBLIQUE AXES

552. WEB CONSTRUCTIONS
BASED ON 4:4:3 AXES

553.
CONSTRUCTION
FOR OCTOPUS

554.
CONSTRUCTION FOR BOAT

measured if you wish. Draw the long axes of the ellipses through
these centers and perpendicular to the short axes. You can then
sketch the ellipses. Add the straight lines of the cylinders, making
them tangent to the ends of the ellipses. This is a much quicker
method than constructing rectangular blocks and fitting the cylinders and wheels inside these.

Fig. 557]   Controlling Distortion   259

When source shows many
circles, base your sketch
on the short-axis law and
ignore the tangent law.

Draw the ellipses first.
Then make sides of the
cylinder perpendicular
to ends of the long axis.

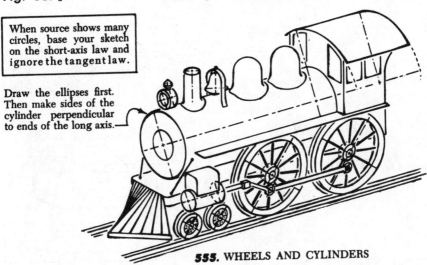

555. WHEELS AND CYLINDERS

Prepared Grids. If you find squared paper helpful as an all-purpose construction when sketching direct views, you may prefer to sketch isometrics over a grid like that used for Figs. 556 and 557. Similar grids are available for trimetric and perspective drawings. I have never had any luck with these, but many people consider them valuable time-savers. If you do much three-dimensional sketching and have any trouble with it, you should certainly experiment with these special grids. They may give you exactly the assistance you need.

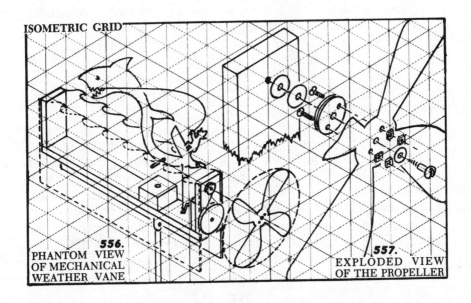

ISOMETRIC GRID

556.
PHANTOM VIEW
OF MECHANICAL
WEATHER VANE

557.
EXPLODED VIEW
OF THE PROPELLER

15

PROJECTION IN THREE DIMENSIONS

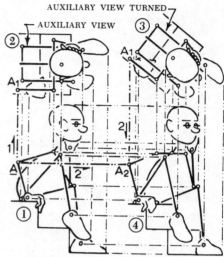

FIG. 558. CHANGING VIEWPOINT BY THE USE OF PROJECTION

CONSTRUCTION is adequate for all normal situations that involve the third dimension. However, there are many special problems which can be solved only by projection. Thus, it would be almost impossible to construct the turned view in Step 4, Fig. 558, so that it corresponds exactly to the side view in Step 1, but this becomes easy when we use projection.

FUNDAMENTALS

Projection is a tool with which we can solve any problem in three-dimensional drawing. In parallel projection—the only type that concerns us here—every ray is drawn on the same principle. You must learn how to apply this principle in your work, but the devices involved are few and simple. Thus, the method of projecting the turned stick figure in Fig. 558 is the same as that used for the birdhouse in Fig. 465, except that I actually turned the top view of the stick figure instead of using a reference line as I did with the birdhouse.

Visualization. Although the principle and the methods of projection are easy enough, we cannot apply them unless we are able to visualize what we are drawing. As this normally requires visualizing two or three views of the source at once, it often puzzles the beginner. Even the expert has trouble at times. You cannot expect to read the illustrations in this chapter until you completely understand the simple projections in Figs. 456, 465, and 467 and have acquired some ability to think in three dimensions by making axial drawings.

Fig. 558]   Projection in Three Dimensions   261

Procedure. If you know how to project one point in any given situation, you know how to project them all. Figs. 559–562 show what happens when we project a point [P] from the side view of a half-cylinder to the front view of the same half-cylinder. All four illustrations depict the same set of drawings. Figs. 559 and 561 represent the actual drawings. Figs. 560 and 562 are imaginary axial views in which the half-cylinders are depicted in three dimensions. In all four cases, the side, top, and front views have been drawn by construction. They are, therefore, considered as given. The only problem is to project Point P from the side view and fix its correct position on the front view.

Try to follow the whole process in the illustrations without referring to the text. This will be good practice and will test your powers of visualization. If you find that you can read the illustrations with complete understanding, congratulate yourself and skip to the next heading. If you have any doubts, either work your way through the ray-by-ray account given below or skip the whole chapter until you have improved your ability to visualize in three dimensions by making more axial drawings.

We begin by projecting any given point on the side view (in this case Point C_S) upward. The corresponding point on the top view is then projected sidewise [Point C_T]. This fixes Point C_R, and we draw our reference line through that by construction (*not* projection) at 45° [Line 3].

There are several details to note here. The reference line is constructed; it is therefore designated by a numbered circle and not by a numbered half-arrow. However, the numbering is consecutive; Line 3 follows Ray 2. The arrowhead near Point C_R shows that Line 3 is drawn through this point. The 45° reference line has the effect of turning the top view 90° on the height axis and tilting it 90° on the breadth axis at the same time.

We are now ready to project Point P. In Fig. 560, Ray 4 projects this point vertically upward to fix Point P_1 on the rim of the cylinder. Ray 5 projects Point P_1 perpendicular to the picture plane and locates Point P_2 on a breadth line through Point C_S. Line 6 then projects Point P_2 vertically to fix Point P_3 on the reference line.

If we now turn to Fig. 559, we see that our drawing automatically projects Point P_1 onto Point P_2. This eliminates Ray 5 and turns Rays 4 and 6 into one continuous ray. I have retained both numbers for the purpose of identification. In practice, you would simply make a tick at Point P_3 on the reference line.

Ray 7 projects Point P to the rim of the top view and fixes Point P_4. In Fig. 560, Rays 8, 9, and 10 reverse the process fol-

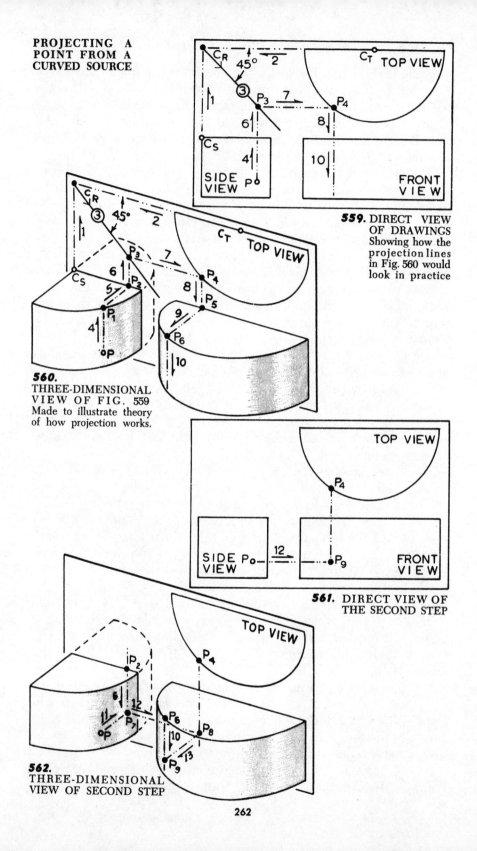

PROJECTING A POINT FROM A CURVED SOURCE

559. DIRECT VIEW OF DRAWINGS
Showing how the projection lines in Fig. 560 would look in practice

560.
THREE-DIMENSIONAL VIEW OF FIG. 559
Made to illustrate theory of how projection works.

561. DIRECT VIEW OF THE SECOND STEP

562.
THREE-DIMENSIONAL VIEW OF SECOND STEP

Fig. 563]   Projection in Three Dimensions   263

lowed by Rays 4, 5, and 6. In Fig. 559, Ray 9 is eliminated, and Rays 8 and 10 become one line.

We now know that our wanted point [P$_9$] will fall somewhere along Ray 10. The method of fixing its height is illustrated in Figs. 561 and 562. In Fig. 562, we must continue Rays 6 and 8 downward. We must also draw Rays 11 and 13. In Fig. 561, however, Ray 12 does the whole job.

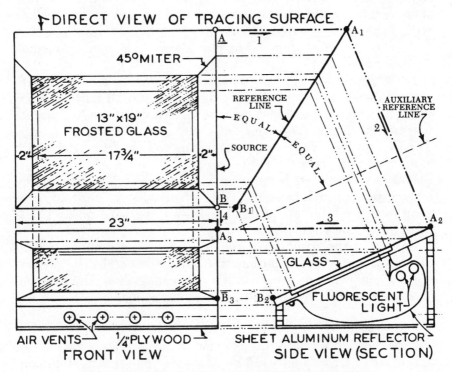

563. DRAWING AN OBLIQUE PLANE BY PROJECTION

I first drew the direct view of the tracing surface. Line A$_2$B$_2$, which represents this surface in the side view, was then drawn in any convenient place. The auxiliary reference line is parallel to A$_2$B$_2$ and forms an angle with AB. The reference line bisects that angle. Depth measurements from the tracing surface were projected to the reference line and from there to A$_2$B$_2$. With these as a guide, I designed the side view. Lastly, I drew the front view by projecting the width measurements downward from the tracing surface and projecting the height measurements sidewise from the side view.

Complications. In an elaborate drawing, the number of points to be projected may run into the hundreds—or even into the thousands. Projection then becomes extremely laborious. If you do not draw the rays but merely represent their key points by ticks, you soon have trouble remembering which tick is which. If you do draw the rays, they create a network that is difficult to distinguish from the lines of the drawing itself.

In some cases, such as a detailed perspective drawing of a skyscraper, these difficulties must be accepted as the price we pay for accuracy. Usually, however, we can dodge much of this work and confusion without any material loss.

You will often save time and effort by projecting only the key points and locating the rest by eye. The number of points to be projected will, of course, depend partly on the degree of accuracy required and partly on how far you can trust your eye. Another short cut is to project the main forms first, using ticks. When these forms have been sketched in, they provide a kind of reference map of the drawing and help to identify the points projected for the minor forms.

If the source is complex, try drawing the rays and ticks with colored pencil. Lay in the lines of the drawing itself fairly heavily, using a graphite pencil. When the drawing gets too cluttered, make a tracing of the object lines but omit the rays and ticks. Then go on with your work, putting in new rays and ticks with a pencil of a different color.

You can usually save time on a really elaborate drawing by making several such tracings. Tracing is much quicker than puzzling over a jumble of rays and ticks—and perhaps making mistakes by getting your ticks mixed up.

Projecting the irregular curves of a free-line drawing would be almost impossibly laborious. We can get around it by preparing a straight-line construction and projecting that. The drawing can then be made over this projected construction.

APPLICATIONS

Projection is normally used when we have one or two views and want to make another. The new view may be three-dimensional, but more often it represents a compromise between two- and three-dimensional drawing. Thus, the drawing of the turned stick figure [Step 4, Fig. 558] shows only two axes, height and breadth. Such a drawing cannot represent the depth dimension. In spite of this, we are so accustomed to seeing a figure as three-dimensional that the lines appear to recede into the paper. They thus suggest the dimension of depth without representing it. Similarly, the front view of the tracing box in Fig. 563 contains vertical lines that represent the sloping face of the box. These lines slant in the source. Hence, we must think of them as having depth and must visualize them as receding into the paper.

Oblique Planes. The source-drawing in Fig. 563 is an oblique plane instead of a front or top view. This should give you no trouble. The only new feature is the fact that the reference line is placed at half the angle between the oblique plane and the vertical. I located this reference line by drawing an auxiliary reference line and then bisecting the angle by the method in Fig. 141. However, as the angle of the oblique plane (22°) was given, I could have computed the angle of the reference line by arithmetic—($[90° - 22°] \div 2 = 34°$). Hence, the reference line must be 34° from the vertical or 56° from the horizontal.

PROJECTING SINE CURVES
A direct, side view of a wire
spring would be a sine curve.

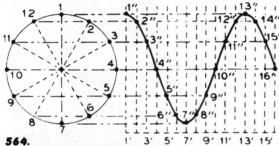

564.
PROCESS OF PROJECTION
Points evenly spaced around
a circle are projected in
sequence onto evenly spaced
parallel lines. Join these
points to draw the sine curve.

565.
SIDE VIEW OF A
BARBER'S POLE
Example showing a
practical applica-
tion of sine curves.

Helices. The curve seen in a spiral staircase or a barber's pole is technically known as a *helix*. A direct side view of a helix is called a *sine curve* [Fig. 564]. Sine curves occur frequently in the graphs used by scientists and engineers [Fig. 404]. Both three-dimensional helices and sine curves are difficult to draw accurately without the aid of projection, but the methods shown are easy to use though somewhat tedious.

To project the sine curve, we draw a circle and divide it into, say, twelve equal parts [Fig. 564]. The points on this circle are numbered. We then draw a set of evenly spaced parallel lines, which are also numbered.

The first point of the circle is then projected onto the first line, the second point is projected onto the second line, and so on. We can continue this as long as we like. Thus, I have projected Point 1 onto Line 13' to fix Point 13", Point 2 onto Line 14' to fix Point 14", and so on. Note that the spacing of the parallel lines determines whether the waves of the sine curve are bunched up or spread out.

The three-dimensional helix in Fig. 566 is projected on much the same principle. We begin by drawing an ellipse and dividing it into equal segments by the method in Fig. 549. We then project the points by parallel rays. Point 1 is projected an arbitrary distance (a). Point 2 is projected a distance equal to $a + b$. Point 3 is projected $a + 2b$, and so on. If b is small, the loops will be close together. If b is large, they will be far apart.

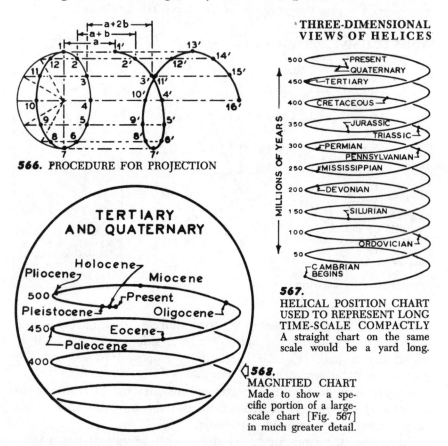

566. PROCEDURE FOR PROJECTION

THREE-DIMENSIONAL VIEWS OF HELICES

567. HELICAL POSITION CHART USED TO REPRESENT LONG TIME-SCALE COMPACTLY A straight chart on the same scale would be a yard long.

568. MAGNIFIED CHART Made to show a specific portion of a large-scale chart [Fig. 567] in much greater detail.

In certain fields, such as Geology and Astronomy, we sometimes need diagrams that cover an enormous range but that must nevertheless show details as well. The helical time chart in Fig. 567 lends itself to situations of this sort by crowding the maximum length of line into a limited space. This is essentially the same as the position chart in Fig. 93 except that the line is much longer and is coiled instead of straight.

When we want to show small details, we can supplement our first chart with a *magnified chart* like Fig. 568. This represents a selected portion of the first chart as it might look through a

Fig. 570]   Projection in Three Dimensions   267

magnifying glass. Actually, the magnification is imaginary; it shows details that do not exist in the original chart.

We can carry the magnification principle as far as we please. A popular work on physics might start with a map of the nearby universe. It could then give a magnified map of our galaxy, then one of the solar system, then one of the earth. This could be continued until the last diagram showed the particles within an atom.

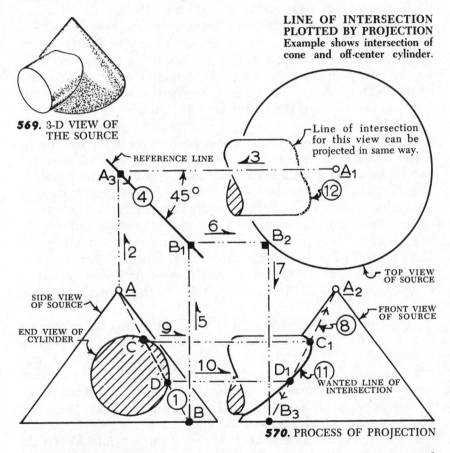

LINE OF INTERSECTION PLOTTED BY PROJECTION
Example shows intersection of cone and off-center cylinder.

569. 3-D VIEW OF THE SOURCE

Line of intersection for this view can be projected in same way.

REFERENCE LINE

A_3 3 A_1

4   45°   12

6   B_2

B_1 2

7

A A_2

SIDE VIEW OF SOURCE   TOP VIEW OF SOURCE

FRONT VIEW OF SOURCE

END VIEW OF CYLINDER   9   5   8

C C_1

D 10 D_1 11

1   B B_3 WANTED LINE OF INTERSECTION

570. PROCESS OF PROJECTION

Intersections. When a curved surface meets another curved surface or an oblique plane, the line of intersection can be drawn accurately only by projection [cone and cylinder in Figs. 569 and 570].

To make such a projection, begin by drawing three views as we did in Fig. 559. Omit the line of intersection in the top and front views, as these must be plotted by projection. Note that the side view must show one of the elements (in this case, the cylinder) head on.

In this side view, draw a construction line [1] on the surface of the second element (the cone) and passing through the first element (the cylinder). Mark points [A and B] at the ends of this line. Also, mark points [C and D] where the line cuts the first element (the cylinder). I have shown only one such construction line in order to keep the diagram simple, but in practice it is necessary to draw several.

Establish a 45° reference line [4] by the method in Fig. 559. Then project the construction line [1] onto the front view where it becomes Line 8. You can then draw horizontal rays [9 and 10]. These will project Points C and D onto Line 8 as Points C_1 and D_1. Project enough points in this manner to fix the line of intersection and then draw that line [11] through the points. Problems of intersection can tax your powers of visualization to the utmost, but they can all be solved on the same principle.

Development. Anyone who works in sheet metal, or who builds cardboard models, needs to make patterns for flat material that can be bent to form three-dimensional objects like the funnel in Fig. 571. The only practical way to draw such patterns is through the technique known as *development*. This is largely a process of construction, but projecting the key points saves time and trouble.

I began to develop the body of the funnel by extending AC [Line 1] to fix Point E on the center line. Line 2 was then drawn parallel to AE, and Points A, C, and E were projected onto it by Lines 3, 4, and 5. This fixed Point E_1 as the center of Arcs 6 and 8.

The length of the outer arc [6] was established by drawing a top view [Fig. 572] and marking off one-twelfth of the circumference (30°). This length was then measured by dividers, and twelve spaces were stepped off along Arc 6 [Fig. 573]. As dividers measure straight lines rather than curves, the method is not strictly accurate. However, it will serve in most cases. If greater accuracy is required, you can use eighteen steps (20° in the top view). A larger number of steps is rarely worth while. When the length of the outer arc is fixed, Line 7 determines the length of the inner arc [8].

The pattern for the spout was drawn by exactly the same method. Do not forget to add *tabs* for the seams.

Once you know how to project the patterns for a funnel, you should be able to work out a method of development for any form into which a flat surface can be bent. However, some of the more complex forms present difficult problems that combine both construction and projection. If you have much occasion to use

Fig. 573]   Projection in Three Dimensions   269

development, it will pay you to study the examples given in a book on mechanical drawing.

ADVANCED PROJECTION

We have now considered the main uses of projection in general drawing. There are a number of other applications, but these are restricted to more or less specialized fields. Also, although they are simple enough in theory, they raise many problems in practice. Short outlines of the methods involved would be misleading, and extended treatments would require more space than these subjects deserve in a book on general drawing. All I can do here is to mention each type briefly. If you are interested in any of them, the bibliography [p. 330] lists books that will prove helpful.

Cast Shadows. In the rare cases where cast shadows are needed for practical drawing, the required standard of accuracy is usu-

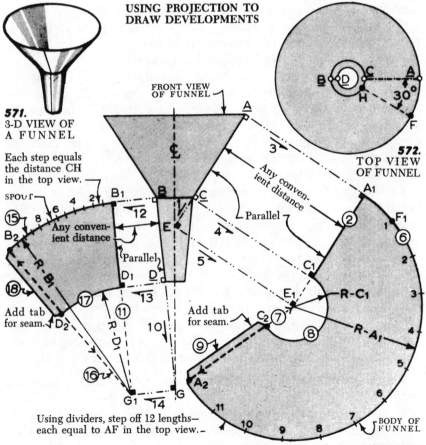

USING PROJECTION TO
DRAW DEVELOPMENTS

FRONT VIEW
OF FUNNEL

571.
3-D VIEW OF
A FUNNEL

Each step equals
the distance CH
in the top view.

SPOUT

Any conven-
ient distance

Parallel

Add tab
for seam.

Using dividers, step off 12 lengths—
each equal to AF in the top view.

572.
TOP VIEW
OF FUNNEL

30°

Any conven-
ient distance

Parallel

Add tab
for seam.

R-C₁

R-A₁

BODY OF
FUNNEL

573. PROCEDURE FOR DEVELOPMENT

ally so low that you can probably sketch the shadows by eye without much trouble. Accurate shadows must be drawn by projection. If you really understand projection, you should be able to work out the process for yourself. If that is too difficult, you must either be content with a rough approximation or study the subject in detail from a textbook.

Perspective. Axial drawing is much simpler and quicker than perspective. Furthermore, the finished work is easier to read, and its measurements can be scaled without difficulty. For these reasons, the use of perspective is largely confined to art drawing and to the semi-art sketches made by architects and scene designers. In my own practical work, I have encountered exactly two situations where I was forced to use perspective because axial drawing was inadequate. In one case, I needed to depict a house in some detail and at the same time indicate the location of a second house half a mile away. In the other, I wanted to show the proscenium, gridiron, and rigging of a stage; this required representing the ceiling, floor, and three walls in their proper relations. Neither drawing could have been made by axial methods, but perspective handled them nicely.

Although the theory of perspective is simple, methods of applying this theory vary enormously with the source and the conditions under which the drawing is made. Thus, methods favored by artists are so different from those used by architects that even a master of art-perspective like Norman Rockwell was occasionally forced to have an architect lay out the architectural-perspective of the background for one of his paintings.

As the practical draftsman needs perspective only in exceptional cases, an extended treatment of the subject is not justified in a book like this. As the cases where he does need perspective are likely to require exceptional methods, a brief discussion of the subject could not hope to cover these exceptional methods and hence would have little value. For these reasons, I feel that the space in this book can be put to better use. In the rare instances where you need perspective, you may be able to trace on glass [Fig. 193] or to take a snapshot and trace from that [Fig. 253]. If you want to pursue the subject more deeply, I can only refer you to the books listed in the bibliography (p. 330).

Mapping. Map-makers employ more than a dozen forms of projection to represent areas of the globe on a flat surface. Each type distorts the source in a different way. You cannot completely understand any map until you know something about the projection on which it was based.

Fig. 574]   Projection in Three Dimensions   **271**

Crystallography. *Clinographic projection* is a type of trimetric drawing used to make realistic pictures of crystals. Crystallographers also employ two abstract types of projection called *stereographic* and *gnomonic*. These bear almost no resemblance to any other kind of drawing. I suspect that if they were better known, the principles on which they are based could be put to good use in many fields.

16

PEOPLE
AND ANIMALS

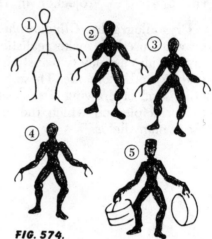

FIG. 574.
DRAWING A SCRIBBLE FIGURE

Y OU have no doubt discovered by now that easy ways of learning to draw are not the same thing as easy ways of making drawings. This chapter, however, offers an approach to figure drawing that combines a method of learning so completely with a method of drawing that it is hard to say where one stops and the other begins.

SCRIBBLE FIGURES

Scribble drawing is like modeling in clay. A stick figure takes the place of the sculptor's armature [Step 1, Fig. 574]. We then build on this by adding scribble to scribble until the sketch is done. Try to think like a sculptor and to visualize each scribble as a three-dimensional mass rather than as a flat mark on the paper. Unlike clay, however, these masses can be pushed into each other just as we did with the interlocking blocks of the church in Fig. 472.

There is no set rule about the forms of the scribbles. Nevertheless, the ellipsoids shown in the sketch of the bellhop are recommended for the beginner; they are easy, and they prepare you for the more elaborate method of drawing to be explained later.

Sources. Use sources for your early experiments. You cannot expect your memory and imagination to supply correct data about the proportions and positions of the parts. Professional artists, including cartoonists, employ sources for all of their serious work. You are only making trouble for yourself if you attempt to draw without the aid that experts require.

Drawings or photographs are better sources for your early efforts than a live model; they never change their positions and are easy to measure. If you have any difficulty, make your first scribbles on tracing paper laid over the source.

Fig. 581]   People and Animals   273

USES OF SCRIBBLE FIGURES

575. AUTHOR'S ROUGH SKETCH TO GUIDE THE ARTIST IN MAKING AN ILLUSTRATION

576. DOODLE CARTOON

BRACHIOSARUS
The largest animal that ever walked the earth.

577. SCRIBBLE-FIGURE ANIMAL
Note use of man to show scale.

578. HOBBYIST'S DESIGN SKETCH
Drawn as a guide for modeling a "military miniature" (tin soldiers) to represent a hand-to-hand fight between a trapper and an Indian.

Start with cartoon figures. They are easier than realistic figures because their proportions need not be exact. They are also more amusing and better suited to the scribble technique.

PROGRESSIVE DOODLING

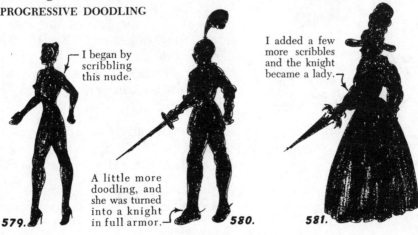

I began by scribbling this nude.

A little more doodling, and she was turned into a knight in full armor.

579.

580.

I added a few more scribbles and the knight became a lady.

581.

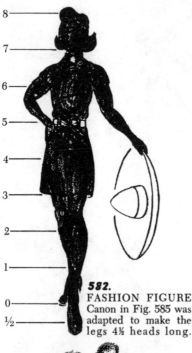

582.
FASHION FIGURE
Canon in Fig. 585 was
adapted to make the
legs 4½ heads long.

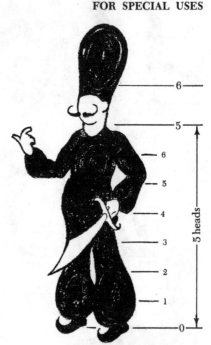

583. CARTOON FIGURE
The canon in Fig.
585 was adapted to
make the little Turk
only 6 heads high.

584.
PROFESSIONAL METHOD OF
DRAWING SCRIBBLE FIGURES
This takes much more skill, but
it is ideal for advertising layouts.

Poses. If you have not already discovered from your experiments with stick figures that finding effective poses is a matter of major importance, you should certainly learn it now. Make your figures do something. Arty poses like that of the model in Fig. 576 have few practical applications and are apt to seem dull—no matter how skillfully they are drawn.

Clothing and Props. These add materially to the interest of your sketches. Clothing the usual type of figure requires more skill than the figure itself. With scribble people, however, cloth-

585.
SKLINE TEMPLATES AND A CANON OF
MEASUREMENTS FOR AN IDEAL FIGURE
The units of measurement are head heights.

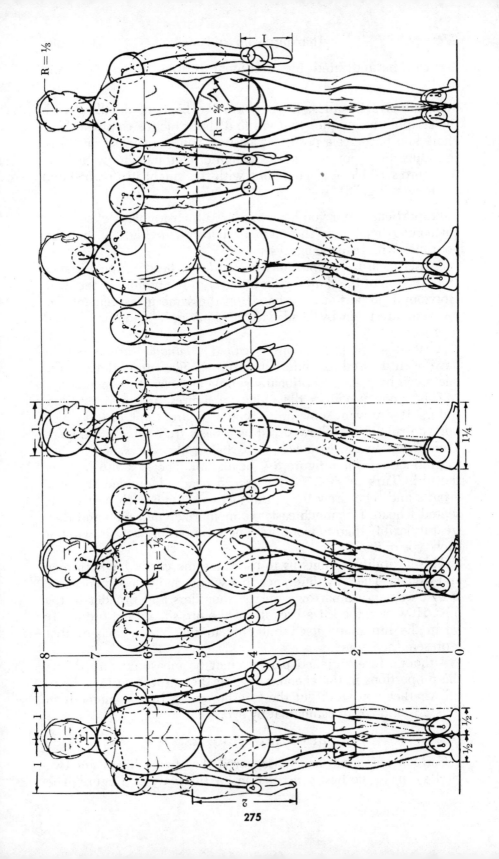

ing can be indicated by additional scribble [Figs. 582 and 583].

Progressive Doodles. If you form the habit of doodling with the scribble technique, you will find that practice ceases to be a chore and becomes a positive pleasure. You can correct mistakes, introduce props, or change the design of clothing simply by adding more scribble as I have done with the knight in Fig. 580 and the lady in Fig. 581.

Proportions. After you have mastered the rudiments of scribble cartooning, memorize the main proportions in Fig. 585 and try your luck with realistic figures.

Artists measure proportions in *heads*. A head is the distance from the top of the skull (without hair) to the bottom of the chin. Horizontal proportions are based on the same measurement. Do not compare them by head widths; think only in terms of head heights.

A stock set of proportions is called a *canon*. Various canons have been devised for different purposes. The proportions of the one given here are exceptionally simple and easy to remember.

This canon produces the idealized figures preferred by illustrators. If you want some other type of figure, think of the canon not as a rule to be followed but as a basis from which to depart. Thus, I added an extra half head below the knees of Fig. 582 to produce a fashion figure 8½ heads tall. The legs and body of the little Turk in Fig. 583 measure 5 heads. I divided this into 7 parts and then drew the figure just as though each part represented 1 head. It is much easier to memorize one canon and then treat it flexibly than to work out a new canon for each drawing or each type of figure.

This flexibility permits us to use the same canon for both men and women. The only difference that we normally need to observe is that women are narrower in the shoulders and broader in the hips. However, the extra breadth of the hip should not ordinarily be in the hip shape itself but only in the muscle masses that represent the haunches.

Although foreshortened parts cannot be measured directly by the proportions in the canon, knowing their true lengths is helpful whether you work out the foreshortening by the methods in Figs. 237 and 239 or estimate it by eye.

BUILDING FIGURES

Cartoon animators have discovered that two ellipses (or two circles) make the best construction for the body of a figure. The sizes and positions of these shapes vary widely and depend on whether the sketch represents a man or an animal and whether

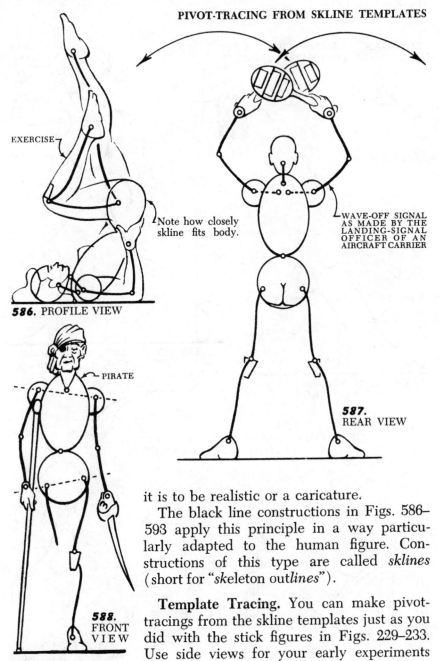

PIVOT-TRACING FROM SKLINE TEMPLATES

EXERCISE

Note how closely skline fits body.

WAVE-OFF SIGNAL AS MADE BY THE LANDING-SIGNAL OFFICER OF AN AIRCRAFT CARRIER

586. PROFILE VIEW

PIRATE

587. REAR VIEW

588. FRONT VIEW

it is to be realistic or a caricature.

The black line constructions in Figs. 586–593 apply this principle in a way particularly adapted to the human figure. Constructions of this type are called *sklines* (short for "*sk*eleton out*lines*").

Template Tracing. You can make pivot-tracings from the skline templates just as you did with the stick figures in Figs. 229–233. Use side views for your early experiments [Fig. 586]. This avoids problems of foreshortening. An endless array of profile poses may be drawn in this way. You can have lots of fun with it, and it will teach you a great deal about the art of posing figures. You will also familiarize yourself with the proportions of the parts.

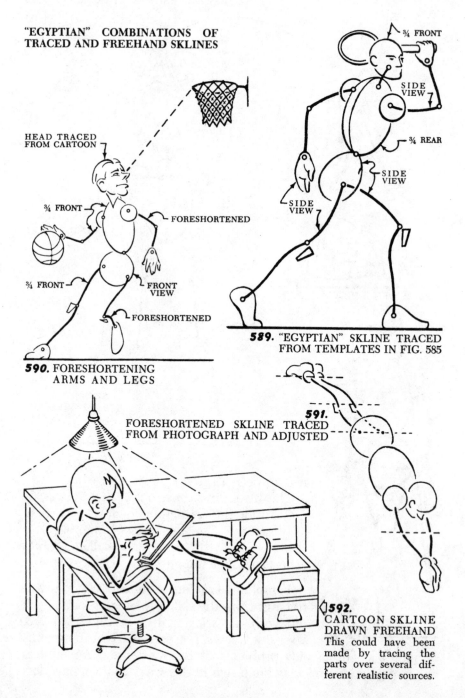

"EGYPTIAN" COMBINATIONS OF TRACED AND FREEHAND SKLINES

¾ FRONT

SIDE VIEW

¾ REAR

SIDE VIEW

SIDE VIEW

589. "EGYPTIAN" SKLINE TRACED FROM TEMPLATES IN FIG. 585

HEAD TRACED FROM CARTOON

¾ FRONT

FORESHORTENED

¾ FRONT

FRONT VIEW

FORESHORTENED

590. FORESHORTENING ARMS AND LEGS

591. FORESHORTENED SKLINE TRACED FROM PHOTOGRAPH AND ADJUSTED

592. CARTOON SKLINE DRAWN FREEHAND This could have been made by tracing the parts over several different realistic sources.

Fig. 592]					People and Animals					279

When you have acquired proficiency in handling profiles, try creating a few front and back views [pirate in Fig. 588 and landing-signal officer in Fig. 587]. You will find that it is almost impossible to produce interesting poses either in these or in three-quarter views if you limit your tracing to one template. However, you can easily get around this by applying the Egyptian principle and taking parts from other views. Thus, I traced the right arm of the pirate from the three-quarter front view, and I had to use side views for the arms of the landing-signal officer. The latter drawing also brings out the fact that shoulders are not confined to one position but can be moved up, down, or forward by pivoting the collar bones at points near the center of the chest. The pirate's right shoulder would have seemed more natural if I had raised it slightly in this way.

The tennis player in Fig. 589 carries the Egyptian principle further and combines parts traced from three different templates. The free use of this principle greatly extends the range of poses that you can work up from templates. It also results in more interesting positions. This type of tracing should be easy if you have already mastered the technique with stick figures [Figs. 234–236].

When you can handle "Egyptian tracings," try foreshortening one or more limbs. My tracing of the basketball player in Fig. 590 was produced in this way. A little foreshortening will enable you to draw many poses that you could not achieve by tracing alone.

Although template tracing is primarily a device for learning to draw, you will find it useful whenever you want to construct a figure in an unusual pose and cannot find a satisfactory source.

Tracing Sklines from Pictures. Working from templates will teach you the parts of the skline and how they fit together. After you have learned these things, lay tracing paper over a picture of a nude or lightly clad figure and construct the skline by tracing. The procedure is identical with that used for the stick figure in Fig. 208. When you can do this from simple sources, go on to figures like the diver in Fig. 591 where the masses are foreshortened.

Tracing a skline may be worth while even when you want to trace the whole figure. Thus, my skline for the diver in Fig. 591 shows parallel lines drawn through the principal joints. This is the pose that a real diver takes in a perfect dive. Unfortunately, the diver in my source did not show ideal form. I therefore traced a rough skline and corrected it to bring the joints onto parallel lines. With this construction firmly established, I could then have

BUILDING A FIGURE

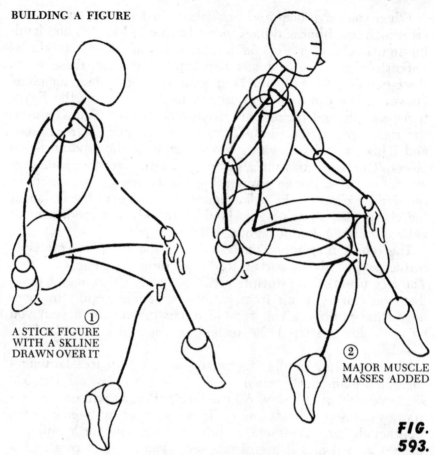

① A STICK FIGURE WITH A SKLINE DRAWN OVER IT

② MAJOR MUSCLE MASSES ADDED

FIG.
593.

gone back and traced the whole figure, making the necessary adjustments as I went along. This may seem like a complicated procedure. But once you acquire the knack, you will find it quick and easy—provided that you have a clear idea of what you are trying to do.

Although Fig. 592 was sketched freehand, you can create similar cartoon figures by combining sklines from several sources with different proportions. The method is similar to that used for drawing the careless woodworker in Fig. 253. However, as you are now dealing with sklines rather than figures, trace only the required parts of each skline and do not let yourself be distracted by the details of your source.

Thus, the body and legs of Fig. 592 might have been traced over a photograph of a bathing beauty, and the head traced from an advertisement. The arms and hands would probably have needed to be added freehand. Combining sklines in this way greatly increases the number of sources available for tracing.

Fig. 593]   People and Animals   281

When my skline was complete, I used it as a construction and turned it into a conventional cartoon by drawing clothes over it [title page]. This is much easier than drawing a cartoon figure in a difficult pose entirely freehand.

When you can visualize and trace a skline from lightly dressed figures, try working from pictures where the clothing hides parts of the body. The first time I attempted this, I expected to have trouble. Actually, I found it surprisingly easy. Such tracing is good practice. It also enables you to work from a much wider range of sources; lightly clad figures are rarely depicted in poses that are good for anything but pin-ups.

After you have familiarized yourself with the shapes and proportions of sklines, try sketching them freehand. Begin by drawing a stick figure as a construction. This will set the pose and proportions. Adding the body masses will then be easy.

BUILDING A FIGURE (Cont.)

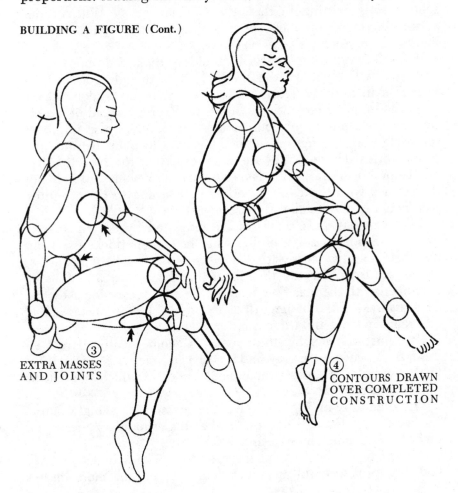

③
EXTRA MASSES
AND JOINTS

④
CONTOURS DRAWN
OVER COMPLETED
CONSTRUCTION

You will learn more quickly in the long run if you start free-hand drawing with simple profile poses. Proceed to Egyptian poses. Then, add minor foreshortening. Do not attempt poses like those of my diver and sketcher [Figs. 591 and 592] until you can handle simpler poses without difficulty.

Muscle Masses. Sklines make good figures for rough diagrams like that of the boy in the soap-box racer [Fig. 153]. However, their main function is to serve as constructions for complete figures. Not only are they ideal for this purpose, but they permit us to build up a figure by adding one *muscle mass* at a time [Fig. 593]. The process is essentially a refinement of that used for drawing scribble figures.

This building method is easier than simply drawing contours but it is much more than that. It forces you to think in terms of solid masses existing in three-dimensional space. Without this approach, your people are apt to look like flat patterns that outline two-dimensional shapes on the paper.

If you learn to draw figures by building them, I do not believe that you will abandon the method even though you acquire enough skill to draw figures offhand with no construction at all. With the building technique, you create figures instead of merely copying the contours of your model. The method also improves the design of your figures by enabling you to plan them around simple forms. These virtues are more important for the artist than for the practical draftsman. Nevertheless, as they are a free bonus that comes with the easiest method of learning to draw figures, you should certainly take advantage of them.

The principal muscle masses are indicated by dotted lines in Fig. 585. Study these carefully. Note how their thicknesses, but not their lengths, vary with the viewpoint. The haunch masses are separate from those that form the thighs instead of being combined with them as they were in the cruder scribble sketches. This distinction is not important in profile, but it makes a real difference in front and three-quarter views.

The illustrations show the masses as geometrically correct ellipsoids. However, you may find it easier in practice to make them fit the figure if you use streamlined shapes in which one end is slightly sharper than the other.

The diagrams in Fig. 585 give the masses for a male figure. To construct female figures, make the shoulders narrower, broaden the haunch masses, and add breasts.

If the figure is more than three or four inches high, you will find it helpful to build up minor details by adding more masses

Fig. 595]   **People and Animals**   **283**

(see arrows in Step 3, Fig. 593). There is no system for this. Simply draw an ellipsoid for any bump that you observe in your source.

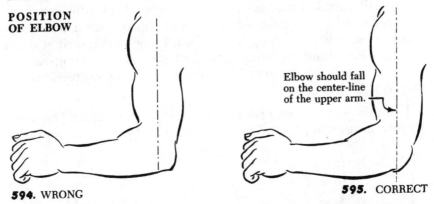

POSITION OF ELBOW

Elbow should fall on the center-line of the upper arm.

594. WRONG   **595.** CORRECT

Joints. Where the drawing is small and the standard of accuracy is low, joints cause little trouble; with larger drawings and a higher standard of accuracy, they become a study in themselves. Elbows and knees show small projections of bone, muscle, and fat. These vary in subtle ways depending on the angle at which the joint is bent and on the viewpoint from which it is seen.

The elbow is part of the forearm and moves with it. Hence, bending the arm brings the point of the elbow in line with the bone of the upper arm [Fig. 595]. If you draw the elbow in line with the back of the arm, it will look like a corner on a picture frame [Fig. 594].

The kneecap is attached to the shinbone by a ligament and moves with the bone in much the same way that the elbow moves with the forearm. However, the movement of the kneecap ceases when the heel reaches a point about 6" from the buttock. If the leg is bent still farther, the kneecap remains stationary.

These are the chief details to watch, but minor forms also deserve careful attention. The only general advice that I can give is to pay especial attention to the joints in your sources. Get the joints right, and the larger masses will almost take care of themselves.

Contours. When you intend to clothe a figure, you need not carry it beyond the muscle-mass stage. For nude parts, however, the muscle masses must be treated as a faint-line construction over which contours are drawn [Step 4, Fig. 593]. If you have not already learned how to draw accented contours on traced constructions [Fig. 189], I suggest that you master this before attemping to contour original sketches.

Although sklines provide a remarkably easy and accurate method of figure drawing, we cannot expect the procedure to be completely straightforward. Unless you have an unusually good eye, small mistakes may occur at any stage. Check your construction constantly and make whatever adjustments seem necessary. Thus, when I finished Step 3, Fig. 593, I saw that the right thigh was too long, and that the right foot should be swung farther forward and twisted toward the observer. These corrections are shown in Step 4.

Feet. Experience with stick figures should have given you some facility in drawing feet. The diagrams in Figs. 596–602 may also

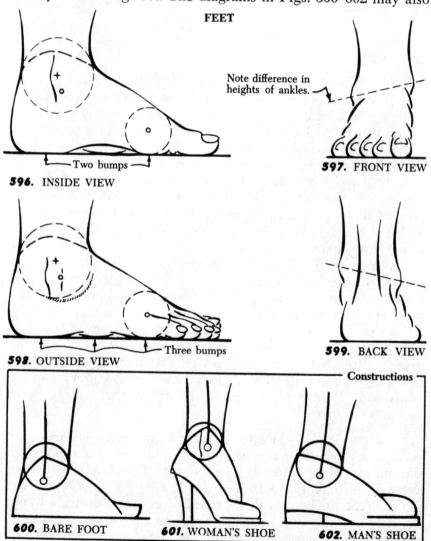

FEET

Note difference in heights of ankles.

596. INSIDE VIEW — Two bumps

597. FRONT VIEW

598. OUTSIDE VIEW — Three bumps

599. BACK VIEW

Constructions

600. BARE FOOT

601. WOMAN'S SHOE

602. MAN'S SHOE

Fig. 608]   People and Animals   285

FEET IN THREE DIMENSIONS

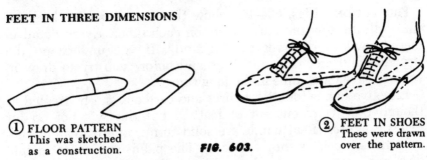

① FLOOR PATTERN
This was sketched
as a construction.   *FIG. 603.*   ② FEET IN SHOES
                                                 These were drawn
                                                 over the pattern.

prove helpful. Feet are easy except for the problem of making them stand flat on the ground. The best way to do this is to sketch footprints as constructions and then draw the feet on the prints [Fig. 603]. You may have trouble in making the footprints lie flat, but at least the construction itself is simple and you can see what you are doing. If you try to draw feet (or feet attached to a body) without the footprints, you are apt to go wrong—and making corrections is much harder.

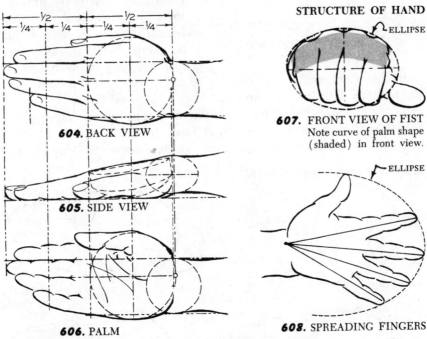

STRUCTURE OF HAND

604. BACK VIEW

605. SIDE VIEW

606. PALM

607. FRONT VIEW OF FIST
Note curve of palm shape
(shaded) in front view.

608. SPREADING FINGERS

Hands. Hands give more trouble than all the rest of the figure put together, but they richly repay the effort required to master them. Well-drawn hands add greatly to the appearance of any figure. Furthermore, hands by themselves serve many uses as notes and illustrations.

PROPORTIONS. Figs. 604–608 show the proportions of the hand and indicate how the parts move on each other. Every detail in these drawings deserves careful study. If you understand the structure and mechanism of the hand before you try to draw it, you will save much time in the long run.

Effective hands for stick figures and cartoons can be treated as though they were cut out of leather, but this will not do for realistic figures. Real hands are solid forms, approximately one-seventh as thick as they are long. The palm mass is not a thin disk but is more like a large biscuit. This "biscuit" is always slightly bent [Fig. 607], and it can be bent still more when the thumb and little finger are brought together. It cannot be bent lengthwise. Also, remember that the fingers do not curl but bend only at the joints [Fig. 609].

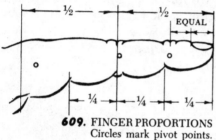

609. FINGER PROPORTIONS
Circles mark pivot points.

THE MITTEN METHOD. The hands in Figs. 610–619 were drawn by the *mitten method* used by cartoon animators. This represents a major breakthrough in the hand problem. With its aid, you can not only draw hands in half the time you would otherwise need, but you can learn to draw them with half the amount of practice and study.

Draw the wrists and palm shapes first. The wrist shape is important. If you omit it, you will have trouble in making your sketches convincing. Next add the "mitten" as a construction for

MITTEN METHOD OF CONSTRUCTING HANDS

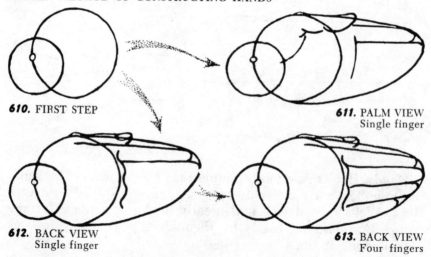

610. FIRST STEP

611. PALM VIEW
Single finger

612. BACK VIEW
Single finger

613. BACK VIEW
Four fingers

Fig. 614] **People and Animals** 287

the fingers. Note that this is drawn around the palm circle and ignores the thumb. When the mitten has been placed, draw the thumb as a separate form. Show the knuckle line in back views. This can be simply a slight curve if the hand is small. In larger drawings, it is better to represent the knuckles of the middle and ring fingers by bumps [Figs. 612].

For small figures or rough sketches, you rarely need to separate more than one finger from the mitten [Figs. 611 and 612]. In such cases, hands look better if the details are kept to a minimum. Fig. 614 shows a woman's hand with index and little fingers separated from the mitten.

Drawing fingernails tends to give hands a fussy appearance. Sketch your hands without them at first; then decide whether or not nails are needed. I usually find that the thumbnail helps except in the smallest hands. When you do show the nails, give only the barest indication; it is rarely desirable to outline the whole nail [Fig. 618].

The same principle applies to drawing wrinkles on the palm and at the knuckles. Leave them out unless you are convinced that they are really needed; then keep them to a bare minimum.

To the palmist and the portrait painter, every hand is different and the differences are important. For practical purposes, however, we can safely use the same proportions for the hands of all figures under 3″ or 4″ in height. If you sketch many figures larger than this, you will need two types of hands—one for men and one for women.

Women's hands should be narrower than men's; you can get this effect without difficulty by constructing them with ellipses instead of circles. Women's fingers should be more pointed than men's. Try to place your women's hands in graceful positions. This is more than half the secret of drawing hands for fashion ads. The hands in such ads are often faulty in structure, but they almost never take awkward poses.

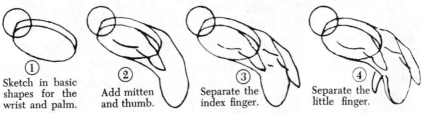

① Sketch in basic shapes for the wrist and palm.
② Add mitten and thumb.
③ Separate the index finger.
④ Separate the little finger.

FIG. 614. CONSTRUCTING ACTION VIEW OF WOMAN'S HAND

LEARNING TO DRAW HANDS. Begin by studying the proportions and mechanics of the hand in Figs. 604–609. Then trace the hands in Figs 615–619 to gain a clearer idea of the mitten method. Recopy these examples freehand in order to be sure that you understand the procedure.

Next, select drawings in which the hands are 3″ or 4″ long. Supplement these by taking snapshots of hands in various positions. Pose the hands as close to the camera as possible, so that they will show up well in the prints. Trace mitten constructions from these drawings and photographs. After you have sketched a dozen or so mittens, go back and separate the fingers from the mittens—one at a time. Do this freehand, but use the mitten as a construction and have the source before you as a guide.

Finally, redraw the hand over your constructions. Pay especial attention to the way the contours overlap [Fig. 617]. Accents make hands more interesting [Fig. 619]. The simplest way to accent a hand is to fill the hollows along the upper lines and to thicken the centers of the curves that mark the lower lines.

You will not learn to draw hands overnight. However, do not let that discourage you. The knack comes suddenly. You may make little progress for some time and then discover almost between one drawing and the next that hands no longer give you trouble.

SKLINES IN MECHANICAL DESIGN

Many mechanical devices, ranging from space capsules to soap-box racers, are intended to fit the human form. Many of them fail to do this. Men over 5′11″ and women under 5′2″ are uncomfortable in the average automobile. Printing presses and theatrical control boards are provided with levers and pedals which only an acrobatic operator can reach.

These faults are often due to the designer's belief that the comfort and convenience of a device cannot be tested without building a costly full-scale *mock-up* (a model which works like the real thing, but which need not look like it). This is partly true, and a certain amount of guesswork is inevitable. Nevertheless, many misfits could be corrected on the drawing board by tracing simplified sklines over the engineer's preliminary sketches.

Proportions. The idealized proportions in Fig. 585 will not help the mechanical designer. He needs the measurements of real people, which are often far from ideal. The measurements in Fig. 623 were compiled from all the published data I could find. Unfortunately, much of this was gathered for the benefit of tailors and dressmakers and is not well adapted to the needs of the mechanical designer. Furthermore, most available tables relate to army air force personnel. This automatically weeds out those who are seriously over- or under-weight. Nevertheless, as such people drive cars and operate machines, the designer should take them into account. I have tried to allow for these factors in my table. I cannot hope that the results are completely satisfactory. However, I feel confident that the designer will find Fig. 623 more useful than any other table available at the present time.

No average measurements are given because no average person exists to fly a plane or play an organ. Even if this mythical being did exist, a device designed for him would not fit a 6′2″ man or a 5′0″ woman. Hence, the designer must plan for a range of people. This means that he should consider 95 percent of the population. The population may include all adults or be restricted to a specific group: designers of air-force bombers can ignore small women and fat men.

APPLICATIONS OF THE MITTEN METHOD

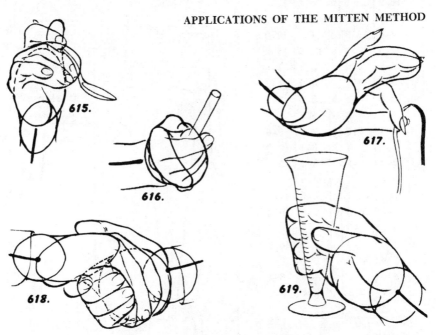

615.

616.

617.

618.

619.

Preparing Templates. Decide on the scale at which the mechanical drawings are to be made. Redraw the sklines in Figs. 621, 624, and 625 on sturdy tracing paper or acetate, using the procedure in Fig. 327. Take the dimensions for each skline from the appropriate column in the table [Fig. 623]. The number of sklines needed will depend on the problem. A designer of automobiles will probably require only two sklines—one profile for a tall man and one for a short woman. The design of a control board like that in Figs. 626–628 would call for six sklines—those for tall and short men in each of the three principal views.

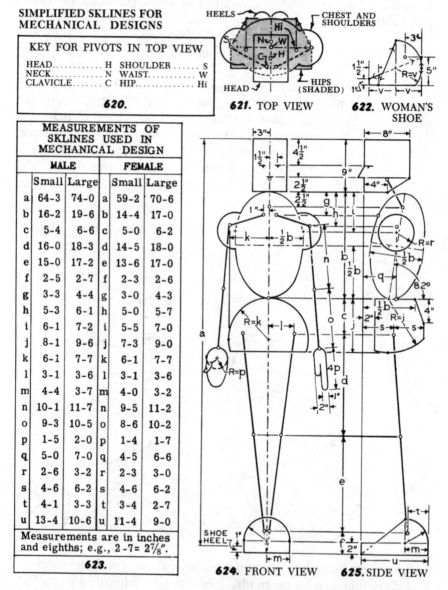

SIMPLIFIED SKLINES FOR MECHANICAL DESIGNS

KEY FOR PIVOTS IN TOP VIEW

HEAD............ H   SHOULDER ...... S
NECK............ N   WAIST.......... W
CLAVICLE....... C   HIP............. Hi

620.

621. TOP VIEW

622. WOMAN'S SHOE

MEASUREMENTS OF SKLINES USED IN MECHANICAL DESIGN			
MALE		**FEMALE**	
Small	Large	Small	Large
a 64-3	74-0	a 59-2	70-6
b 16-2	19-6	b 14-4	17-0
c 5-4	6-6	c 5-0	6-2
d 16-0	18-3	d 14-5	18-0
e 15-0	17-2	e 13-6	17-0
f 2-5	2-7	f 2-3	2-6
g 3-3	4-4	g 3-0	4-3
h 5-3	6-1	h 5-0	5-7
i 6-1	7-2	i 5-5	7-0
j 8-1	9-6	j 7-3	9-0
k 6-1	7-7	k 6-1	7-7
l 3-1	3-6	l 3-1	3-6
m 4-4	3-7	m 4-0	3-2
n 10-1	11-7	n 9-5	11-2
o 9-3	10-5	o 8-6	10-2
p 1-5	2-0	p 1-4	1-7
q 5-0	7-0	q 4-5	6-6
r 2-6	3-2	r 2-3	3-0
s 4-6	6-2	s 4-6	6-2
t 4-1	3-3	t 3-4	2-7
u 13-4	10-6	u 11-4	9-0
Measurements are in inches and eighths; e.g., 2-7= 2⅞".			

623.

624. FRONT VIEW   **625.** SIDE VIEW

Procedure. Draw the basic elements of the device on one sheet of paper. Place tracing paper over this, attaching it only at the top. Manipulate the skline template between the two sheets and make a pivot-tracing on the upper sheet. Any needed corrections can also be indicated on the upper sheet. This process minimizes erasure. It also permits you to make two or more pivot-tracings from different sklines on the same basic drawing.

Straight lines will ordinarily do for the arms and legs when you trace these experimental sklines. Occasionally, as in Fig. 628, the

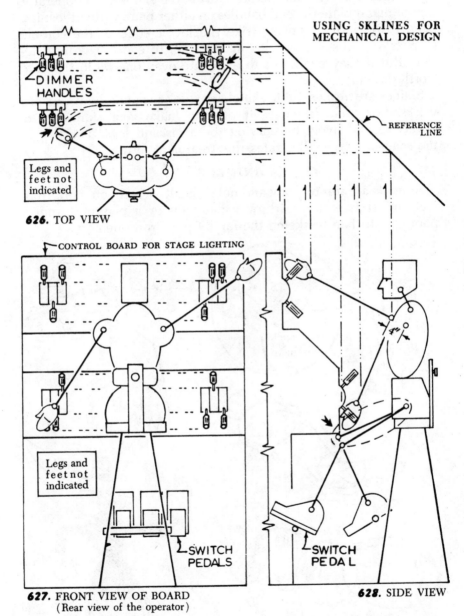

USING SKLINES FOR MECHANICAL DESIGN

DIMMER HANDLES

REFERENCE LINE

Legs and feet not indicated

626. TOP VIEW

CONTROL BOARD FOR STAGE LIGHTING

Legs and feet not indicated

SWITCH PEDALS

627. FRONT VIEW OF BOARD
(Rear view of the operator)

SWITCH PEDAL

628. SIDE VIEW

The "glass box" [Fig. 458] would place this side view on the left of the front view, but I have put it on the right because this arrangement seems clearer. Although it is foolish to ignore the rules, it is equally foolish to follow them without thinking.

thickness of a limb may be important (note arrow). You can then indicate this roughly by an ellipse—as I have done in the illustration.

The little arrows in Figs. 626 and 628 point to flaws in my design which I overlooked before I drew the sklines. The operator cannot manipulate the end handles on either bank without leaning [Fig. 626], and his knees strike the lower edge of the console [Fig. 628]. Sklines may not call attention to every flaw in a design. But if they enable us to eliminate even one fault, they are worth drawing.

Sklines are also useful in sketches made to explain how a device works. For such drawings, it pays to make your sklines more attractive and lively by curving the arms and legs. The boy in the soap-box racer illustrates this treatment [Fig. 153].

ANIMALS

Animals are fun to draw and not difficult—when you work from pictures. It is easier to draw a pangolin or a platypus from a photograph than to sketch the family pup from memory.

ANIMAL SKLINES

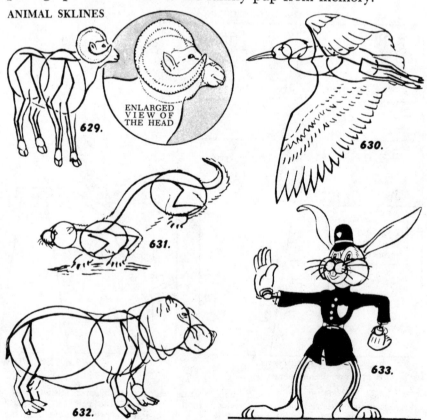

ENLARGED
VIEW OF
THE HEAD

629.

630.

631.

632.

633.

Fig. 638]   People and Animals   293

ANIMAL HEADS

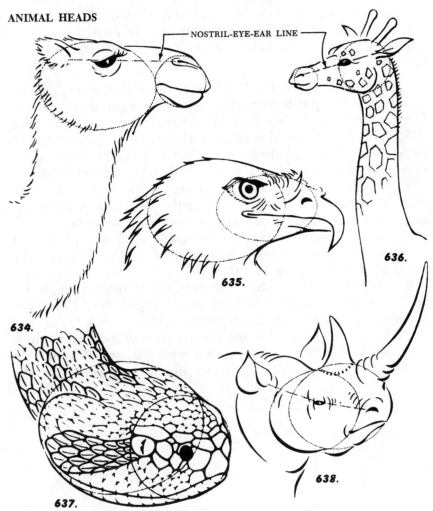

NOSTRIL-EYE-EAR LINE

636.

635.

634.

637.

638.

If you are not prepared to make a serious study of animal drawing, you will be wise to confine yourself to tracing and adapting pictures. Finding the right source may be difficult, but the drawing itself should give you no trouble—provided that you show only the main features and do not attempt to include minor details. If you want to draw from life, begin with a stick-figure construction [Figs. 369–374]. Unless the animal is unusually active, you have a good chance of getting this far before it moves.

Body Masses. The next step is to construct the body masses. These vary in size, proportions, and relative positions, but they are always ellipsoids or spheres [Figs. 629–633].

As animal legs are largely bones and tendons, there is little point in trying to build them up with muscle masses as you do with human figures. A skline provides all the construction you need.

Heads. Construct a head with two circles or ellipses [Figs. 634–638]. Add lines to mark the top and bottom of the muzzle. Draw a construction line through the nostril, eye, and ear [Fig. 634]. This line is usually straight [hippopotamus in Fig. 632; camel in Fig. 634, and giraffe in Fig. 636]. However, it sometimes curves up or down [sheep in Fig. 629 and rhinoceros in Fig. 638]. The shape of this construction line may vary with the point of view. A line that is straight when the head is seen in profile may show a decided curve when viewed from an angle.

The last step in a construction is to add any special projections such as the cheek pouches of the rabbit in Fig. 633 and the horns of the rhinoceros in Fig. 638.

If the animal stands still long enough, or often enough, for you to draw the construction and check it, you should not have much trouble in adding details one at a time. Nevertheless, this sort of drawing is not for the novice. You will proceed much faster if you first familiarize yourself with the animal by tracing drawings or photographs before you attempt to sketch from life.

17

RENDERING

639. LANDSCAPE

WHEN an object can be recognized by its shape, a contour drawing is easier (and normally better) for practical purposes than an elaborate rendering. When the shape is not enough, we may be able to identify an object by its relationship to other objects in the same drawing. Thus, the clouds, trees, bushes, and boulders in the landscape above have the same general shape. If they were sketched separately, they would be meaningless; when we combine them, each one explains the others.

The little landscape also demonstrates that the simplest symbol can provide a satisfactory picture of a bird if the meaning of the symbol is explained by a recognizable landscape. The same symbol on a blank sheet or in an interior scene would mean nothing at all.

Cases occur, however, where neither shape nor position is adequate to explain the object drawn. We must then fall back on devices of rendering. These act as graphic labels and notes to identify the object or to specify the materials from which it is made. Thus, we can distinguish between a blonde and a brunette by the way the hair is rendered.

The best way to learn rendering is to trace good examples. Trace only the details that involve the technique in which you are interested, and avoid tracing too many drawings by the same artist. When you can trace recognizable renderings of some material, say fur or foliage, lay tracing paper over a photograph of the same material and attempt to apply your newly acquired technique. This lets you concentrate on rendering without worrying about shapes and proportions.

There is no one right way to render any object or material. The methods given below were chosen because they are the easiest and quickest ways that I have found for achieving adequate results with the sharp-pencil technique. These methods will get you started, but you should make a point of experimenting with others. As neither your personality nor your problems match mine, it is unlikely that the same types of rendering will exactly suit us both.

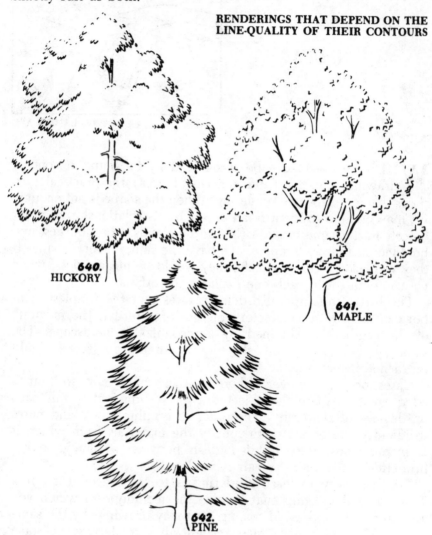

RENDERINGS THAT DEPEND ON THE LINE-QUALITY OF THEIR CONTOURS

640.
HICKORY

641.
MAPLE

642.
PINE

PRINCIPLES

Tricks in rendering are not substitutes for a knowledge of structure. On the contrary, rendering techniques seldom work unless the structure is drawn correctly. Even this is not enough. You can get the structure right by tracing, but you cannot render it effectively without understanding the nature of the structure

Fig. 643]   Rendering   297

and keeping this clearly in mind while you draw. If you make rendering lines blindly, they never turn out to be the right lines.

Contour Quality. Most of the illustrations in the earlier chapters of this book show contours that are either straight lines or simple curves. However, contours permit infinite variation, and we can take advantage of this to render materials more vividly. Thus, the trees in Figs. 640–642 are roughly the same size and shape, but the species are clearly differentiated by the way the foliage-contours are rendered.

643. METHODS OF RENDERING TEXTURES
WITH THE SHARP-PENCIL TECHNIQUE

Details. Keep details to a minimum. Where they are needed, they can often be made to do double duty. Thus, the leaf details just inside the contours of Figs. 640 and 641 accent the edges and also serve as shading to make the trees seem round. Again, the scattered leaves in the large blank spaces *break up* these spaces both to give them interest and to keep them from seeming flat.

The secret of rendering foliage and grass is not to draw every leaf but to make every line that you do draw suggest a leaf.

If you are seriously interested in landscape sketching, you should investigate the *blunt-pencil technique* described in books with titles like "Pencil Drawing and Sketching" (see bibliography, p. 330). This technique is extremely effective and is *much* easier than you are likely to believe until you try it.

I have never found a book that deals with rendering by the sharp-pencil technique. Fortunately, this technique is sufficiently similar to rendering in pen and ink so that you can pick up many useful hints from books on the latter medium.

Symbols. You can often save time and make your drawings clearer by using arbitrary symbols instead of more realistic renderings. I have employed such symbols to render part of the sketch in Fig. 643. See how long it takes you to spot them. The hands and eyes in Figs. 217 and 218 illustrate other symbolic renderings.

Such symbols are valuable shorthand devices for quick sketching. Try to collect all you can. Unfortunately, they are not easy to find or invent because they often achieve their ends by improbable means. For example, no tree has a square leaf, but it may have taken you some time to discover that each leaf in Fig. 643 is a rough square.

Hair. Animal hair is rendered on the same principle as foliage. Do not draw every hair, but make each line represent one hair or part of a hair. When the fur is long and bushy, the contours themselves are made up of hair lines [skunk in Fig. 644]. Render dark hair by shading it with additional hair lines. Leave blank patches for high lights. For smooth-coated animals, draw curved contours and add one or two short hairs where contour lines meet [dog in Fig. 645].

RENDERING ANIMAL HAIR

644. DARK, BUSHY FUR   **645.** PALE, SMOOTH COAT

The easiest approach to rendering human hair is to make study-tracings of the examples scattered throughout this book and those that you find in comic strips. Choose one blonde and one brunette rendering for each sex, and experiment with these until

Fig. 648]   Rendering   299

you can apply them to any position of the head. While studying
men's hair, pay especial attention to the treatment at the back of
the neck.

**LEARNING HOW TO
RENDER HUMAN HAIR**

646.
SOURCE DRAWING
This also serves as
an example of how
to render blond hair.

647.
TRACED STUDY-DIAGRAM
Use source as construction
and outline each lock from
the beginning to the end.

648.
RENDERING DARK HAIR
This was redrawn over the
study diagram in Fig. 647.

If you want to go more deeply into the subject of hair, you
must be prepared to make a thorough investigation of its structure. Choose a blonde source [Fig. 646] and trace each lock lightly
from beginning to end [Fig. 647]. Lay this diagram on white
paper and draw hair over it. For blondes, leave the high lights
blank and draw only enough hairs—or parts of hairs—to give the
desired effect [Fig. 646]. For brunettes, leave small high lights
and blacken most of the space between them [Fig. 648]. Study
your source carefully to learn where the high lights and shadows
fall.

This is not recommended as a method for drawing hair; it is a method for *learning* to draw hair. You will probably have to make a number of such studies before you get the knack. However,

SHADING TUBES AND RODS

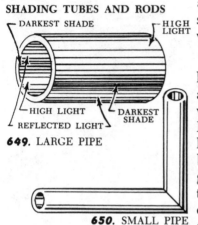

649. LARGE PIPE

650. SMALL PIPE

after you do get it, rendering hair suddenly becomes easy and you will not need any special method.

Parallel Shading. Rendering is largely a matter of indicating color and texture. This can often be done with parallel shading. The house in Fig. 643 illustrates how the parallel technique is used to render brick, stone, clay, shingles, and glass. Shading is mainly confined to the shadows, and the directions of the lines are varied to distinguish the materials and to avoid monotony. Note the use of accents to suggest minor irregularities.

Flat surfaces present no problem, but curved surfaces require some skill [pipes in Figs 649 and 650]. Three effects are combined here: (1) edges are darkened to round them off; (2) parts turned away from the light are shaded; (3) a pale area is left

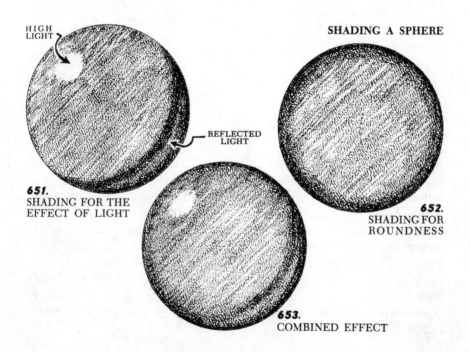

SHADING A SPHERE

651.
SHADING FOR THE
EFFECT OF LIGHT

652.
SHADING FOR
ROUNDNESS

653.
COMBINED EFFECT

Fig. 655]   Rendering   301

in the darkest shade to represent light that is supposed to be reflected from some surface below the object.

Figs. 651–653 apply the same principles to a sphere. If you study these diagrams, you should have no difficulty in locating the areas to be shaded. Unfortunately, the effect will be missed unless the areas blend into each other. This is not easy; you may have to practice for some time before you can do it well.

SHADING TECHNIQUES

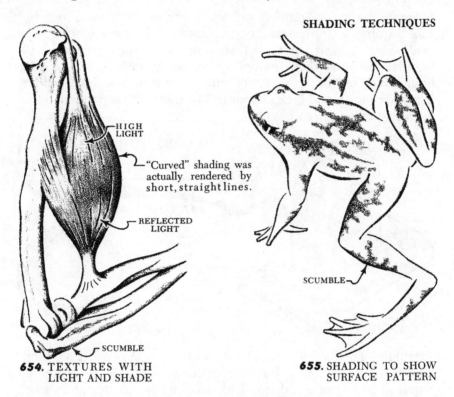

HIGH
LIGHT

"Curved" shading was actually rendered by short, straight lines.

REFLECTED
LIGHT

SCUMBLE

SCUMBLE

654. TEXTURES WITH
LIGHT AND SHADE

655. SHADING TO SHOW
SURFACE PATTERN

Curved-line Shading. The muscle in Fig. 654 shows another type of shading. Here, the lines follow the curve of the surface. Theoretically, the lines should actually curve. But if your skill is limited, you can shade with short straight lines. Try to space them evenly and be careful to make their directions follow the curve of the surface. The muscle in Fig. 654 was shaded in this way. I do not believe you can tell that the lines are not curved. This type of shading is fairly easy when the subject is dark, and you can disguise your mistakes by blackening parts of the area. However, on light surfaces—where each line is distinct—it requires skill of a high order.

The fact that the shading follows the curve of the surface tends to make the muscle look round. Nevertheless, we must also use high lights and dark shading according to the principles illustrated by the sphere in Figs 651–653.

Scumbling. In this type of shading, the pencil wanders loosely over the paper. It is especially adapted to cases like the bones in Fig. 654 where the shaded areas are narrow and tend to taper off into lines. It can also be used to indicate color patterns [frog in Fig. 655].

Some draftsmen render smooth surfaces by scumbling, but this requires extreme care or the result will seem patchy. You can save time and trouble by shading the surface roughly with parallel lines and then smudging the pencil with the tip of your finger. Pick out the high lights with an eraser. Smudged renderings look messy and lack crispness, but they are easy to make and perfectly clear to read.

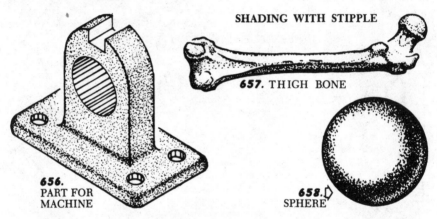

SHADING WITH STIPPLE

657. THIGH BONE

656.
PART FOR
MACHINE

658.
SPHERE

Stipple. This is not a practical technique for pencil sketching. However, if you draw for reproduction, you will probably be required to use pen and ink. Line shading in ink demands more skill than I have ever been able to develop. Fortunately, stipple is much easier and works well with both biological and mechanical subjects, as Figs. 656–658 illustrate.

DRAPERY AND CLOTHING

A knowledge of structure is essential in rendering drapery. Even a dishrag can take an infinite number of forms; we need to know what factors influenced its form before we can draw it. Here again, study-tracing is the best way to learn. Several "adventure comic" strips are brilliantly drawn and provide ideal models. Vary your sources. You are learning to render. Do not imitate the techniques of any one artist—not even someone whom you admire.

Fig. 658]　　　　　　　Rendering　　　　　　　303

Once you have mastered the principles, you should not have much trouble with drapery and clothing—if you have a source to show where the folds appear. Unfortunately, visualizing drapery without a source requires long experience and practice. Do not be disappointed if your first attempts are unsuccessful.

Support. The folds in a drapery depend largely on the way it is supported. In many cases, each part of the material is supported at two definite points [Figs. 659 and 660]. A wide drapery may show several panels, each with its own pair of supporting points. The folds in one panel have little effect on those in the other panels.

Clothing may be supported by pairs of points, but the support is often a rounded surface like the thighs of the girl in Fig. 661. A support is not necessarily at the top of the drapery. In Fig. 661, for example, the skirt is pulled around the figure in such a way that the lower part of the buttocks acts as a "support." When the material is fairly stiff and pressed together, it may be supported from below. Thus, the upper material in the girl's sleeves rests on her arms at shoulder, elbow, and wrist.

Folds. Although folds apparently occur in bewildering variety, they can be classified into four types. One type may be influenced by another, but this gives little trouble.

Pleated folds are evenly spaced. In all other cases, the spacing is irregular. This is important; *uniform spacing produces a mechanical effect that contradicts the spirit of drapery.*

HANG. The folds immediately below a point of support hang almost straight down. In light materials, the folds are shallow and comparatively numerous. The lines stop part of the way down and new lines begin [B, Fig. 659]. Some lines from the top should overlap those from the bottom, but some should stop short. In heavy material, the folds are deep, there are not many of them, and the fold lines run from the top to the bottom of the drapery [G, Fig. 660].

SAG. A chain supported at two points always forms a *catenary* [curve in Fig. 454]. Cloth supported in this way tends to *sag* into catenaries, but the curves are never quite perfect geometrically. Although sag-folds in flimsy materials approach the true curves closely [A, Fig. 659], those in stiff, or heavily lined, draperies break in almost straight lines and sharp angles [E, Fig. 660]. Sometimes, the line bends back on itself to form a hook [F]. Even in such cases, however, the lines tend to follow the basic catenary pattern. Every variation between smooth curves and nearly straight lines can be found. Each material has characteristic folds. Success in rendering it depends on drawing the folds with the appropriate degree of smoothness or angularity.

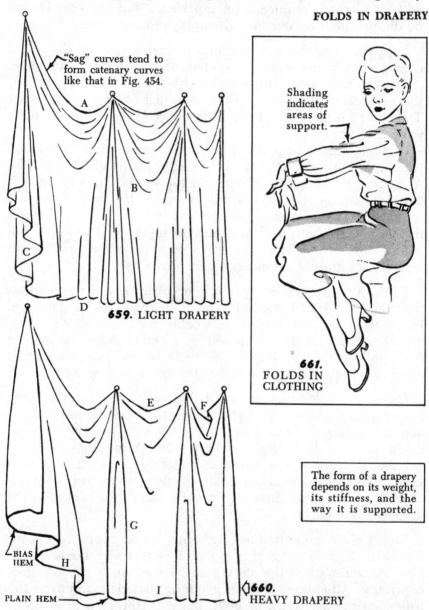

FOLDS IN DRAPERY

"Sag" curves tend to form catenary curves like that in Fig. 454.

659. LIGHT DRAPERY

Shading indicates areas of support.

661.
FOLDS IN
CLOTHING

BIAS HEM

PLAIN HEM

660.
HEAVY DRAPERY

The form of a drapery depends on its weight, its stiffness, and the way it is supported.

In both light and heavy material, the sag-folds are fairly flat and close together at the top but grow sharper and more widely spaced as they go down. Observe that folds from one point alternate with those from the other [Figs. 659 and 660].

Fig. 661]   Rendering   305

PULL. When two supporting points are spread apart, the catenaries are pulled until they become more or less straight lines. The turban in Fig. 662 is an extreme example. In this case, there are no points of support; the cloth is merely wrapped tightly around the head. Nevertheless, the effect of pull is the same. Note the irregularities of the folds and the way in which they interlace. Pull-folds are especially common in sleeves, where they usually spiral around the arm from high to low points of support [Fig. 663].

Do not hesitate to show seams. They reveal the structure of the garment and normally follow curves that increase the three-dimensional effect. Render seams with thin lines of constant width to distinguish them from the accented contours.

CRUSH. When the material is crushed together, it is supported from below and stands by its own stiffness [Fig. 663]. As crushed folds have no definite points of support, they can begin anywhere. This makes them particularly difficult to visualize. It is almost impossible for the beginner to draw them without a source.

Hems. If the material hangs so that the threads are vertical and horizontal, the drapery is said to be *plain* and the hem line makes a series of characteristic horizontal curves [D, Fig. 659 and I, Fig. 660]. When the threads slant, the material is said to hang *on the bias* or *circular* [C, Fig. 659 and H, Fig. 660]. This also produces characteristic curves in the hem line.

Figs. 666 and 667 illustrate how the type of drapery affects a skirt. Fig. 666 is a plain skirt, which is a simple tube of cloth gathered at the waist. Fig. 667 is a *fitted* or circular skirt made of *gores*, each of which is narrow at the top and wide at the bottom.

In drawing the hem line of a skirt, an elliptical construction line is helpful [dashed line in Fig. 668]. Some folds may not touch this line, but if any of them miss it too far, the effect will be unsatisfactory [Fig. 669].

Always construct the whole hem line, including those parts that are hidden by folds [dotted lines in Fig. 668]. This makes it easy to avoid unnatural curves [Fig. 669].

Whenever the hem line bends back on itself, a vertical fold line should be drawn. These fold lines—and the side lines of the skirt —should be tangent to a curve of the hem [Figs. 668 and 669]. Show more fold lines at the sides than in the center. This helps to make the skirt seem round [Figs. 666–668].

Simplifying Folds. The folds in most actual drapery are extremely complex. Draw just enough of them to indicate the nature of the material. This is especially important in rendering crushed folds as these tend to bunch. If you draw a line for each one, you will get an effect of shading where you do not want it.

PULL AND CRUSH

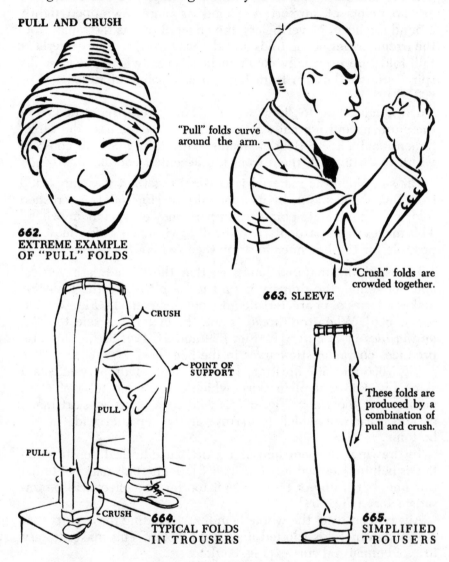

"Pull" folds curve around the arm.

662.
EXTREME EXAMPLE OF "PULL" FOLDS

"Crush" folds are crowded together.

663. SLEEVE

CRUSH

POINT OF SUPPORT

PULL

PULL

CRUSH

664.
TYPICAL FOLDS IN TROUSERS

These folds are produced by a combination of pull and crush.

665.
SIMPLIFIED TROUSERS

Encircling Folds. When one point of support is behind the figure so that part of a pull-fold is hidden, place your pencil at the hidden point of support and then move it as though you were actually pulling the cloth around the body [Fig. 671]. Do not let the pencil touch the paper until it passes the edge where the fold becomes visible. This is more of a psychological trick than a drawing trick, but you will find it extremely helpful.

Fig. 669]   Rendering   **307**

Shading. Try to avoid shading when you use the fine-line technique. In most cases, it will be enough to accent your contours and to show folds, creases, and seams [Figs. 659-669]. Drawing a hidden contour of a figure will sometimes take the place of a fold that would not show in real life [left thigh of girl in

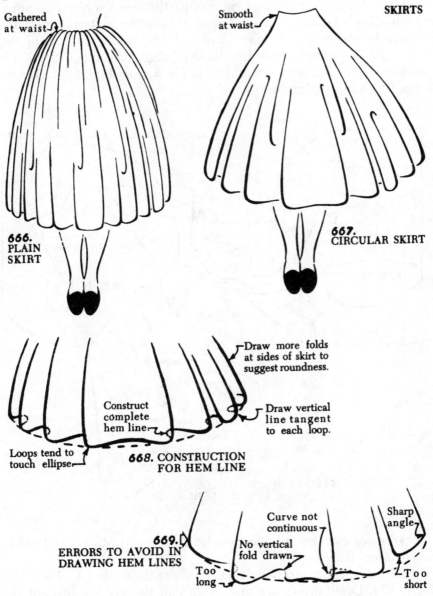

Gathered at waist

Smooth at waist

SKIRTS

666. PLAIN SKIRT

667. CIRCULAR SKIRT

Draw more folds at sides of skirt to suggest roundness.

Construct complete hem line

Draw vertical line tangent to each loop.

Loops tend to touch ellipse

668. CONSTRUCTION FOR HEM LINE

669. ERRORS TO AVOID IN DRAWING HEM LINES

Curve not continuous

Sharp angle

No vertical fold drawn

Too long

Too short

Fig. 661]. Shallow folds in broad, blank spaces may occasionally require a little shading, but keep it simple and be careful not to

overdo it [670-672]. Shading never looks well unless the underlying drawing is sound.

Draw the lines first. Pay especial attention to the places where
contours overlap. Use accents freely, especially in the "corners"
and below "bumps." This helps to bring out the three-dimensional
nature of the drapery and minimizes the need for representing
folds. Hold shading to a minimum. Where the material overlaps,
a line is normally sufficient. Shallow folds, where no part of the
material is hidden, must be shaded [Figs. 670 and 672]. Keep
shading uniform. Any attempt to grade it from light to dark may
result in a messy drawing.

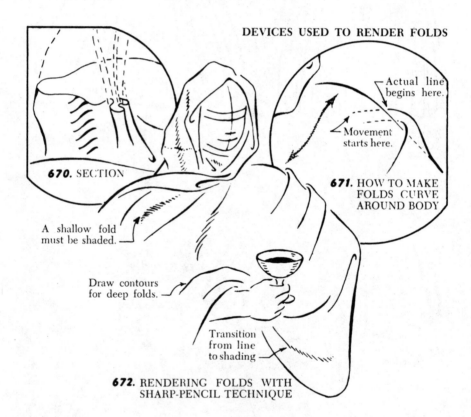

DEVICES USED TO RENDER FOLDS

Actual line
begins here.

Movement
starts here.

670. SECTION

671. HOW TO MAKE
FOLDS CURVE
AROUND BODY

A shallow fold
must be shaded.

Draw contours
for deep folds.

Transition
from line
to shading

672. RENDERING FOLDS WITH
SHARP-PENCIL TECHNIQUE

Accessories. The only accessories that are apt to cause trouble
are hats and shoes.

The method of drawing men's hats is illustrated in Figs. 673
and 674. Draw the crown first. Note that the vertical lines of the
crown extend the lines of the head. The brim normally forms a
figure-of-eight. Remember that a brim is not flat; wherever its
internal contours are visible, they must be shown [Fig. 674].

DRAWING HATS AND CAPS

½ head height

① Construct crown by continuing the lines of the head.

Draw brim as a figure-of-eight.

Add details.

② ③

FIG. 673. SIDE VIEW

674. THREE-QUARTER VIEW Note curves at the points indicated by the arrows.

Begin with the band.

①

Add the top and a visor.

②

FIG. 675. CAP

Start with the band when drawing a cap [Fig. 675]. Once this is placed, the other parts can easily be added.

The secret of rendering shoes is to draw a separate line for the sole [Figs. 661 and 664]. This may not seem important, but shoes without sole lines are apt to look like shapeless lumps.

ALL-CAP LETTERING
Ⓐ Made with LeRoy "Doric" guide

18

LETTERING
AND LAYOUT

CAPS AND SMALL CAPS
Ⓑ Made with "Slotletter" guide

Initial-Cap Lettering
Ⓒ Made with "Rapidograph" guide

Caps and lower case
Ⓓ Lettered freehand

676. MODES OF LETTERING

NEAT *lettering* and *layout* can do much to improve the clarity and appearance of your drawing. "Lettering" is a technical term that refers to the handmade letters sometimes incorrectly called "printing." As used here, "layout" means the effective arrangement of several drawings and blocks of lettering on a single sheet. A type of engineering drawing that is midway between a rough and a detailed working drawing is also called a layout, but we shall not employ the word in this sense.

LETTERING

Fine lettering is an art in itself. It requires skills that differ greatly from those needed for drawing. Many people who draw well letter badly and vice versa. The material here does not pretend to deal with the art of lettering; it is confined to methods that make the work easier and the results more legible.

As the examples in Fig. 676 illustrate, lettering may be either *vertical* or *inclined*. The individual letters may be capitals (*caps*) or lower case. They may be arranged in four ways: (A) *all caps*; (B) *caps and small caps*, in which the important words begin with large caps (you will have to decide for yourself what words to capitalize as the experts do not agree); (C) *initial caps*, in which all words except articles, prepositions, and conjunctions begin with capitals; (D) *caps and lower case*, in which only proper nouns and the first word of each sentence are capitalized.

LETTERING—A. TECHNICAL

If your handwriting is legible, you can use it to label rough sketches. If it is not legible, you can make it so by ruling guide lines and taking extra pains. Typewriting is excellent when the size and material of your rough or semifinished drawing permit.

Fig. 677]   Lettering and Layout   311

Mechanical Lettering. Several devices are available which control the forms of letters through the use of plastic guides. These require special pens and—in spite of some advertisements—do not work really well with pencil. Such devices are an excellent substitute for skill; A and C, Fig. 676, were done with the aid of guides. Unfortunately, the guides give no help in spacing.

A semimechanical device, called a Slotletter, speeds rough lettering and can be used with a pencil or a Rapidograph pen. The Slotletter is a strip of plastic with a slot cut in it to regulate the heights of the letters. All it does is to aline the tops and bottoms of the letters, but this is a great convenience [B, Fig. 676].

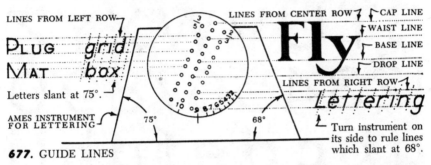

677. GUIDE LINES

Freehand Lettering. I once knew a man who could letter neatly without guide lines, but unless you are exceptionally gifted it is a waste of time to try. The lines can be ruled quickly with the aid of a special *lettering triangle* or with an *Ames Lettering Instrument* [Fig. 677]. The latter is especially handy, as it can be adjusted to draw letters of any height up to 1⅝₆″. It can also be used to rule evenly spaced pencil lines for any other purpose.

ALPHABETS. An enlarged view of the vertical alphabet recommended by the American Standards Association (ASA) is shown in Fig. 678. This alphabet is also standard when the characters are inclined at a slope with a rise of 5 for a run of 2 (approximately 68°). Vertical lettering looks better and is more legible, but the inclined variety saves time and occupies less space. A good practical rule is to use vertical caps for captions and labels and inclined caps-and-lower-case for notes.

The ASA alphabets lack distinction, but this is an advantage in large plants where several draftsmen may work on the same drawing. Unfortunately, the letters are not easy to form, and a number of the characters may be mistaken for each other if they are not made accurately.

The alphabet in Fig. 679 is far from beautiful by expert standards, but it has three practical virtues: it is easy to make, it remains legible even when hurriedly made, and nearly all of the characters are sufficiently distinct to be identified when used separately as reference letters or numbers. It is not an alphabet for the skillful but has real merit for offhand lettering.

678. ALPHABET RECOMMENDED BY AMERICAN STANDARDS ASSOCIATION

STROKES. The arrows in Fig. 678 show how to build up the characters by separate strokes. The alphabet in Fig. 679 should be lettered in the same way. You may find that another arrangement of strokes is more convenient for you—especially when you use a different alphabet. If you are left-handed, you may get better results by reversing the directions of some strokes.

Do not try to reduce the number of strokes. It is possible to letter a word like "cues" in four strokes, but doing this neatly requires much more skill than when you use ten.

To make strokes that begin straight and then curve or vice versa, as in "g," "h," "j," "m," "n," "u," and "y," pause an instant where the straight part joins the curve. This gives you more control.

Fig. 679] **Lettering and Layout** 313

Take your time at first. If you have natural ability for lettering, speed will come with experience; if you lack natural ability, you cannot afford speed.

LETTERING—B. FOR DISPLAY

The display lettering used for practical purposes is largely confined to placards, posters, and advertising layouts. If these are an important part of your work, study this type of lettering in books by authors who have more space—and more knowledge of the subject—than I can boast. This section is for readers who have only an occasional need for display lettering, and who want to do an adequate job with a minimum of time and effort.

ABCDEFGHIJKLM
NOPQRSTUVWX
YZ¢1234567890
aabcdɛefghijklmn
opqrstuvwxyz?$¢

679. ALPHABET FOR MAXIMUM LEGIBILITY WITH MINIMUM SKILL

Prepared Letters. Alphabets containing several examples of each character are printed on sheets of transparent acetate with an adhesive backing. The letters can be cut apart and stuck onto a drawing to form words. The shiny patches of acetate are visible to the eye but disappear when the work is reproduced by some photographic process. Acetate lettering was used for Figs. 682–684. A wide range of styles is available in either black or white.

Transfer letters are printed on the back of waxed paper and behave like pressure-sensitive decals. This type of prepared lettering is excellent for placards and posters without any photographic process. If you get a letter in the wrong place, you can scrape it off with a sharp knife. Transfer letters come in black, white, and several colors. They adhere to plastic as well as they do to paper.

The main captions for the posters in Fig. 265 were produced with this kind of lettering.

Freehand Display Lettering. Freehand letters are made with a brush or a broad-pointed pen. They can be indicated in rough layouts by using a *carpenter's pencil* sharpened to a chisel point. Freehand display lettering requires a degree of skill that is acquired only by long and constant practice.

EXPRESSIVE LETTERING
Each of these alphabets
suggests a different mood.

AIRPORT

680. PRACTICALITY

FULL SPEED

681. QUICK ACTION

Important Vote!

682. ATTENTION PLEASE!

Tomorrow's Fashions

683. SMART STYLES

St Philip

684. ECCLESIASTICAL

COMICAL

685. CLOWN CAPERS

A much easier (but slower) method is to draw the outlines of the letters. The areas within these outlines can be left blank [top row, Fig. 686], filled in with show-card color [second row], or filled in solid [lower-case letters]. When the lettering is solid, thin lines ruled in a contrasting color can make them even more eye-catching [third row].

These drawn letters can be constructed freehand or by tracing. Even when the construction is done freehand, follow a source. If you letter from memory, you are apt to include inconsistent details—or worse still, to use thick strokes where · you should use thin ones and vice versa.

Display Alphabets. The most legible display lettering is done in caps and lower case with a vertical, undecorated, Roman alphabet similar to Fig. 686. There are many good Roman alphabets from which to choose. These vary in weight, refinement, and the relative proportions of the parts of the letters. By selecting wisely, you can usually find one that will suit the placard or poster you wish to make.

Omitting the small spurs or *serifs* on the ends of the letters produces a *sans-serif* alphabet [Figs. 678 and 680]. This type of lettering is used in working drawings because it is quick and easy, but it is definitely less legible than Roman.

Deliberately fancy alphabets, like Figs. 681–685, can express ideas or emotions. Thus, the slant, the fancy "S," and the "speed" lines in Fig. 681 all emphasize the meaning of "FULL SPEED."

Fig. 687]   Lettering and Layout   315

686. AN EASY ALPHABET FOR DISPLAY LETTERING

A few of these special alphabets are not only expressive but easy to make [Figs. 681 and 685]. Nevertheless, you should think twice before using one. The advantages of special lettering are accompanied by a loss of legibility. This is usually too high a price to pay when the drawing is made for a purely practical purpose.

687. VARYING AN ALPHABET
Capital "G" contains nearly all of the elements used in forming the other letters.

SUBTLETIES. Optical illusions play a large part in the appearance of display lettering. If the letters are all the same width, like those on a typewriter, they will seem awkward. If they are all the same height, pointed letters (A, N, V) and those with round tops (O, Q, S) will look shorter than those with square tops (B, E, H).

Furthermore, forms that harmonize with some alphabets seem out of place in others. Thus, the alphabet in Fig. 686 employs unusual forms for eight characters (J, M, U, a, g, y, 3, and &).

The best alphabets observe many more subtleties than those mentioned. However, the one in Fig. 686 was designed for simplicity of execution and therefore reduces subtleties to a minimum. Except for fourteen of the sixty-six characters (S, s, $, h, m, n, u, y, 3, 5, 6, 7, 8, and 9) all the lines can be drawn with ruler and compass.

VARIATIONS. If you like this alphabet, you need not copy it exactly. Some of the ways in which it can be varied are illustrated in Fig. 687. "G" is the key letter of the alphabet. When you know the design of the "G," you can form a fairly accurate picture of all the other letters.

SPACING

688. WRONG SPACING BASED ON DISTANCES

Note that a part of the area belongs to the letter and has no influence on the spacing.

689. CORRECT SPACING BASED ON AREAS

SPACING. This is as important, and as subtle, as the letter forms themselves. The principle involved is simple. The areas between each pair of letters should be the same, even though this makes the horizontal distances vary [Figs. 688 and 689]. Unfortunately, area is hard to estimate by eye, and part of the area belongs to the letters rather than to the space separating them. The matter is further complicated by the fact that some letters (FA) fit neatly together, whereas others (FT) leave unpleasant gaps [Fig. 690].

The optimum amount of space that should be left between letters varies so widely with the alphabet and the situation that no specific rule can be given. For caps and lower case, the letters should normally be placed as close together as possible without seeming to be crowded. All-cap items need more space between letters; half the width of an "N" is a fair average. The space between words should be about an "N," and that between sentences should be about two "N's."

Fig. 690]   Lettering and Layout   **317**

The best procedure is to space the letters lightly in pencil. If the first attempt is not satisfactory, it can be corrected as often as necessary until a pleasing result is achieved.

LAYOUT

Artistic layout is a study for a lifetime. Practical layout is less demanding. Your layouts will be adequate if they present the material clearly and seem reasonably well balanced.

All the illustrations in this book are examples of practical layout. This does not mean that they are examples to follow. Study them to note what (if anything) you like and also to decide how they could be improved.

LAYOUT—A. FOR CLARITY

Clarity and interest go hand in hand. A confused drawing is not likely to hold attention; a monotonous one is hard to follow.

Variety. This is the key to interest in a layout. If carried too far, variety may end in confusion. However, there is not much risk of this in practical drawing. The sample advertisement in Fig. 83 shows how dull a formal arrangement can be as compared with the irregular arrangement in Fig. 84. The layout would be still more interesting if one or two of the figures were larger than the rest.

Emphasis. Whenever possible, the most important item should be the largest. If this is impractical, emphasize the chief item by contrast. Thus, the brunette in Fig. 648 takes attention from the blonde and the line diagram. Similarly, a single free-line sketch will stand out from a page of mechanical drawings [Fig. 460].

FAT
AFT

690. LETTER ORDER
Some arrangements require more width than others do.

When the main item must be smaller than the others and cannot be contrasted with them, set it off by surrounding it with white space or a cartouch. The cartouches around Figs. 568 and 674 were not used for emphasis but to separate these items from the other drawings on the same plates. Nevertheless, they illustrate how much emphasis is provided by a cartouch. Note also the contrast-emphasis in Fig. 674. Another device is to stress the important item with an eye-catcher such as a cartoon figure or an arrow. The head in Fig. 455 has the same effect. Observe how it takes attention away from Fig. 456.

Sequences. Items that have a definite sequence should be arranged as nearly as possible from left to right and from top to bottom [Fig. 574]. When an item such as a head or an automobile faces in a definite direction and is part of a sequence, it should point to the next item [hands in Fig. 614]. The scribbled doodles in Figs. 579–581 break this law. The plate would have been more effective if I had turned the figures the other way so that the girl looked at the knight and the knight looked at the lady. Pointing of this sort is especially important when the objects are shown in motion [Fig. 365].

When no sequence is involved, objects should normally face the center of the layout. If they face outward, they carry the eye off the sheet. The fist-shaker in Fig. 663 illustrates this. I placed him in this position because the turbaned head was mentioned first in the text. However, the layout would look better if the drawings were reversed.

Organization. In most layouts, the items are arranged either at random or in sequence. But many cases occur where the relationships are more complex. The arrangement should then take on the qualities of an organization chart [Figs. 505–511 and 610–613]. Sometimes you must not only indicate the connections between related items but also avoid suggesting connections that do not exist. Cartouches are helpful here. They can set off items that are distinct from the main organization [Fig. 661]. At the other extreme, they can enclose details and associate these with the main item either by overlapping the main item or by the use of a leader line [Fig. 671].

LAYOUT—B. FOR APPEARANCE

Placards and posters require attractive layouts. In the case of working drawings it would be more accurate to say that awkward layout should be avoided. In practice, however, seeking attractiveness and avoiding awkwardness amount to much the same thing.

Spacing. When we have plenty of room, spacing is comparatively easy. Items should not be so far apart that they seem to leave gaps nor so close that they appear crowded. A little experience will make it easy for you to find this happy medium.

Generally speaking, space should be uniformly distributed over the whole layout. However, important items may be emphasized by giving them extra space. Closely related items should be grouped and may even overlap. Each group is then treated as a

Fig. 691]   Lettering and Layout   319

separate item, and the space between groups is equalized as much as possible.

Balance. The easiest way to make a layout is to arrange the items symmetrically. The poster or placard will then balance automatically [Fig. 691].

Unsymmetrical layouts are more interesting and are usually necessary when arranging a sheet of technical drawings. The items in an unsymmetrical layout should seem to balance. The principle here is that of the seesaw. A "heavy" object near the center will balance a "light" object at the side. Large, dark items seem "heavier" than small, pale ones.

Fig. 692 illustrates this principle. As the figure is "heavy" and the football is "light," they balance near Point B. This is to the left of center. The words "COME OUT" also weigh down this side. I, therefore, introduced the dark area in the lower right corner to balance it. This proved so "heavy" that I tried to lighten it by introducing white lettering. When the corner still seemed too heavy, I made the area gray instead of black.

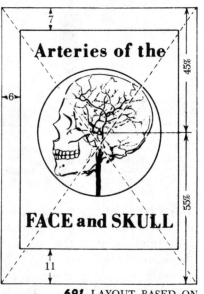

691. LAYOUT BASED ON FORMAL BALANCE Note height of optical center and the method of spacing the border.

Stability. A layout should be stable as well as balanced. Otherwise, it may seem as though it might either topple over or fly away.

One secret of stability is the fact that the *optical center* of a drawing is about 5 percent above the true center [Fig. 691]. The exact position of this optical center probably varies with the shape of the layout, but this is not important as we never have to locate it precisely. For practical purposes, all we need to remember is that the center of interest is slightly above the geometrical center of the layout.

Stability is improved by keeping most of the "weight" at the bottom. The capitals in Fig. 691 make the words "FACE" and "SKULL" more emphatic, but their chief function is to get plenty of black into the lower part of the placard.

Placing "weight" in both lower corners is an especially effective means of achieving stability. The little patch of gray in the lower left-hand corner of Fig. 692 may seem unimportant. However, if you cover it with a scrap of white paper, the layout will appear to topple over to the left.

692. A LAYOUT BASED ON INFORMAL BALANCE

The "center of gravity" of kicker is at **A.**   The words "COME OUT" also add weight
The football has its "center of gravity" at   on the left. Both weights are balanced by
D. These balance on an imaginary seesaw at   the combined effect of the word "for" and
B, which is left of the optical center, **C.**   by the dark area in the lower right corner.

Borders. Engineers and architects normally rule a rectangle around a sheet of drawings to serve as a border. This improves the appearance of the work and tends to minimize any flaws in the layout. Unfortunately, a border wastes a great deal of space. Over 35 percent of the area in Fig. 691 is occupied by the narrow frame of white between the border and the edge of the placard. We cannot afford to use borders unless we have plenty of room to spare.

To eliminate the need for a border, rule a faint rectangle the size of the layout. Then make all the drawings and blocks of lettering near the edges of the plate touch the rectangle. This creates an imaginary border and provides an acceptable substitute for a real one. Most of my layouts were arranged on this principle.

The widths of the margins outside the border (real or imaginary) can make or break the appearance of a placard or poster.

Fig. 692]   Lettering and Layout   321

Ideally, the margins should vary with the size, shape, and nature of the layout. For practical purposes, however, those shown in Fig. 691 will prove adequate. Choose a unit (say ¼″). Make the top margin 7 units (1¾″), the side margins 6 units (1½″), and the bottom 11 units (2¾″).

The best way to produce a good layout, or to study layouts in general, is to draw each item on a separate sheet of tracing paper. Rule blocks for the lettering like those in Fig. 84. Draw a rectangle the size and shape of the layout or border. Place the items on this rectangle and shift them around until you find the best arrangement. When approached in this way, layout can become a fascinating study. I hope you enjoy it as much as I do.

Equipment and Materials Supplement

Dealers in draftsman's supplies carry most of the items listed here. Art and stationery stores are also good sources. When an item is not normally available at one of these stores, the most likely source is suggested.

Acetate. The matte surface of tracing acetate is highly transparent, takes both pencil and ink beautifully, and permits easy, clean erasure. Unfortunately, the acetate is expensive. The clear type has no advantage over tracing acetate except that it is *slightly* more transparent. You may need it to trace fine detail from a photograph. Also, you can place it over glass and trace on it from life [Figs. 190 and 193]. This is not possible if the acetate has a matte surface. Acetate comes in several weights. The .003″ weight is the most satisfactory. Thinner acetate tends to buckle; the heavier weights are unnecessarily expensive and uncomfortably stiff. New *technical films* come on the market fairly often. Most of them are too costly to be used for anything but exceptionally precise engineering drawings. However, it will pay you to ask your dealer about them. They may have virtues you need, or a film cheaper than acetate may be developed tomorrow.

Adhesives. Rubber cement is ideal for paste-ups. If you smear the back of the drawing with cement and put it on the backing immediately, you can slide the drawing around until it is in the exact spot where it belongs. All of my plates were prepared in this way. When the cement is dry, any excess can be rubbed off with a finger. However, if you do much work of this kind, a *rubber-cement eraser*, made by the Craftint Mfg. Co., is a great help. The consistency of the cement affects both the adhesive quality and the ease of handling. The cement that you buy is too thick and must be diluted with rubber-cement thinner. If cement is applied to both the drawing and the backing and allowed to dry, you will get a stronger bond when the drawing is put in place. However, the position must be exactly right the first time. No correction is possible. Unfortunately, rubber cement turns yellow with age. If your drawings have lasting value, they must be *dry mounted.* This requires heat. You can have it done by a photographer, or you can buy *dry-mounting sheets* at a camera store and do the mounting yourself with a warm iron *if you are careful.* Never use paste, glue, or any other watery adhesive on drawings as they make the paper wrinkle.

Alcohol. Rubbing alcohol, sold by drugstores, is an inexpensive and effective way of making paper temporarily transparent. Most clear liquids, such as lighter fluid or energine, which are neither watery nor oily, can be used in the same way. Do not use either wood alcohol or carbon tetrachloride; their fumes are poisonous.

Boards, Drawing. If you must move it frequently, the lightweight "So-

Lite" board is ideal. If you can leave the board on your drawing table, get the type with metal edges. When you have room, choose a 24" x 36" board unless you expect to make exceptionally large drawings. For most purposes, however, a 16" x 21" board is adequate.

Bricks. These are ideal for supporting the glass used for tracing from life shown in Fig. 190. They can be obtained from dealers in building supplies. Bricks are steady and permit you to adjust the height of the glass at will, but they are hard to store. Books may be substituted. All four piles must be exactly the same height, or the glass will be unsteady and may crack.

Brushes. Drawings with accented lines like those in Figs. 659-675 are best made with a brush. Unfortunately, this requires a level of control that I have never acquired. Hence, I was forced to use a sharp-pointed pencil. Broad areas must be painted with a brush. Red sable brushes are considered standard for ink or water color work. Nevertheless, brushes with man-made bristles, sold as "white sable," seem to be equally satisfactory.

Chalk. This is available at dime stores in both white and pastel shades. Vivid hues are available in *lecturer's chalk*, which comes in square sticks. Unfortunately, these are expensive and are fragile. They are sold by art stores and sometimes by stationers.

Chalkboards. Toy departments carry inexpensive, portable boards. You can make your own by painting a sheet of ⅛" *hardboard* with a special paint sold by paint and hardware stores for the purpose. The hardboard itself may be bought at a lumber yard.

Compasses. The most useful type is shown in Figs. 23-25. It should be about 6" long when closed and equipped with an extension bar and three points—pen, pencil, and needle. The needle point converts the compass into a pair of dividers. This compass can be used for circles with radii from ⅜" to 10½" and serves nearly all the needs of the occasional draftsman. Smaller circles

require either a *circle template* (*see* Templates) or a *drop bow compass*. The latter is equipped with pen and pencil points but not with a needle point. An intermediate type called, for some reason, a "bow compass" is equipped with a screw which permits accurate setting and keeps the instrument from getting out of adjustment. The kind with the thumbscrew on the side can be set more quickly; when the thumbscrew is in the center, the instrument can be adjusted with one hand. As the points are not ordinarily interchangeable, the pen compass, the pencil compass, and the dividers are separate instruments. Compasses 3¾" long permit radii from ³⁄₁₆" to 1½". The dividers of this size can be adjusted from almost nothing to 1½". Although bow instruments are not really necessary, they are extremely convenient. In fact, if you do much work, you will find use for two or three bow dividers so that you can measure stock widths without changing the settings. Large, accurate arcs require a *beam compass*. These have interchangeable pen, pencil, and needle points. (*See also* Drafting Instruments.)

Copies. Methods of copying drawings have changed greatly and will probably continue to do so. Explore the processes available in your area. The choice of the most appropriate method can make a great difference in both the cost and the quality of the work.

Office copiers in good condition can turn crisp, dark, pencil lines into lines that look like ink and can be used to illustrate books or magazine articles. They do not work with large black areas. Most of them do not permit changes of scale. Professionally-made Xerox copies are cheap and permit standard reductions (such as one-half). Reductions to a specific size are also possible but are much more expensive. Xerox color prints are of high quality and comparatively inexpensive. The problem is to find a place that makes them.

This book was illustrated with professionally-made copies by reducing the originals on photographic film and then enlarging them to the desired size. If many drawings that are to be reduced in the same proportion are grouped together on the same sheet, the cost of this process is not prohibitive. Unfortunately, it is not available in all areas.

Tracings can be reproduced in small quantities cheaply by having them blueprinted (white lines on a blue background). Whiteprints are also available. The lines may be black or blue. Unfortunately, the blue lines cannot later be reproduced photographically, and prints with black lines are rarely crisp.

Crayons. If you lecture with a large newsprint pad [Fig. 48], you may find crayons superior to chalk. They are less messy. They have brighter colors than pastel chalks and are much less expensive than lecturer's chalks. *Wax crayons* are sold as school supplies. *Lumber crayons* are available in hardware stores.

Curves, French. [Fig. 454.] These come in all shapes and sizes. Only experience can tell which is the best for your work. *Logarithmic spiral curves* are sold for making graphic computations, but I use mine as a French curve and find that it serves that purpose well.

Dividers. (*See* Compasses.)

Drafting Films. Most professional drafting is now done on film. It is much more transparent and durable than tracing paper. It has almost no tendency to shrink or expand. Films come in a variety of weights and offer types suited to different purposes. Unfortunately, they cost several times as much as tracing paper.

Drafting Instruments. These include compasses, dividers, and ruling pens. They come in a large variety of grades and prices. The cheapest grade is made of bent tin and is worthless. However, I own some inexpensive solid instruments and some of the most costly type available. For all ordinary purposes, both types do equally good work. Excellent instruments may be purchased at low prices from pawn shops. To test instruments, insert needle points in the 6″ compass-dividers. Bend the legs at their hinges to bring the points together. They should meet exactly. Try to force the points apart sidewise with light pressure. The best dividers are rigid. If there is any

loose play at all, or if you can bend the points as much as ⅛″ apart without meeting stiff resistance, the quality is low. If the dividers meet this test, other instruments of the same make are probably satisfactory. Examine each instrument for rust. New ones should show none. Pinpoints of rust, even if numerous, on second-hand instruments are harmless, but do not buy those with large or deep rust spots.

Dry-cleaning Pads. (*See* p. 30.) The Craftint Mfg. Co. sells pulverized Art Gum under the name of Draw Clean. This is dusted over the drawing and picks up dirt when it is wiped away with a soft cloth.

Dyes. These are used for making permanent charts on white window shades. Use drugstore dyes for large areas. Lines can best be drawn with Magic-Marker type ink, which comes in small cans with built-in felt-tipped pens.

Ellipsographs. An ideal instrument should be accurate, easy to set, and capable of drawing small ellipses as well as large ones. Prepare at least three or four sheets of paper with perpendicular axis lines and accurately measured axis lengths. Use different axis lengths for each sheet. Take these with you to the store. Set the device on a sheet. Note how difficult this is to do. The axis adjustments must be made separately. There is some advantage in a device that permits setting the long axis first as you may want to draw different views of the same circle [Fig. 321]. Then draw an ellipse. The end of the line should run smoothly into the beginning, so that no joint is perceptible. A device which fails to do this is almost worthless. If you find an ellipsograph which is both convenient and accurate, please let me know. (*See* Templates.)

Erasers. (*See* p. 30.) There is no really good device for removing ink. The Jet type, which is an adjustable ink eraser in a plastic holder, is as good as any and quite convenient. Electric erasers are quick but must be used with care if they are not to remove the paper with the ink. Chalkboard erasers are sold by dealers in school supplies. Crayon, dye, and

Magic-Marker type ink cannot be erased. Rubber cement can be removed with the finger or with a *rubber-cement eraser* made by the Craftint Mfg. Co.

Erasing Shields. Buy these from a dealer in draftsman's supplies. The type sold for stenographers does not have a wide enough variety of openings.

Files. These are for sharpening pencils [Fig. 58]. I prefer the magneto files sold for automobiles. However, any fine file can be used, and files made especially for draftsmen are available. (*See* Sandpaper.)

Flannelboards. (*See* Figs. 83-85 and 157, also text pp. 82-83 and 116.) Cotton flannel can be bought at any dry-goods store. Molding for the frame and ¼" wallboard for the backing are available at lumber yards. You will also need screws to attach the backing and flannel to the frame. Hardboard, ⅛" thick, can be used as a backing and is more rigid than wallboard. Unfortunately, it is also heavier.

Glass. Window glass, sold in paint and hardware stores, does nicely for tracing frames [Figs. 190 and 193] and tracing boxes [Figs. 518 and 563]. The edges of the glass should be smoothed with coarse emery cloth, available at hardware stores.

Ink. Black, waterproof, India ink is required for all drawings which are intended to be permanent or are used for reproduction. There are many good brands on the market. I can recommend Higgins Super Black, which I consider better than Higgins Regular Black. Pelikan white ink is superior to any other similar product that I have tried. Most colored drawing inks are transparent dyes. The colors are weak, and the inks do not take well—at least not on the papers I use. Weber's Waterproof Pigment Drawing Ink is opaque, and the colors are brilliant. However, you may have trouble using it for fine lines. The inks sold for use on acetate are usually too thick for pen drawing and become watery when thinned. However, Koh-i-noor Rapidograph Drawing Ink is excellent in every way. It works even with stylographic pens and ruling pens. The

only fault I have found with it is that the bottle is not equipped with a device for filling ruling pens. To fill a ruling pen with this ink, dip an ordinary steel pen into the ink and insert the point between the blades of the ruling pen. The ink will then flow into the ruling pen. Rapidograph ink works equally well on paper or on the special *tracing cloth* used by draftsmen.

Lamps. (*See* Figs. 55 and 56 and text p. 26.) The lamps recommended can be bought from dealers in electrical supplies. You can also get good results from an ordinary 100 watt bulb mounted in a spun aluminum reflector. Do not believe anyone who says that working under a concentrated light is bad for the eyes. I have done it for years without ill effects.

Lettering, Prepared. The Para-Tone, Artype, and Craftint companies all make a wide variety of acetate letters. Transfer lettering has come on the market recently. Most of the manufacturing firms are small, the quality of their output varies widely, and their choice of alphabets is far from ideal. However, this type of prepared lettering is basically so practical that I expect it to supersede acetate lettering in a few years. I also expect it to be used in many cases where lettering guides are now employed.

Lettering Guides. Wricoprint guides are inexpensive but require special pens and provide only four styles of lettering —although these come in several sizes. Rapidograph guides can be used with any stylographic pen but are limited to one alphabet in eight sizes, and each size can be used with only one pen. Guides of the Doric type [A, Fig. 676] are more expensive but provide a wide variety of alphabets. It will pay you to investigate the Unitech and Varigraph brands. The latter has an adjustable scriber which produces lettering of various heights and slants from the same guide. This feature is especially valuable when lettering three-dimensional drawings like Fig. 150, although I did that freehand. (*See* B, Fig. 676, Fig. 677, and text p. 311 for devices which aid lettering, but which do not actually form the letters.)

Liquid Paper. This is a liquid sold in stationery shops for use by typists to correct errors. I find it ideal to correct small mistakes in drawings. It cannot be applied accurately, as you must dab it on instead of using a pointed brush. On the other hand, it has many virtues. It dries almost instantly. It can cover black lines completely, and colored inks will not "bleed" through it.

Ozalids. These are inexpensive reproductions made on opaque paper from tracings. A similar process is called Diazo. The lines show blue or black. Blue-line Ozalids are sharper and should be preferred unless you have a definite reason for choosing black. Reddish brown Ozalids are made on tracing paper and can be used as masters from which other Ozalids can be made. The Xerox process makes inexpensive copies from opaque masters, but the size is usually limited to 9″ x 14″. Several firms manufacture machines similar to the Xerox. If you need to alter the size of a drawing, investigate the Micromaster process. It is not cheap, but a good operator can produce clean lines that look like ink from a pencil original.

Paper. Inexpensive types suitable for rough sketches are discussed in the text [pp. 27-28]. *Bristol board* is the traditional paper for finished drawings, but it is fairly expensive. I use a *ledger paper* called Navaho made by Bienfang. The stock intended for white index cards is cheap and almost ideal for pencil renderings similar to those in Figs. 643 and 653-655. Unfortunately, this is not normally sold except in the 3″ x 5″ size. Larger sizes must be obtained from a paper supply house.

Paper, Artist's Carbon. This is available only at art stores, where it is sometimes known as *graphite carbon paper.*

Paper, Squared and Statistical. Squared papers are of two kinds. Ruled paper, called quadrille, is cheap but not highly accurate. Printed papers are accurate but expensive. Ruled lines normally run to the edge of the paper. This is also true of some printed papers made by Clearprint. However, most printed papers have a white border. Tracing paper is more convenient than opaque paper for many purposes, but I have been unable to find ruled tracing paper. Regular graph paper has ten squares to the inch and is usually called "10 x 10." Each tenth line is made heavier to facilitate counting [Fig. 395]. Other papers have four, five, six, eight, or ten lines to the inch and may or may not have accented lines. I prefer the unaccented, 8 x 8 kind for all-purpose constructions [Fig. 28] and rough charts [Figs. 410 and 411]. Many other types of printed papers are available. Figs. 421, 434, and 556-557 illustrate some of these. The isometric paper in Figs. 556-557 can be used for triangular graphs like Fig. 423.

Paper, Tracing. The cheapest tracing papers are so flimsy that they are almost worthless. In the next higher grade, Bienfang's 101 Parchment (not the 100) is quite white, highly transparent, and has a fine surface for drawing. Craftint 48 has more body, but it is slightly yellow and less transparent than the 101 Parchment. It takes pencil well but is not really satisfactory for ink. Expensive rag papers are white. They resist tearing and show little discoloration with age. On the other hand, most of them are not sufficiently transparent. Their drawing surfaces are unpleasant and do not permit easy erasure. Finally, carelessness in handling them leaves rumpled areas which affect the drawing surface. Clearprint 1000H avoids most of these faults, but it is definitely less transparent than 101 Parchment. (*See* p. 28.)

Paper, Backing Sheets. A special plastic is sold for this purpose. However, any smooth paper, such as Bienfang's Navaho, does nicely. I get excellent service from the paper which is used to print "slick" magazines, and which I secure from a friendly printer.

Pencils. For most sketching, you need a mechanical pencil with a *sturdy* eraser. Thinline pencils with 0.036″ leads work especially well if you can get 2B leads to fit. Pencils that take 0.5 mm leads are better for narrow lines. Holders for this lead may be hard to find, but several brands—including *Autopoint* and *Pentel* are on the market. Leads for these pencils range from 2B to 6H. Accented lines, like those in Figs. 659-675 require leads that can be sharpened. Standard "thick" leads (0.045″) can be treated in this way. If you need leads softer than 2B or harder than 6H, you will need draftsman's pencils—either the wooden variety or the type with screw clutches to hold the lead. Colored leads are made for mechanical pencil, but I have never found them satisfactory. Venus *Col-erase* wooden pencils have the virtue of being erasable, but the colored lines they draw are not as sharp as you may wish. Watercolor pencils come in many shades and make clear marks. *Mephisto* pencils are strong and brightly colored but are not always available. Unfortunately, watercolor pencils smudge if they get even slightly damp. Waterproof pencils avoid this fault, but the colors are duller and their lines less crisp.

Pens. For most purposes, felt-tip pens are probably the most useful. They draw lines of uniform width and come in a fair range of sizes and colors. They draw on most surfaces—including glass and clear acetate. The ink dries almost instantly. Pens with erasable ink are now available. The erasing quality is excellent, but the writing quality is less satisfactory. Drafting pens are of two types; stylographic pens, each of which makes a line of some standard width; and adjustable pens with points made of steel blades. If you do much drafting, you should experiment with both types and see which one suits you best.

Photostats. These are copies made by most firms that do blueprinting. They provide the cheapest way to have a drawing or photograph enlarged or reduced. A paper negative, showing white lines on black, is made first. For some purposes, this may be all you need, but a paper positive, with the lines in black, can be made from the negative.

Projectors. Slide projectors can be obtained from camera stores, dealers in optical equipment, and wholesalers of school supplies. These firms may carry opaque projectors as well. This type is also available in toy departments and from companies which handle supplies for sign writers. For overhead projectors,

see your telephone book under "Visual-Educational Equipment and Supplies."

Protractors. Those made of clear plastic are superior to the metal ones. Keuffel & Esser Co. makes an exceptionally convenient model which reads to 210° instead of the usual 180°.

Push Pins. (*See* Fig. 57.) These are not favored by most draftsmen. However, the fact that they can be inserted and withdrawn instantly is a great convenience for the person who makes many quick sketches.

Rubber-cement Thinner. (*See* Adhesives.)

Rulers. I strongly recommend the squared, transparent rulers in Figs. 26 and 283. These are a C-Thru product. The 1″ x 6″ type (No. W-10) can be carried in the pocket and is an indispensable aid to the student who does any drawing at all. As this is a cheap model, the edges are likely to be rough. They should be rubbed lightly on fine sandpaper. The 2″ x 12″, No. B-70 ruler is of much better quality than the No. W-10. I use mine almost as much as I do my pencil. C-Thru also makes other rulers that are worth investigating. (*See also* Tapes, Steel.)

Rules, Flexible. These can supposedly be bent to any desired shape and used for drawing curves without unwanted bumps. Many designs have been put on the market. Unfortunately, none that I have tried proved satisfactory.

Rules, Scale. The best scales are made of boxwood and have plastic edges. All plastic scales are much cheaper, but those I have used chip easily. The cheapest scale rules available today are 12″ triangular rules made of wood. The scales will wear off these in time, but the rules meet every need of the beginner.

Sandpaper. The blocks usually sold are intended for sharpening charcoal and are too coarse for graphite. If you prefer paper to a file, get the finest garnet or emery paper that you can find at your hardware or paint shop and glue this onto a tongue depressor bought at a drugstore. The sandpaper strips used to hold items on a flannelboard should be fairly coarse [Fig. 85].

Stands, Laboratory. Nearly all laboratories possess stands like that in Fig. 190. If you do not have access to one, you can either make a wooden substitute or purchase a metal stand from a wholesale dealer of school or laboratory supplies.

Stik-Tacks. (*See* Fig. 57 and text p. 28.) Cellophane tape that is sticky on both sides can be substituted for Stik-tacks, but I find the latter more satisfactory.

Straightedges. These are rulers without graduations. They are sold by stores carrying draftsman's supplies and are employed for ruling long lines or fixing alinements. For all ordinary purposes, a T square turned upside down makes an adequate straightedge.

Tape, Drafting. As Fig. 57 shows, short bits of drafting tape can be used to attach paper to a drawing board. Paint and hardware stores sell this as masking tape. The use of tape for this purpose has never appealed to me, but many professional draftsmen consider it a major convenience.

Tape, Statistical. This comes in various widths, colors, and patterns. It is used to make charts and graphs for display purposes. The narrower tapes can be bent into smooth curves. I have had no experience with it myself, but the results —at least in expert hands—are extremely neat.

Tapes, Steel. Steel tapes and flexible steel rules are used for making long measurements. The flexible rules are much better than the folding rules used by carpenters. All types are available in hardware stores.

Templates. Glyph templates are made for a wide variety of fields. It is also possible to buy templates for drawing squares, triangles, and circles. At first sight, a template for circles seems useless when it is so easy to draw them with a compass. Nevertheless, if you buy one, I believe you will find that you use it constantly. Ellipse templates are de-

scribed in the text pp. 248-249. Several companies make them. It will pay you to examine as many as you can to see just what combinations of shapes and sizes are available before you buy. Do not overlook C-Thru's No. E-10 templates. These are adjustable to any size within their range. They are not really satisfactory for small ellipses, and they are limited to the 15°, 30°, 35°, 45°, and 60° shapes. However, for ellipses from $1\frac{1}{2}''$ to $12''$ long, the adjustable feature is a major asset.

Thumb Tacks. These come in a surprising variety of styles. If you do much mechanical drawing, it may pay you to look through those listed in manufacturers' catalogs.

Triangles. The edges of a good triangle should be sharply cut, not molded. The inner edges must be notched so that it is easy to pick up the triangle with a fingernail. The material should be between $\frac{1}{16}''$ (0.06") and $\frac{5}{64}''$ (0.08") thick. Thinner triangles cannot be used with a ruling pen; thicker ones will not work with either stylographic pens or ball points. Triangles of brightly colored plastic are coming on the market. I have not used them, but the color should be a good feature; clear triangles are surprisingly easy to mislay when they are mixed with a pile of papers. I find small triangles much more convenient than large ones. Most of my work is done with a 6", 45° triangle, a 6", 30°-60° triangle, and a special triangle like Fig. 546 cut from a 10", 30°-60° triangle. If you make many large drawings, you will also need a 12", 30°-60° triangle. Several types of adjustable triangles are available, but that shown in Fig. 453 is the only one that I can recommend. The 8" size is the most convenient for general use.

T Squares. (*See* Figs. 441-444.) The blade should be of wood with edges of transparent plastic. Blades made entirely of wood are a nuisance as they often hide points that you need to see while ruling a line. Blades of clear plastic should be convenient, but those I have seen are too thick for use with either stylographic or ballpoint pens. The thickness should not be over $\frac{5}{64}''$ (0.08"). The blade should be as long as the greatest measurement of your drawing board. If you have boards of several sizes, you will need a different T square for each one. A number of mechanical substitutes for T squares are available. These are essentially devices for making a straightedge slide up and down the drawing board while always remaining parallel to the same axis. Each type has its faults and virtues, but the faults do not always appear until the instrument has been in use for some time. However, if you can find a device of this type that fits your needs and your purse, it will prove a real convenience.

Window Shades. These come in both paper and cloth. They are carried by dime stores and department stores.

Publisher's Note: Many of the titles in the following Bibliography are no longer available from the original publishers or most bookstores, but may still be obtained from libraries, publishers who specialize in classic reprints, or dealers in antiquarian books.

Bibliography

During the past eleven years, I have examined every book I could find that dealt with any aspect of drawing. The majority of these were art books. No matter how good they were in themselves, only a few contained anything of value to the practical draftsman except a few scattered hints. Texts dealing directly with the practical aspects of our subject are largely confined to the fields of lettering and mechanical drawing. Each of these contains more good books than do all the other phases of the subject combined. I have searched in vain for adequate works on the selection and use of schematics, creative tracing, or construction.

GENERAL DRAWING

Scrogin, Everett, and William Bettencourt. *Applied Drawing and Design,* 4th ed. Bloomington, Ill: McKnight & McKnight, 1959.
I have not seen this edition. However, the first edition was crowded with interesting examples and suggested applications although the material on methods was rather skimpy.

ANATOMY

Lutz, F. G. *Practical Art Anatomy.* New York: Charles Scribner's Sons, 1941.
Out of print, but the best book for the beginner. Also worth studying as a fine example of drawing for communication.

Peck, Stephen Rogers. *Atlas of Human Anatomy for the Artist.* New York: Oxford University Press, 1951.
Much more detailed than the Lutz book and therefore less suited to the needs of the beginner. However, for anyone who wants to go deeply into the subject, it could hardly be bettered.

Bridgman, George B. *Constructive Anatomy.* New York: Barnes & Noble, 1966.
———. *Heads, Features, and Faces.* New York: Barnes & Noble, 1966.
Originally included in "Bridgman's Complete Guide to Drawing from Life."
———. *The Human Machine.* New York: Barnes & Noble, 1966.
———. *Book of 100 Hands.* New York: Barnes & Noble, 1966.
These Bridgman books are an inexpensive but beautifully printed reissue of a classic series. *Constructive Anatomy* is the volume that will prove most helpful to the practical draftsman.

Perard, Victor. *Anatomy and Drawing,* 4th ed. New York, Toronto, London: Pitman, 1955.
Uninspired drawings but valuable because it shows anatomical figures from many angles and in many positions.

Hogarth, Burne. *Dynamic Anatomy.* New York: Watson-Guptill, 1958.
An inspiring book with magnificent drawings. His treatment of muscles as masses is especially valuable.
———. *Drawing the Human Head.* New York: Watson-Guptill, 1965.

Damon, Albert, Howard W. Stoudt, and Ross A. McFarland. *The Human Body in Equipment Design.* Cambridge, Mass.: Harvard University Press, 1966.

This contains much valuable data and presents it well. It deals exhaustively with the fallacy that average measurements can be used for design, and points out that allowances must be made for clothing and equipment. Unfortunately, it confines itself to external measurements and virtually ignores pivot points. Also, it fails to give measurements for the distance from the seat to the small of the back. As that distance is a basic element in seat design, this is a serious omission.

Hertzberg, H. T. E., ed. *Annotated Bibliography of Applied Physical Anthropology in Human Engineering.* Washington: Office of Technical Services, Department of Commerce, PB151447, WADC-TR-56-30, 1958.

This is a digest of the most important studies in human measurement made prior to the date of publication. It also contains generous samples of the data and illustrations provided by the works covered. Mr. Hertzberg is a leader in this field and has prepared a number of monographs and books on special phases of it.

(*See also* Figure Drawing.)

ANIMALS

Hultgren, Ken. *The Art of Animal Drawing.* New York: McGraw-Hill, 1950.
This is a major contribution. It covers both realistic and cartoon figures. The material on action is especially good.

Ellenberger, W., H. Baum, and H. Dittrich. *An Atlas of Animal Anatomy for Artists.* 2nd revised and expanded ed. New York: Dover, 1956.
Magnificently illustrated but confined to the larger animals.

Luard, Lowes D. *The Anatomy and Action of the Horse.* Woodstock, Vt.: The Countryman Press, 195 .
Contains information not available elsewhere and useful to those interested in drawing any hoofed animal.

(*See also* Cartooning.)

ARCHITECTURAL DRAFTING AND RENDERING

Guptill, Arthur L. *Color in Sketching and Rendering.* New York: Reinhold. 1935.
Although the text deals with color rendering in general, the illustrations are almost exclusively confined to architectural subjects. Mr. Guptill's works on pen and pencil also contain invaluable material for the architect (*see under* Rendering).

Goodban, William T., and Jack J. Hayslett. *Architectural Drawing and Planning.* New York, Toronto, London: McGraw-Hill, 1965.
This is an excellent and unusually complete book on the technical side but gives very little information on rendering architectural sketches.

Ray, J. Edgar. *Graphic Architectural Drafting.* Bloomington, Ill.: McKnight & McKnight, 1960.

Waffle, Harvey W. *Architectural Drawing.* Milwaukee: Bruce Publishing Co., 1962.
(*See also* Perspective.)

CARTOONING

Blair, Preston. *Animation.* Laguna Beach, Cal.: Walter T. Foster, 1949.
Sold in art stores. This is a new version of the book formerly called *Advanced Animation,* but do not let the word "Advanced" frighten you. The book is packed with material that will prove useful to anyone who wants to draw either people or animals. Much of it is applicable to realistic figures as well as to cartoons.

Hamm, Jack. *Cartooning the Head and Figure.* New York: Grosset & Dunlap, 1967.
A storehouse of practical ideas and helpful suggestions. It contains over 3,000 illustrations in every conceivable style.

(*See also* Figure Drawing and Animals.)

CLOTHING AND DRAPERY

Young, Cliff. *Drawing Drapery from Head to Toe.* New York: House of Little Books, 1947.
This is one of the best books in any field of drawing. Although it is an out-of-print paperback, the effort required to find a copy will be well repaid.

Bridgman, George B. *The Female Form Draped and Undraped.* New York: Barnes & Noble, 1966.
Originally published as *The Seven Laws of Folds.*

Doten, Hazel R., and Constance Boulard. *Fashion Drawing.* New York and London: Harper & Bros., 1953.
Contains advice on drawing and rendering fashion figures and clothing for both sexes.

CRYSTALLOGRAPHY

Although books in this field contain many axial drawings of crystals, I have been unable to learn what axis angles and axis ratios are used or even whether these have been standardized. If any reader can supply this information, I will be grateful.

Terpstra, P., and L. W. Codd. *Crystallometry.* New York: Academic Press, 1961.

Wahlstrom, Ernest E. *Optical Crystallography,* 3rd ed. New York and London: John Wiley & Sons, 1960.

FIGURE DRAWING

Hamm, Jack. *Drawing the Head and Figure.* New York: Grosset & Dunlap. This has just been reprinted, and I have been unable to obtain a copy. However, if it is even half as good as the same author's *Cartooning the Head and Figure,* it should not be missed.

Loomis, Andrew. *Fun with a Pencil.* New York: Viking, 1939.
An unusually helpful and inspiring book for the beginner. It covers cartoon heads, figures, and backgrounds. The material on heads is especially valuable. If you have any trouble with heads, the approach provided by Loomis will solve all your problems. The book also includes rules of thumb for perspective. These are helpful when sketching but are not always theoretically correct.

———. *Figure Drawing for All It's Worth.* New York: Viking, 1943.
This is both practical and inspiring. It contains much information not available elsewhere.

(*See also* Cartooning.)

GRAPHIC COMPUTATION

Crowhurst, Norman H. *Graphical Calculators and Their Design.* New York: Hayden Book Company, Inc., 1965.
This gives a detailed description of slide rules, graphs, and nomograms. It explains how to make them and contains numerous examples. Unfortunately, the treatment makes unnecessary demands on the reader's knowledge of mathematics. Thus, anyone wanting to make a nomogram to solve simple problems of the form $x = ab$ cannot learn how to do it without plowing through a great deal of technical matter that does not interest him at the time.

Richards, J. W. *Introduction to Graphs and Nomograms.* London: Heywood Books, 1966.
This is like the preceding item, but it omits slide rules and goes into greater detail on nomograms. Anyone seriously interested in graphic calculations should examine both books.

LAYOUT

Felten, Charles J. *Layout.* New York: Appleton-Century-Crofts, 1954.
Deals with advertising layout but gives principles that apply to all forms.

Young, Charlotte H. *Fashion Advertising Layout and Illustration.* Laguna Beach, Cal.: Walter T. Foster, 1950.
Out of print but exceptionally good. Contains fine examples of scribble figures like those in Fig. 584 and useful hints on rendering drapery in wash.

LETTERING

Almost all the texts on lettering are excellent. An exhaustive list would serve no purpose, and it would be unfair and misleading to name only a few and omit others equally valuable. Books in this field vary widely in price, completeness, and emphasis. Examine those available in your local library and select any that fit your purposes and your purse.

George, Ross F. *Speedball Text Book.* Camden, N.J.: Hunt Pen Co.
New editions appear frequently, but the latest is not always the best. Sold in art stores. Low cost and wide range of material make this the first choice for the beginner.

MAPPING

Greenwood, David. *Down to Earth*. New York: Holiday House, 1944.
An exceptionally clear and interesting treatment of a complex subject.

MECHANICAL DRAWING

The note under Lettering applies here with equal force. Besides the books listed below, there are a number of encyclopedic works in this field. These are all clearly written, magnificently illustrated, and so inadequately indexed that much of their value as reference works is wasted.

Lombardo, J. V., L. O. Johnson, and W. I. Short. *Engineering Drawing*. New York: Barnes & Noble, 1956.
This inexpensive work gives a clear treatment of the major drafting techniques used in mechanical engineering. It also contains the complete text of *Drawings and Drafting Room Practice*, which shows the drafting conventions recommended by the American Standards Association.

Katz, Hyman H. *Handbook of Layout and Dimensioning for Production*. New York: Macmillan, 1957.
"Layout" here applies to a type of preliminary working drawing. Problems in dimensioning often arise in elaborate technical work where space is at a premium. This book solves them in an encyclopedic manner.

Blakeslee, H. W. *Illustrators' Ellipse Tips*. Baltimore, Ohio: Timely Products Co., Inc., 1964.
Blakeslee covers much the same material as my Chapters 13 and 14. However, he treats it from the standpoint of projection. Advanced readers will find this approach interesting. His book also contains ideas on using ellipse protractors, on tip, turn, and tilt, and valuable suggestions on drawing special items ranging from bent pipe to springs.

PERSPECTIVE

Books on perspective vary greatly in quality. Some are hopelessly complex. Some achieve simplicity by omitting important facts or by introducing rules which usually work but which are not strictly true. A book in this field is not really adequate unless it passes two tests: (1) it should show how to find the *measuring points*, and (2) it should *not* state that the short axis of an ellipse which represents a circle is always in line with the "axle" of the circle (see p. 242).

Morehead, James C., and James C. Morehead, Jr. *A Handbook of Perspective Drawing*. New York, Toronto, London: Van Nostrand, 1952.
Although this is not ideal, it seems to be the best book of its kind that is now in print.

Schaawächter, Georg. *Perspectives for Architecture*. New York and Washington: Frederick A. Praeger, 1967.
A difficult book to study, but accurate and full of valuable information.

Ramsey, Charles George, and Harold Reeve Sleeper. *Architectural Graphic Standards*. New York: John Wiley & Sons, and London: Chapman & Hall, all editions.
Contains excellent but highly compressed explanations of straightline perspective. Curves are not treated.

Hoelscher, Randolph P., Clifford H. Springer, and Richard F. Pohle. *Industrial Production Illustration*. New York and London: McGraw-Hill, 1946.
Contains a great deal of material on axial drawing that is not available elsewhere. The chapters on Perspective and Shades and Shadows also have much to recommend them.

(*See also* books by Loomis listed under Figure Drawing.)

PROJECTION

Slaby, Steve M. *Engineering Descriptive Geometry*. New York: Barnes & Noble, 1956.
"Descriptive Geometry" has little connection with ordinary geometry. It is merely the name under which projection is taught in schools of engineering. This book is exceptionally clear, and the illustrations are all that could be asked. Anyone who has trouble with projection or who wishes to go into the subject thoroughly will find this book almost ideal.

Books on Crystallography, Mapping, Mechanical Drawing, Perspective, and Shadows usually contain valuable material on projection. *See* Blakeslee under Mechanical Drawing and *see also* Levens under Graphic Computation.

RENDERING

Guptill, Arthur L. *Drawing with Pen and Ink*, rev. ed. New York: Reinhold, 1961.
This is probably the best source of techniques that can be adapted to the sharp-pencil technique. It is a reprint of the original 1930 edition. Do not confuse it with the edition which was revised by Henry C. Pitz.

————. *Pencil Drawing Step by Step*, 2nd ed. New York: Reinhold, 1959.

Most books on this subject are little more than portfolios of examples. This one is a real textbook.

SCHEMATICS

The works listed deal with rendering schematics for display or reproduction and give little advice on their selection and use.

Lutz, R. R. *Graphic Presentation Simplified*. New York: Funk & Wagnalls, 1949.

Smart, L. Edwin, and Sam Arnold. *Practical Rules for Graphic Presentation of Business Statistics*, rev. ed. Columbus, Ohio: Ohio State University, 1951.

Spear, M. E. *Charting Statistics*. New York: McGraw-Hill, 1952.

SHADOWS

The books named here give detailed instructions for drawing accurate shadows on curved surfaces. They are intended only for the serious student. An elementary treatment is contained in Loomis, *Fun with a Pencil* (*see under* Figure Drawing.)

Holmes, John M. *Sciagraphy*. London: Pitman, 1952.

Turner, William W. *Shades and Shadows*. New York: Ronald Press, 1952.

TRACING

Staniland, L. N. *The Principles of Line Illustration*. Cambridge, Mass.: Harvard University Press, 1953.
Contains some information on rendering biological subjects in ink, but its real merit consists in its exhaustive treatment of techniques for tracing from life on the principle illustrated in Figs. 190–197.

TREES

Cole, Rex Vicat. *The Artistic Anatomy of Trees*. New York: Dover Publications, 1951.
Cole's literary style is leisurely by modern standards, but his advice is as sound as ever. No one interested in landscape drawing can afford to be without his book.

Index

Text references are in lightface and indicate pages. Boldface entries are figure numbers.

Notes

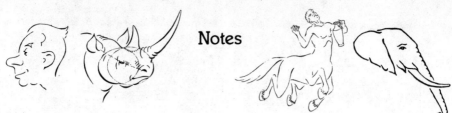

Notes

  # Notes

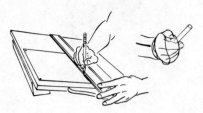

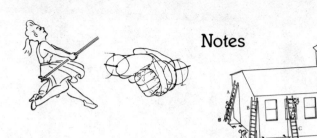

Notes

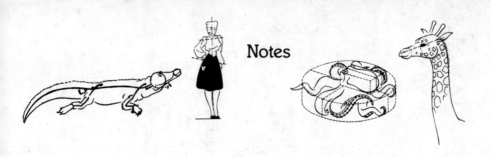

Notes

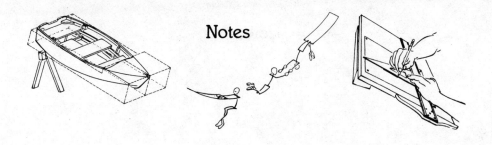

Notes

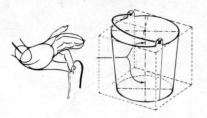

Notes